SHELVING
–AND–
STORAGE

25 Easy-to-Build Projects for Every Part of Your House

TIM SNYDER

Coauthor, *The New Yankee Workshop*

Illustrated by Vince Babak

Rodale Press, Emmaus, Pennsylvania

To Barbara. No author could ask for a better book designer;
no husband could ask for a more understanding and supportive wife.

Printed in the United States of America on acid-free ⊗, recycled paper ♻

If you have any questions or comments concerning this book, please write:
Rodale Press
Book Reader Service
33 East Minor Street
Emmaus, Pa 18098

Senior Managing Editor: Margaret Lydic Balitas
Senior Editor: Jeff Day
Editor: David Schiff
Copy Editor: Barbara Webb
Book Designer: Barbara Snyder
Cover Designer: Lisa Carpenter
Cover Photographer: Mitch Mandel
Illustrator: Vince Babak
Interior Photographers: Barbara Snyder,
   Tim Snyder, and Carmine Presti

Text copyright © 1992 by Tim Snyder

Design, illustration, photography
   copyright © 1992 by Barbara Snyder

Library of Congress Cataloging-in-Publication Data
Snyder, Tim
   Shelving and storage: 25 easy-to-build projects for every part
of your house / Tim Snyder.
   p. cm
   Includes bibliographical references.
   ISBN 0–87857–998–2 hardcover
   1. Cabinet-work.   2.Shelving (Furniture).   3.Storage in the home.
I.Title
TT197.S653 1992
684.1'6—dc20   91–36321 CIP

Distributed in the book trade by St. Martin's Press
   2   4   6   8   10   9   7   5   3   1   hardcover

Contents

Acknowledgments

Like a well-made cabinet, a book comes together from many parts, demanding close attention to detail and careful step-by-step assembly. Teamwork is important, too, and I'd like to acknowledge the individuals and organizations that made these pages possible. Thanks first to Rodale Press, whose infusions of publishing know-how, financial recompense, and (last but not least) faith sustained the project from beginning to end. My editor, David Schiff, chose just the right times to be insistent or compliant, never allowing his friendship to lag or his aim for an exceptional book to waver.

I owe a great debt to the woodworkers who have come before me, especially those who have taken the time to offer advice and encouragement to those of us with less skill and experience. Particular thanks go to Phil Andrews and David Tasher who worked on several of the book's projects.

Artwork is a critical element in any woodworking book, and for producing such fine drawings, I want to praise Vincent Babak. In transforming my sketches into final art, Vince created visuals that are beautiful as well as informative.

With hard work, good photography, and great layouts, Barbara Snyder put the book back on schedule and skillfully assembled the vast puzzle of text, photographs, and drawings that you'll find on the pages ahead. She has earned the book's dedication in more ways than I could possibly describe.

Many of the projects in this book were built using a Kity K-5 Wood Machining Center. This compact combination machine (incorporating table saw, jointer/planer, shaper, and horizontal mortiser) offered the precision, versatility, and mobility that I needed in my small workshop. I'm grateful to Jeff Farris, of Farris Machinery, for educating me on the K-5's attributes. Thanks also to the Bosch Power Tool Company, Cascade Tools, Inc., Sears, Roebuck, and Company, and Woodhaven.

Introduction

Most of us never have enough storage. We just never seem to reach that ideal state where there's a place for everything. Although the goal may be unattainable, the aim of this book is to help you come as close as possible. Here you will find projects that will solve storage problems all over the house, from the basement to the bedroom and every room in between.

These first few pages of the book constitute a sort of "operator's manual." Follow the advice given here and you'll be able to make the most of each project. In addition to gaining valuable storage space, you'll save plenty of money by not having to pay someone else to do the work. You'll also expand your woodworking abilities, learn new techniques, build jigs, and gain skills that you can take far beyond these pages. So dig in, work carefully, and enjoy every project.

Safe Hands, Safe Head

In an instant, an accident can wipe out all the satisfaction of creating a well-crafted project. To prevent this from happening, make sure that safety is your first concern. Keep your workshop organized so that scrap wood, sawdust, or other debris are not underfoot. Follow standard procedures to prevent electrical shock:

1. Never use electrical tools in wet or damp conditions.
2. Plug into a circuit that has ground-fault-interrupt (GFI) protection.
3. Don't use power cords with frayed or loose wires.
4. Adhere to the maintenance and safety instructions in the owner's manual for each power tool you use.

You'll notice that in this book, the table saw's blade guard has been removed. This has been done to facilitate special operations, such as milling dadoes or using a tenoning jig. With the blade guard removed, it's also possible to photograph exactly how various cuts are made. Be aware that whenever you remove blade guards or other safety attachments, you do so against the manufacturer's recommendations.

Always wear eye protection when you work with power tools. If you wear eyeglasses, make sure that they have shatterproof lenses. Otherwise, wear safety goggles. A dust mask to cover your nose and mouth is also a good idea, especially if you're sanding, sawing, or doing other work that puts dust in the air. If you're applying stain, varnish, or other finish, work in a well-ventilated space.

In addition to following safety procedures for specific tools and conditions, it's important to work with a "safe" head. This means quitting when you're tired or when distractions such as children or other visitors make it difficult to concentrate. If a project calls for a technique that you haven't tried before, practice on some scrap material. Completing a trial run or two will give you confidence and skill before you tackle the actual project. It's much better to make mistakes in scrap stock than to ruin a part that you have carefully sized to fit your project.

Measure Twice, Cut Once

This carpenter's adage is always useful advice. It takes on even more meaning when you're following written instructions. When you decide to tackle a project from these pages, read through the entire step-by-step text before you cut a single board. This way, you'll discover ahead of time if there's a special router bit you need to order or if you should begin by building a helpful jig. Speaking of

jigs, you'll find quite a few in this book, along with shop-proven shortcuts and other advice. So as you read each project's step-by-step text, take time to look over the "Shop Savvy" tips and the boxed features that cover jigs and special accessories or procedures. These extras will enable you to work more quickly and more precisely.

Another reason to go over a project's step-by-step procedures is that you may want to use an alternative technique. For example, you can cut a dado with a straight bit in a router, or you can produce exactly the same joint with a dado cutter on the table saw. Throughout the book you'll find different methods of achieving the same results. In many of the projects, you'll be able to choose the method that you're most comfortable with or that suits the tools you own.

Custom-Designing Your Projects

Good design combines form with function, while also embracing pleasing proportions and well-crafted construction. Some of the projects in this book, such as the Magazine Rack (see page 278), have dimensions that are fairly standard. But for other projects, you may want to adjust the depth of a drawer, or change the distance between shelves, in order to fit your particular storage needs. On a larger scale, built-in projects like the Storage Wall (page 208) or Building a Closet (page 94) demand that you adjust numerous dimensions to fit the space you're working with.

Dimensional adjustments won't affect the step-by-step construction process. Proportions will change, however, and this will affect the finished appearance of your project. So it's a good idea to make a scale drawing when you're customizing one of the projects shown here. To do this, start with a good mechanical pencil. For fine lines, use a pencil that takes a .5 lead. Pencils that hold .7 and .9 leads are good for broader lines. You'll find that these pencils are also helpful in the workshop. They never need sharpening, and they give you a constant line width that's excellent for layout work.

You can do your drawing on graph paper, which is available at most stationery and art supply stores. Grid paper allows you to use a variety of scales. For example, you can let a single square equal 1 square inch, or you can allow four squares to equal 1 square foot. To get an exact idea of a project's overall proportions, you'll need to draw a plan view (from above, where the line of sight is vertical) and at least one elevation (with a horizontal line of sight), showing how a side, front, or back will look when it's finished.

Another way to make scale drawings is to use an architect's rule. This three-sided ruler has many different scales to choose from, such as ⅜ inch equals 1 foot, and 1½ inches equals 1 foot. To make precise angles in a scale drawing, you'll need a 45-45-90 drafting triangle, a 30-60-90 drafting triangle, and a protractor.

Using Patterns

Some projects in this book include down-scaled patterns for curved parts. The patterns are shown against grids in which one square represents 1 square inch. So to enlarge the patterns to full-scale size, you'll need paper that is divided into a grid of 1-inch squares. You'll find this paper at art supply stores and stationery stores. You can also make your own

master grid on a sheet of 11 × 17-inch paper. Photocopy the master to make as many 1-inch grid sheets as you need to enlarge different patterns.

Every pattern in the book supplies at least a few crucial dimensions, such as the overall length of a curved part, or widths at different locations along the curve. Start making your full-scale pattern by plotting these given dimensions on your grid paper. Draw in all the straight lines, and carefully plot the location of important details like joints or centers for holes. While these dimensions are critical, it's not necessary for you to reproduce a curved line exactly if it doesn't need to fit against another part. So plot a few points along a curved section, then connect the points, tracing a graceful curve that pleases your eye. This strategy should give you fine results without affecting joinery details.

If a curved piece is symmetrical, it's only necessary to make a pattern for half of the curve. On a curved backsplash, for example, make a pattern for the right half of the backsplash. Trace the curve onto the stock, flip the pattern over to the left end of the backsplash, and trace it again. The layout lines on each end of the stock will be identical.

You can make a pattern more durable and easier to trace against by mounting it on some cardboard or even on a scrap of hardboard. Spray-on contact adhesive (available at art supply stores) does a good job of adhering the pattern to either material. If you're using hardboard, cut out the pattern with a jigsaw, using a fine-cutting blade.

Tools, Techniques & Materials

Getting Equipped for the Job

With good tools and well-chosen materials, woodworking projects can go smoothly and safely, maximizing your satisfaction in completing each job. As you take on the projects on the pages ahead, you'll find you can produce professional quality cabinets, using a basic selection of tools and working with commonly available lumber and hardware. In this chapter, we'll have a look at the basic tools and materials you'll need. We'll also cover some helpful techniques, including tips on applying different finishes.

The rule in equipping a workshop is a familiar one: More often than not, you get what you pay for. In durability, precision, and quality, there are important differences between so-called "handyman" tools and "professional quality" tools. In a chisel or screwdriver, the difference might be as simple as the quality of the steel used in making the tool. In a power tool, differences multiply. A cheap electric drill, for example, will have sleeve bearings instead of ball bearings, and aluminum wiring instead of copper. You can't see these differences, but you can feel them. Inexpensive switches can wear out prematurely, and cheap bearings will be noisier than good ones, causing excessive friction and heat that can shorten tool life.

With the prevalence of established mail-order tool and woodworking suppliers (see "Sources" on page 360), you can price-shop for good deals on name-brand tools. This is a smart strategy, especially if you don't have a nearby home center or hardware store that carries a large selection of merchandise. Used tools also can offer good value if they've been well cared for. Garage sales and flea markets tend to yield the best deals on hand tools. For used power tools, consult the classified ads in local newspapers or in woodworking publications. However you go about tooling up, buy the best equipment you can afford.

Basic Hand Tools

Let's begin with hammers and mallets. You'll do well with the following trio: a standard 16-ounce hammer, a 10-ounce or 12-ounce tack hammer, and a wooden mallet. The smaller hammer will give you more control when driving tacks, brads, and small nails. The standard 16-ounce model will handle everything else. The wooden mallet comes in handy when you're assembling a project. With the mallet, you can tap wood parts together without marring wood surfaces. You can use a steel hammer instead of the mallet, if you protect the workpiece by tapping against a piece of scrap wood.

Used with the hammer, a nail set lets you drive finishing nail heads below the wood surface. When assembling a project with finishing nails, don't drive the nail flush with the wood, since this risks marring the wood with the hammer head. Instead, stop when the head is about ⅛ inch above the wood surface. Then use the hammer and nail set to drive the nail about ⅛ inch below the wood surface. After setting the nail, fill the resulting hole with wood putty, and sand the putty smooth after it has dried.

Layout tools occupy an important niche in any cabinetmaking shop, since they're used on virtually every project. Start with a good tape measure. It should have clear markings that haven't been worn away with use, and the first 12 inches should be divided down as far as ¹⁄₃₂ inch. It's good to have several different squares for layout work: a framing square, a try square, and an angle square. (See *Photo 1*.) To transfer angles other than 90 degrees and 45 degrees, you'll need a bevel gauge.

Even in a workshop full of power tools, chisels and planes still do important work. Have a block plane on hand to chamfer edges quickly and to shave down the occasional proud edge or corner. The jack plane will do the same work on a larger scale, and you can also use it to give a traditional hand-planed appearance to raised panels and other parts of a project. Your selection of chisels should include blade widths of ¼ inch, ½ inch, ¾ inch, and 1 inch.

To round out your hand tool collection, you'll need a few saws. For general-purpose use, have a crosscut saw with between 9 and 12 teeth per inch. For finer work, you'll need a backsaw. The fine teeth and reinforced backs on these saws make them excellent tools for precise cutting work.

Photo 1: Layout tools (top to bottom): a framing square, an angle square, a combination square, a bevel gauge, and a try square.

Basic Power Tools

You can accomplish the projects in this book with just three power tools; a table saw, a router, and a drill.

The Table Saw

The table saw is the most important stationary power tool you'll use for woodworking projects. You rely on this workhorse mainly for cutting parts precisely to their finished dimensions. But with certain accessories and jigs, you'll also be able to use your table saw for milling rabbets, dadoes, and grooves, or for cutting tenons, raising panels, and duplicating angled parts. Detailed instructions on these and other table saw techniques are featured throughout the book.

Quality and price vary greatly among table saws. Commercial cabinet shops use large saws with heavy cast-iron tables, expensive fences, and 220-volt motors. If, like many of us, you don't have the budget or space for such a behemoth, you can still find professional features and quality in a machine priced in the $400–$800 range. If you can afford it, avoid buying a direct-drive saw, which uses the motor's driveshaft as the arbor for the saw blade. A direct-drive saw sacrifices some depth of cut because the arbor is centered on the motor, preventing it from rising as close to the table as a belt-driven arbor can. Belt-driven saws suffer less from vibration, and they're usually quieter, too. Likewise, the cast aluminum tables on a lightweight "bench-top" table saw can't offer the stability or precision of a cast-iron table that is machined smooth and flat. If you're shopping for a saw, keep in mind that table extensions are often useful; you'll need them when cutting larger pieces of wood. Also, be sure to check out the rip fence and miter gauge that come with a table saw. You'll rely on these two components to guide the workpiece for different cutting and milling operations; both should be easy to adjust and should operate precisely.

Regardless of the table saw you're using, you'll do better work if you make it standard procedure to true up the blade angle, as well as the miter gauge and the rip fence adjustments. To square the blade to the table, don't rely on the angle measurements that are printed or stamped on the angle adjustment mechanism. Instead, raise the blade to its maximum height, and place a square between the blade and the table surface, checking the blade angle against the square. (See *Photo 2*.) Make sure that the leg of the square extends between the blade's teeth, coming into full contact with the body of the saw blade.

For a table saw to cut accurately, the blade must also be perfectly parallel to the miter gauge grooves in the table. This truing-up procedure varies from one saw to another, so consult your owner's manual. If you know that the blade is parallel to the table grooves, you can use a square as shown in *Photo 3*, to set the miter gauge at an exact 90 degrees. Alternatively, you can square the gauge to the miter gauge groove.

To complete your table saw tune-up, lock the rip fence in position over a miter gauge groove, and make sure that the fence is perfectly parallel to the groove. If the fence needs adjustment, follow the instructions in your owner's manual.

Blades and Dado Cutters

For smooth, straight cuts on the table saw, you'll need a high-quality blade. Here it's smart to select a carbide-tipped "combination" blade designed for supersmooth "finish" cutting. The "combination" designation means that you can use the blade for cutting with the grain of the wood or against it. Carbide teeth will stay sharp far longer than steel teeth, especially if you are cutting much plywood, particleboard, or hardwood. Finish-cutting blades have more teeth than general-purpose blades. While they can't cut as quickly as general-purpose blades, finish-cutting blades leave the extremely smooth surface that cabinetmaking demands. So don't scrimp when buying blades for your table saw. It's a good idea to have one or more general purpose blades on hand so you don't have to use your expensive finish-cutting blade if you're just cutting stock to rough sizes.

To tackle many of the projects in this book, you'll need a dado cutter (also called a dado head or dado set) for your table saw. With this accessory mounted on your saw's arbor, you can make the wide cuts necessary for dadoes, rabbets, and grooves. Many cabinetmakers prefer to use stack-type dado sets, because the multi-blade setup of these cutters ensures flat-bottomed cuts. Wobble-type dado cutters are less expensive than stack dadoes but will cut flat-bottomed dadoes at only one setting. A good compromise between stack dado cutters and wobble dadoes can be found in a *V-wobble* dado that uses a pair of carbide-tipped blades. All three types of dado cutters are shown in *Drawing A.*

Most dado cutters can be adjusted for cutting widths between ¼ inch and ¹³⁄₁₆ inch. If your cutter has a narrower maximum setting, you can still make wide cuts by making additional passes through the cutter. As with con-

Photo 2: When squaring your table saw blade to the table, make sure that the leg of the square extends between the saw teeth.

Photo 3: Square the miter gauge to the blade to ensure square cuts.

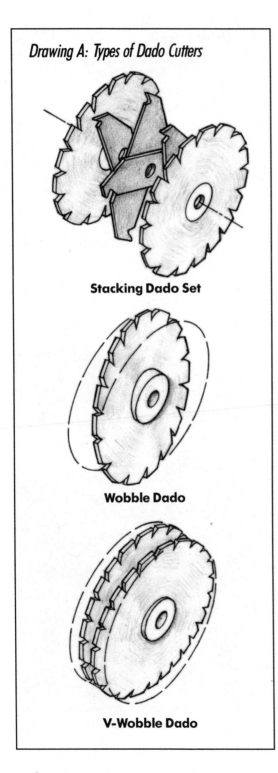

Drawing A: Types of Dado Cutters

Stacking Dado Set

Wobble Dado

V-Wobble Dado

ventional table saw blades, you'll find dado cutters with steel teeth, as well as cutters with carbide teeth. The more expensive carbide-tipped sets will last longer, especially if you're cutting plywood, particleboard, and hardwood.

The Router

Compact and powerful, routers earn their keep by doing all kinds of shaping, trimming, and joint-cutting work. Two types of routers are used in this book: a fixed-base router and a plunge router. (See *Photo 4.*) Fixed-base routers have a simple depth adjustment that is set before a particular routing operation takes place. With a plunge router, you can turn on the tool and plunge the bit into the wood, stopping at one or more preset depths. Plunge routers are more expensive than their fixed-base counterparts, but they are also more versatile, since they can duplicate most fixed-base operations. Many models of fixed-base and plunge routers are available. Smaller, less-powerful routers will accept bits with 1/4-inch-diameter shanks, while larger routers can handle shank diameters of 1/4 inch, 3/8 inch, and 1/2 inch.

No matter what type of router you have, it's a good idea to equip it with an edge guide. Edge guides typically consist of a straight fence attached to a pair of parallel steel arms. The arms fit into holes in the router base. Thumbscrews in the base lock the arms in position, fixing the distance between fence and bit. Some fences have a micro-adjustment screw near the fence. This is a good feature that lets you fine-tune the fence position without loosening the thumbscrews. With the edge guide on your router, you can mill straight lines quickly and easily.

The router table is another important accessory. Mounted upside down in a router

Photo 4: Turning the motor housing adjusts the depth on the fixed-base router (left). The larger plunge router (right) can move up or down on a pair of steel arms.

table, your router can function as a small shaper. (See *Photo 5*.) This added versatility lets you cut contours in stock that is too small or narrow to work on with a hand-held router. You also can handle large workpieces, as long as they can be supported on the table surface. Manufactured router tables come with a fence and usually have a miter gauge and miter gauge slot. You'll use the fence for many shaping operations; the miter gauge is needed only infrequently. If you're buying a router table, make sure that it will fit your particular router. If it doesn't, look for a different factory-made table, or make your own.

Of course, a router isn't any good without bits, and your bit collection will determine the milling and shaping operations you can per-

Photo 5: With your router mounted upside down in a router table, you can perform shaping operations.

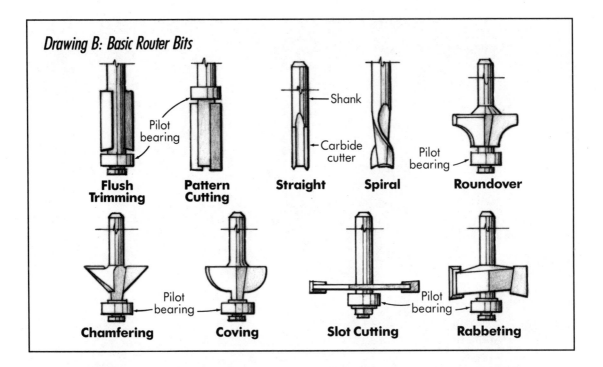

Drawing B: Basic Router Bits

Flush Trimming — Pilot bearing

Pattern Cutting

Straight — Shank, Carbide cutter

Spiral

Roundover — Pilot bearing

Chamfering — Pilot bearing

Coving — Pilot bearing

Slot Cutting — Pilot bearing

Rabbeting — Pilot bearing

form. With the bits shown in *Drawing B,* you'll be able to tackle most projects in this book. But with the ever-growing variety of bits available today, you'll be tempted to expand your bit collection, and thus your shaping capabilities. (See "Sources" on page 360.) As a rule, you're better off buying carbide bits or carbide-tipped bits. Harder and more heat-tolerant than high-speed steel (HSS), carbide cutters will actually save you money by outlasting HSS bits several times over.

Drilling and Driving

Few cabinetmaking projects go together without screws, which pull parts together more securely than nails. In this book and in many woodworking shops, drywall screws are universally used for cabinet assembly. These remarkably useful, relatively inexpensive screws have sharp threads, a non-tapered shank, and a bugle-shaped Phillips head that is self-countersinking in drywall and soft woods. Available in lengths from ¾ inch to more than 3 inches, these fasteners are designed to be driven using a Phillips bit in a variable-speed drill or screwgun. If you do any woodworking at all, it's smart to stock up on drywall screws and have a few extra #2 Phillips bits on hand. For cabinetmaking, you'll also find that trim-head screws are useful. (See the Shop Savvy on page 11.)

In woodworking projects, most screws are either countersunk or counterbored. As shown in *Drawing C,* counterboring leaves the screw head recessed below the surface of the wood. Use a dowel plug to fill the resulting hole. Dab the dowel with glue and tap it into place. After the glue dries, trim and sand the plug flush. This will leave a telltale circle of contrasting wood grain.

Countersinking a screw leaves the top of the screw head flush with the wood surface, or just slightly below it. It's standard practice to leave the screw head exposed when it will be out of sight in the finished project.

Whether you're countersinking or counterboring screws, in most situations you'll need to drill pilot holes. A pilot hole has a slightly smaller diameter than the screw's shank. The pilot hole guides the screw and prevents the wood from splitting, while still allowing its threads to seat in the wood. Combination countersink/counterbore bits are specially designed to drill both types of holes. These bits come in sizes that are matched to commonly used wood screws (screw gauges #5, #6, #8, #10, and #12). Because drywall screws have sharp threads, you can drive them into smaller pilot holes than you'd drill for other wood screws. So use a #5 or #6 size bit for drilling pilot holes for #8 or #10 drywall screws.

A selection of conventional drill bits should also be close at hand in your workshop. Standard "twist" drill bits are relatively inexpensive and will do a fine job of making holes in wood. To prevent a twist bit's tip from wandering when drilling into wood or other material, start the hole with an awl or a punch. For more precise drilling, you can move up to brad-point bits and Forstner bits. While more expensive than twist bits, these bits will leave cleaner, more uniform holes.

To install shelves and other cabinetry against a masonry wall, you'll need masonry bits to drill holes for different fasteners. (See "Against the Wall" on page 10.) Most hardware stores and mail-order suppliers carry a full range of bits, so you shouldn't have trouble finding exactly what you need.

Buying Wood

Most of the projects in this book can be made using the wood and wood products that you'll find at lumberyards and home centers. At these outlets, you will find a good selection of softwood lumber and sheet goods including plywood, particleboard, and hardboard.

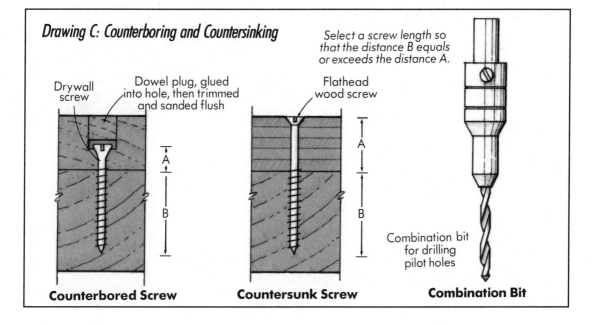

Drawing C: Counterboring and Countersinking

Select a screw length so that the distance B equals or exceeds the distance A.

Drywall screw

Dowel plug, glued into hole, then trimmed and sanded flush

Counterbored Screw

Flathead wood screw

Countersunk Screw

Combination bit for drilling pilot holes

Combination Bit

Against the Wall

Fastening Strategies for Different Wall Types

If you're just hanging pictures, a hammer and nail will work fine. But to secure heavier objects such as shelves and cabinets, you'll have to consider the wall type and a few different fastening options. If you're working with a wood-frame wall, drive support screws through the plaster or drywall and into a wall framing member: a stud, header, or plate. Make sure that at least half the screw's length extends into the framing member.

For masonry walls, you can choose from several wall anchors. Toggle bolts work well in concrete block walls, providing you drill your installation holes into a void in the block. For brick walls, poured concrete walls, and other solid masonry, you can use expansion shields, and lead or plastic anchors for solid masonry walls. These fasteners are available in different sizes, and usually carry a load rating. Small and medium-sized anchors will do well for most shelving and storage projects.

To install any masonry anchor, you'll have to drill a hole in the wall, using a masonry bit in your drill. The required bit size is usually given on the box or package containing the anchors. If you're working on a brick or stone wall, it will be easier to drill into the mortar than into brick or stone, so try to locate your installation holes in mortar.

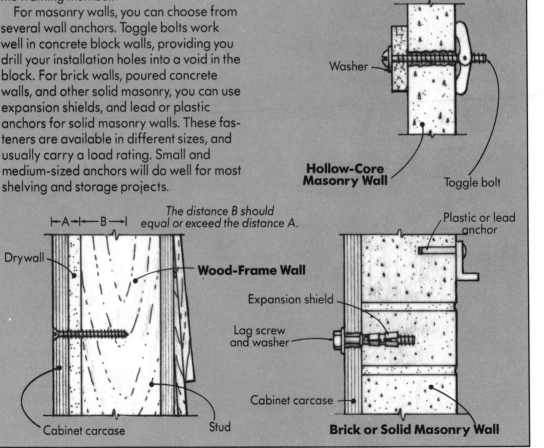

Washer

Hollow-Core Masonry Wall

Toggle bolt

The distance B should equal or exceed the distance A.

├─A─┤├─B─┤

Drywall

Wood-Frame Wall

Plastic or lead anchor

Expansion shield

Lag screw and washer

Cabinet carcase

Stud

Cabinet carcase

Brick or Solid Masonry Wall

Softwood lumber is divided into three categories: *boards,* which are less than 2 inches thick; *dimension lumber,* which is at least 2 inches thick and less than 5 inches thick; and *timbers,* which are at least 5 inches thick. Dimension lumber is used chiefly to frame up the walls, floors, and roofs of buildings. (See "Building a Closet" on page 96.) Softwood boards are used for everything from siding and paneling to cabinetmaking. Lumberyards and home centers usually stock boards that are planed, or *surfaced,* on all four sides (*S4S*). For furniture and cabinetmaking projects, you'll want to use boards that are straight and clear, or relatively free of defects such as knots and pitch pockets. Cracks, cupping, warped or twisted boards, and wormholes are other undesirable features to avoid when selecting lumber. Softwood is graded according to the presence of these and other defects, and you'll want to use higher grades when building cabinets and furniture. Select grades include *B and better* and *C Select.* It's also possible to

find acceptable softwood boards graded as *#1 Common.*

Hardwood boards are also graded by appearance. Cabinetmaking grades of hardwood include *Firsts, Seconds, Select,* and *#1 Common.* If you haven't bought hardwood lumber before, you'll find that it's more difficult to come by than softwood lumber and more expensive, too. Most lumberyards aim to serve the construction industry, not cabinetmakers. So it's unlikely that you'll find a wide selection of cherry, oak, walnut, maple, or other hardwoods at the average lumberyard. Specialty lumber dealers carry hardwoods, however, and these companies frequently advertise in woodworking publications. Unlike softwood boards, hardwood lumber is often sold *S2S,* or surfaced on two sides only.

The process of surfacing wood reduces its thickness and width, but not its length. But surfaced lumber still is sold according to its *nominal* preplaned size. This practice holds true for dimension lumber and also for soft-

Shop Savvy

Use Trim-Head Screws instead of Finishing Nails

Like their close cousins, the drywall screws, *trim-head* screws also have non-tapering shanks and sharp threads. But the heads of these specialized screws are small and have a square recess instead of the Phillips recess found on drywall screws. Power-driven with a square bit, trim-head screws can be used instead of finishing nails, offering greater holding power and joint-tightening capabilities than nails. Like drywall screws, trim-head screws are available in

a number of different lengths. Usually, no pilot hole is required when driving trim-head screws into softwoods. Drive the head of the screw about ⅛ inch into the wood, then fill the resulting hole with wood putty. Sand the putty flush after it has dried.

wood and hardwood lumber that is used for cabinetmaking and finish carpentry. Thus an 8-foot-long 2 × 4 will actually measure 1½ inches thick, 3½ inches wide, and 8 feet long. Likewise, a poplar board with nominal dimensions of 1 × 8 × 12 will measure ¾ inch thick, 7¼ inches wide, and 12 feet long. The nominal thickness of cabinet lumber often is described in ¼-inch increments. For example, a ⁵⁄₄ (five-quarter) S2S board will actually measure 1 inch thick. For a more complete comparison of different nominal and actual measurements, see the table below.

If you have access to a thickness planer, and don't mind the extra work of surfacing boards yourself, you can buy your boards rough-sawn from a saw mill and save some money over the cost of S2S or S4S boards. When you buy wood rough-sawn, you can expect to get at least the full thickness and width you ask for. So a rough sawn 2 × 4 will actually measure 2 inches by 4 inches, or maybe a little more.

Whether you're buying pine or walnut, it pays to be discriminating when selecting boards. Make sure to purchase lumber that has been properly seasoned. This can be lumber that has been kiln-dried, or lumber that has been air dried for at least 1 year per inch

of thickness. Regardless of the grade designation given by the dealer, avoid stock with knots and cracks, or boards that are warped or bowed. When buying boards for a particular project, it's good practice to get all your stock from the same lumberyard, and even from the same stack or pallet load. This way, you can be more certain of uniform thickness and seasoning.

Strength and dimensional stability make plywood useful for everything from exterior siding to drawer parts, cabinet sides, and shelves. By using different types and qualities of wood plies, or *veneers,* plywood manufacturers can tailor the thickness, surface quality, durability, and price of these composite panels to many different uses. There are strict rules that govern the grading of plywood, so you can be reasonably sure of consistent quality if you know what type of plywood to order. The plywood used in this book's projects should be readily available at most lumberyards.

Plywood used for interior cabinetwork usually is made with a non-waterproof adhesive that is less expensive than the glues used for manufacturing exterior grades of plywood. It's chiefly the face veneers that determine the quality and cost of cabinet-grade plywood.

Nominal and Actual Dimensions

Nominal Thickness	Actual Thickness	Nominal Thickness	Actual Thickness
S4S 1× board	¾″	2″	1½″
4/4 (four-quarter)	¾″	3″	2½″
5/4 (five-quarter)	1³⁄₁₆″	4″	3½″
6/4 (six-quarter)	1⁷⁄₁₆″	5″	4½″
8/4 (eight-quarter)	1¹³⁄₁₆″	6″	5½″
10/4 (ten-quarter)	2³⁄₈″	8″	7¼″
		10″	9¼″
Note: Actual dimensions will usually be accurate to within ¹⁄₃₂ inch.		12″	11¼″

Shop Savvy

Cut or Scribe to Fit for Tighter Joints

"Don't build the door until you've framed and finished the opening." Such advice summarizes the wisdom of cutting parts to fit. It's risky to cut by the numbers, running down the Materials List of a project and cutting every part to its listed dimensions. No matter how carefully you measure and cut, you can never be absolutely accurate. Every measurement adds a bit of error and if you try to cut all the parts at once, the error will accumulate. Instead, complete one subassembly at a time, and let actual distances and clearances determine the finished lengths, widths, and thicknesses of joining parts. For example, wait until you've completed a cabinet's *carcase* (the assembly of sides, top, bottom, and back) before you cut the face frame members (stiles and rails) to their finished dimensions. The result will be an exact fit, even if the carcase is slightly larger or smaller than planned.

A good way to minimize error is to scribe parts to fit instead of measuring whenever possible. To scribe a cut, lay the piece over or next to its installed position and mark the cut with a sharp pencil, or better yet, by nicking the piece with a sharp knife. In the photo below, a rail is being scribed to fit between two stiles. The left end of the rail has been cut square and is butted against the stile, while the right end was left long and is being scribed for the cut. Notice that the squared end hasn't been pushed down into place; this would create a diagonal, so a cut at the scribe mark would leave the piece too long.

Where appearance is important on both sides of the plywood and a painted finish is planned, you can use a softwood panel with an "A-A" rating. "A" grade denotes a smooth-sanded surface where defects (no more than 18 in a 4 × 8 panel) have been repaired with wood patches. On an "A-A" panel, you'll find A-grade veneer on both faces.

If only one side of the plywood will be seen in the painted project, you can use an "A-C" panel, or an "A-C plugged" panel. The "C" designation means that limited splits in the surface are permitted, along with face veneer holes as large as 1½ inches in diameter. "C plugged" means that these imperfections are filled—usually with synthetic patches.

For some projects, you'll want to use hardwood plywood. Birch-veneered plywood is less expensive than other hardwood-veneered plywood, and it takes a better painted finish than softwood plywood. A and B grades of hardwood plywood don't have plugs or patches. This means you can make them look like solid wood by covering the edges with solid wood.

When you're shopping for wood, you'll discover that quality and price vary from one lumberyard to the next. Some yards store their better grades of lumber indoors, while other yards will just keep them under cover outdoors. And one dealer's "Select" pine may be comparable to another's "#1 Common." Some dealers will allow you to handpick your boards, while others won't.

You may find it best to deal with one supplier for plywood, and another for solid stock. For hardwood boards, you're likely to find the best selection and price at a saw mill or specialty lumber dealer. To get a good price, or to justify a dealer delivery, you may have to put together a larger order with one or more fellow woodworkers. If you do find a reliable source for any or all of your lumber, inquire about setting up an account. This should entitle you to standard discounts on wood, hardware, and even tools.

Once you've bought your wood, store it in a dry place so that it can retain its dimensional stability until you're ready to use it. It's best to store boards flat and up off the floor. If space allows, build a lumber rack which will enable you to separate boards by species or project.

Joinery and Dimensioning Details

Woodworking joints have simple names, and it's easy to understand how each joint fits together. It's more difficult to define a joint in terms of length, width, thickness, and depth. In *Drawing D,* you'll find examples of the basic joints that are used in this book. You'll also see how the specifics for thickness, length, width, and depth vary for different types of joints. Notice, for example, that tenon width usually corresponds to mortise length, while tenon length corresponds to mortise depth. Refer to this drawing if you're uncertain about references to joinery dimensions while doing a project.

Once you've ordered the lumber and hardware for a particular project, you'll begin the construction process by *dimensioning* your stock. For most of the projects in this book, you'll start off with boards that are already planed to uniform thicknesses. However, a few projects demand stock in thicknesses that you won't find at the lumberyard. For information on planing boards to different thicknesses, see "Thicknessing Boards" on page 16.

When all your boards are the proper thickness, dimensioning work continues as you cut parts to width and length. Cutting a piece to *rough* length or width means that you'll be cutting it slightly (at least ¼ inch) longer or

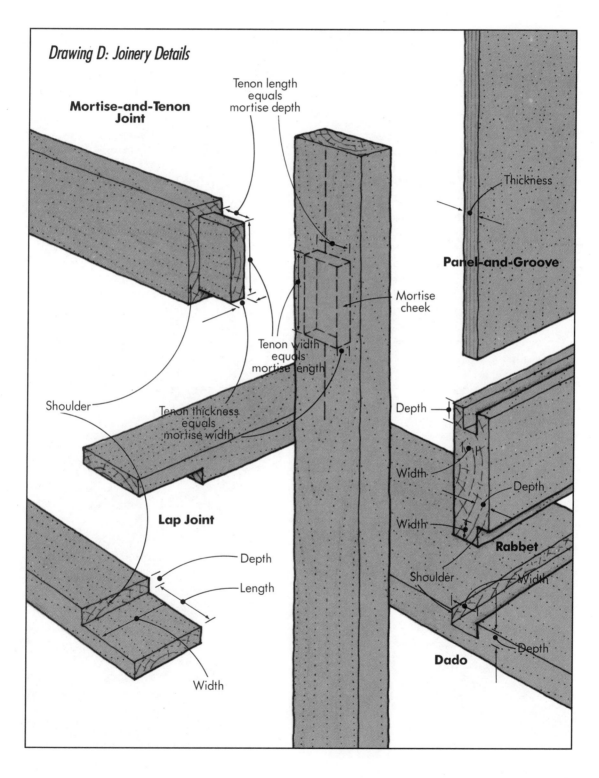

Drawing D: Joinery Details

Mortise-and-Tenon Joint

Tenon length equals mortise depth

Mortise cheek

Tenon width equals mortise length

Tenon thickness equals mortise width

Shoulder

Lap Joint

Depth

Length

Width

Panel-and-Groove

Thickness

Depth

Width

Depth

Width

Rabbet

Shoulder

Width

Depth

Dado

Thicknessing Boards

Rough-sawn boards, cupped boards, and boards that are too thick or not uniformly thick all require thicknessing before they can be used for cabinetmaking. The jointer and the thickness planer are the tools required for this dimensioning work, and the step-by-step procedure usually is the same. If you can't thickness boards in your workshop, you can have a cabinetmaking or millwork shop do the work for you.

The first step is to cut your boards into rough lengths, so that you won't be *surfacing* stock that won't be used in your project. This is the time to trim off sections of wood that have loose knots, splits, and other imperfections. Give a final check to boards to be planed, making sure that

each board is free of dirt, embedded nails, and other foreign material that can damage planer blades.

Step two is to flatten the concave side of the board on the jointer. It would be more difficult and dangerous to joint the convex side because the board would be able to rock from side to side. When flattening or jointing a surface, move the board slowly and steadily over the cutters to produce the smoothest possible cut. Use a push stick at the back of the board to move the board forward. Use your left hand to hold the board down against the infeed table as the board begins to travel over the cutters. Do not, however, let your left hand travel over the cutters; if the board breaks you could

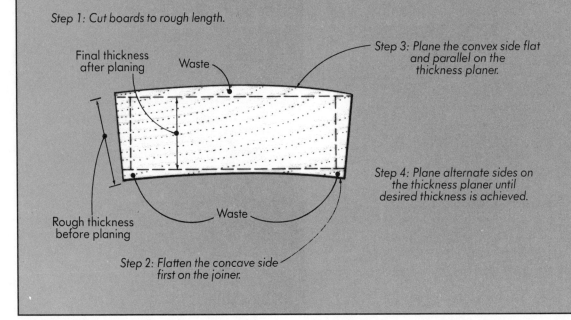

Step 1: Cut boards to rough length.

Final thickness after planing

Waste

Step 3: Plane the convex side flat and parallel on the thickness planer.

Rough thickness before planing

Waste

Step 4: Plane alternate sides on the thickness planer until desired thickness is achieved.

Step 2: Flatten the concave side first on the joiner.

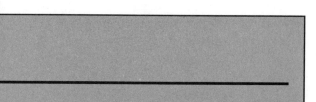

be seriously injured. When 8 or 10 inches of the board is on the outfeed table, move your left hand there to hold the board down. Continue pushing down and forward with the push stick until the pass is completed.

Remove no more than 1/16 inch of wood with each pass. On some boards, irregular or sloping grain may cause the cutters to leave small chips instead of the smooth surface you're after. You can usually correct this by reducing the depth of cut and/or running the opposite end of the board through the jointer first. You'll know the board is flat on one side when the cutters have contacted the entire face of the board.

When you've jointed the side flat, turn to the thickness planer. Run the flat side of the board against the planer bed, and plane away the convex side in 1/16-inch increments, raising the table and removing a little more wood with each pass. Once both sides of the board are flat, you may still want to reduce the board's thickness. If this is the case, plane alternate sides so that you'll be removing equal ammounts of stock from each side of the board. This offers good insurance against warping. If you are planing more than one board to the same thickness, run them all through the planer at one setting, adjust the machine, and run them all through again on the other side. Continue this process until the boards reach the thickness you want. This will guarantee that all the boards are precisely the same thickness.

wider than the *final,* or *finished,* dimensions given in the Materials List and shown on the drawings. Cutting a part to its rough dimensions at an early stage in the project enables you to cut it to fit later. (See the Shop Savvy on page 13.)

For all dimensioning and joinery work, you need to start off with surfaces that are flat, and with at least one edge that is straight and square. (See "Straight, Square Edges" on page 22.) When these conditions are met, you shouldn't have any trouble maintaining precision throughout a project.

Finishing

Creating a good finish is a process that should begin with the materials you order for a project. Your decision to paint or stain all or part of your project will determine your choice of solid wood and plywood. Even the type of hardware you select (brass knobs or turned wood knobs, for example) will be influenced by the color or shade of your finish.

There are some general rules that apply to most finishing options. Then there are specific rules for different types of finish. We'll cover the general rules first.

During a project's construction, take precautions to ensure that glue stains and squeezed-out glue won't cause problems when it comes time to sand and finish your project. If a painted finish is planned, you can wipe off excess glue using a damp cloth. If you plan to use stain or a clear finish, it's best to avoid wiping off excess glue, since this can actually spread a thin film of glue over the wood surface, causing an uneven reaction to the finish. Instead, allow squeezed-out glue to harden. Then use a paint scraper or a chisel to scrape off the hardened adhesive.

It's often important to apply finish to part of a project before construction is complete, or to disassemble a completed project so that parts can be finished separately. For example, the top of a chest should have equal coats of finish applied on both sides and all edges. This will help to prevent the top from warping due to an uneven reaction to temperature and humidity changes. So finish the top before you screw it to the carcase.

For a quality finish, always remove hardware before applying finish coats. It's difficult to finish around hinges, handles, latches, and other items, and hardware with drops of finish on it doesn't look good. Your project will look more professional if the hardware sits on top of the finish.

Surface Preparation

Time spent in sanding and cleaning a wood surface is your best way to ensure a first-rate finish. Sanding isn't as exciting as joinery work, but it's every bit as important in terms of the overall appearance of your woodworking project.

You can speed the sanding process if you know when to switch from one abrasive grit to another, and if you have some power sanding equipment. Portable electric sanders shown below have greatly reduced the time and effort that stands between final assembly and finish application. But hand sanding is important, too. It's often the only way that you can smooth difficult-to-reach areas, and sanding by hand gives you a feel for the wood surface that isn't possible when power sanding. To sand flat surfaces by hand, wrap your sandpaper around a sanding block, and work the abrasive paper back and forth over the wood, always smoothing with the grain, not against or across it. You can buy a sanding block at your hardware store, or simply make one from a scrap piece of wood. To smooth contoured areas, use hand or finger pressure alone, con-

Photo 6: Power sanding tools (left to right): a random-orbit sander, an orbital sander, and a belt sander.

Make a Straight-Cutting Guide for Your Circular Saw

The circular saw is most commonly used for rough carpentry. But with this jig and a finish-cutting blade, you can make cuts that are straight, precise, and smooth. Unlike the straightedge guides that must be positioned parallel to the cutting line (see "Cutting Plywood Panels" on page 25), this jig has a "working" edge that can be quickly positioned directly on the cutting line. The photo at the right shows a 4-foot-long version of this jig at work. For longer cuts, you can make a longer jig. If you cut a lot of plywood, you might want to make a 4-foot version for crosscutting and an 8-foot version for full-length rips.

The jig consists of a straightedged board that is glued to a hardboard base. For your straightedge, use any length of plywood or solid lumber with a straight edge. The straightedge should be at least ¼ inch thick and at least 2 inches wide. Glue the straightedge to a length of ⅛-inch-thick tempered hardboard, allowing at least an 8-inch width of hardboard to show along the straightedge side. Clamp the straightedge onto the hardboard until the glue dries, or tack it into place with brads.

Once the glue has dried, you can make the trim cut with your circular saw to complete the jig. Square the blade to the base of the saw, adjust the depth of cut to about ³⁄₁₆ inch, and place the hardboard on a piece of scrap wood. Then cut away the waste hardboard, running the edge of the circular saw's base against the straight-

edge. This will create a straight base edge that shows the saw's exact cutting line.

Use the jig with the same blade on the saw that was used to trim the base. Clamp the jig onto the workpiece, aligning the base edge along the cutting line. After adjusting your saw's depth of cut, make the cut by guiding the saw base against the straightedge.

forming the sandpaper to the contour.

Three different types of portable electric sanders are shown in *Photo 6*. The belt sander is designed for smoothing flat surfaces, and it's the best sander to use if you need to remove a substantial amount of wood (or hardened glue) quickly. It's easy to go overboard when belt sanding, however—removing too much wood, digging into the wood by applying uneven pressure, or causing gouges and scrapes with a sanding belt that's too coarse. So be careful. Many belt sanders can also be used for shaping smaller parts if you can clamp the tool in a stationary position and engage a switch lock. Don't use your belt sander this way if the manufacturer doesn't recommend it.

The orbital sander, or pad sander, is designed for finer sanding. Use this tool on flat surfaces, or to smooth curves and edges. The vibrating orbital motion of this sander will leave swirls in the wood surface. So always follow orbital sanding with hand sanding to remove the swirls. Use the same grit when sanding by hand, or use a finer one.

The random-orbit sander will remove wood quickly when medium-grit and coarse-grit pads are used; but it will also produce supersmooth surfaces with fine-grit pads. Unlike orbital sanders, random-orbit sanders leave no swirl marks. Newer to woodworking than belt or orbital sanders, this tool is the one to buy if you can only afford one electric sander.

Sanding should be an ongoing process throughout a project's construction. It's always a good idea to give parts an initial sanding before you join them together. It won't take you long to "soften" sharp corners that will be exposed once the project is finished, and to smooth off any stains or rough spots that you find. Do this preliminary sanding with 100-grit or 120-grit sandpaper. You'll find that aluminum oxide sandpaper, which is light brown, lasts longer than reddish-brown garnet sandpaper.

Parts such as shelves and drawer sides should actually be finish-sanded before final assembly. This way, you can reach corners and edges that will be *very* difficult to sand once the project is together. The abrasive grit you use for final sanding depends on the wood, the planned finish, and even the location of the part in the project. If a painted finish is planned, finish sanding with 150-grit or 180-grit abrasive. You can also use these abrasive grades to finish sand unseen or secondary surfaces (the insides of drawers, for example) before varnishing or staining.

Primary surfaces like chest sides and tops deserve more careful sanding, especially if clear or stained finishes are planned. You'll find that it's much less tiring to have flat surfaces horizontal for sanding. If you're turning a project on its side, rest it on wood pads instead of directly on the workshop floor or ground. (See *Photo 7*.)

After preliminary sanding with 120-grit sandpaper, switch to 150-grit or 180-grit sandpaper, and finish up with 220-grit sandpaper. For a supersmooth wood surface, brush off loose sawdust, and then dampen a clean cloth and wipe down the wood, moving the cloth with the grain. When the wood dries after a few minutes, the grain will be raised slightly, and you can sand down these swollen wood fibers by hand, again using 220-grit sandpaper.

There are several ways to remove loose sawdust once you've finished sanding. You can use a vacuum equipped with a soft brush nozzle, or you can blow the sawdust off the wood with compressed air. Still another technique is to brush the wood down by hand, and then go over the surface with a tack rag. Available at

Photo 7: Sanding outdoors reduces your sawdust exposure significantly. Sanding is easier if you work on a horizontal surface, but be sure to protect your project by placing it on wood blocks.

any hardware store, tack rags are cloth impregnated with varnish to make them tacky.

Environmentally Safe Finishes

Concern over volatile organic compounds (VOCs) and toxic waste disposal has fostered a new generation of finishing products that are more friendly toward the environment. In some areas, new laws have mandated the use of low-toxicity finishes, while in other regions, the choice is left up to the customer. Wherever you live, you should know that a wide

range of safe finishes is now available. (See "Sources" on page 360.)

In addition to being environmentally benign, most of these finishes offer the convenience of cleanup with water. It's important to note, however, that surface preparation and application details often differ from those associated with old-fashioned solvent-based finishes. You might not be able to thin down a water-based varnish, for example. Intervals between finish coats and compatibility with other finishes (stains, sealers, and primer coats, for example) will vary as well. So be sure to read the manufacturer's instructions before you make a final finish selection.

Selecting a Finish

Commercial cabinet shops usually spray on their finishes to save time and produce uniform results. With spray equipment, you can apply quick-drying sealer and finish coats in thin layers, building up a uniform finish with none of the hardened drips or runs that can occur in a brushed-on finish. If you have spray-painting equipment, as well as good ventilation and safe working conditions, this is a good option to consider. Just make sure to select finishes that can be used in spray form.

If spray finishing isn't possible, you can still produce a professional-quality finish. You'll have to select your finish carefully, and follow the manufacturer's instructions for surface preparation and application.

Brush-on finishes, including paint and varnish, are the toughest ones to do well. This is because these so-called on-the-wood finishes rely on good brush technique to produce even applications that are free of brush marks, runs, or drips. On-the-wood finishes are also very susceptible to contamination by airborne dust; so when applying paint or varnish, be

(continued on page 24)

Straight, Square Edges

Try Out One or More of These Jointing Strategies.

Every cabinetmaking operation needs to begin with straight, square edges. Without a straight, square reference edge, it's difficult to rip parts to width without transferring irregularities to the freshly sawed edge. As a result, tight-fitting joints become an impossibility, threatening the soundness and quality of even the smallest woodworking project.

Sheet goods such as plywood, particleboard, and drywall are manufactured to consistently exact dimensions, and their *factory edges* are usually straight and square. But the solid wood boards you buy at the lumberyard, home center, or saw mill usually aren't straight and square. Even

when you get the opportunity to handpick boards, changes in moisture content can cause them to twist, cup, and bow after you get them home. So it's important to have at least one reliable method of producing good edges as you begin to dimension wood for a project. The process of creating straight, square edges is called *jointing*. In the days before power tools, jointing was done with long, heavy hand planes and required plenty of skill and elbow grease. Fortunately, today we have several different ways to joint a board using power tools. One of these methods should work with the tools you have on hand.

The easiest way to straighten an edge is

Using a jointer

Guiding a router against a straightedge

with a jointer, a stationary power tool designed specifically for the job. The heart of this power tool is a fast-spinning cylindrical cutterhead positioned between the *infeed* and *outfeed* tables. The top of the outfeed table is level with the top cutting radius of the planer knives that are held in the cutterhead. Adjusting the infeed table up or down determines how much wood the knives remove with every pass. For a smooth cut, remove 1/16 inch or less with each pass. An adjustable fence guides the workpiece as you move it through the cutter. In addition to excelling at edge-straightening work, a jointer enables you to flatten and smooth a warped board by

Guiding a straightedged board against the table saw's rip fence

running the full width of the board through the cutter. (See "Thicknessing Boards" on page 16.) Some manufacturers make machines that incorporate a jointer and a planer into one machine. These combination machines are popular in small workshops where space is limited.

If you don't have the space or budget for a jointer, you can joint with a portable power plane. Like a traditional hand plane, the portable power plane is designed to be moved along the edge of a stationary workpiece.

You can also joint boards using a router, a straight bit, and a straightedge. Clamp the straightedge onto the board, positioning it parallel to the finished edge you want to mill with the router. When the router base runs against the straightedge, the bit should remove no more than about 3/16 inch of wood, leaving a straight, square edge along the full length of the board.

Finally, you can square and straighten edges like a pro even if your only power tool is a table saw. You will need to find a straightedged guide board, however. A piece of plywood with a factory edge works well. Temporarily fasten the guide board to the workpiece with finishing nails or drywall screws. Position the guide board's straightedge parallel to the cutting line on the workpiece. Extend the straightedge beyond the edge of the workpiece, so that it can run against your saw's rip fence. Adjust the position of the rip fence to make your straight, square cut where you want it.

sure to work as dust-free as possible.

When a painted finish is planned over bare wood, your first coat will be a primer and sealer coat. Its purpose is to seal the wood surface and create a smooth, uniform base for the paint. Make sure to select a primer-sealer that is compatible with your paint. When applying this initial coat, resist the temptation to brush on a thick layer. Being overgenerous with your brush will cause runs and drips that will need to be sanded out if you don't want them to show up on the painted surface.

The paint you select can show a flat finish, a semigloss finish, or a high gloss. Semigloss is usually used on woodwork. It gives a more subdued finish than high gloss, but is more durable and easier to wipe clean than flat paint. If you're selecting a latex paint, be aware that *acrylic* latex formulations will give a better and longer lasting finish than simple latex paints. The acrylic resins are well worth the extra expense.

When painting bare wood, most manufacturers recommend an undercoat, or primer coat, followed by two coats of paint. If you're after a supersmooth finish, wait for the first coat of paint to harden completely; then go over it with 240-grit sandpaper. Smooth out all the bumps, bubbles, drips, and other irregularities that you can find; then wipe the surface clean before applying the next coat.

Stains and penetrating oil finishes are more foolproof than paint. Both of these treatments are "in-the-wood" finishes, which means that application technique is less important. Wood stain is available in numerous colors and wood tones. At most paint and hardware stores, you'll find displays that include small wood samples that have been treated with different stains. This will give you some idea of what to expect on your own project. But to be certain of your choice, it's a good idea to test a prospective stain on a piece of scrap wood from your project.

Wipe on stain, or brush it on. Then wipe off the excess stain that isn't absorbed into the wood. Increasing the interval between application and wipe-down usually creates a darker finish. If, after wiping, you want a darker finish, just add a second or third coat of stain. When applying stain, remember that endgrain absorbs stain more easily. To avoid excessive darkening in these areas, apply less stain, and wipe the end grain down right away.

Stain won't fully seal or protect the wood, so you should plan to follow up a stain application with one or more coats of clear sealer or varnish. Make sure to select a product that's compatible with the stain. As an alternative to varnish or sealer, you can apply wax over stain. Use a furniture-quality paste wax if you decide to go this route.

Penetrating oil finishes give wood a soft luster, highlighting and protecting the wood surface without covering it. These finishes are designed to be applied generously so that they can soak into the wood pores. When the wood surface is thoroughly saturated, excess finish is removed by rubbing the wood with a clean cloth. Resins in the oil harden in the wood, creating a very durable surface. Both clear and tinted versions of this finish are available.

Whatever finish you choose, be sure to follow the manufacturer's instructions, from surface preparation through final coats. If you have any uncertainties about how the treatment will look on your project, go through a test run on some scrap stock that is identical in species or composition to what you've used in your project.

Cutting Plywood Panels

At lumberyards and large cabinetmaking shops, 4 × 8 panels of plywood, particleboard, and other sheet goods are cut to size on panel-cutting machines. These large, specialized, and expensive tools hold the plywood panel on edge, while cuts are made with a circular saw mounted on steel tracks. If you don't like handling full-sized panels on your own, it's smart to have a few cuts made at the lumberyard, on the panel cutter. (Some yards charge a nominal fee for this service.) If you have your parts cut to rough size, you can handle the smaller pieces more easily, making finish cuts in your workshop.

Sometimes, however, you can't avoid dealing with large panels in your own workshop. When this is the case, there are a few techniques you can use to ensure safety and precision. First, don't attempt to cut full-sized panels on your table saw unless you have a helper and sufficient table surface to support at least half the width of the panel you're cutting.

If you have to cut down a large sheet of plywood, particleboard, or hardboard, it will be safer to keep the sheet stationary and move the saw to make the cut. Support the panel on sawhorses, or rest it on two-by boards placed on the floor. Whichever option you choose, make sure that the sheet is evenly supported on both sides of the cutting line to prevent binding and kickback. Adjust the circular saw's depth of cut so that it's about ⅛ inch greater than the thickness of the plywood. Then make the cut, keeping the blade moving along the layout line on the sheet. It often makes sense to use the circular saw for cutting plywood parts to rough size, about ¼ inch larger than their final dimensions. Then you'll be able to make precise final cuts on the table saw with relative ease, guiding smaller pieces against the rip fence or miter gauge.

Of course, there are situations when you'll need to make straight, precise final cuts using the circular saw instead of the table saw. When this is the case, you'll need to guide the base of your circular saw against a straightedge that is clamped to the panel. At hardware stores and home centers, you'll find aluminum edge guides designed for this purpose. These guides can also be used with a router or jigsaw when straight cuts are needed. Alternatively, you can make your own edge guide from a straight length of plywood. Both versions work the same way. Clamp or tack the straightedge to the plywood, parallel to the cutting line and offset from it by a distance that equals the measurement between the blade and the edge of the circular saw base. Make the cut, keeping the circular saw base and the straightedge together for the full length of the cut. For a modified version of this straightedge guide that can be positioned directly along the cutting line (rather than offset from it), see "Make a Straight-Cutting Guide for Your Circular Saw" on page 19.

Garage & Workshop

Utility Shelves

By definition, utility shelves should be sturdy and inexpensive to build. But there's no reason they can't look good, too. The shelves shown here offer 32 square feet of storage space, spread evenly over three levels. The design makes maximum use of a single plywood panel. The plywood edges are hidden and reinforced by pine trim. Easily built in an afternoon, these shelves will do well in the garage, in the workshop, or, with a coat of paint, even in the office. You can choose shelf levels to suit your needs. The shelves will even accommodate an uneven floor.

1 Locate studs for anchoring ledger boards. If you're installing your shelves against a masonry wall, you can skip this step, since you'll be securing ledgers with masonry anchors. (See "Against the Wall" on page 10.) For installation against a wood-frame wall, mark each stud location along the planned 96-inch length of the shelves. For tips on locating studs in a wood-framed wall, see the Shop Savvy on page 32.

2 Lay out lines for ledger boards. The top edge of each ledger will be ¾ inch below the finished level of each shelf. Ledger heights for the shelves shown here are given in *Drawing B*. Using a four-foot level, mark a level line on the wall where the top edge of each ledger board will be. Then mark plumb lines through the ledger lines to lay out the shelf ends. Finally, mark where studs cross the ledger lines. These marks will tell you where to drive

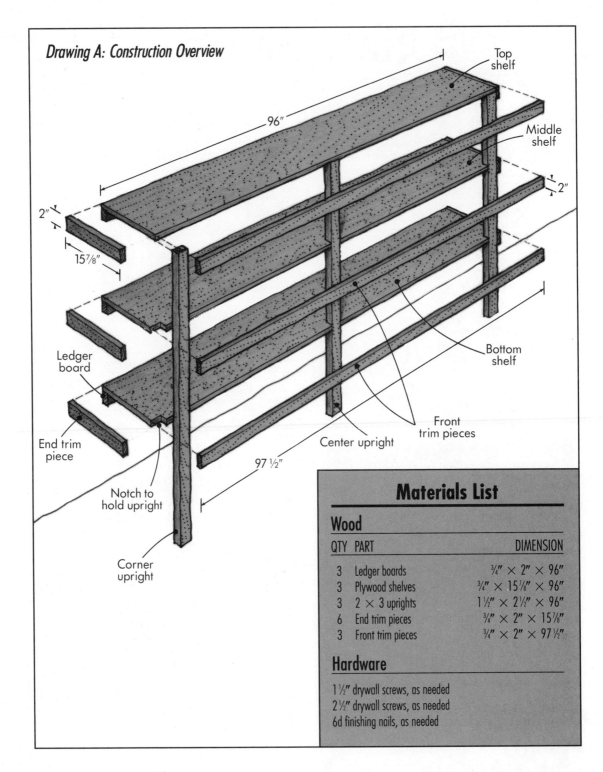

Drawing A: Construction Overview

Top shelf

96"

Middle shelf

2"

2"

15⅞"

Bottom shelf

Ledger board

Front trim pieces

End trim piece

Center upright

Notch to hold upright

97½"

Corner upright

Materials List

Wood

QTY	PART	DIMENSION
3	Ledger boards	¾" × 2" × 96"
3	Plywood shelves	¾" × 15⅞" × 96"
3	2 × 3 uprights	1½" × 2½" × 96"
6	End trim pieces	¾" × 2" × 15⅞"
3	Front trim pieces	¾" × 2" × 97½"

Hardware

1½" drywall screws, as needed
2½" drywall screws, as needed
6d finishing nails, as needed

screws when installing the ledger boards. Make sure they extend above the lines you drew for the ledgers.

3 Fasten the ledger boards to the wall. Run two beads of panel adhesive along the back face of each ledger board. Then use 2½-inch drywall screws to secure the ledgers against the wall. (See *Photo 1*.) Keep the top edge of each ledger against its layout line, and make sure that the ends of the ledgers line up plumb.

4 Cut the plywood shelves to size. All three shelves can be cut from a single sheet of ¾-inch AC plywood. Considering the size and weight of the plywood, it's a good idea to make your first cut with a circular saw and edge guide. (See "Cutting Plywood Panels" on page 25.) Rip this shelf to a rough width of 15¹⁵⁄₁₆ inches. Then set up the rip fence on the table saw to cut all three shelves to a finished width of 15⅞ inches.

With two or three nails, temporarily tack two shelves together, one on top of the other,

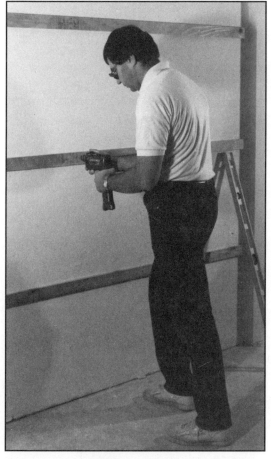

Photo 1: Screw ledger strips to the wall, driving 2½-inch screws into studs.

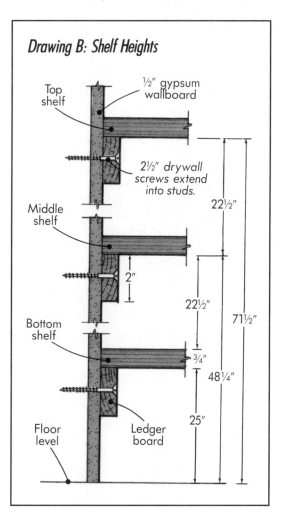

Drawing B: Shelf Heights

Shop Savvy

Low-Tech and High-Tech Strategies for Finding Studs

Locating studs is a frequent problem whenever shelves or cabinets need to be installed against a wood-frame wall. At most hardware stores and home centers, you'll find magnetic stud locaters that detect screws or nails in the studs. There are also electronic detectors that search for variations in the wall density. These devices are reliable and useful in many remodeling projects. But you can also locate studs by doing some simple detective work. Follow the step-by-step procedure outlined below.

If you're working with a wall where gypsum wallboard is installed over studs, examine the wall surface for signs of nails, screws, or drywall tape used on vertical joints between wallboard panels. Slight depressions and irregularities in surface texture are good indicators of fasteners and taped vertical joints which always fall over studs. Also, look for nails in the baseboard molding. Nails near the bottom of the molding (within 3 inches of the floor) extend into the wall's bottom plate, not into studs. But nails near the top of the molding do indicate studs. Once you've found that telltale nail, you can usually find adjacent studs on 16-inch centers.

To confirm a stud location, drive a 4d nail into a section of the wall that will be covered when the shelves or cabinets are installed. For the project shown here, test-nailing was done just below the line marking the top of a ledger. You'll know right away if you are just popping through drywall or hitting solid wood.

with all edges flush. Now lay out and cut the notches for the 2 × 3 uprights. (See *Drawing C.*) Corner notches can be cut with a portable jigsaw or by hand with a crosscut saw. To cut out the center notches, use a portable jigsaw or a coping saw.

5 Install the shelves. Use a board at least 72 inches long as a temporary support for installing the shelves as shown in *Photo 2.* Start by resting the bottom shelf on top of its ledger board. Shelf ends should be flush with ledger ends. Hold the front edge of the shelf level, and nail the temporary support against the edge. At this stage, don't worry if the shelf hangs below level at either end. Near the back edge of the shelf, drive 1½-inch drywall screws through the shelf and into the ledger. Use five or six screws per shelf, spacing them evenly. Repeat this procedure to install the two remaining shelves.

6 Cut and install the uprights. As shown in *Drawings A and D,* 2 × 3 uprights fit in notches in the two lower shelves. The top end of each upright butts against the bottom of the uppermost shelf. To determine the height of each upright, hold the upright vertically against the front edge of the top shelf at one of the three notches. Place a level on the top shelf near the upright, and move the top shelf's front edge up or down until the shelf is level across its width. Then mark the cutoff line for trimming the upright to its finished length.

This method will give you level shelves even if the floor isn't level. Repeat this technique to cut the remaining two uprights to length, and label all three uprights so that you'll install them in the right place.

To install corner uprights, align the front corner of each upright with the front corner of the top shelf. Then secure the upright by

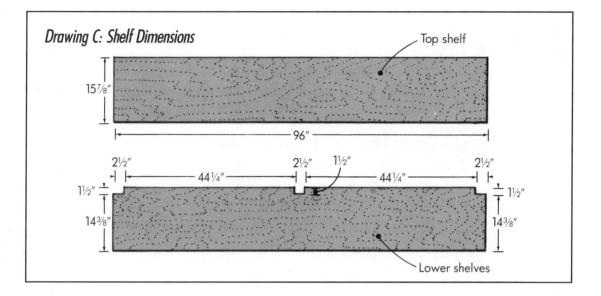

Drawing C: Shelf Dimensions

Top shelf

15⅞"

96"

2½"   2½" 1½"   2½"

1½"   1½"

44¼"   44¼"

14⅜"   14⅜"

Lower shelves

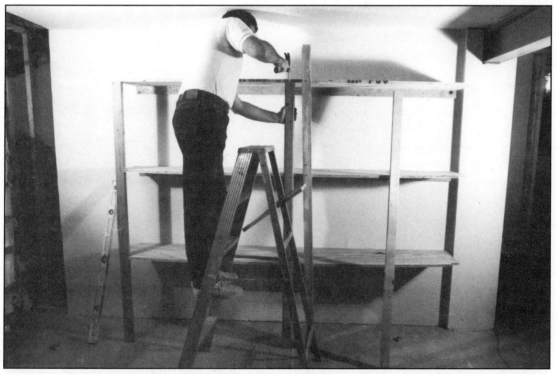

Photo 2: A temporary upright, tacked to the front edge of each shelf, keeps the shelves in position while you cut permanent uprights. Secure each upright by driving two 6d nails through the top shelf and into the top of the upright.

Photo 3: Glue and nail each end trim piece to the shelf edge and to the upright, using 6d finishing nails.

driving two 6d finishing nails through the top shelf and into the top of the upright.

To install the center upright, position this 2 × 3 in its notches so that the front face of the upright is flush with the front edges of the shelves. Then drive a pair of 6d finishing nails through the top shelf and into the upright. (See *Photo 2.*)

7 **Install the end trim pieces.** In this design the trim pieces are structural, keeping shelf edges stiff, level, and secured to the uprights. Use glue and 6d finishing nails to fasten each end trim piece to the end of a shelf. On the two lower shelves, make sure that the shelf is level across its width before nailing the end trim piece to the upright. (See *Photo 3.*)

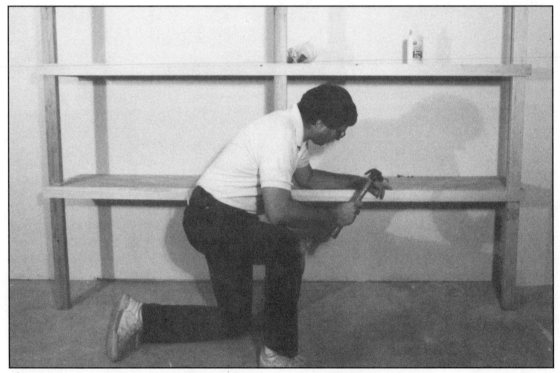

Photo 4: Nail the trim pieces to the uprights and to the shelf edges.

8 Install the front trim pieces. Remove the temporary upright. Before installing the front trim pieces on the two lower shelves, make sure that each of these shelves is level along its front edge. To do this, place a 4-foot level on the shelf, just behind the center upright and parallel with the front edge. Hold the front edge of the shelf level while toenailing a 6d finishing nail through the edge and into the upright. Now install the front trim piece using glue and 6d finishing nails. Nail the trim piece to the shelf edge as well as to the uprights and to the ends of the end trim pieces. (See *Photo 4*.) Finish the project by installing the remaining trim piece along the front edge of the top shelf.

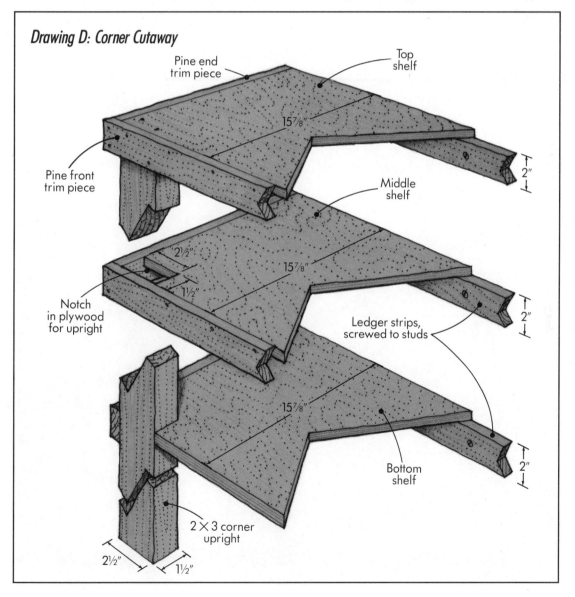

Drawing D: Corner Cutaway

Pine end trim piece

Top shelf

15⁷⁄₈"

Pine front trim piece

Middle shelf

2"

2½"

1½"

15⁷⁄₈"

Notch in plywood for upright

Ledger strips, screwed to studs

2"

15⁷⁄₈"

Bottom shelf

2"

2 × 3 corner upright

2½"

1½"

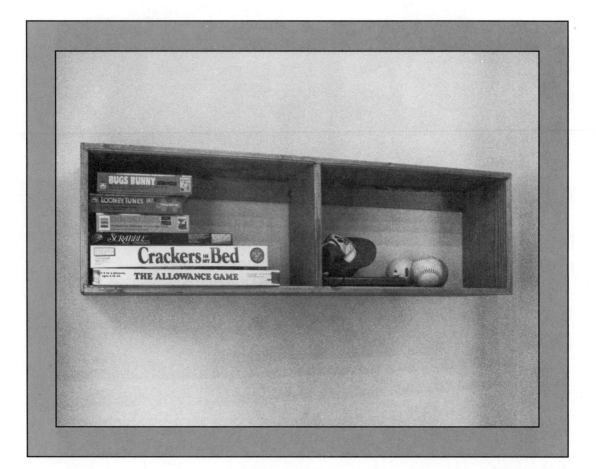

Basic Wall Shelves

These basic wall shelves are simple but elegant, and could do well in quite a few locations throughout the house. Essentially a long rectangle with a center divider, this design is modular enough to repeat easily, both in the workshop and on the wall. You might want to build several units at once. They could be used singly, or in groups on the same wall.

These shelves combine the strength and stability of plywood with the fine appearance of solid wood. One must look carefully to discern the solid-wood edge pieces that cover the plywood edges. As for its strength, when properly installed a single wall unit like the one shown here will easily support more than 100 pounds.

Making Shelves and Sides

1 **Cut plywood shelves to size.** The grain of the face veneers should run parallel to the length of the shelves. Cut each shelf to its finished width (8⅝ inches), and to a rough length of about 48 inches. (See "Cutting Plywood Panels" on page 25.)

2 **Fasten edge strips to the shelves.** As shown in *Drawing A,* each shelf has a front edge of solid pine. Cut the two edge strips from a straight, clear pine board, and choose the straightest edge on each plywood shelf to make the glue joint. Spread glue along one edge of each strip, and join strips to shelves. Don't worry if the edging extends beyond the end of the shelf; you'll cut it to size later. A few 4d finishing nails, driven through each strip and into the plywood, will secure strips until clamps are applied.

As an alternative to fastening with finishing nails, you can *biscuit-join* these parts, using a slot-cutting bit in your router to mill grooves for wood biscuits. (See "Biscuits and Splines"

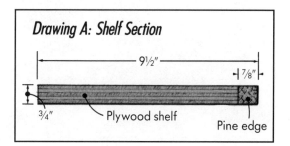

Drawing A: Shelf Section

9½"

⅞"

¾"

Plywood shelf

Pine edge

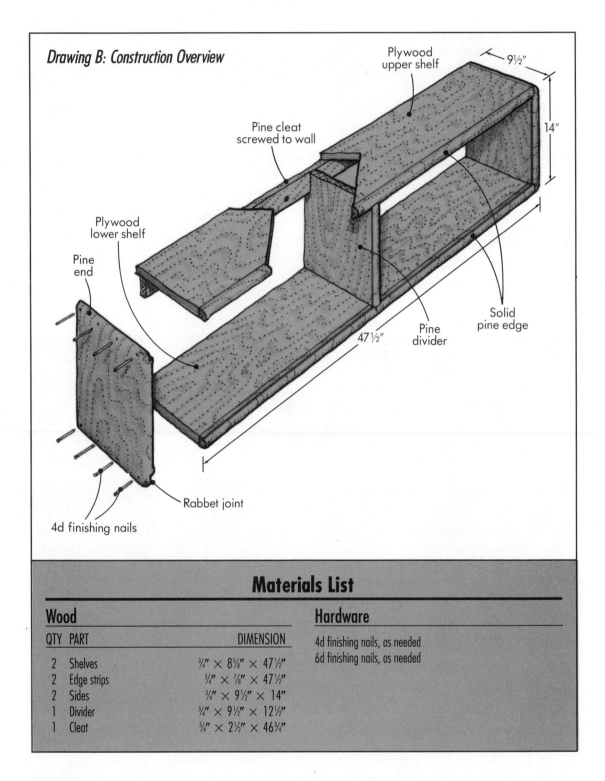

Drawing B: Construction Overview

Plywood
upper shelf

9½"

14"

Pine cleat
screwed to wall

Plywood
lower shelf

Pine
end

47½"

Pine
divider

Solid
pine edge

Rabbet joint

4d finishing nails

Materials List

Wood

QTY	PART	DIMENSION
2	Shelves	¾" × 8⅝" × 47½"
2	Edge strips	¾" × ⅞" × 47½"
2	Sides	¾" × 9½" × 14"
1	Divider	¾" × 9½" × 12½"
1	Cleat	¾" × 2½" × 46¾"

Hardware

4d finishing nails, as needed
6d finishing nails, as needed

on page 42.) Either way, these glue joints should be clamped firmly until the glue dries. The easiest way to do this is to butt the pine strips edge-to-edge, and apply pressure with pipe clamps, as shown in *Photo 1*.

3 **Smooth the edge strips flush with the shelves.** Unclamp the shelves when the glue has dried, and sand the joints using an 80-grit sanding belt. The purpose of this step is to remove hardened glue and to sand the edge strips flush with the plywood faces of the shelves. Apply even pressure with the belt sander to avoid gouging the work. Then finish smoothing by hand, using 150-grit paper. There's no need to round-over the front edges

of each shelf; the important thing is to smooth the joint between the edging and the plywood.

4 **Cut shelves to length.** Trim a slight amount (about ¼ inch) from the ends of each shelf to yield a final length of 47½ inches. (See *Photo 2*.) Make sure that both shelves are identical in length.

5 **Cut and rabbet the side pieces.** Rabbet the ends of the sides with a dado cutter on the table saw. Adjust cutter width to about ⅝ inch (the widest setting on most dado cutters) and height to exactly ⅜ inch. (See *Drawing C*.) Set the rip fence so that it is ¾ inch from

Photo 1: After gluing pine edges to both plywood shelves, clamp the shelves together with the pine edges butting against each other.

the outside of the blade. Run the sides over the cutter, supporting the piece with the miter gauge and running the end against the fence. To complete the rabbet, slide the piece away from the rip fence. Make another pass to complete the rabbet as shown in *Photo 3*.

Assembling the Parts

1 Assemble shelves and sides. Spread glue on the rabbet joints, and drive 4d finishing nails through the side pieces into the ends of the shelves. (See *Photo 4*.) The front edges of the sides should be flush with the front edges of the shelves. With the shelves and sides together, nail a temporary diagonal brace across the back edge of one shelf and one side to keep the shelf square.

2 Cut and install the center divider. This piece not only divides the cabinet in half, it ties the lower shelf to the cleat and prevents the lower shelf from bowing. Cut a notch for the cleat in the upper back corner of the divider. (See *Drawing D*.) Then glue the divider between the shelves.

Before securing the divider by driving 6d finishing nails through the shelves, make sure that the front edges of shelves and divider are flush. Then use a square to make sure that the divider's edges meet the shelves at right angles. (See *Photo 5*.)

3 Cut and install the cleat. It's important for this piece to be straight. After ripping the cleat to a width of 2½ inches, cut it to fit

(continued on page 44)

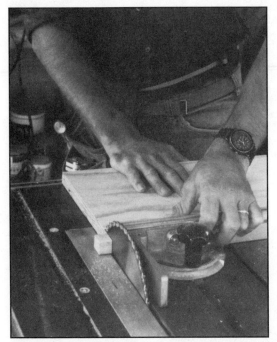

Photo 2: Trim the shelf ends square on the table saw. Here, the miter gauge is reversed to improve stability while cutting.

Photo 3: Rabbet side pieces on the table saw, using the dado cutter. Guide the edge of the side against a wood auxiliary fence to mill the dado.

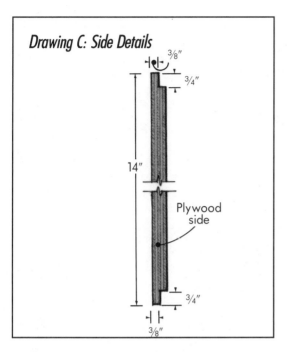

Drawing C: Side Details

3/8"

3/4"

14"

Plywood
side

3/4"

3/8"

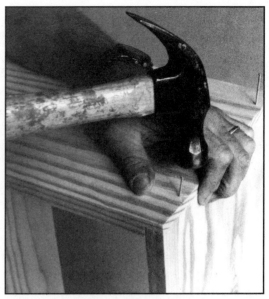

Photo 4: Glue and nail the side pieces to the shelves, using 4d finishing nails.

Photo 5: When installing the divider, keep it square with both shelves. The cleat, installed next, will fit in the notch.

Biscuits and Splines

With a router, a slot-cutting bit, and some wood *biscuits,* you can make edge-to-edge joinery go quickly and precisely. You'll soon find that biscuits eliminate the need for nailing edge strips in place. They also make dowels obsolete when edge-joining narrow boards to form a larger panel. Biscuit joinery not only adds strength, it also aligns the joining parts.

Many commercial cabinetmaking shops have expensive biscuit-joining machines. But you can buy reasonably priced biscuit-joinery "kits" for the router (see "Sources" on page 360) that work just as well. Included in each kit are a piloted slot-cutting bit and a number of football-shaped biscuits made from solid wood or waferboard.

To use this biscuit-joinery kit, first align the planned edge-to-edge joint. In the example shown here, a solid pine edge strip is being joined to a plywood shelf. Make a pencil line across the joint at each planned biscuit location. For edge-to-edge joinery like this, biscuits can be spaced every 10 inches or so.

The first time you use the biscuits, you'll discover that they are slightly thinner than the slot. The wood in the biscuits is compressed during manufacture. During assembly of a project, the moisture in the glue causes the biscuit to expand slightly,

Slot-cutting bit with biscuits

Laying out biscuit locations

creating an extremely solid joint.

Chuck the slot-cutting bit in the router, and adjust the router's depth of cut so that the slot cutter contacts the edges to be joined near the center of their thickness. Then turn on the router, and mill slots at each layout mark, as shown in the photo below. By sighting through the opening in the base of the router, you can center the shaft of the bit on each layout line. Move the bit slightly to either side of the layout line to ensure that slot length will exceed biscuit length by about ¼ inch. The pilot

bearing on the bottom of the bit controls the depth of the slot. Repeat the slot-cutting operation on the solid-pine edging, again milling slots at each layout line.

Apply glue along the joint, taking care to spread some in the biscuit slots. Then insert the biscuits and join the parts together. Clamp them snugly and wait for the glue to dry. As a variation on biscuit joinery, you can use the slot-cutting bit to mill a groove along the full length of joining edges; then use a full-length spline when gluing the joint together.

Milling slots

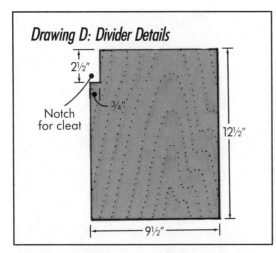

Drawing D: Divider Details

2½"

Notch for cleat

¾"

12½"

9½"

snugly between the side pieces. Then spread glue on the divider notch and on the ends and top edge of the cleat. Tap the cleat into position, and secure it by driving 6d finishing nails through the top of the upper shelf and into the top edge of the cleat. Also nail the side pieces to the cleat, and nail the cleat to the divider.

4 Round-over front edges. (See *Photo 6*.) Some quick work with the router will embellish the front edges of your project nicely. The edge treatment shown in *Drawing E* is done using a router and a ¼-inch roundover bit. Adjust the router's depth of cut until the bit routs a delicate shoulder in addition to the roundover. Now mill this profile on the inner front edges of shelves, sides, and divider. Once this is done, adjust the router's depth of cut to rout a roundover without the shoulder. Then mill a simple roundover on the outside edges of the shelves and sides.

Installing the Shelves

These shelves should be fastened into studs, or secured to a masonry wall with heavy-duty masonry anchors. In either case, drive the screws through pre-drilled pilot holes in the cleat. If you use flathead screws, countersink the screw heads. If you use roundhead or hexhead screws, place a washer between the head and the cleat. Two fastening points should provide sufficient holding power, but they should be as far apart as possible. When installing the shelves against a wood-frame wall, make sure that each screw is at least 2¾ inches long, so that it can extend through the cleat, through the drywall or plaster, and at least 1½ inches into the stud.

To install the shelves against a masonry wall, use screws and masonry anchors rated

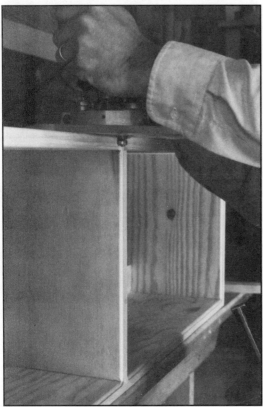

Photo 6: Finish off the front edges of the shelves, sides, and divider using a ¼-inch roundover bit in the router.

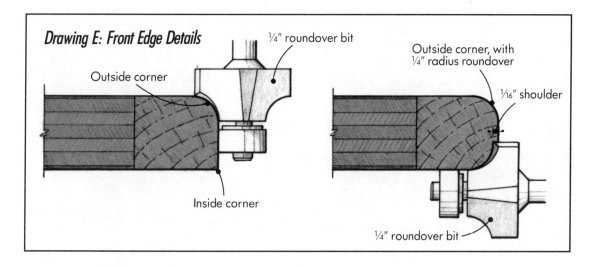

Drawing E: Front Edge Details

Outside corner

¼" roundover bit

Inside corner

Outside corner, with ¼" radius roundover

¹⁄₁₆" shoulder

¼" roundover bit

to support at least 50 pounds. For detailed information on wall-fastening hardware and techniques, see "Against the Wall" on page 10.

Sandpaper Storage Case

S andpaper is a neglected item in many home workshops. Too often, fine-grit paper is mixed up with medium-grit or coarse-grit paper, and used sheets are stored with new ones. This project, easily completed in an afternoon, should solve sandpaper storage problems for good. The design shown here contains six separate compartments for 9 × 11-inch sheets of different grits. Below the compartments is a drawer for storing used and partial sheets.

Milling Rabbets and Dadoes

1 **Cut the parts to size.** For a small project like this one, it makes sense to cut all your parts first. This way, you'll be able to complete the rabbets and dadoes on the table saw, without switching back and forth between the dado cutter and a conventional table saw blade.

To simplify the joint-cutting process for the two sides and for the top and bottom pieces, temporarily fasten each pair of pieces together after ripping them to their finished widths. Put the faces you want on the outside of the cabinet against each other, and keep side edges flush. Drive a couple of 1-inch drywall screws to hold each pair of pieces together. Then cut the paired pieces to their finished lengths. Leave these parts screwed together through Step 4.

2 **Mill dadoes in the sides.** As shown in *Drawing B,* the dadoes for the dividers are ¼ inch wide and ¼ inch deep; they're spaced to allow a compartment 1½ inches high in the finished case. Using a tape measure and a square, lay out each dado along one edge of the sides. Also lay out the dado for the ⅝-inch-thick bottom shelf. When the layout is complete, make sure that the screws holding the sides together aren't located inside a dado. Relocate the screws if necessary.

Square your table saw's miter gauge to the saw blade; then replace the blade with a dado cutter. Adjust the cutter's width to ¼ inch, and raise the cutter ¼ inch above the table. Now attach a wood auxiliary fence to your miter gauge. Use a straight piece of ¾-inch-thick stock for the fence, and make it about 1½ inches high and 16 inches long. Fasten the fence to the gauge so that one end extends at least several inches beyond the cutting width of the dado.

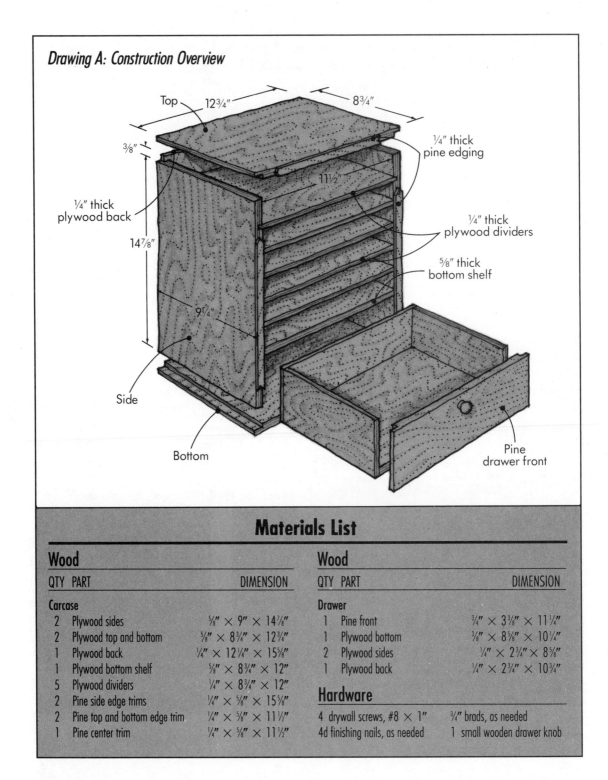

Drawing A: Construction Overview

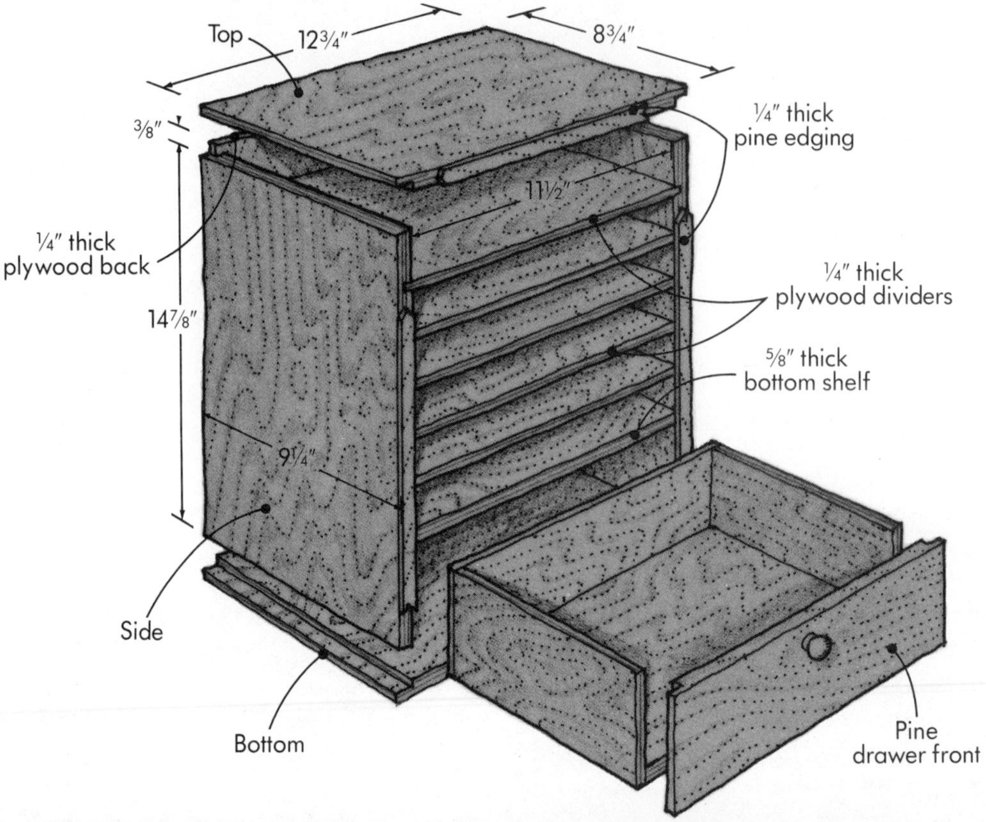
Top
12¾″
8¾″
⅜″
¼″ thick
pine edging
11½″
¼″ thick
plywood back
14⅞″
¼″ thick
plywood dividers
⅝″ thick
bottom shelf
9¼″
Side
Bottom
Pine
drawer front

Materials List

Wood

QTY	PART	DIMENSION
Carcase		
2	Plywood sides	⅝″ × 9″ × 14⅞″
2	Plywood top and bottom	⅝″ × 8¾″ × 12¾″
1	Plywood back	¼″ × 12¼″ × 15⅝″
1	Plywood bottom shelf	⅝″ × 8¾″ × 12″
5	Plywood dividers	¼″ × 8¾″ × 12″
2	Pine side edge trims	¼″ × ⅝″ × 15⅝″
2	Pine top and bottom edge trim	¼″ × ⅝″ × 11½″
1	Pine center trim	¼″ × ⅝″ × 11½″

Wood

QTY	PART	DIMENSION
Drawer		
1	Pine front	¾″ × 3⅜″ × 11¼″
1	Plywood bottom	⅜″ × 8⅝″ × 10¼″
2	Plywood sides	¼″ × 2¾″ × 8⅝″
1	Plywood back	¼″ × 2¾″ × 10¾″

Hardware

4 drywall screws, #8 × 1″

4d finishing nails, as needed

¾″ brads, as needed

1 small wooden drawer knob

Now mill the side dadoes as shown in *Photo 1*, guiding the workpiece against the auxiliary fence, with one end butted against a stop block that is clamped to the fence. The block enables you to mill corresponding dadoes in each side, precisely duplicating the location of each pair of dadoes at each block setting. Position the block to the left or right of the miter gauge to align the workpiece. Mill each bottom shelf dado by making several passes through the cutter.

3 **Rabbet the top and bottom.** As shown in *Drawing B*, the top and bottom are rabbeted to house the sides. Mill these joints the same way you milled the dadoes. Adjust the

Photo 1: A stop block, clamped to the miter gauge auxiliary fence, enables you to duplicate dado locations on both sides.

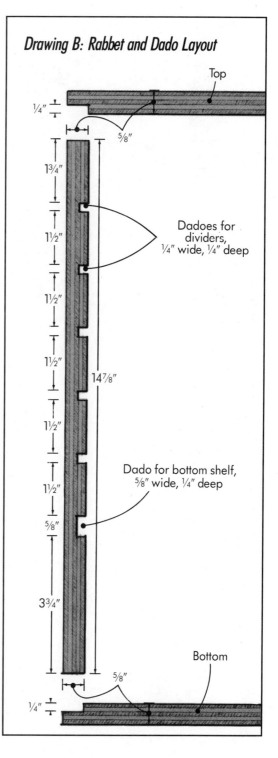

Drawing B: Rabbet and Dado Layout

Top

¼"

⅝"

1¾"

1½"

Dadoes for dividers, ¼" wide, ¼" deep

1½"

1½"

1½"

14⅞"

1½"

1½"

Dado for bottom shelf, ⅝" wide, ¼" deep

⅝"

3¾"

Bottom

⅝"

¼"

Photo 2: Rabbet the top and bottom with both pieces temporarily screwed together. Position a stop block on the miter gauge auxiliary fence to align the shoulder cut for all four rabbets.

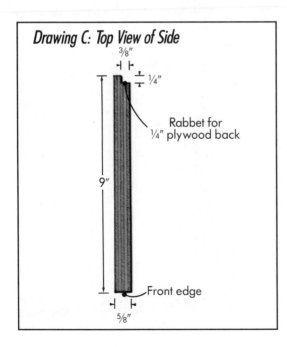

dado cutter's width to ½ inch, while keeping cutter height at ¼ inch. Now position the stop block on the auxiliary fence to align the top and bottom for the rabbet's shoulder cut. To mill each rabbet, guide a long edge of the workpiece against the auxiliary fence. Make one pass through the cutter with the work-piece end about ⅜ inch from the working edge of the stop block. Finish the joint as shown in *Photo 2*, with the end of the work-piece butted against the stop block. Mill all four rabbets this way.

4 **Rabbet the back edges of the sides.** These rabbets are ⅜ inch wide and ¼ inch deep, as shown in *Drawing C*. Mill them with the cutter width at ½ inch, as in the previous step, but adjust the cutter height to ⅜ inch. Then position the rip fence 8¾ inches from the cutter. Turn on the saw, and mill each rabbet by running the front edges of the sides against the rip fence. Don't adjust your dado cutter's width or height after completing this step; you'll need these settings later.

Assembling the Case

1 **Assemble the sides, top, bottom, and bottom shelf.** Remove the screws that hold the paired parts together. Spread glue along the rabbets in the top and bottom pieces, and in the dadoes where the bottom shelf will fit. Then nail the case together, using 4d finishing nails. Make sure that all front edges are flush with each other. (See *Photo 3*.)

2 **Attach the back.** As shown in *Drawing A*, the back fits in the rabbets milled in the sides, and over the back edges of the top and bottom. Install the back with glue and ¾-inch brads. Make sure that the case stays square as you drive the brads.

3 **Install the dividers.** These pieces don't need to be glued into their dadoes; simply slip them into place. Divider front edges should be flush with the front edges of the sides.

4 **Install the trim pieces.** These thin pine edge strips will give the case a more finished appearance, while also preventing the splintering that can occur when plywood edges are left exposed. Secure each strip with glue and ¾-inch brads. (See *Photo 4*.)

Making the Drawer

When rummaging in the drawer for used sandpaper, you'll find it easiest to pull the drawer out of the cabinet and set it on your bench. For this reason, this drawer is designed for a much looser fit at the sides than the drawers in other projects in this book. The loose fit makes it easy to remove and replace the drawer with one hand. The flush-fit design of the drawer front hides the loose fit of the sides.

1 **Rabbet the drawer front.** As shown in *Drawing D*, the drawer front is rabbeted along three edges to hold the sides and bottom. Mill these rabbets with the dado cutter adjusted to ½-inch width and ⅜-inch height. To align the workpiece for its end rabbets, clamp a stop block against the miter gauge auxiliary fence, as shown in *Photo 5*. To rabbet the bottom edge of the front, position the rip fence 2⅞ inches from the dado cutter. Guide the top edge of the front against the rip fence to cut the rabbet.

2 **Install the drawer bottom.** Spread glue on the rabbet that runs along the bottom edge of the drawer front. Then nail the bottom

Photo 3: Glue and nail the top and bottom of the case to the sides.

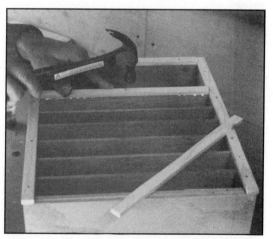

Photo 4: After slipping the dividers into their dadoes, glue and nail pine edging into place.

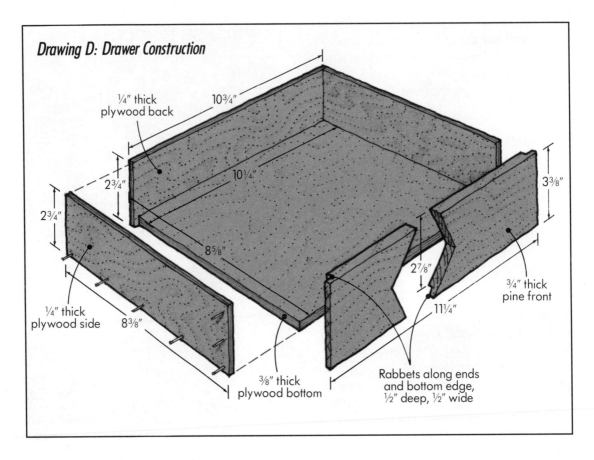

Drawing D: Drawer Construction

¼" thick plywood back

10¾"

10¼"

2¾"

2¾"

8⅝"

3⅜"

¼" thick plywood side

8⅜"

2⅞"

11¼"

¾" thick pine front

⅜" thick plywood bottom

Rabbets along ends and bottom edge, ½" deep, ½" wide

to the rabbet with 4d finishing nails. You'll use 4d finishing nails for the entire drawer assembly.

3 **Install the drawer sides.** Glue and nail each side to the front and to an edge of the bottom. (See *Photo 6*.) Make sure that the side's bottom edge is flush with the bottom face of the drawer bottom.

4 **Install the drawer back.** Glue and nail the back against the back edges of the bot-

tom and sides. Now set all the nails used in assembling the drawer. Then smooth all corners and edges with 120-grit sandpaper.

5 **Install the drawer knob and apply finish.** Drill a hole centered in the drawer front for the screw that secures the knob, and screw the knob into place. Then seal the inside and outside of the drawer with a coat of polyurethane. When this finish has dried, rub wax on the bottom of the drawer.

Photo 5: A stop block, clamped to the miter gauge auxiliary fence, aligns each end of the drawer front for its rabbet cut.

Photo 6: After gluing and nailing the drawer bottom to the drawer front, fasten the sides to the front and bottom. The block of wood raises the drawer front off its edge, steadying the drawer for nailing.

Mudroom
&
Entry

Coatrack

Traditional proportions and construction details give this hat and coatrack a timeless appeal that will dress up any hallway or entry area. Though this rack is small enough to fit just about anywhere, it has enough room to hold the hats and coats of the whole family. Very little wood is required to build this project, so you might consider making more than one of these. A second hat and coatrack, mounted lower on the wall, enables children to stow their own outerwear.

Making the Parts

1 **Cut the shelf and rails to size.** Except for the two brackets, all parts for the hat and coatrack can be cut to size on the table saw. For strength, cut the peg rail from clear wood.

Photo 1: After making a pattern, use it to trace the bracket shape onto ¾-inch-thick stock.

Drawing A: Construction Overview

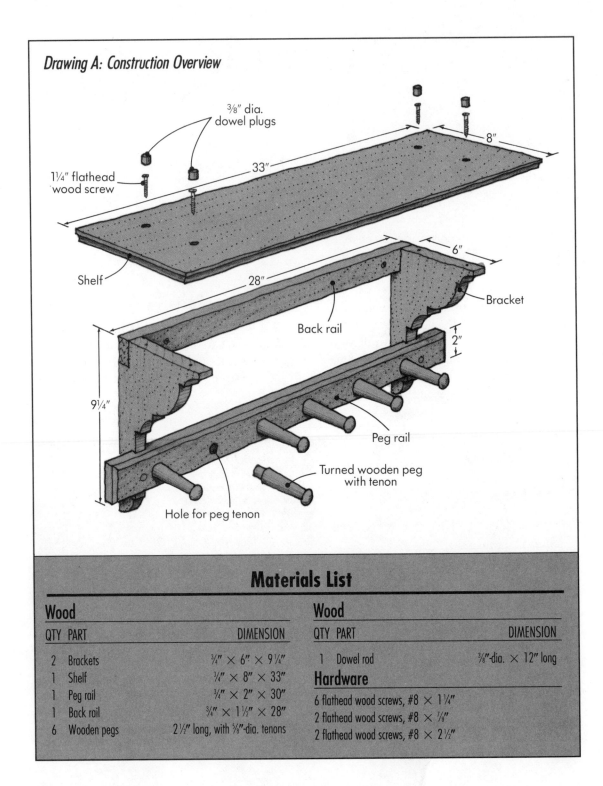

⅜" dia. dowel plugs

1¼" flathead wood screw

33"

8"

Shelf

28"

6"

Back rail

Bracket

2"

9¼"

Peg rail

Turned wooden peg with tenon

Hole for peg tenon

Materials List

Wood

QTY	PART	DIMENSION
2	Brackets	¾" × 6" × 9¼"
1	Shelf	¾" × 8" × 33"
1	Peg rail	¾" × 2" × 30"
1	Back rail	¾" × 1½" × 28"
6	Wooden pegs	2½" long, with ⅝"-dia. tenons

Wood

QTY	PART	DIMENSION
1	Dowel rod	⅜"-dia. × 12" long

Hardware

6 flathead wood screws, #8 × 1¼"
2 flathead wood screws, #8 × ⅞"
2 flathead wood screws, #8 × 2½"

2 **Lay out the brackets.** Use the scaled-down pattern shown in *Drawing B* to make a full-scale pattern of the bracket. Then trace the bracket shape onto the stock so the wood grain runs along the length of the bracket. (See *Photo 1*.)

3 **Cut and shape the brackets.** First, cut each bracket to length on the table saw. The top edge of each bracket should be straight and square with the bracket's back edge. Cut out the curves with a bandsaw or with a portable jigsaw. When both brackets have been cut out, clamp them together in your bench vice so that the top and back edges are flush with each other. A round sanding stick, which you can easily make in the workshop (see the Shop Savvy on page 60), does a good job of smoothing out the saw marks. (See *Photo 2*.) Take care to keep the sanding stick perpendicular to the bracket sides. In this way, both brackets will come out with the same profile.

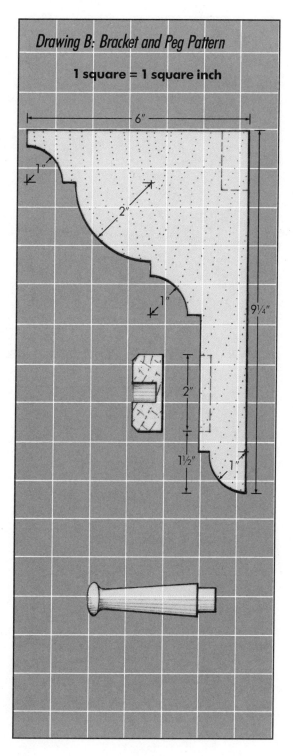

Photo 2: Clamp the cut-out brackets together in the bench vice, and use a sanding stick to smooth out saw marks from curved edges.

Shop Savvy

Sanding Sticks--Smooth Results from Shop-Made Tools

Steel rasps and files are commonly used to smooth and shape wood. But you can often get smoother results with a shop-made sanding stick. All you need to make a sanding stick are contact cement, some sandpaper, and the stick itself--in this case, a short length of dowel rod. Use an inexpensive brush to spread a thin layer of contact cement on the back of the sandpaper and on the surface of the stick. When the cement has dried to the touch (no longer sticking to your finger), apply the sandpaper to the stick.

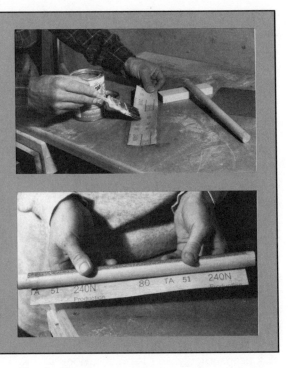

Photo 3: Cut out notches for the back rail on the table saw, using the miter gauge to guide the bracket.

4 **Notch the brackets for the back rail.** Each bracket has two notches--one to hold the back rail and the other to hold the peg rail. First, cut the back rail notches using the miter gauge to guide the stock across the table saw. These notches measure ¾ inch deep and 1½ inches long. Adjust the miter gauge for a 90-degree cut, then adjust the blade height to ¾ inch. Make the first cut with the back edge of the bracket against the table surface. Then raise the blade height to 1½ inches, and make the second cut to complete each notch. For this cut, the top edge of the bracket runs against the table surface. (See *Photo 3*.)

5 **Notch the brackets for the peg rail.** The notches for the peg rail are cut a little differently. Since these are located on the front edges of the brackets, they need to be cut by hand instead of on the table saw. Lay out each ⅜-inch-deep, 2-inch-long notch with a

Photo 4: To make the peg rail notch, use a backsaw to make a series of closely spaced kerfs inside the notch layout lines.

combination square, marking both sides of each bracket. Then clamp a bracket in the bench vice so the notch faces up and the back edge of the bracket is level.

Making each notch is a two-step process. First, use a backsaw to make a series of cuts, or kerfs, inside the layout lines, as shown in *Photo 4*. Then chisel away the waste. You'll find that the closely spaced kerfs make it very easy to chisel away the wood. Remove most of the waste with the chisel's bevel facing down. If necessary, use a hammer to tap the chisel. To clean up the joint, flip the chisel over and pare the joint smooth and square. (See *Photo 5*.) Test fit the peg rail in each notch; pare the notch as necessary to achieve a firm fit.

6 Chamfer the peg rail. The front edges of the peg rail are chamfered for appearance and feel. Clamp the rail on the workbench with its top side facing up. Use a hand plane

Photo 5: Carefully break out the waste between kerfs; then use a chisel to pare the notch flat and square.

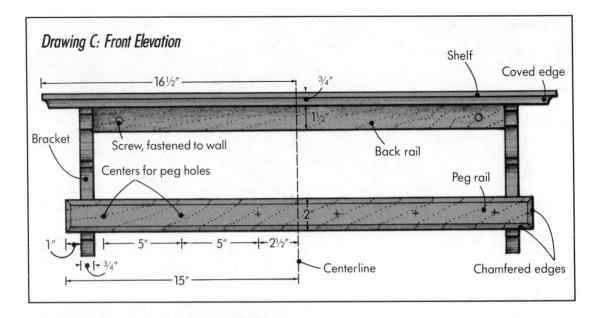

Drawing C: Front Elevation

Shelf

Coved edge

16½"

¾"

1½"

Bracket

Screw, fastened to wall

Back rail

Centers for peg holes

Peg rail

2"

1"

5"

5"

2½"

¾"

Centerline

Chamfered edges

15"

Photo 6: Holes for six pegs are spaced equally along the length of the peg rail. Keep the shank of the bit perpendicular to the rail when drilling each hole.

(or a router and chamfering bit) to chamfer the ends and long edges.

7 Lay out and drill the holes in the peg rail. Lay out six holes for the pegs, beginning from the center of the rail, as shown in *Drawing C*. After making six vertical center marks, make horizontal marks across the verticals to center each hole on the 2-inch-wide rail.

Now drill holes with a brad-point bit whose diameter matches that of the peg tenons, as shown in *Photo 6*. Make the holes slightly deeper than the tenon length to ensure that the shoulders of the tenon contact the face of the peg rail.

8 Rout the edge of the shelf. A cove, routed on the front and side edges of the shelf, complements the curves on the brackets. Clamp the shelf to the workbench with the bottom of the shelf facing up. Rout the cove with a ½-inch cove bit, as shown in *Photo 7*.

Assembling and Installing the Rack

1 Attach the brackets to the back rail. The back rail is glued and screwed in its notch. To attach the rail, clamp a bracket in the bench vise with the back rail notch facing up. Put glue in the notch and put the rail in position. While holding the end of the rail flush with the outside edge of the bracket, drill and countersink for a #8 × 1¼-inch screw. Screw the rail in place. Repeat to attach the other bracket, as shown in *Photo 8*.

2 Attach the shelf to the brackets. Since glue won't hold well in the end grain along the top edges of the brackets, secure these joints with screws only. Center the shelf on the brackets. Then drill two pilot holes through the shelf and into each bracket. Counterbore each hole to about ⅜ inch. Then secure the shelf to the brackets with four #8 × 1¼-inch flathead wood screws.

Plug the counterbored holes with plugs cut from a ⅜-inch diameter dowel. Cut each plug slightly long so it will stand proud of the shelf top by about ¼ inch. Dab glue on each plug before tapping it into its hole.

3 Install the peg rail. Put glue in the bracket notches where the peg rail will fit. Then fit the rail in the notches. Each rail end should overhang a bracket by 1 inch, as shown in *Photo 9*. Check that the entire assembly is square and not racked. Drill a counterbored pilot hole at each connection, taking care to center the hole on the rail. Then secure each joint with a single #8 × ⅞-inch flathead wood screw.

Fill counterbored holes with dowel plugs. When the glue has dried, use a backsaw to trim the plugs so they extend just slightly above the surface of the rail. Saw carefully so that you don't leave marks in the rail. Then

Photo 7: Rout the cove along the bottom edge of the shelf with a piloted cove bit.

Photo 8: Begin assembly by attaching the back rail to the brackets. Glue each joint and secure it with a single countersunk screw.

Photo 9: Glue and screw the peg rail so that it overhangs the bracket by 1 inch. Counterbore pilot holes for the screws, and cover screw heads with dowel plugs.

Photo 10: Install the pegs last. Spread glue onto each peg tenon before turning the tenon into its hole.

use a sharp chisel to shave the plugs flush with the rail.

4 **Sand the rack thoroughly.** Round-over any sharp edges that remain on the shelf or brackets.

5 **Install the pegs.** Test fit the pegs in their holes to make sure that the hole depth is correct. Then spread glue evenly on the peg tenons, and insert the pegs in the holes as shown in *Photo 10*. Use a damp rag to wipe away any excess glue that squeezes out around the pegs.

6 **Install the rack.** Install your hat and coat-rack by driving two screws through the

back rail and into the wall. Flathead or round-head screws can be used, depending on taste. Be sure to use washers if you are using round-head screws.

If the wall is framed with wood studs, the screws should extend through the back rail, through the plaster or gypsum board of the wall, and into two studs. For most walls, #8 × 2½-inch flathead wood screws will do the job. (For instructions on locating studs, see the Shop Savvy on page 32.) Drive one screw and then place a level on the shelf or against the bottom edge of the top rail. Keep the rack level as you drive the second screw.

Recycling Center

This outdoor recycling center provides a neat and easy way to separate and store household recyclables. Sturdy and compact, the center has a slanted top that swings up on a pair of hinges. Two doors on the front of the unit open to reveal six plastic bins stored on two levels. Three bins can be used for glass (clear, green, and brown), one bin can hold aluminum cans, and the remaining two bins hold newspapers and plastic containers.

The frame is constructed from 2 × 4s, with a base of pressure-treated 2 × 8s. The sides are sheathed with Textured 1-11 (commonly called T1-11), a style of exterior plywood siding that is manufactured to look like rough-sawn boards. The top is made from BC exterior-grade plywood because it is smoother and sheds water better than T1-11. The back is also BC exterior grade, only because it won't be seen and is less expensive than T1-11.

You can change this mix of plywoods to suit your needs. Just be sure to use plywood that is stamped "exterior," which means that the plywood is designed for permanent outdoor use. Don't use plywood stamped "exposure" or "x." Exposure-grade plywood is designed to be covered with siding, not to be left permanently to the weather.

The bins in this center measure 14½ inches wide, 17 inches long, and 11¼ inches high. If you prefer to use larger or smaller bins, you'll need to adjust the dimensions of your recycling center accordingly. The construction details presented here can stay the same.

Building the Horizontal Frames

The recycling center is built around a 2 × 4 frame. Four 2 × 4 uprights are joined by two

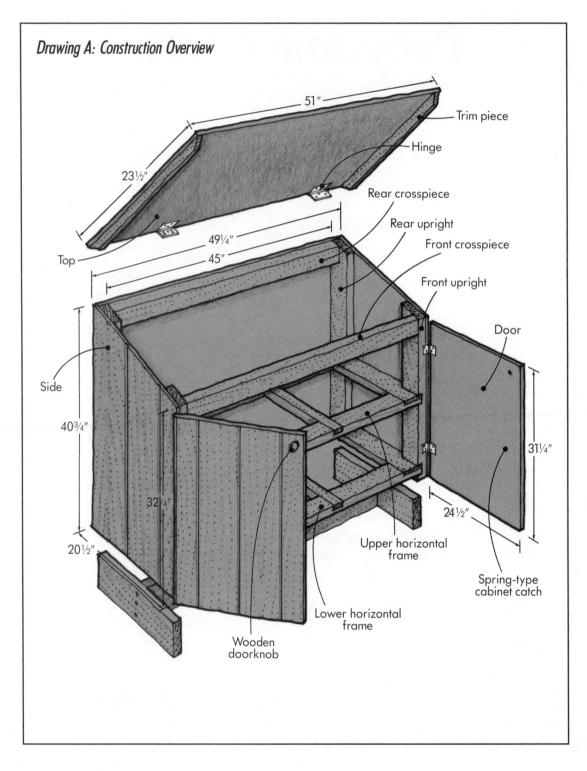

Drawing A: Construction Overview

51"

Trim piece

Hinge

23½"

Rear crosspiece

Rear upright

Front crosspiece

49¼"

45"

Front upright

Top

Door

Side

31¼"

40¾"

32¼"

20½"

24½"

Upper horizontal
frame

Spring-type
cabinet catch

Lower horizontal
frame

Wooden
doorknob

Materials List

Wood

QTY	PART	DIMENSION
Horizontal Frame Members		
4	Front/back members	1½″ × 3½″ × 46½″
4	Side members	1½″ × 3½″ × 20″
4	Center members	1½″ × 1¹¹⁄₁₆″ × 20″
Uprights and Crosspieces		
2	Front uprights*	1½″ × 3½″ × 34″
2	Rear uprights*	1½″ × 3½″ × 42″
2	Front and rear crosspieces	1½″ × 3½″ × 45″
Cladding, Top, and Doors		
2	T1-11 plywood sides*	⅝″ × 20½″ × 40¾″
1	Plywood back	½″ × 40¾″ × 48⅝″
1	Plywood top	½″ × 23½″ × 51″
2	Pine trim	¾″ × 1⅛″ × 23½″
2	T1-11 plywood doors	⅝″ × 24½″ × 31¼″

*Dimensions before angled top cut

Wood

QTY	PART	DIMENSION
Base (pressure treated wood)		
2	Cross members	1½″ × 7¼″ × 19½″
1	Connecting piece	1½″ × 7¼″ × 43″

Hardware

48 galvanized decking screws, 1¼″
16 galvanized decking screws, 2″
8 galvanized decking screws, 2½″
4d galvanized buttonhead nails, as needed
2 butt hinges, 3″ × 3″
4 butt hinges, 1½″ × 3″
2 wooden doorknobs, with mounting screws
2 spring-type cabinet catches
6 galvanized decking screws, 3″
6 plastic bins, 14½″ × 17″ long × 11¼″

---

identical horizontal frames and by crosspieces that connect the front and rear uprights. The first step is to build the horizontal frames.

1 Cut frame members to size. Each of the two horizontal frames requires two 46½-inch-long 2 × 4s and three 20-inch-long 2 × 4s. On the table saw, rip two of the six 20-inch-long 2 × 4s in half to make four center frame members. (See *Drawing B*.) Cut the front and rear uprights to the length given in the Materials List, and set them aside.

Incidentally, 2 × 4s usually measure 1½ × 3½ inches when you buy them at the lumberyard, because they have been planed so that the surface is smooth. The Materials List and drawings assume that you are working with lumber that measures 1½ × 3½ inches.

2 Set up a right-angle jig. This simple jig speeds the work of cutting numerous lap joints in horizontal frame members. To make it, start with a large, flat work surface (such as a sheet of ¾-inch-thick plywood) and a pair of straight-edged boards, each at least 30 inches long. Using a framing square as a guide, screw the boards to the work surface to form a perfect 90-degree angle.

3 Cut lap joints in horizontal frame members. As shown in *Drawing B*, the depth of each lap joint is ¾ inch, or exactly half the thickness of a standard 2 × 4. Adjust your circular saw to make a ¾-inch-deep cut. Clamp the four front and back frame members in the jig, with edges butted together and the ends against one arm of the jig.

Photo 1: With 2 × 4 frame members clamped in a right-angle frame, make closely spaced kerfs inside layout lines for lap joints. Depth-of-cut adjustment is ¾ inch.

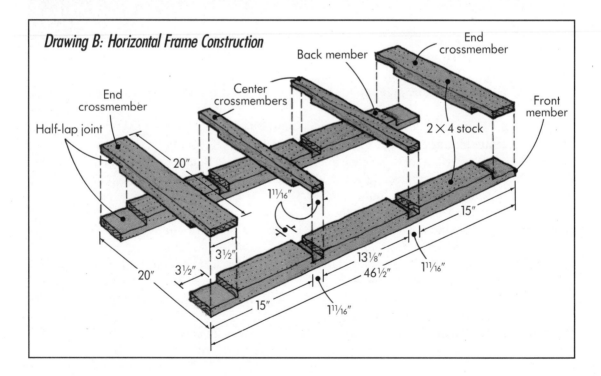

Drawing B: Horizontal Frame Construction

End crossmember

Back member

End crossmember

Center crossmembers

Front member

Half-lap joint

2 × 4 stock

20″

1¹¹⁄₁₆″

3½″

15″

20″

3½″

13⅛″

46½″

1¹¹⁄₁₆″

15″

1¹¹⁄₁₆″

Lay out the shoulder cuts for the lap joints in these members, following the dimensions given in *Drawing B*. Then make a series of closely spaced kerfs inside the layout lines for each joint. (See *Photo 1*.) Repeat this procedure for the four 20-inch-long 2 × 4s.

4 **Chisel the lap joints flat.** First, break out the waste material that remains between the saw kerfs. You can do this quickly and easily using a hammer or mallet and a 1-inch chisel. Tap the chisel into the joint with its bevel facing down to chop out the major portion of the waste. Then pare the joint flat, using the chisel with its bevel facing up.

5 **Assemble horizontal frames.** For this step, return to the right-angle jig, and use it to maintain a 90-degree angle when joining the short side members to the long front and back members. (See *Photo 2*.) Secure each corner joint with three 1¼-inch galvanized decking screws. Use a pair of screws where each center frame member joins a front or back frame member.

Making Uprights and Crosspieces

1 **Dado and rabbet the uprights.** As shown in *Drawing C*, each upright is dadoed for the upper horizontal frame and rabbetted for the lower horizontal frame. The dadoes and rabbets are spaced to allow the lower set of recycling bins to be removed easily, even if they're brimming with material.

Cut the dadoes and rabbets using the same technique you used in Steps 3 and 4 for the lap joints. Adjust the circular saw's depth of cut to ¾ inch, and make closely spaced kerfs inside the dado and rabbet layout lines. Then break out the waste between the kerfs, and

chisel each dado and rabbet flat.

2 **Join uprights and horizontal frames.** Screw the uprights to the upper horizontal frame with 2-inch galvanized decking screws. (See *Photo 3*.) Make sure each upright stays square with both the long and short edges of the frame as you drive the screws. Use two screws at each connection. Drill pilot holes to prevent splitting when joining the lower horizontal frame to the uprights. For a quick way to drill pilot holes without remov-

Photo 2: Use the right-angle frame when assembling horizontal frames. Drive 1¼-inch decking screws to secure lap joints.

ing the Phillips bit from your drill, see the Shop Savvy on page 76.

3 **Lay out and cut the top ends of the uprights.** The slope for the recycling center's top is marked and cut after you've installed the uprights. Lay out these cuts as shown in *Drawing C* and *Photo 4*. Mark the front outside edge of both front uprights 31½ inches from the bottom. Mark the back outside edge of both rear uprights 40 inches from the bottom. Use a straightedge to connect these points on each end of the frame, mark-

ing cut-off lines on all four uprights. Make the slanted cuts with a circular saw or hand saw.

4 **Cut and install crosspieces between uprights.** Make the bevel cut along the top edge of each crosspiece to match the angle on the uprights. (See *Drawing C.*) Use a bevel gauge to transfer this angle from the upright to the table saw. (See *Photo 5*.) When the blade angle is right, rip a bevel along each of two 2 × 4s that is at least 46 inches long. Cut each crosspiece to fit between front or rear uprights. Then fasten crosspieces to uprights

Photo 3: Drive 2-inch decking screws to fasten front and back uprights to horizontal frames.

Photo 4: With the frame right-side up, use a straightedge to lay out angled cuts on tops of uprights.

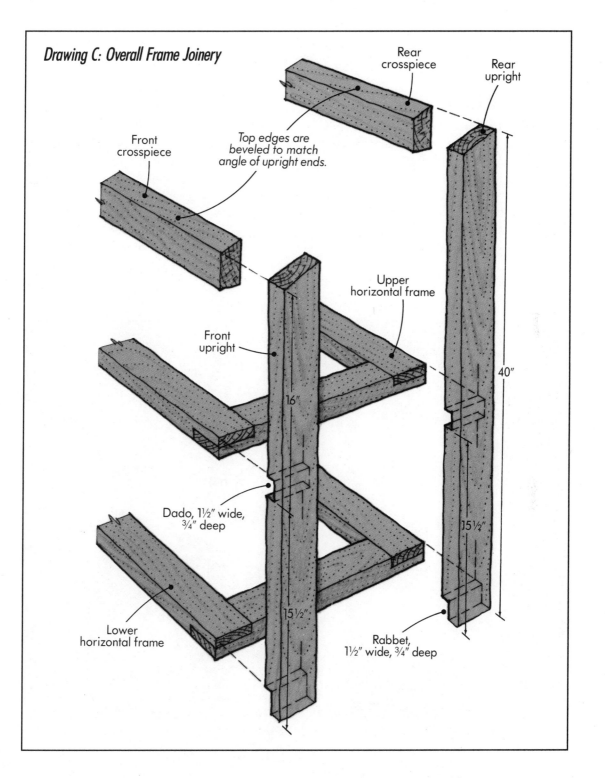

Drawing C: Overall Frame Joinery

Rear crosspiece

Rear upright

Front crosspiece

Top edges are beveled to match angle of upright ends.

Front upright

Upper horizontal frame

16"

40"

Dado, 1½" wide, ¾" deep

15½"

Lower horizontal frame

15½"

Rabbet, 1½" wide, ¾" deep

with 2½-inch-long galvanized decking screws. (See *Photo 6*.) Use two screws per joint.

Cladding the Frame

1 **Install the back and sides of the recycling center.** Take the outside dimensions of the completed frame, and use these to lay out the plywood panels for the back and sides of the recycling center. (See *Drawing D*.)

T1-11 panels have a factory-milled rabbet along each long edge. On one edge the rabbet is in the front face, and on the other edge it's in the back face. (This is to form lap joints when the panels are installed side by side.) In laying out the sides for the recycling center, position a back face rabbet along the back edge of each side. Position the shoulder of the rabbet flush with the back frame so that the rabbet will house the plywood back as shown in *Drawing D*.

Cut the top edge of each side panel to match the slope of the recycling center's top. Size all three panels so that their tops are flush with the tops of the uprights and their bottoms extend ¾ inch below the lower horizontal frame. Fasten the plywood panels to the frame with galvanized 4d "buttonhead" nails. (See *Photo 7*.) These nails are made for installing exterior siding, and will "set" below the wood

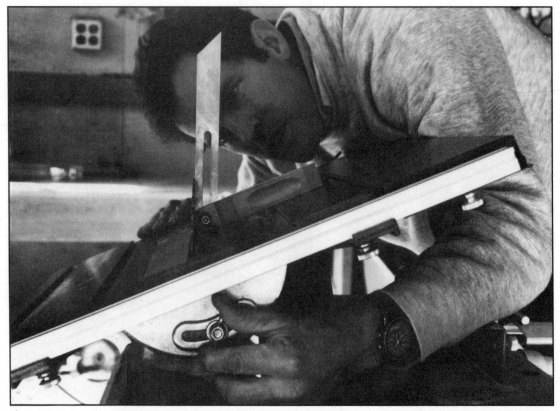

Photo 5: Use a bevel gauge to set the cutting angle on the table saw for beveling the crosspieces to match the slope of the top.

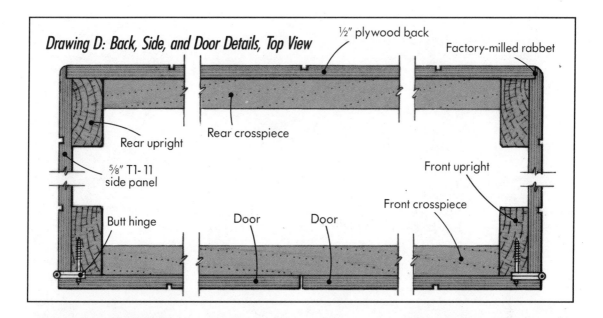

Drawing D: Back, Side, and Door Details, Top View

½" plywood back

Factory-milled rabbet

Rear upright

Rear crosspiece

⅝" T1-11 side panel

Front upright

Front crosspiece

Butt hinge

Door

Door

Photo 6: Fasten front and rear crosspieces between uprights with 2½-inch decking screws.

Photo 7: Nail back and side pieces to the frame with 4d galvanized nails. Bottom edges of back, sides, and doors should extend ¾ inch below the lower horizontal frame.

Shop Savvy

Drilling and Driving

This handy drill accessory enables you to drill pilot holes and drive screws quickly with one drill. You'll find this auxiliary chuck in hardware stores and mail-order tool catalogs. One end of the chuck fits over a Phillips or square-drive bit that is already chucked in your drill. The other end of the chuck holds the drill bit of your choice.

To use the auxiliary chuck, put a bit in it and then slip it over the Phillips bit in your drill. Now bore the pilot holes. As soon as these are done, slip off the auxiliary chuck and use the Phillips bit to drive the screws.

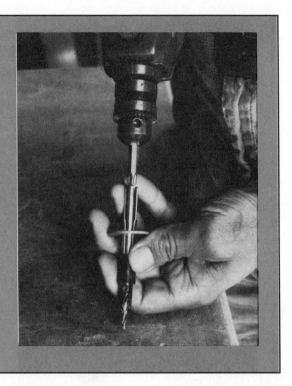

surface when you hammer them. If you can't find buttonhead nails, use galvanized 4d common nails.

2 Cut the top to size and install trim pieces. The measurements given in the Materials List allow the top to overhang the front crosspiece by about 1½ inches and each side by about ⅞ inch. Cut the top to size.

From ¾-inch-thick pine, cut a pair of trim pieces 1⅛ inches wide and as long as the top is wide—23½ inches. The top end of each trim piece is cut plumb, while the bottom end is cut level. Temporarily clamp the trim in place, and lay out the cuts as shown in *Drawing E*.

Drill counterbored pilot holes in the top for 1¼-inch galvanized decking screws. Then secure each trim piece to the top by driving the screws through the top and into the top edge of the trim piece. Fill the counterbored holes with waterproof wood filler, and sand the filler flush after it has cured.

3 Hinge the top to the rear crosspiece. The 3-inch-wide butt hinges are attached to the underside of the top and to the rear crosspiece. It's not necessary to mortise the top hinges.

Here's a quick way to position the hinges accurately. First, place the top in its installed position. Temporarily secure it in this position by driving a couple of 3d or 4d finishing nails through the top and into the tops of the front or rear uprights. Now place the hinges on the top, 6 inches from each side. Close each hinge, and hold it so that the hinge barrel extends over the back edge of the top. While holding the hinge in this position, drill pilot holes for hinge screws, as shown in *Photo 8*. Make sure to center the drill bit in each hole, and keep the bit perpendicular to the top. Drill all the way through the top and into the rear crosspiece. Now you've drilled perfectly aligned pilot holes for both leaves of the hinge.

Remove the top, and attach the hinges to it by driving screws into the pilot holes. Then attach hinges to the rear crosspiece by driving screws into the remaining pilot holes.

4 Cut and install doors. Like the back and sides of the recycling center, the plywood doors should fit so that their bottom edges extend ¾ inch below the lower horizontal frame. Allow the top edges of the doors to fall about 1 inch below the top edge of the front crosspiece. This way, the doors can swing open without lifting the top.

Position the 1½-inch-wide door hinges the

Photo 8: To drill pilot holes for top hinges, first secure the top in its installed position. Then hold the top hinge closed and 6 inches from the top corner while drilling through the top and into the rear crosspiece.

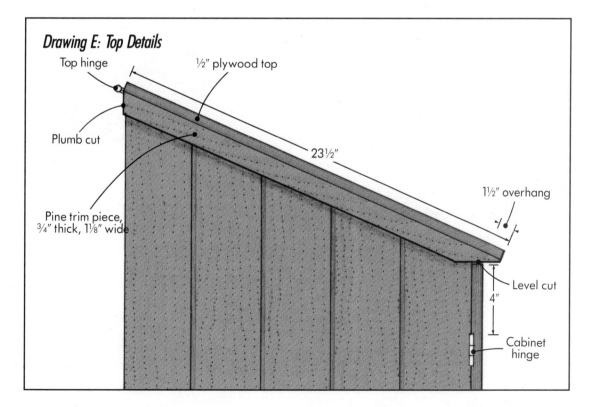

Drawing E: Top Details

Top hinge

½" plywood top

Plumb cut

23½"

1½" overhang

Pine trim piece, ¾" thick, 1⅛" wide

Level cut

4"

Cabinet hinge

same way you positioned the hinges in Step 3. First, place the recycling center on its back, and temporarily tack the doors in place against the front of the unit. Then use a closed hinge as a guide for drilling pilot holes for hinge screws. Make sure to drill through the plywood door and into the upright. Take the doors off and use the pilot holes in the uprights to register the position of the hinges. Scribe the top and bottom of the hinges and use a chisel to cut mortises for the door hinges. (See "Mortising for a Butt Hinge" on page 93.) Then screw the hinges to the doors and to the frame.

5 **Install knobs and catches.** Drill a hole for each knob 2 inches from the inside edge of the door and 4 inches from the top edge. Install catches so that the female half of each catch is screwed to the underside of the front crosspiece.

Building the Base and Applying Finish

1 **Assemble the base.** From pressure-treated 2 × 8 stock, cut a pair of cross members 19½ inches long. Cut the connecting piece 43 inches long. With 3-inch galvanized decking screws, fasten the connecting piece between the two cross members, as shown in *Drawing F*. Note that the base is ½ inch shorter and narrower than the inside dimensions of the plywood sides. This makes it easy to set the center on its base.

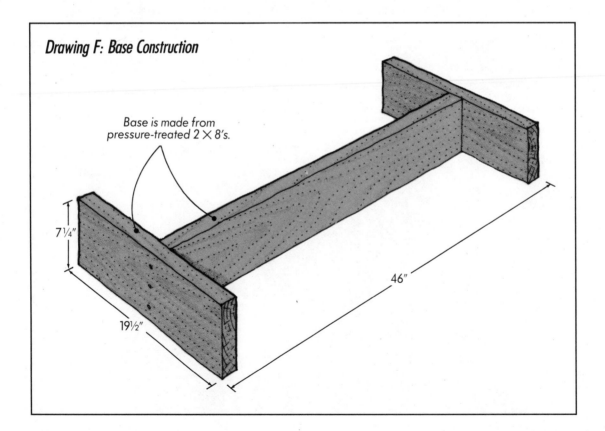

Drawing F: Base Construction

Base is made from pressure-treated 2 × 8's.

7¼"

46"

19½"

2 **Smooth corners and edges.** Plywood is especially susceptible to splintering when sharp-cornered edges are left exposed. Use a block plane to shave a chamfer along exposed plywood edges, then round the chamfer with 80-grit sandpaper. Pay particular attention to the doors and top of the center.

3 **Apply a protective finish.** The recycling center is designed for outdoor use, so it needs a good outdoor finish. The rough-sawn surface of the T1-11 plywood is more receptive to stain than to paint. A semitransparent exterior stain that includes a sealer or water repellent is a good finish for this project. A wide selection of colors is available, and the sealer or water repellent in the finish will help to prevent moisture damage.

Apply finish both inside and outside the center. To prevent warping, be sure to coat the underside of the top and the inside face of each door. Take time to coat all edges as well.

Sports Locker

You shouldn't have to go to a health club or to the "Y" to have your own sports locker. This home-based locker would be a fine addition to an exercise room, but you might also consider using it in a garage, breezeway, or hallway. It has some notable extras that you won't find at the health club. The design incorporates a seat, as well as extra shelf space and a peg rack. The construction is sturdy, and the configuration is versatile, so you can add your own hardware for storing anything from bicycle gear to ski equipment. Also, the design is modular, so you can build more than one unit and then gang them together. (See *Drawing A*.)

The plywood parts of the locker shown here are made of birch-veneered plywood because it takes paint very well. Masonite, another superb base for paint, would be an excellent substitute for the plywood door panels. Poplar is a good choice for any solid wood parts that will be painted.

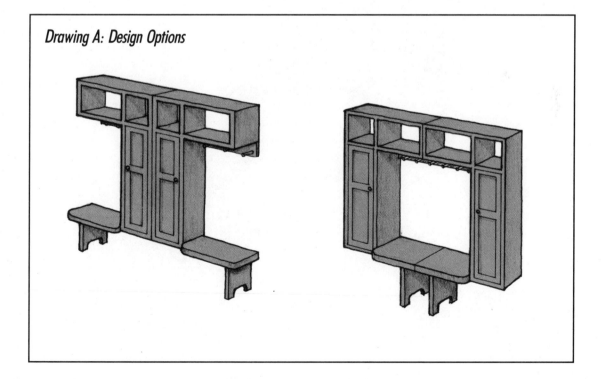

Drawing A: Design Options

Drawing B: Construction Overview

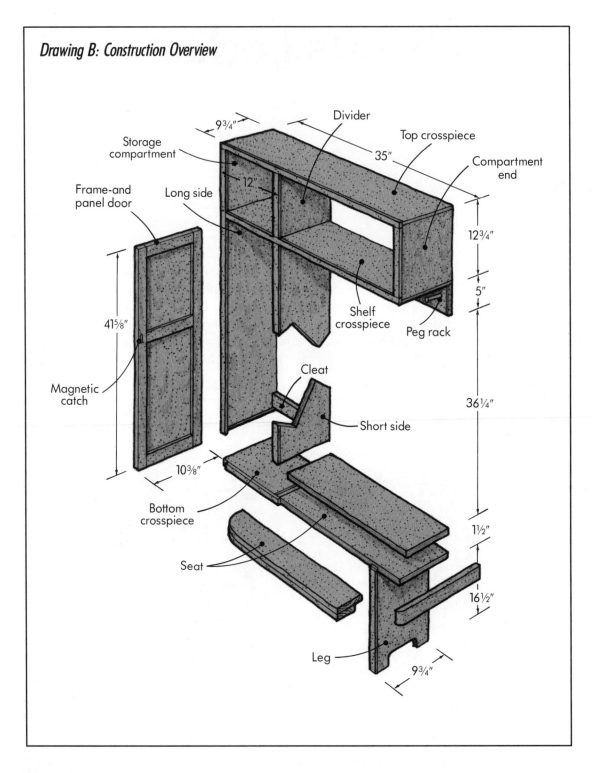

Storage compartment

Divider

Top crosspiece

35"

9¾"

12"

Compartment end

12¾"

5"

Frame-and panel door

Long side

Shelf crosspiece

Peg rack

41⅝"

Magnetic catch

36¼"

Cleat

Short side

10⅜"

Bottom crosspiece

1½"

Seat

16½"

Leg

9¾"

Materials List

Wood

QTY	PART	DIMENSION
Carcase		
1	Plywood long side	$\frac{3}{4}'' \times 9\frac{3}{8}'' \times 55\frac{1}{4}''$
1	Plywood short side	$\frac{3}{4}'' \times 9\frac{3}{8}'' \times 42\frac{1}{4}''$
3	Plywood crosspieces	$\frac{3}{4}'' \times 9\frac{3}{8}'' \times 34\frac{1}{2}''$
1	Plywood divider	$\frac{3}{4}'' \times 9\frac{3}{8}'' \times 11\frac{3}{4}''$
1	Plywood end	$\frac{3}{4}'' \times 9\frac{3}{8}'' \times 11\frac{3}{4}''$
1	Plywood leg	$\frac{3}{4}'' \times 9\frac{3}{8}'' \times 16\frac{3}{4}''$
1	Plywood brace	$\frac{1}{4}'' \times 6\frac{1}{2}'' \times 6\frac{1}{2}''$
2	Poplar cleats	$\frac{3}{4}'' \times 2\frac{1}{2}'' \times 10\frac{1}{2}''$
Seat		
1	Plywood seat top	$\frac{3}{4}'' \times 8'' \times 22\frac{1}{4}''$
1	Poplar front trim	$\frac{3}{4}'' \times 4\frac{3}{4}'' \times 22\frac{1}{4}''$
1	Poplar front trim	$\frac{3}{4}'' \times 3\frac{3}{8}'' \times 22\frac{1}{4}''$
1	Poplar end trim	$\frac{3}{4}'' \times 1\frac{1}{2}'' \times 12\frac{3}{4}''$
Trim		
2	Poplar edge strips	$\frac{3}{8}'' \times \frac{3}{4}'' \times 35''$
3	Poplar edge strips	$\frac{3}{8}'' \times \frac{3}{4}'' \times 11\frac{1}{4}''$
2	Poplar edge strips	$\frac{3}{8}'' \times \frac{3}{4}'' \times 41\frac{3}{4}''$
1	Poplar edge strip	$\frac{3}{8}'' \times \frac{3}{4}'' \times 12''$
1	Poplar edge strip	$\frac{3}{8}'' \times \frac{3}{4}'' \times 16\frac{1}{2}''$
Rack		
1	Oak peg rack	$\frac{3}{4}'' \times 5'' \times 23''$

Wood

QTY	PART	DIMENSION
Door		
2	Poplar door stiles	$\frac{3}{4}'' \times 1\frac{3}{4}'' \times 41\frac{5}{8}''$
3	Poplar door rails	$\frac{3}{4}'' \times 1\frac{3}{4}'' \times 7\frac{7}{8}''$
1	Plywood door panel	$\frac{1}{4}'' \times 7\frac{3}{4}'' \times 15\frac{1}{8}''$
1	Plywood door panel	$\frac{1}{4}'' \times 7\frac{3}{4}'' \times 23''$
2	Poplar door stops	$\frac{3}{4}'' \times 1\frac{1}{4}'' \times 1\frac{1}{4}''$

Hardware

3 drywall screws, 2"

1⅝" drywall screws, as needed

1¼" drywall screws, as needed

3 pairs butt hinges, 1½" × 1½"

1 metal door handle, with mounting screws

1 magnetic catch

3 double clothes hooks

4d finishing nails, as needed

1" paneling nails, as needed

6 turned oak pegs, ½" dia. × 2½"

  Available from Woodworker's Supply,
  5604 Alameda Place NE, Albuquerque, NM 87113;
  (800) 645-9292. Part #824-262

Making the Carcase

1 Cut the plywood parts to size. Start by ripping all carcase parts to a finished width of 9⅜ inches. Then cut the seat top to 8 inches wide. Cut the parts to the finished lengths given in the Materials List.

2 Mill the rabbets and dadoes. Square your table saw miter gauge to its blade before replacing the blade with a dado cutter. Adjust the cutter width to match the thickness of the carcase parts. The plywood is nominally ¾ inch thick, but measure it: It could be slightly less. Then raise the cutter to ¼ inch.

Fasten a wood auxiliary fence to your miter gauge. Make the fence from a straight board or piece of plywood at least ¾ inch thick, 2 inches high, and 30 inches long. The auxiliary fence will help you keep large parts steady and square as you guide them through the cutter. It also lets you use a stop block to duplicate dado locations in the crosspieces.

First, run the fence over the cutter to make a notch that is the same height and width as all the rabbets and dadoes in this project. As shown in *Drawing C,* the top and seat cross-

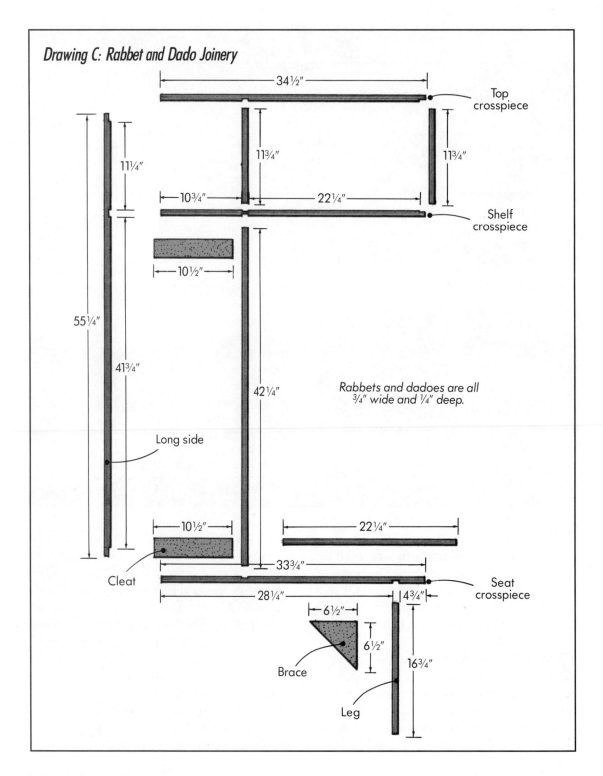

Drawing C: Rabbet and Dado Joinery

34½"

Top crosspiece

11¾"

11¾"

11¼"

10¾"

22¼"

Shelf crosspiece

10½"

55¼"

42¼"

Rabbets and dadoes are all ¾" wide and ¼" deep.

41¾"

Long side

10½"

33¾"

22¼"

Cleat

28¼"

Seat crosspiece

6½"

4¾"

6½"

16¾"

Brace

Leg

pieces each are dadoed 10¾ inches from the long side. The dadoes on the top and bottom of the shelf crosspiece are also 10¾ inches from the end. Clamp a stop block to the fence 10¾ inches from the notch and mill these four dadoes.(See *Photo 1*.)

Lay out the dado for the leg in the seat crosspiece as shown in *Drawing C*. Cut this dado by aligning the layout line with the notch.

To mill the rabbets shown in *Drawing C*, align the end of the workpiece to the fence notch and make one pass.

3 **Assemble the carcase.** Join the three crosspieces to the long side first, making sure that the front edges are flush. Glue and nail the divider and compartment end into place next. Put glue on the ends of the short side and fit this piece into its dadoes. To secure the top of the short side to the shelf crosspiece, drive 4d finishing nails into this edge at an angle, as shown in *Photo 2*. If you have a long bar clamp, you can skip these nails and secure the joint by clamping across the carcase. Check the overall assembly and make sure that the crosspieces meet the sides and

Photo 1: *To duplicate rabbet and dado locations in the crosspieces, clamp a stop block to an auxiliary fence that is fastened to the miter gauge.*

Photo 2: *To fasten the shelf crosspiece to the short side, drive 4d finishing nails at an angle into the side's top edge.*

the divider at right angles. When everything is square, reinforce the bottom joint by predrilling and driving three 2-inch drywall screws through the bottom crosspiece into the short side. Set all nails, and fill the holes with wood putty.

4 **Cut and install the leg.** Lay out the curved cutout on the end of the leg as shown in *Drawing D*. Cut the curve with a jigsaw. Then glue the leg into its dado on the underside of the seat crosspiece. Pull this joint tight by driving three 1⅝-inch drywall screws into the top edge of the leg from the opposite side of the crosspiece.

5 **Cut and install the brace.** Cut a square blank to the dimensions given in the Materials List. First, rip a piece of plywood to

Photo 3: Glue and screw a triangular brace between the leg and the seat crosspiece.

6½ inches. Then, to ensure that the brace has a right angle, crosscut it to 6½ inches. Draw a line between diagonal corners and cut the blank in half with a jigsaw.

Install the brace as shown in *Photo 3,* using glue and 1⅝-inch drywall screws. Hold the brace squarely against the crosspiece and leg while driving the screws. It shouldn't be necessary to drill pilot holes for these screws. Drive them so that their heads are recessed about 1⁄16 inch below the surface. Cover the screwheads in the leg with wood putty.

6 **Cut and install the cleats.** These two cleats fit inside the locker, stiffening its construction and also providing fastening points for securing the finished unit against the wall. The cleat ends butt against the locker sides. One cleat fits up against the shelf crosspiece, and the other fits against the bottom crosspiece, as shown in *Drawings C and D*. Cut the cleats to fit inside the locker. Secure them with glue and by driving 4d finishing nails through the sides and the crosspieces. Set these nails.

7 **Cut and install the edge trim strips.** This poplar edging covers the front edges of the carcase. It meets at corners with butt joints.

Rip the trim strips to the width and thickness given in the Materials List, but leave the parts at least ½ inch long. It's easiest and most accurate to lay out the cuts directly from the locker. Begin with the crosspiece trim. Square one end of the trim, and hold the piece in place on the carcase. Mark the exact length with a utility knife, and cut the piece to length.

Attach each piece with glue and 1-inch paneling nails. When you are done with the crosspieces, repeat this process with the side trim and the compartment end trim. Then trim the bottom edge of the locker and the front edge of the leg. Set the nails and fill the holes with wood putty.

Assembling the Seat

1 **Fasten the seat top to the seat crosspiece.** Spread glue on the underside of the seat top and on the edge that butts against the short side. Clamp the seat in place. Then drive 1¼-inch drywall screws through the underside of the crosspiece and into the seat top. Use six to eight screws, spacing them evenly.

2 **Complete the seat.** As shown in *Drawing D,* the seat is wider than the rest of the locker. This is done by applying poplar front and end trim, which hides the plywood edges of the seat and seat crosspiece. As shown in *Drawing E,* the trim is applied in layers, forming a lap joint. Cut both seat front pieces to their finished dimensions, and lay out a curved cut in the corner that will be next to the locker opening. A curve with a 2¼-inch radius will look good. Make the curved cut in both pieces, using a jigsaw.

Glue and screw the top trim in place, driving four or five 1¼-inch drywall screws

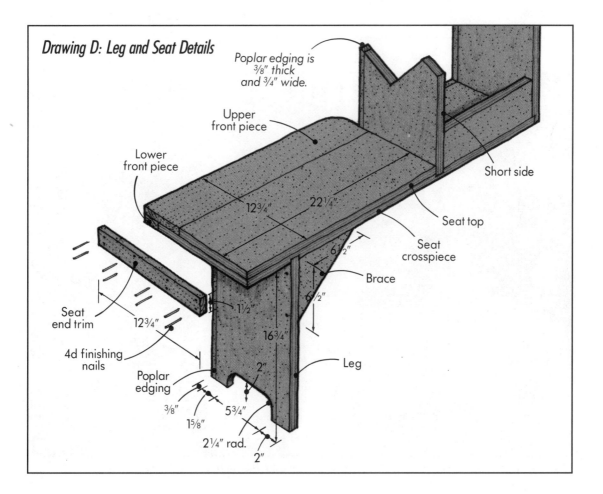

Drawing D: Leg and Seat Details

Poplar edging is ⅜" thick and ¾" wide.

Upper front piece

Lower front piece

Short side

12¾"   22¼"

Seat top

Seat crosspiece

6½"

Brace

6½"

Seat end trim

12¾"   1½"

16¾"

4d finishing nails

Poplar edging

2"

Leg

⅜"   5¾"

1⅝"

2¼" rad.

2"

through the seat crosspiece and into the trim. Then install the lower front piece with glue and screws. (See *Photo 4*.) Recess the screwheads, and cover them with wood putty.

Next, cut and install the seat end piece. Use glue and 4d finishing nails to fasten this piece to the seat top, seat crosspiece, and seat front pieces. Set the nails and fill the holes with wood putty. Lay out and cut a 2¼-inch-radius curve in the outside front corner, as shown in *Photo 5*.

When the glue and wood putty have cured, carefully sand the seat. You want the edges to be especially smooth, so file a slight roundover into the corners. After filing, sand with 100-grit sandpaper. Switch to progressively finer grades, finishing up with 220-grit paper.

Making the Door

1 **Cut the stiles and rails to size.** The locker's frame-and-panel door is sized to

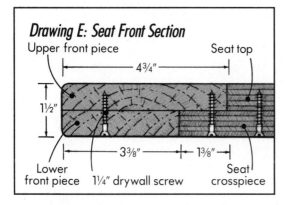

Drawing E: Seat Front Section

Upper front piece — Seat top
4¾"
1½"
Lower front piece — 1¼" drywall screw — 3⅜" — 1⅜" — Seat crosspiece

Photo 4: Attach the lower front seat piece with glue and 1¼-inch drywall screws.

allow for about ¹⁄₁₆ inch of clearance between the door and locker edges on all four sides. Before cutting the stiles and rails to size, check the measurements of your locker opening, and adjust the Materials List dimensions if necessary. Then cut the frame members to width and length. Save a few frame member cutoffs to use in testing the next step's setup.

2 Groove the stiles and rails. As shown in *Drawing F,* the frame members are grooved to hold two plywood panels. Cut a groove in one long edge of each frame member. Groove both long edges of the center stile.

Adjust the dado cutter in your table saw to a width that matches the thickness of your plywood door panels. The plywood is nominally ¼ inch thick, but measure it because it's likely to be slightly less. Then position your rip fence to guide the frame member sides when milling panel grooves. (See *Photo 6.*) It's important for grooves to be centered on the frame edges. To test your fence position, turn on the saw and guide a scrap cutoff against the fence and through the cutter. Now turn the piece around, and with the groove facing down, guide its opposite side against the fence to make a second pass. Your fence is set correctly if the cutter doesn't enlarge the width of the groove. Cut grooves on the inside edges of the stiles and the top and bottom rails. Groove both edges of the center rail as shown in *Drawing F.* Leave the dado cutter on the saw for the next step.

Photo 5: Use a jigsaw to round the seat's outside front corner.

Photo 6: Groove the door stiles and rails on the table saw, using the dado cutter. Position the fence carefully so that the groove is centered.

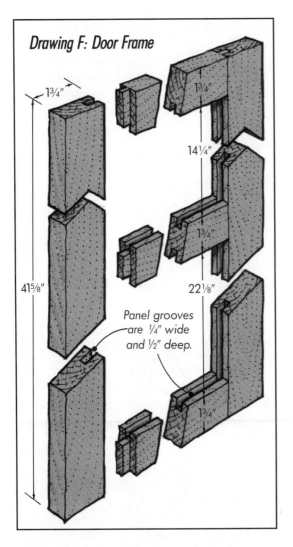

Drawing F: Door Frame

1¾"

1¾"

14¼"

41⅝"

1¾"

22⅛"

Panel grooves are ¼" wide and ½" deep.

1¾"

complete the tenon. Check its fit in the groove. Adjust the stop block position or blade height until you get a perfect test fit. Then cut tenons on both ends of each rail.

4 Cut the panels to size. The surest way to determine panel sizes is to test fit the door frame, and measure the openings where the panels will fit. This trial assembly also gives you a chance to see how the door's tenon-and-groove joints fit together. Position the rails as shown in *Drawing F*. Square up the frame as you assemble it. Then measure the height and width of each opening, and add ¹⁵⁄₁₆ inch to each dimension to get the finished dimensions of each panel. Cut the panels to finished length; then cut them to their finished widths.

5 Assemble the door. Spread glue evenly on the rail tenons and in the stile and rail grooves. Clamp one stile horizontally in your bench vice, with its groove facing up. Fit the

Photo 7: To align the door rail tenon shoulders, clamp a stop block to the auxiliary miter gauge fence.

3 Make the rail tenons. Each rail tenon is as thick as the door groove is wide, and is ½ inch long. Lay out a sample tenon shoulder on a scrap piece of the rail stock.

Adjust the dado cutter's height to ¼ inch. Align the shoulder layout line to the blade. Butt a stop block against the rail and clamp the block to the fence as shown in *Photo 7*. Make a cut, and then move the shoulder away from the stop block to make a second pass. Flip the sample rail over and repeat the process to rails into the groove. Tap these joints together until they're fully closed. Then fit the panels in the assembly. Once the panels are in place, fit the remaining stile over the rail tenons, while fitting the stile's groove over the panel. Use three pipe clamps to pull the stiles tightly against the rails. Place the clamps vertically, with one at each rail, as shown in *Photo 8*. Tighten the clamps gradually, checking to make sure each stile-rail connection is square as you do so.

6 Install the door. This door swings on three hinges. One is centered on the stile. The other two are located 2½ inches from the top and bottom of the door. Mortise the hinges to the door; then lay out mortise locations on the locker. Cut these mortises, and attach the door. (See "Mortising for a Butt Hinge" on page 93.)

7 Add corner stops. From ¾-inch-thick poplar, cut a pair of triangular door stops. Attached to the inside corners of the locker,

these pieces will act as stops on the top and bottom corners of the door. Close the door until it is flush with the front of the locker. Put each stop in place through the back, open the door, and mark the stop's position. Predrill a ¹/₁₆-inch-diameter nail hole in each stop; then glue and nail the stop in place, using a single 4d finishing nail. (See *Photo 9*.)

8 Install the handle and catch. Position the handle so that it's centered on the door's right stile, and on the centerline of the middle rail. Drill installation holes ¹/₁₆ inch larger than the diameter of the installation screws.

Install the catch next, positioning the catch magnet between the installation holes for the handle. Position the steel catch plate on the locker's short side so that the door closes firmly against its stops.

9 Install the double clothes hooks. Screw one hook to the upper cleat and one to each of the locker sides.

Photo 8: Check to make sure the door frame is square as you tighten clamps across the stile-and-rail joints.

Photo 9: Glue and nail triangular door stops inside the locker after installing the door. Position each stop so that the door can close flush with the locker's front edges.

Making the Peg Rail

1 Cut and chamfer the oak rail. Cut the rail from a straight, clear piece of oak. Rout a 45-degree chamfer on the bottom and right edges of the peg rail as shown in *Drawing G*.

2 Drill peg holes and install the pegs. The rail holds six pegs. Lay out holes in two rows as shown in *Drawing G*. Drill the holes to the same diameter as the peg tenons, drilling about ⅛ inch deeper than the tenon length. Use a piece of tape wrapped around the drill bit as a depth guide. Put glue on each peg tenon, and fit the tenon into its hole. Clean up excess glue with a sponge.

Finishing and Installing the Locker

1 Remove the hardware. Unscrew the handle, hinges, hooks, and catches, and set them aside. Then give your project a thorough sanding, slightly rounding all sharp edges. Finish up with 150- or 180-grit sandpaper.

2 Apply the finish. Prime the whole project, except the peg rail and pegs, with interior primer-sealer. When the primer dries, sand it lightly with 220-grit sandpaper, smoothing out any drips, runs, or raised grain. Wipe the wood free of dust, and apply two coats of high-gloss enamel, sanding lightly with 220-grit sandpaper between coats. Give the pegs and peg rail a clear finish. You can use a penetrating oil finish, or a varnish in either satin or high gloss.

3 Install the peg rail. Drill three countersunk pilot holes, and drive 2-inch drywall screws through the shelf crosspiece and into the top edge of the peg rail. Drive a single 2-inch drywall screw into the end of the rail from inside the locker. Counterbore this screw hole as well.

4 Install the locker. With the leg resting on the floor and the crosspieces level, drive screws through the cleats and peg rail and into wall studs. Use at least one screw in each cleat, and at least one screw in the peg rail. Counterbore all screw holes, and make sure that the screws are long enough to penetrate at least 1¼ inches into the wall studs. If you're fastening this project against a masonry wall, use masonry anchors.

5 Reattach the hardware. Install the door by reattaching the hinges. Then screw on the handle, catch, and hooks.

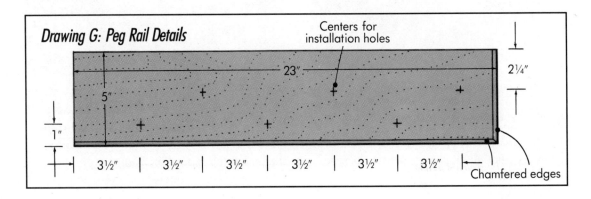

Drawing G: Peg Rail Details

Centers for installation holes

23"

2¼"

5"

1"

3½" | 3½" | 3½" | 3½" | 3½" | 3½"

Chamfered edges

Mortising for a Butt Hinge

The butt hinge is the most commonly used hinge in cabinetmaking. Here is how to position and mortise these hinges.

First, position the hinge on the door as shown in the first photo. If your hinge is the right size, the leaf will be slightly narrower than the door thickness. Holding the hinge firmly in place on the door, drill pilot holes for the hinge screws. When doing this, it's crucial to center the drill bit in the hinge leaf hole. You can do this by eye, or you can use a special self-centering "VIX" bit (available at hardware stores and home centers). Screw the hinge to the door.

Cut the border of the hinge mortise with a sharp utility knife. Run the edge of the knife blade hard against the edges of the hinge, cutting straight down. Remove the hinge and put the edge of the hinge against the side of the door. Make a light pencil mark under the hinge to scribe its thickness onto the door. This line will guide the depth of your mortise. Deepen the cuts with the utility knife until they touch this line.

Divide the waste area into smaller sections, tapping a chisel straight down as shown in the second photo. Cut across the grain, not with it, and be careful not to tap down deeper than the line on the side of the door. Finish up the mortise by paring out the waste, section by section. For this work, hold the chisel with the bevel facing up. Move the chisel so that it is perpendicular to the face of the door, as shown in the third photo. Test fit the hinge. It should fit flush with the door edge. Do extra paring as necessary for a good fit.

After screwing the hinges to the door, bring the door to its opening, and use shims at the bottom and sides to position the door with equal clearance around all its edges. Mark the height of the top of each hinge on the carcase frame by making a little nick with your utility knife. Take the door out and extend the nicks into lines across the inside edge of the carcase frame. Once this is done, repeat the three steps to complete the carcase mortises.

Scribing the mortise outline   *Dividing waste area with a chisel*   *Paring the mortise flat*

Building a Closet

B uilding a closet is a great way to add permanent storage to your house. It's cost-effective, too—you'll get more storage volume for your dollar than from any other project, and you'll add value to your home. It's the perfect first carpentry project. You'll try your hand at framing, drywall work, hanging a door, and trim carpentry, all on a small scale.

The bare wall you want to transform into a closet may not look like the space in *Photo 1,* but you can still use the step-by-step techniques presented here to build your own version of this project. If you want your closet to be in a corner, all the better—you'll have one less wall to frame.

Before you begin, there are a few things to note about the Materials List. Obviously, your lumber and drywall order will depend on the size of your planned closet. You can use the specifications given in this project's Materials List as a guide when putting together your own order. Likewise, the length dimensions given assume a ceiling height of exactly 96 inches and framing lumber that is exactly 1½ inches thick. Since these measurements may vary, take measurements before cutting any vertical framing members. Door jambs and casing trim come in standard lengths. You'll have to cut these pieces to fit, so the Materials

Photo 1: This wall space will soon be put to work as a closet. Note the door chimes (near the ceiling) and light switch on the back wall. Both will have to be moved to a side wall of the new closet. The electrical outlet will be left in the closet.

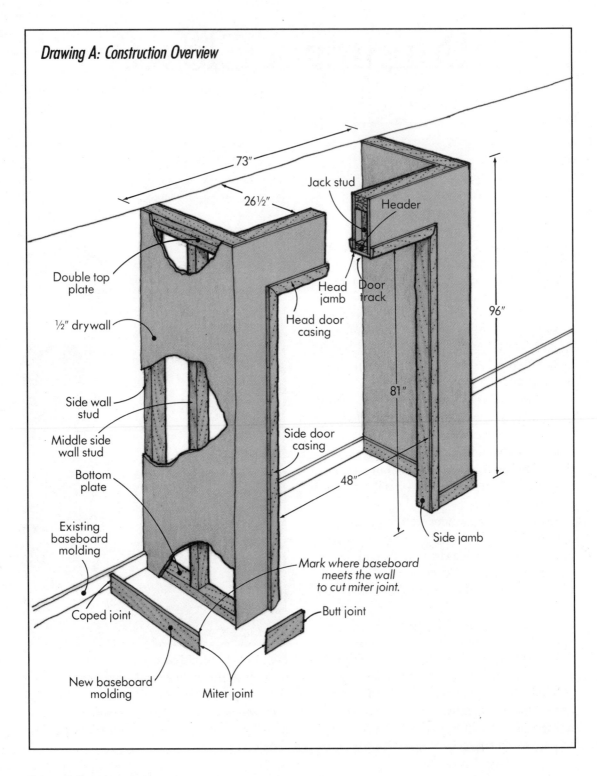

Drawing A: Construction Overview

73"

26½"

Jack stud

Header

Double top plate

½" drywall

Head jamb

Door track

Head door casing

96"

Side wall stud

81"

Middle side wall stud

Side door casing

Bottom plate

Existing baseboard molding

48"

Side jamb

Mark where baseboard meets the wall to cut miter joint.

Coped joint

Butt joint

New baseboard molding

Miter joint

List gives the standard lengths, not finished dimensions.

The closet shown here will be used as a coat closet, so it's very helpful to have a wide door opening. According to space or taste, you may choose to make your door opening a different size. And when it comes to doors, you can choose between a conventional hinged door, sliding doors (also called bypass doors), and bi-fold doors, which are used here. It's best to buy your door before you begin framing so you can follow the manufacturer's directions regarding rough and finished opening sizes.

Finally, if you are planning to paint your closet's trim, you can save money by ordering finger-jointed trim instead of clear trim. Finger-jointed trim is made of small pieces of wood joined into long strips. The joints are invisible under paint, so there's no need to spend the extra money on clear stock unless you plan to stain or varnish your trim.

Laying Out the Plates

When you are laying out framing for new walls in an existing house, it's important to tie the new framing to the old. More often than

---

Materials List

Wood

QTY	PART	DIMENSION
Framing Lumber		
2	Side wall studs	$1\frac{1}{2}'' \times 3\frac{1}{2}'' \times 96''$
1	Upper top plate (front)	$1\frac{1}{2}'' \times 3\frac{1}{2}'' \times 65''$
2	Upper top plates (sides)	$1\frac{1}{2}'' \times 3\frac{1}{2}'' \times 24\frac{1}{2}''$
1	Lower top plate (front)	$1\frac{1}{2}'' \times 3\frac{1}{2}'' \times 69''$
2	Lower top plates (sides)	$1\frac{1}{2}'' \times 3\frac{1}{2}'' \times 21''$
2	Bottom plates (sides)	$1\frac{1}{2}'' \times 3\frac{1}{2}'' \times 24\frac{1}{2}''$
2	Bottom plates (front)	$1\frac{1}{2}'' \times 3\frac{1}{2}'' \times 7\frac{1}{4}''$
2	Outside corner studs	$1\frac{1}{2}'' \times 3\frac{1}{2}'' \times 93''$
4	Inside corner studs	$1\frac{1}{2}'' \times 3\frac{1}{2}'' \times 91\frac{1}{2}''$
2	Middle side wall studs	$1\frac{1}{2}'' \times 3\frac{1}{2}'' \times 91\frac{1}{2}''$
2	Trimmer studs	$1\frac{1}{2}'' \times 3\frac{1}{2}'' \times 91\frac{1}{2}''$
2	Cripple studs	$1\frac{1}{2}'' \times 3\frac{1}{2}'' \times 80\frac{3}{4}''$
1	Header	$1\frac{1}{2}'' \times 3\frac{1}{2}'' \times 53\frac{1}{2}''$
5	Jack studs	$1\frac{1}{2}'' \times 3\frac{1}{2}'' \times 9\frac{1}{4}''$
Trim		
2	Side jambs	$\frac{3}{4}'' \times 4\frac{9}{16}'' \times 84''$
1	Head jamb	$\frac{3}{4}'' \times 4\frac{9}{16}'' \times 50''$
2	Door casing side trim pieces	$\frac{3}{4}'' \times 2\frac{1}{4}'' \times 84''$
1	Door casing head trim piece	$\frac{3}{4}'' \times 2\frac{1}{4}'' \times 60''$

Wood

QTY	PART	DIMENSION
	Baseboard molding	$\frac{5}{8}'' \times 4\frac{1}{2}'' \times 20'$
	Quarter round molding	$\frac{3}{4}'' \times \frac{3}{4}'' \times 48''$
	Wood shims, as needed	

Drywall Materials
4 sheets ½" drywall, 4 × 8
1 roll drywall tape
2 outside corner beads, 96" long
2 gallons drywall compound

Hardware

4d finishing nails, as needed
6d finishing nails, as needed
8d common nails, as needed
8d finishing nails, as needed
10d common nails, as needed
1" drywall screws or $1\frac{1}{4}''$ drywall nails, as needed
$2\frac{1}{2}''$ drywall screws, as needed (optional)
3" drywall screws, as needed (optional)
1 set bi-fold closet doors for 48" × 81" opening, with door track and associated hardware

not, existing walls will be out of plumb, or floors and ceilings won't be perfectly level. Other conditions that will vary from house to house include flooring or carpeting, baseboard or cornice trim, and the spacing of wall studs and ceiling joists to which the new framing will be fastened. The framing scheme used in this project accommodates most situations where existing wood-frame walls are involved.

1 **Lay out the top plate and side walls.** Using your tape measure and a framing square, mark the outside edges of the top plate on the ceiling. For this closet, the plates extend 26 inches from the wall. This allows for 22 inches of depth inside the finished closet. Any depth less than this won't be ade-

quate for hanging clothes. More than 27 inches of depth tends to waste space. Take these figures into consideration when determining the depth of your closet.

Make sure the ends of the closet are at right angles to the wall by laying them out with a framing square. Measure to make sure the front layout line is parallel to the wall. Where the plate lines meet the back wall, use a level to mark a plumb line down the wall and across the baseboard trim, to the floor. (See *Drawing B.*)

2 **Locate the bottom plate.** Drop a plumb bob to the floor from the outside corners of the ceiling plate lines. Drive a nail partway into the floor where the point of the plumb bob touches the floor. (See *Photo 2.*) These

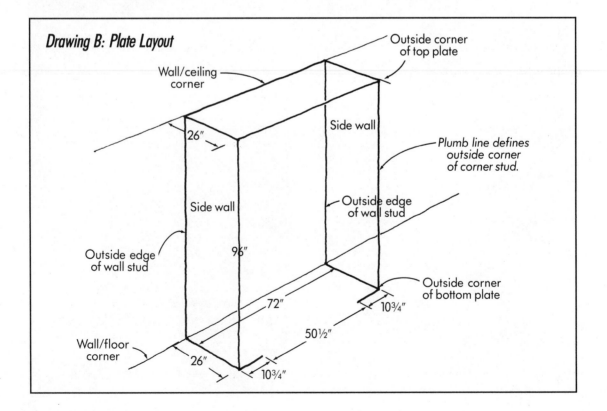

Drawing B: Plate Layout

Outside corner of top plate

Wall/ceiling corner

Side wall

26"

Plumb line defines outside corner of corner stud.

Outside edge of wall stud

Side wall

96"

Outside edge of wall stud

Outside corner of bottom plate

72"

10¾"

Wall/floor corner

26"

50½"

10¾"

two points mark the outside front corners of the bottom plate, corresponding to plate corner points on the ceiling.

3 Cut and remove the baseboard trim. Lay out cutting lines ½ inch outside the side wall lines marked in Step 1. This ½ inch will allow the drywall on the side walls to fit behind the trim running along the existing wall. To remove the trim between the lines, start by deeply scoring the lines with a utility knife. Then make the cuts with a backsaw. The knife cut will guide the saw blade and prevent the trim from splintering as you cut it. Make sure to cut all the way through the trim so that it comes off cleanly. After making both cuts in the trim, pry off the waste section carefully. Work the trim loose with a prybar or putty knife; then pull it free.

4 Re-route electrical wires. With the closet's outline defined on the wall and ceiling, you'll be able to see what electrical fixtures (switches, receptacles, door chimes, etc.) will have to be relocated for safety and convenience. By replacing a standard switch or receptacle plate with a solid outlet box cover, you can convert an outlet box to a junction box. This way, you can run wire from the old box to a new box that will be installed in the new closet wall or elsewhere. If you're not experienced with household wiring, have an electrician handle this work for you.

Framing the Closet

The framing plan for this closet, shown in *Drawing C,* is designed to accommodate a pair of standard bi-fold doors that require a finished opening 48 inches wide and 81 inches high. If you're planning for a door of a different size, find the rough opening dimensions

by adding 1¼ inches to the required finished height and 2½ inches to the required finished width. These calculations allow for ¾-inch-thick jambs and ½-inch-wide shim spaces (this will be explained later).

Before you start framing the closet, check the Shop Savvy on page 109 for helpful tips on toenailing. If you are installing your closet against plaster and lath walls, use drywall screws instead of nails wherever you are attaching to framing members behind the plaster and lath. This avoids hammer blows,

Photo 2: After marking the top plate's outside edge on the ceiling, drop a plumb line from each outside corner to the floor, and drive a nail into the floor to mark the bottom plate's corner.

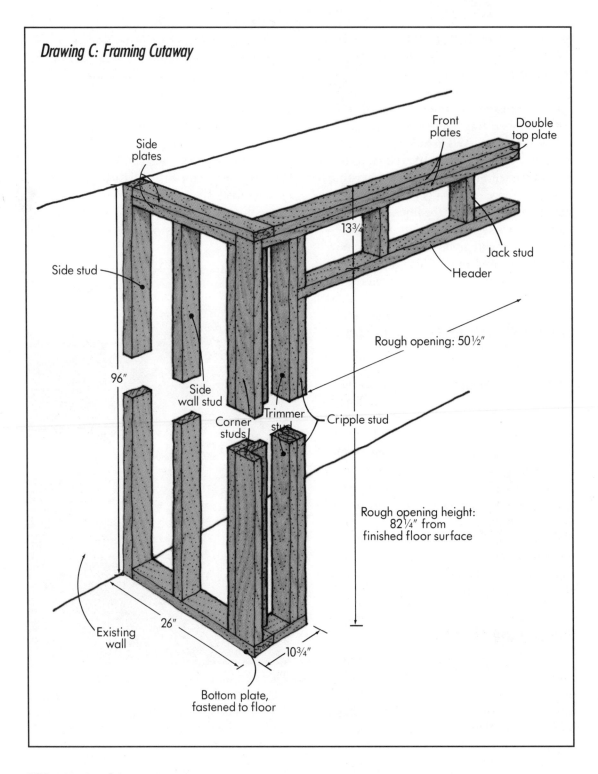

Drawing C: Framing Cutaway

Side plates

Front plates

Double top plate

Side stud

13¾"

Jack stud

Header

Rough opening: 50½"

96"

Side wall stud

Corner studs

Trimmer stud

Cripple stud

Rough opening height: 82¼" from finished floor surface

Existing wall

26"

10¾"

Bottom plate, fastened to floor

which can cause the plaster to break loose. Use 2½-inch drywall screws in place of 8d nails and 3-inch screws instead of 10d nails.

1 **Nail the side wall studs to the wall.** If you're working on a carpeted floor (as is the case here), you'll first have to cut back and remove the carpet so that the bottom of each wall stud and bottom plate can fit directly on the floor. (See *Photo 3*.) Using a sharp utility knife, cut a line from each bottom corner point (made earlier with a nail) to the layout line for the wall stud's outside edge. Cut another line 4 inches inside of this one and parallel to it. Turn the corner, cutting out a 4-inch-wide strip of carpet beneath each outside corner of the closet.

Cut the two wall studs to length, if necessary. Line up the outside edge of each stud with the vertical layout line on the wall. Using 10d nails, toenail each stud through the existing drywall into the top and bottom plate of the wall. You can also nail into existing wall studs if they're located behind the side wall studs.

2 **Install the double top plate.** As shown in *Drawings C and D,* the corners of the double top plates overlap. As you'll see in this step, this configuration lets you anchor these doubled-up 2 × 4s to the ceiling regardless of which way the ceiling joists run.

Cut all plate members to size. Then fasten the three upper plates to the ceiling. If the ceiling joists run perpendicular to the wall, install the upper front plate first, driving 10d nails through this 2 × 4, through the ceiling drywall, and into each joist. Then toenail each upper side wall plate to the front plate and to a side wall stud. For tips on locating studs in a wood-frame wall, see the Shop Savvy on page 32.

If the ceiling joists run parallel to the back wall, reverse the plate installation order. Install the top side wall plates first, nailing them to the ceiling joists and the side wall studs.

When installing the lower three 2 × 4s that make up the rest of the double top plate, note that each end of the lower front 2 × 4 stops 1½ inches from its corner. (See *Photo 4*.) The corner studs will fit against these indented ends, creating a strong joint at the closet's corners.

Photo 3: Remove the existing baseboard to accommodate the side wall stud and the ½-inch-thick drywall that will go against it. Also remove the carpet so that the side wall stud and the bottom plate can rest on the floor.

3 **Install the bottom plate.** On the floor surface (sheathing, vinyl, or wood) lay out the outside edge of the bottom plate, marking a right-angled corner at each nail point. Also mark where the rough opening will begin on the front of the closet wall. (See *Drawings B and C.*) Then cut and install the 2 × 4s that make up the bottom plate, nailing them into the floor.

4 **Install the corner studs.** As shown in *Drawing D,* each corner requires three studs to create inside and outside edges where drywall can be fastened. Cut and install the outermost stud first, driving 8d nails into the top and bottom plates. Further secure the top of each corner stud by driving two 10d nails through the stud and into the end of the lower

front's top plate. Then install the remaining corner studs. Toenail these studs to the plates, and nail each corner's studs to each other, again using 8d nails.

5 **Install the remaining full-length studs.** In this closet, there are only four remaining full-length studs to install: two middle side wall studs and a pair of trimmer studs. (See *Drawing C.*) Cut and install a stud in each side wall, halfway between the back wall and the front wall of the closet. Use a level to plumb up each side wall stud. Draw lines on the plates, marking where each side of

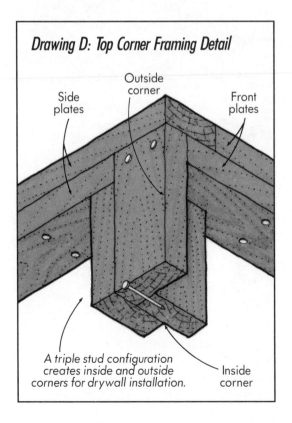

Drawing D: Top Corner Framing Detail

Side plates

Outside corner

Front plates

A triple stud configuration creates inside and outside corners for drywall installation.

Inside corner

Photo 4: The doubled top plate has overlapping joints at the corners. The corner stud will be nailed to the end of the lower top plate, further strengthening the joint. Use 3-inch drywall screws or 10d nails to fasten these framing members to the ceiling and to each other.

each stud should be. Keep the studs on these lines as you toenail them to top and bottom plates with 8d nails.

Cut and install the trimmer studs next. Toenail each trimmer to the bottom plate first, keeping them 1½ inches back from the end of the bottom plate. Then use your level to plumb up each stud before toenailing them to the top plate. (See *Photo 5*.)

6 Cut and install the cripple studs.
These shortened studs form the sides of the rough opening and support the ends of the header. Cut them to the rough opening height

Photo 5: Make sure the trimmer studs are plumb when you toenail them to the top and bottom plates.

you need. Nail them to the trimmer studs and toenail them to the plates.

7 Install the header. Cut the header to fit between the trimmer studs. Holding the header down against the tops of the cripple studs, drive a pair of 10d nails through each trimmer stud and into each end of the header.

8 Install the jack studs. You'll need one jack stud to fit against each trimmer and one every 14 to 16 inches, connecting the header to the top plate. Cut each jack stud to fit between the header and the top plate. Secure each by driving a pair of 10d nails through the bottom of the header and into the bottom end of the jack stud. Then toenail the top of the jack stud to the top plate.

9 Complete the wiring work. If you need to run new or re-routed wiring through the closet walls, now is the time to do it. Install outlet boxes as necessary, allowing the front edge of each box to extend ½ inch beyond the edge of the framing member to which it is fastened. Any holes you drill for wiring should be centered on the width of the framing member. Tack sheet metal plates over the 2 × 4 edges in the hole locations to protect the wiring from nails and screws. These protective plates are available at electrical suppliers and hardware stores.

Installing and Taping the Drywall

If you haven't installed or taped drywall before, take a look at "Drywall Basics" on page 104. Then tackle the inside of the closet first. This way, you'll be able to gain some confidence in drywall techniques before you turn to the more visible outside walls.

(continued on page 107)

Drywall Basics

Hanging and finishing gypsum wallboard (also called drywall or Sheetrock) doesn't require expensive equipment. But it takes time to master the techniques that enable experienced drywall crews to efficiently produce smooth results with minimum mess. So if your drywalling experience is limited, be patient. The advice here will help you to tackle small-scale drywall projects with confidence.

Marking and Cutting Drywall

The tools you'll need for this part of the job are: a tape measure, a chalk line, a pencil, and a sharp utility knife. Always measure and mark on the outside of the panel. Mark the size of the panel on the edges of the sheet, and connect the marks by snapping a line with your chalk line. To lay out cut lines on smaller pieces of drywall, you can mark against a straightedge or framing square.

To cut drywall, run your utility knife along the cut line, cutting through the paper facing and most of the way into the gypsum core of the panel. This usually will take two or three passes with the knife.

Now apply even pressure against the back of the panel, just behind the cut line. The object here is to break the gypsum along the cut line, by "folding" the panel back. Finish the cut by slicing through the folded paper edge.

To make cutouts for outlet boxes, lay out the box location on the outside of the panel. Cut the hole with a drywall saw. Pointed like a small keyhole saw, the drywall saw can be plunged into a panel for cutouts. You can also use it for other cutting work on drywall. If you don't have a drywall saw, you can use a saber saw.

Hanging the "Rock"

To fasten drywall against wood framing, you can use 1¼-inch drywall nails or 1-inch drywall screws (for ½-inch-thick drywall). Screws are a wiser choice when extra holding power is required, such as when you hang ceiling panels. If you elect to use screws, drive them with a screw gun rather than with a variable-speed drill, and space them every 16 inches or so. Equipped with a collar and a clutch, the screw gun will automatically set the head of the drywall screw just slightly below the surface, a feat that's more difficult to achieve with a variable-speed drill.

Nails are a good alternative, especially if you don't have a screw gun. Nails are less expensive than drywall screws, and it's not difficult to master the art of nailing drywall. You want to drive the nail deep enough so that the hammer head leaves a slight dimple in the drywall surface that can later be filled with drywall compound. Space drywall nails about 16 inches apart as well.

Precision isn't crucial when you hang drywall. When installing drywall around the rough opening for a door or window, stop the drywall about ¼ to ½ inch from the rough opening so that the drywall won't get in the way of shims or finished jambs.

When drywall panels are manufactured, the long edges of most drywall panels are tapered slightly. When two tapered edges come together, they create a slight valley, which makes the joint compound work easier. But since you have to cut some panels to fit, you will be creating joints where non-tapered field edges butt together. Never place a field edge against a tapered "factory" edge. The discrepancy between the thicknesses of the two edges will make the joint very hard to hide with joint compound. Two field edges next to each other are a little harder to cover than two factory edges but are much easier than a factory edge against a field edge.

Taping and Applying Joint Compound

This is the messy part of drywall work, and it's the area where experience makes the greatest difference. The goal is to use corner beads, tape, and drywall compound (often affectionately called "mud") to create a smooth, seamless surface suitable for painting. To apply and smooth the compound, you'll need a trowel and a taping knife, tools that are available at most hardware stores.

First, install corner beads on all outside corners. Use metal snips to cut each bead so that it fits along the full height of the corner. Then nail the bead to each side of its corner, spacing nails about 12 inches apart.

After installing a corner bead, you'll notice that the round bead that runs along the corner stands proud of the flat nailing areas on each side of the bead. This makes it easy to cover the nailing areas. Apply a liberal amount of joint compound at the bottom of each side of the corner. Then run your taping knife up the side with one edge riding on the bead and the other edge riding on the drywall outside the bead. Put

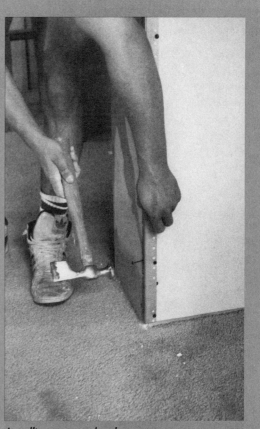

Installing a corner bead

the excess compound back in your bucket, or apply it to another joint.

Cover the inside corners and joints between the panels with drywall tape before applying joint compound. To tape inside corners, scoop up a fist-sized gob of drywall compound on a flat trowel; then use a taping knife to apply a thin layer of compound along both sides of the corner. You will use this compound to paste the tape into the corner. Roll out some tape, and snip off enough length to run the full distance of the corner. Fold the tape along

(continued)

its centerline, creating a profile to match the corner. Now place the tape in the corner, and use the taping knife to bed the paper in the compound. As soon as the tape adheres enough to stay in place, apply a thin layer of compound over the tape, and smooth it out with your taping knife. Go over the tape to smooth out folds and bubbles, applying and smoothing out compound as necessary. Use your excess compound to fill and smooth nail or screw holes.

Joints between drywall panels are also finished with joint compound and tape.

Apply a generous line of compound along a joint prior to placing and bedding the tape that covers it. Apply another layer of compound over the tape; then smooth and flatten the joint and the areas on either side of it, using the long, straight edge on your trowel. With the excess compound that you skim from the joint, cover and smooth over nearby nails or screws.

When taping inside corner joints and joints where panels meet, many do-it-yourselfers prefer to use self-adhering fiberglass mesh tape instead of conventional paper tape. Available in rolls at hardware

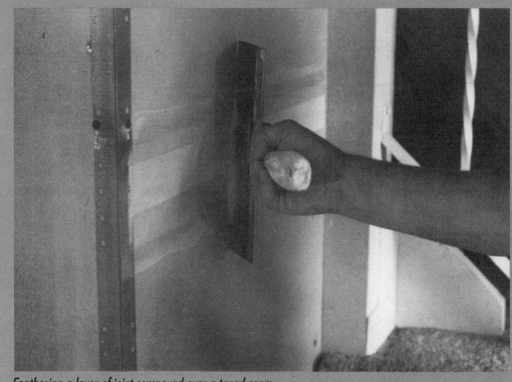

Feathering a layer of joint compound over a taped seam

stores and home centers, fiberglass mesh tape is a little more expensive than paper tape but easier to apply. It sticks directly to the wall, so you don't have to bed it in compound. This eliminates the bubbling that can occur when air gets trapped behind paper tape that isn't properly smoothed into the bed of compound.

When finishing joints and outside corners, the objective is to gradually taper, or feather, the compound so that the finished surface is flat and smooth. Thick applications of joint compound will sag and crack; therefore, a good mud job will usually require three separate applications—each one feathered out a little farther than its predecessor. Depending on the humidity and temperature, you will have to wait at least a day for the joint compound to dry between layers. This progressive feathering work takes time to master, and it's easier if you use progressively longer knives. For example, you might apply the first coat of drywall compound with a 6-inch knife. Then use an 8-inch knife for the second coat and a ½-inch knife for the third.

When two factory edges come together, the tapers form a little valley, so you can fill the joint flush to the surface of the drywall. But field joints are a little more difficult to feather because you have to create a slight mound of compound that feathers out gradually enough to be unnoticeable.

To remove irregularities or unevenness from compounded areas after the compound has dried, you can sand these areas, using 80-grit or 100-grit sandpaper. The better you become at feathering your compound, the less you'll have to sand. Always wear a dust mask when sanding drywall compound, since sanding produces a super-fine white dust that tends to get everywhere.

1 **Install the drywall panels.** Measure and cut your drywall panels to cover the framing members on the closet's walls. If possible, use full sheets on the exterior side walls to minimize the number of joints that require taping and compounding. Secure each panel with drywall screws or nails, driving the fasteners into studs and plates.

2 **Install the corner beads and finish the drywall surfaces with tape and compound.** Install the corner beads on exterior corners as discussed in "Drywall Basics" on page 104. Corner bead provides a straight, durable outside corner that can't be achieved with drywall and tape. It also provides a guide for applying joint compound. "Drywall Basics" will also tell you how to tape and apply compound to the joints and interior corners.

Installing the Trim

You will need three kinds of trim for this closet. Listed according to the order of installation, you will need the finished jambs, the door casing, and the baseboard molding. The finished jambs are square-edged boards that define the closet's finished opening. Door casing trim and baseboard molding are available in different sizes and styles. Choose these moldings to match those already in your house or according to personal taste.

1 **Cut and install the side jambs.** When purchased from the lumberyard, the side jambs are dadoed near their tops to hold the head jamb. Cut the side jambs to length so that the distance between the dado and the bottom of the jamb equals the finished opening height—81 inches in the closet shown here.

Tack each side jamb against a cripple stud

by driving 8d finishing nails about halfway in. Side jambs are usually milled to a width of 4⁹⁄₁₆ inches, so the outside edge of the jamb should be flush with the drywall surface, or slightly proud of it. Place the nails in pairs, with each nail about ¾ inch from a jamb edge. Position the lowermost pair of nails about 2 inches from the bottom of the jamb and the uppermost pair about 2 inches from the dado. Then tack in three more pairs of nails, spaced evenly between the first two pairs.

2 Plumb and straighten the side jambs. To do this, you will need a 4-foot level and some tapered wood shims. Purchase ready-made shims at the lumberyard. The rough opening for this closet allows for ½ inch of shim space between the side jamb and the

cripple stud. Using shims, you can straighten and plumb each side jamb while also precisely fixing the width of the doorway's finished opening.

Use the shims in pairs, as shown in *Drawing E,* inserting them behind opposite edges of the jamb and just above each pair of finishing nails. When used in pairs, the shims can slide against each other, providing solid bearing behind the jamb. Testing the side jamb against the level, tap the shims in against each other, or slide them back to force the jamb in or out. (See *Photo 6.*) You may have to drive the finishing nails deeper into the cripple stud as you make these adjustments. Work your way up and down the jamb until it is straight and plumb. Then drive a single 8d finishing nail through the jamb, through the shim pair, and into the cripple stud. This will lock the shims in place. Drive the side jamb's remaining finishing nails; then set the nail heads. Finish this step by trimming off the waste shim sections that extend beyond the edges of the side jambs. You can do this cutting by hand using a crosscut saw.

Repeat the above operation to fix the position of the remaining side jamb. Remember, in addition to being straight and plumb, the side jambs must also be just the right distance apart (48 inches for this closet).

3 Install the head jamb. Cut the head jamb to fit in the side jamb dadoes. Then slide it into the dadoes, and insert pairs of shims between the header and the head jamb to keep this trim piece straight. Space the shim pairs approximately every 16 inches, pushing or tapping the paired shims against each other, as when securing the side jambs. Lock each pair of shims in place by driving two 8d finishing nails through the head jamb, through the shims, and into the header. Then

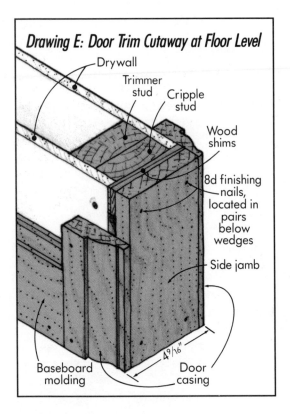

Drawing E: Door Trim Cutaway at Floor Level

- Drywall
- Trimmer stud
- Cripple stud
- Wood shims
- 8d finishing nails, located in pairs below wedges
- Side jamb
- 4⁹⁄₁₆"
- Baseboard molding
- Door casing

trim the waste ends off the shims with a crosscut saw.

4 Cut and install the door casing. As shown in *Drawing F,* the side casing pieces on this closet meet the head casing piece with miter joints. On other types of door casing, corner joints are butted instead of mitered. Either way, it's smart to "case-out" the inside of the closet first, since this will let you try a couple of joints on the less-visible side of the closet.

Make the miter cuts in the head casing piece first. Install this molding piece with 4d finishing nails, driving the nails into the edge of the head jamb, through the the drywall, and into the header. Avoid driving the nails within about 12 inches of each top corner. This will keep the mitered ends of the casing

Photo 6: To straighten and plumb the side jambs, use shims in pairs, driving or withdrawing them from between the jamb and the cripple.

Shop Savvy

Toenailing Tips

To install studs between top and bottom plates, you have to learn how to toenail. The theory behind toenailing studs is simple: Near the end of the stud, you drive nails at an angle so that they extend through the end of the stud and into the plate, fastening the stud in place. To secure the end of a stud firmly, toenail each edge and each side to the plate—a total of four nails.

Most carpenters use 6d or 8d common nails for toenailing framing members. If you're using 8d nails, start your nails about 1½ inches from the stud end (slightly closer to the end for 6d nails). Begin by toenailing both edges, driving the nails at an angle between 45 degrees and 60 degrees. Center the stud on its layout line, and hammer the edge nails alternately, to counteract the shifting of the stud's end that results from hammer blows. Knowing when to switch sides as you hammer will come with a little experience. So will the knack of hitting the nail squarely, even as it seats in the wood. If you find that studs are splitting at their ends, try starting your nails a little higher, or at a wider angle from the stud. A sharp rap with the hammer will usually align a stud over the plate, even after edge toenails are driven home.

Once you've toenailed the edges, the stud should shift minimally as you toenail the sides. Drive these nails slightly off-center in the sides of the studs, so that they don't hit each other.

flexible, so that you can force them tightly against the joining miters of the side casing pieces.

Now cut and install the side casing pieces. Spread a small amount of glue on each side casing's miter before fitting it against the head casing miter. Apply upward pressure on the side casing to force the miter joint tight as you nail the side casing to its jamb and to the cripple stud. If necessary, you can nail the miter joint together by driving a single 4d finishing nail through the top edge of the head casing and into the side casing.

Now that you've had some practice, use the same technique to cut and install the casing around the outside of the doorway. Always wipe off any excess glue with a damp rag.

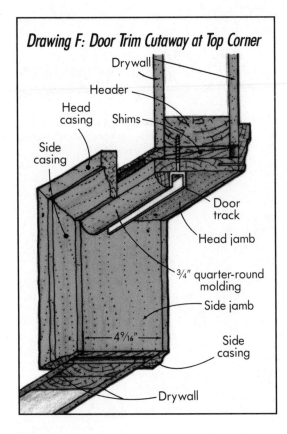

Drawing F: Door Trim Cutaway at Top Corner

Drywall
Header
Head casing
Shims
Side casing
Door track
Head jamb
¾" quarter-round molding
Side jamb
4⁹⁄₁₆"
Side casing
Drywall

5 **Install the door hardware.** Door hardware will vary slightly depending on the door manufacturer. But for all bi-fold doors, your hardware kit will consist of a steel or aluminum track that screws to the underside of the head jamb and two steel bottom brackets that are screwed to the side jambs at floor level. The doors themselves will also have plastic pins, which fit in the door track, and adjustable bottom pivots, which fit the bottom brackets. Follow the manufacturer's instructions for installing this hardware.

6 **Install quarter-round molding in front of the door track.** As shown in *Drawing F,* this molding butts against the door track, concealing it from view in the finished closet. Cut the molding to fit between the side jambs, then use 4d finishing nails to fasten it against the head jamb and against the front side of the track.

7 **Cut and install the baseboard molding.** As was the case when installing the door casing, it's smart to start installing the baseboard inside the closet. Begin by cutting the long piece that will fit against the back wall. Miter the ends of this piece, cutting it to length in the process. Measure and cut the two pieces that fit against the inside side walls. Use miter joints at every corner, and install the molding by driving 6d finishing nails into the studs or bottom plate. Cut and install the short pieces that butt against the door casing.

To install the baseboard molding outside the closet, you'll probably have to join a new piece of closet molding to an existing wall baseboard. If both molding profiles are the same, you can cope the closet baseboard to fit against the wall baseboard. A coped joint, shown in *Drawing G,* fits over the profile of an existing molding. Start with a piece of molding that is 2 or more inches longer than the side wall, in case you have to recut your coped joint. To make the coped joint, first miter the end of the molding as if it were to fit against another inside mitered cut. Then use a coping saw, as shown in *Photo 7,* following the contour of the molding where it meets the angle of the miter. Back-cut the miter so that the front edge of the molding can butt tightly against the profile in place on the wall. Test-fit your coped joint, and fine-tune its fit by trimming the cope with a sharp knife or chisel. A rattail file is also good for this trimming work.

Once a coped joint is done, hold it in its installed position, butting the cope against the existing baseboard molding and allowing the opposite end of the molding to run long, past the closet corner. Now mark the back of the molding at the corner so that you can cut its miter. As shown in *Drawing A,* miter one end

of each front baseboard piece to meet the miter on the side wall baseboards. Square-cut the other end of the front baseboard piece to fit against the door casing. As with the door casings, glue the baseboard's miter joints together. Using 6d finishing nails, attach the baseboard molding to the bottom plates. Wipe away glue squeeze-out with a damp rag.

8 Set the finishing nails and apply wood putty. Using your hammer and nail set, drive the head of each finishing nail so that it's about 1/8 inch below the surface of the wood. Fill the resulting holes with wood putty, and sand the putty smooth after it has dried.

The only trim work left to do is inside the closet. Install shelves and one or more clothes poles, depending on how you wish to use your new storage space. For a versatile closet interior design, see the project "Closet Makeover" on page 312.

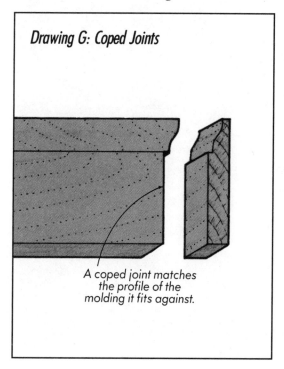

Drawing G: Coped Joints

A coped joint matches the profile of the molding it fits against.

Photo 7: To cut a coped joint in this baseboard molding, first make a miter cut to reveal the molding profile. Then use a coping saw to back-cut the profile, sawing along the miter line at the front of the molding.

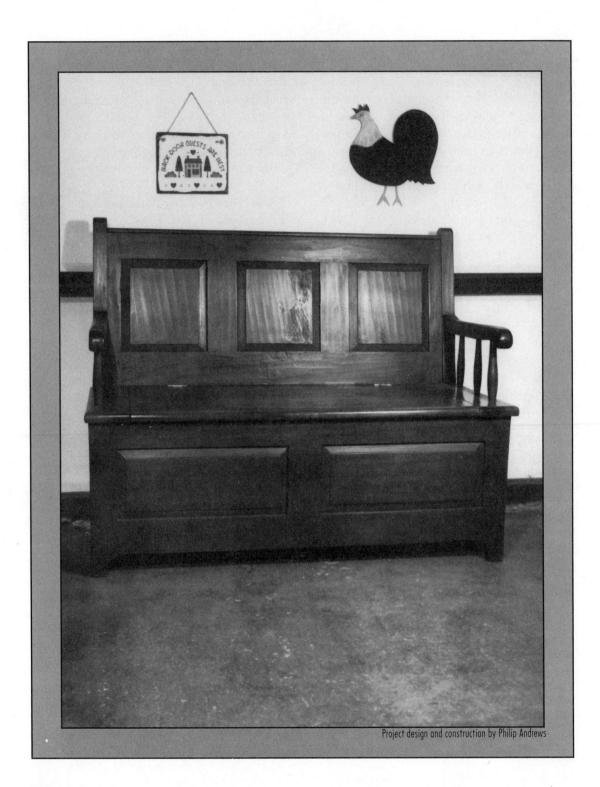

Project design and construction by Philip Andrews

Storage Bench

I n the close quarters of many colonial households, furniture designs became popular if they could perform a couple of different tasks. This practical design ethic still makes sense today. The bench featured here is patterned after an antique and is very traditional in style as well as construction details. Beneath its hinged seat is ample storage space for anything from newspapers and kindling to blankets and boots. This bench could serve well in a hallway, entry foyer, kitchen, or living room.

Like many antiques, this bench is a frame-and-panel design. There are a total of five frame-and-panel assemblies that are joined together to form the front, sides, and back of the bench. Each assembly contains vertical frame members, called stiles, and horizontal frame members, called rails. (See *Drawings A and D*.) Stiles and rails are connected with mortise-and-tenon joints, forming frames that hold raised panels. All four edges of each panel are tapered to fit in grooves cut along the inside of the frame. These taper cuts make the center field of the panel look raised.

You'll begin the project by cutting out the arms and legs. Then you'll build the panels. Finally, you'll join the panels to form the body of the bench and attach the arms and seat.

Like many colonial-style furniture pieces, this bench is made from pine. Three different thicknesses of wood are used. The arms and rear legs are cut from $8/4$ stock that has a finished thickness of $1\frac{3}{4}$ inches after planing. Frame members are cut from planed $5/4$ stock that measures $1\frac{3}{16}$ inches thick. Raised panels are made using one-by pine boards that actually measure $\frac{3}{4}$ inch thick.

Drawing A: Construction Overview

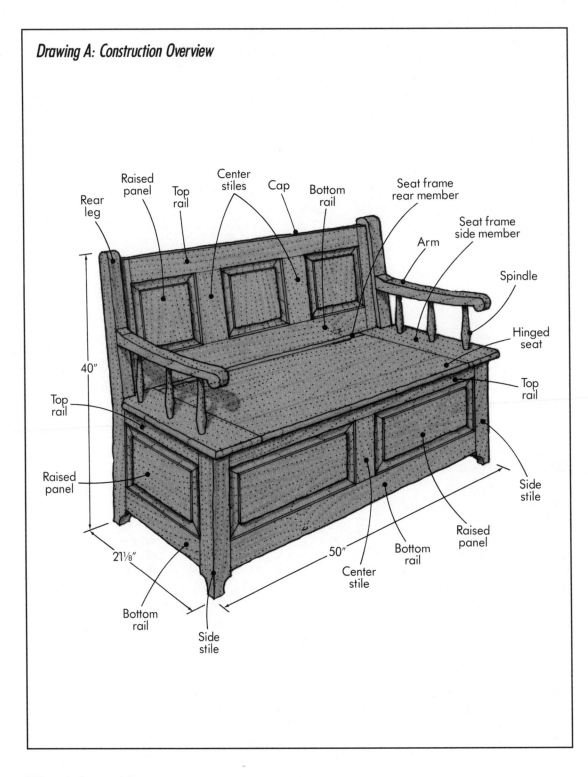

Rear leg

Raised panel

Top rail

Center stiles

Cap

Bottom rail

Seat frame rear member

Seat frame side member

Arm

Spindle

Hinged seat

Top rail

Top rail

Raised panel

40"

21⅛"

Bottom rail

Side stile

50"

Center stile

Bottom rail

Raised panel

Side stile

Materials List

Wood

QTY	PART	DIMENSION
2	Rear leg blanks	$1\frac{3}{4}'' \times 6'' \times 40''$
2	Arm blanks	$1\frac{1}{4}'' \times 2\frac{3}{4}'' \times 20''$

Front Frame-and-Panel Assembly*
QTY	PART	DIMENSION
2	Side stiles	$1\frac{3}{16}'' \times 3'' \times 17\frac{3}{4}''$
1	Center stile	$1\frac{3}{16}'' \times 4'' \times 10''$
1	Top rail	$1\frac{3}{16}'' \times 3'' \times 46''$
1	Bottom rail	$1\frac{3}{16}'' \times 4'' \times 46''$
2	Panels	$\frac{3}{4}'' \times 9'' \times 21''$

Upper Back Frame-and-Panel Assembly*
QTY	PART	DIMENSION
2	Side stiles	$1\frac{3}{16}'' \times 1\frac{1}{8}'' \times 19\frac{9}{16}''$
2	Center stiles	$1\frac{3}{16}'' \times 4'' \times 14''$
1	Top rail	$1\frac{3}{16}'' \times 3\frac{3}{8}'' \times 44\frac{3}{4}''$
1	Bottom rail	$1\frac{3}{16}'' \times 4\frac{5}{16}'' \times 44\frac{3}{4}''$
3	Panels	$\frac{3}{4}'' \times 12\frac{9}{16}'' \times 12\frac{7}{8}''$

Lower Back Frame-and-Panel Assembly*
QTY	PART	DIMENSION
2	Stiles	$1\frac{3}{16}'' \times 4'' \times 15\frac{1}{4}''$
2	Rails	$1\frac{3}{16}'' \times 5'' \times 38\frac{1}{2}''$
1	Panel	$\frac{3}{4}'' \times 6\frac{1}{4}'' \times 39\frac{5}{8}''$

Wood

Side Frame-and-Panel Assembly (2 required)
QTY	PART	DIMENSION
1	Front stile	$1\frac{3}{16}'' \times 1\frac{1}{8}'' \times 17\frac{3}{4}''$
1	Top rail	$1\frac{3}{16}'' \times 3'' \times 15\frac{7}{8}''$
1	Bottom rail	$1\frac{3}{16}'' \times 4'' \times 15\frac{7}{8}''$
1	Panel	$\frac{3}{4}'' \times 8\frac{3}{4}'' \times 14\frac{7}{8}''$

Seat and Bottom Assemblies
QTY	PART	DIMENSION
1	Bottom cleat (back)	$1'' \times 1\frac{3}{16}'' \times 46\frac{1}{2}''$
1	Bottom cleat (front)	$1'' \times 1\frac{3}{16}'' \times 47\frac{5}{8}''$
2	Bottom cleats (sides)	$1'' \times 1\frac{3}{16}'' \times 15\frac{15}{16}''$
1	Bottom	$\frac{3}{4}'' \times 18\frac{1}{2}'' \times 45\frac{1}{4}''$
2	Seat frame side members	$1\frac{3}{16}'' \times 5'' \times 21''$
1	Seat frame rear member	$1\frac{3}{16}'' \times 4'' \times 43''$
1	Seat	$1\frac{3}{16}'' \times 17'' \times 40\frac{7}{8}''$
1	Cap	$\frac{3}{4}'' \times 1\frac{3}{4}'' \times 46\frac{1}{2}''$
1	Bottom	$\frac{3}{4}'' \times 18\frac{3}{4}'' \times 47\frac{5}{8}''$
6	Turned spindles	$9''$ long

Hardware

QTY	PART	
1	pair steel butt hinges, $\frac{3}{4}'' \times 2\frac{1}{2}''$	
1	box trim-head screws, $2\frac{1}{4}''$ long	

*Lengths include tenons. Panel sizes are for reference only, since panel measurements should be taken after each frame assembly is test fit together.

Cutting the Curved Parts

1 Cut out the arms and rear legs. These four parts are the only curved ones in the project. A scaled-down pattern of the arm is shown in *Drawing B;* the rear leg pattern is shown in *Drawing C.* Note that the arm pattern includes a tenon. Enlarge both patterns to full-scale size, and then trace the arm and rear leg shapes onto some clear 8/4 stock.

The bandsaw is the best tool to use for cutting out these parts. (See *Photo 1.*) If you don't have access to a bandsaw, use a portable jigsaw with a sharp blade. Keep the blade just outside the pattern lines. Don't cut the tenon in each arm at this stage.

2 Shape the arms. Use the spokeshave to refine the contour of the arm, creating gentler curves, especially at the fronts, where hands will rest. With an arm clamped in your bench vice, you can transform hard edges into comfortable curves, removing a curl of wood

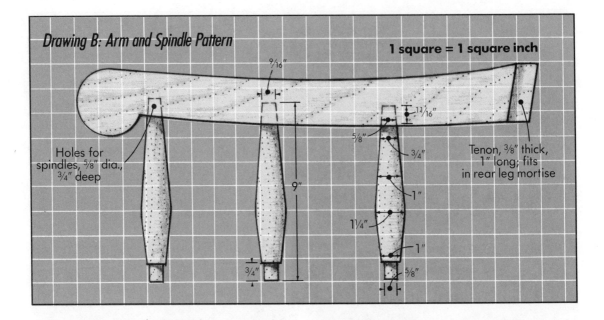

Drawing B: Arm and Spindle Pattern

1 square = 1 square inch

9/16"

Holes for spindles, 5/8" dia., 3/4" deep

9"

3/4"

1 3/16"

5/8"

3/4"

1"

1 1/4"

1"

5/8"

Tenon, 3/8" thick, 1" long; fits in rear leg mortise

Photo 1: The bandsaw makes quick work of cutting out the arms for the bench.

Photo 2: Shape the arm using a spokeshave. Round-over the top edges of each arm to give it a comfortable feel. Later on in the project, a tenon will be cut out of the arm's square bottom end.

with each pass, as shown in *Photo 2*. Test the feel of the arm as you work. Once you finish with the spokeshave, very little sanding should be necessary.

3 **Glue up the bottom panel.** Before turning to joinery work on the stiles and rails, it's a good idea to make the bottom panel, using several one-by boards. Make sure that joining edges are straight and square before gluing and clamping them together. Set this assembly aside to dry.

Making the Stiles and Rails

1 **Cut the stiles and rails to their finished sizes.** Frame-and-panel construction begins with the stiles and rails that are joined together to make the frame. It's best to complete each frame assembly and test fit the parts together so you can cut the panels to fit. Refer to the dimensions given in the Materials List when cutting the stiles and rails to their finished lengths and widths. To avoid confusion as parts receive grooves, mortises, and tenons, label each part as it's cut. This enables you to keep stiles and rails together in their respective frame-and-panel assemblies. These assemblies are detailed in the Materials List and illustrated in *Drawings D, E, F, and G*.

2 **Mill the panel grooves.** Once you've cut the stiles and rails to size, use a dado cutter in the table saw to mill the grooves for panels along the inside edges of all frame members. To set up the cut, adjust the dado cutter width to ⅜ inch and raise the cutter height to 9⁄16 inch above the table. Now adjust the rip fence so that it's ⅜ inch from the dado cutter. This distance corresponds to the ⅜-inch distance between the outside face of the frame member and the shoulder of the panel

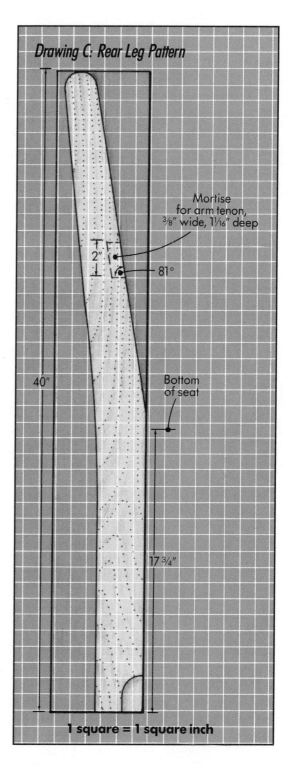

Drawing C: Rear Leg Pattern

Mortise for arm tenon, ⅜" wide, 1¹⁄16" deep

2"

81°

Bottom of seat

40"

17¾"

1 square = 1 square inch

groove. (See *Drawing H.*) Test this setup on some scrap ¾ stock. Adjust the dado cutter and fence, if necessary. Then cut each groove by running the outside face of the rails and stiles against the fence, as shown in *Photo 3.* Remember, only the inside edges of the frame members require grooves.

The rear legs, which also form the stiles on the side frame-and-panel assemblies, require stopped grooves. As shown in *Drawing G,* each rear leg groove extends 17¾ inches from the bottom of the leg. To mill the stopped groove in the right rear leg, run the bottom end of the leg through the cutter, and carefully

lift the leg free of the cutter when the groove has been milled about 17¾ inches from the end. As a guide for stopping the groove, it's helpful to make a mark on the saw table, indicating where the dado cutter emerges from the table. Also mark the stop line on the leg. To mill the groove in the left rear leg, carefully lower the leg down over the cutter at the 17¾-inch mark, and then feed the leg through the cutter until the cutter comes through the bottom end of the leg.

3 **Mortise the stiles and rails.** All of the stile and rail mortises are 1¹⁄₁₆ inches deep

Photo 3: *Stiles and rails require panel grooves, and these can be milled on the table saw, using the dado cutter. Adjust the cutter width to ⅜ inch and the cutter height to ⁹⁄₁₆ inch. The rip fence should be ⅜ inch away from the cutter.*

Photo 4: *Square up the mortises with a chisel after drilling out most of the waste, using a ⅜-inch-diameter bit. The mortise shown here is in the rear leg and will hold the arm tenon.*

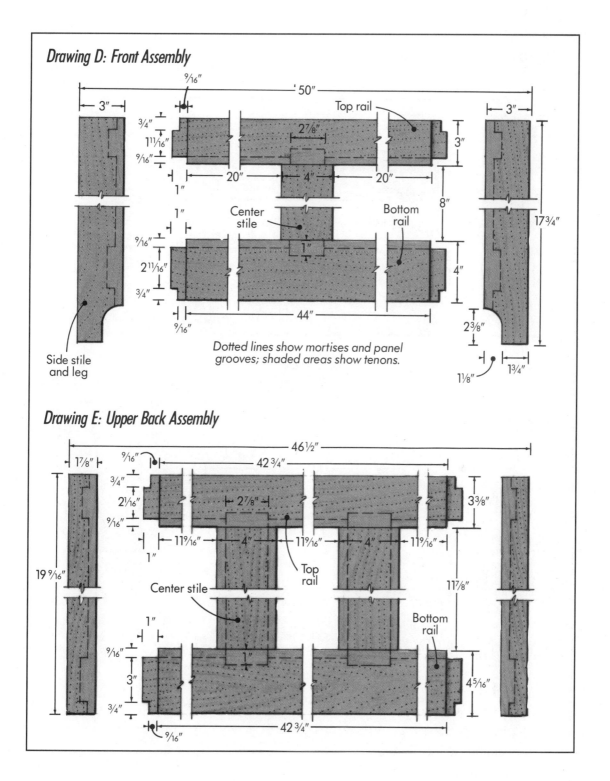

Drawing D: Front Assembly

9/16"

3"

50"

Top rail

3"

3/4"

1 11/16"

9/16"

2 7/8"

1"

20"

4"

20"

8"

Center stile

Bottom rail

17 3/4"

1"

9/16"

1"

4"

2 11/16"

3/4"

44"

2 3/8"

9/16"

Dotted lines show mortises and panel grooves; shaded areas show tenons.

Side stile and leg

1 1/8"

1 3/4"

Drawing E: Upper Back Assembly

1 7/8"

9/16"

46 1/2"

42 3/4"

3/4"

2 1/16"

9/16"

2 7/8"

3 3/8"

11 9/16"

4"

11 9/16"

4"

11 9/16"

1"

Top rail

19 9/16"

Center stile

1"

11 7/8"

9/16"

1"

Bottom rail

3"

4 5/16"

3/4"

42 3/4"

9/16"

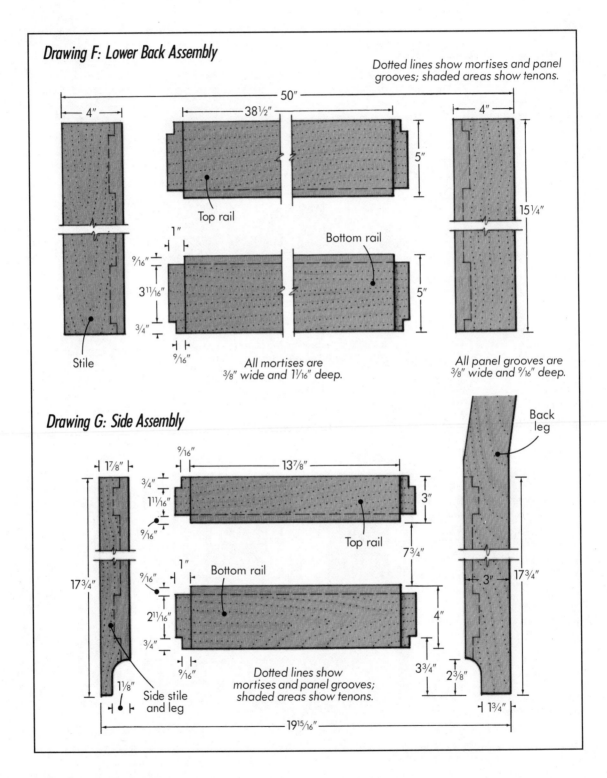

Drawing F: Lower Back Assembly

Dotted lines show mortises and panel grooves; shaded areas show tenons.

50"

4"

38½"

5"

Top rail

4"

15¼"

Bottom rail

1"

⁹⁄₁₆"

3¹¹⁄₁₆"

5"

¾"

⁹⁄₁₆"

Stile

All mortises are ⅜" wide and 1¹⁄₁₆" deep.

All panel grooves are ⅜" wide and ⁹⁄₁₆" deep.

Drawing G: Side Assembly

Back leg

1⁷⁄₈"

⁹⁄₁₆"

13⁷⁄₈"

3"

¾"

1¹¹⁄₁₆"

⁹⁄₁₆"

Top rail

7¾"

17¾"

1"

Bottom rail

⁹⁄₁₆"

3"

17¾"

2¹¹⁄₁₆"

¾"

4"

⁹⁄₁₆"

Dotted lines show mortises and panel grooves; shaded areas show tenons.

3¾"

2³⁄₈"

1⅛"

Side stile and leg

1¾"

19¹⁵⁄₁₆"

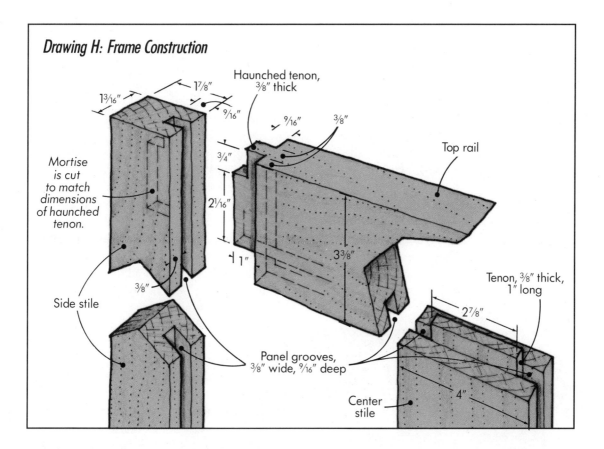

Drawing H: Frame Construction

Haunched tenon, 3/8" thick

1 7/8"

1 3/16"

9/16"

9/16"

3/8"

3/4"

Top rail

Mortise is cut to match dimensions of haunched tenon.

2 1/16"

1"

3 3/8"

3/8"

Side stile

Tenon, 3/8" thick, 1" long

2 7/8"

Panel grooves, 3/8" wide, 9/16" deep

Center stile

4"

and ⅜ inch wide. Mortise locations are shown in *Drawings D, E, F, and G.*

Mortises can be cut quickly and easily using a drill and chisel. Chuck a ⅜-inch-diameter bit in your electric drill. A brad-point bit will do the best job of roughing out these mortises. Wrap a piece of tape around the bit 1¹⁄₁₆ inches from its tip, and clamp the stock to be mortised in your bench vice. Using the panel groove to guide the bit, bore a series of holes inside the layout lines for the mortise. You've drilled deep enough when the taped portion of the bit reaches the edge of the stile. After roughing out the mortise with the drill and bit, use a ⅜-inch chisel to square up the ends of the mortise and pare out the remaining waste. (See *Photo 4.*) In addition to chis-

eling out mortises, use the chisel to square up the stopped grooves in the rear legs.

4 **Mortise the rear legs for the arms.** As shown in *Drawing C,* each of these mortises is ⅜ inch wide, 2 inches long, and 1¹⁄₁₆ inches deep. Lay out each mortise 12 inches from the top of each leg. Drill and chisel the mortises as in the previous step, but take into account the sloped front edge of each rear leg. In the finished bench, the upper edge of each rear leg will slope back 9 degrees from vertical. Instead of meeting the front edge of the leg at a right angle, the ends of the mortise will meet this edge at an 81-degree angle, as shown in *Drawing C.* When laying out the location of each mortise, mark a pair of 81-

degree angles on one side of the leg. Follow these angles when drilling and chiseling the mortise.

5 **Cut mortises in the seat side members.** Each mortise is ³⁄₈ inch wide, 1¹⁄₁₆ inches deep, and 3¼ inches long. Begin each mortise ¾ inch from the back edge of the seat side member, as shown in *Drawing I*.

6 **Cut the tenons in the rails, center stiles, and rear seat member.** Note that all rail tenons are notched, or haunched, so that part of the tenon has a depth of ⁹⁄₁₆ inch. This short section fits into the panel groove instead of into the mortise. This haunched

Photo 5: To mill tenons on the table saw, guide frame members against the miter gauge, and use the dado head to nibble away waste. A stop block, fastened to the wood auxiliary fence in front of the blade, lets you use the rip fence to align each shoulder cut.

tenon detail (see *Drawing H*) is a traditional way to increase strength in frame-and-panel construction by increasing the size of the tenon. Haunched tenons can be milled just like conventional tenons but require a notched cutout. Cut the tenons on the table saw, using a dado cutter.

Remember, tenons aren't centered along rail and center stile edges. Like mortises and panel grooves, tenons are laid out ³⁄₈ inch from the outside face of the frame member. Because of this, shoulder and cheek cuts have to be made with the dado cutter at two different heights. Adjust the cutter to its maximum width. To set up to cut front cheeks, adjust the cutter height to exactly ³⁄₈ inch. Test your height ' adjustment on some scrap stock and fine-tune it if necessary. When you get the right cheek depth, cut it into several scrap ends. You'll use these to fine-tune the back tenon cheeks.

Now screw or clamp a stop block against the rip fence to align the shoulders of the tenon. To reduce the chance of kickback, be sure to position the block on the operator's side of the dado cutter, at least 4 inches from the cutter. When the stop block has been secured, adjust the rip fence so the block aligns the shoulder cut for each frame member 1 inch from the end of the frame member. This setup is shown in *Photo 5*.

Make the first series of cuts with the outside face of the stock flat on the saw table. Make the shoulder cut first, by sliding the frame member against the stop block and guiding it over the dado cutter with the miter gauge. Then position the frame member away from the stop block and make additional passes through the dado cutter to complete the tenon cheek.

To cut the tenon cheeks that will face inside, put the inside face of one of your scrap pieces flat on the saw table. Adjust the height of the dado cutter so the finished thickness of the tenon is ⅜ inch, matching the width of your mortises. Keep the stop block and rip fence in the same position when making this series of shoulder and cheek cuts. Check the scrap tenons against the mortises. When you get the right setting, cut the real tenons.

7 **Cut notches to create haunched tenons.** All of the tenons except those on the center stiles should be haunched. The notch for each haunch is 9/16 inch deep and ¾ inch long, as shown in *Drawing H*. Haunches can be cut by hand, using a backsaw, but with the dado cutter set up in the table saw, notch cutting can be done quickly and accurately. Raise the cutter ¾ inch above the table, and adjust the rip fence (with stop block still attached) so that when the end of the tenon butts against the stop block, a cut is aligned to leave a section of the tenon just 9/16 inch long. Make a test cut on the last scrap tenon you made. Test fit the scrap tenon in a mortise and adjust your setup if necessary.

8 **Make curved cuts for feet.** The front assembly (see *Drawing D*) and side assemblies (see *Drawing G*) require curved cutouts on stiles that extend to become feet. As shown in *Drawings D and G*, each curve should be about 2⅜ inches high and 1⅛ inches wide. Use the bandsaw or a portable jigsaw to make the curved cuts. Use the first curved cutout as a pattern for tracing the curve onto the remaining pieces.

Raising the Panels

In traditional frame-and-panel construction, panels aren't glued or fastened into the frame grooves. Instead, they "float" in their frames. This allows the panels to expand and contract without warping or cracking frame members. When sizing panels, it's best to test fit the frames together and measure the size of each opening. Taking the 9/16-inch groove depth into account, the panel size should be 1 inch greater than the length and width of the opening. This allows about 1/16 inch between the outside edge of a panel and the bottom of the groove that holds it. Once you've written down your panel cutting list, cut the panels to size from ¾-inch-thick stock.

There are several ways to make raised panels. If you have a router table or shaper, you can choose from panel-raising cutters with several different profiles. The panels can also be raised on the table saw, using a carbide-tipped combination blade. The profile of the raised panels for this bench, shown in *Drawing J,* includes a ⅛-inch-high reveal and a simple bevel.

1 **Cut the reveal.** Adjust the blade height to ⅛ inch above the table, and set the rip fence 1⅝ inches away from the blade. Make

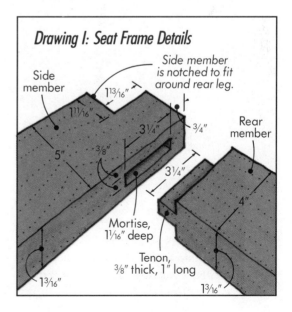

Drawing I: Seat Frame Details

Side member

Side member is notched to fit around rear leg.

1¹³/₁₆"

1¹¹/₁₆"

3¼"

¾"

Rear member

5"

⅜"

3¼"

4"

Mortise, 1¹/₁₆" deep

Tenon, ⅜" thick, 1" long

1³/₁₆"

1³/₁₆"

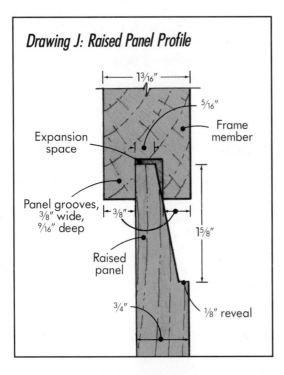

Drawing J: Raised Panel Profile

1³⁄₁₆"

⁵⁄₁₆"

Frame member

Expansion space

Panel grooves, ³⁄₈" wide, ⁹⁄₁₆" deep

³⁄₈"

1⁵⁄₈"

Raised panel

³⁄₄"

¹⁄₈" reveal

four cuts in the outside face of each panel, as shown in *Photo 6*. Make each cut by running an edge of the panel against the rip fence while the outside face of the panel runs against the saw table. In addition to making reveal cuts in all of the panels, cut reveals in a sample panel that can be used to test the bevel setup described in the next step.

2 Cut the bevel. Mount the fence so the blade tilts away from it. On many saws, this will mean putting the fence to the left of the blade. Adjust the blade angle to 78 degrees, or 12 degrees from its vertical position. Adjust the blade height to exactly 1⁵⁄₈ inches. This should be the vertical distance from the table to the top of the blade's cutting radius.

Screw a wood auxiliary fence to the rip fence. Use a straight board at least 14 inches long and 12 inches high, and make sure it

Photo 6: Reveal cuts for each raised panel are made on the table saw, with the blade showing just ¹⁄₈ inch above the table. Position the rip fence 1⁵⁄₈ inches from the blade.

Photo 7: To complete the raised panel profile, make bevel cuts along all four edges of each panel. Tilt the blade 12 degrees off vertical, and position the auxiliary rip fence ⁵⁄₁₆ inch from the blade.

extends at a right angle to the saw table. Adjust the rip fence so the auxiliary fence is 5/16 inch from the blade at the table surface. It's tricky to get all three adjustments just right: blade angle, blade height, and rip fence position. To test your setup, run the sample panel through the blade, holding the edge of the panel against the table surface and the inside face of the panel against the auxiliary fence. The saw blade should remove a triangular section of waste, cutting right to the reveal but not into it. (See *Photo 7*.) Fine-tune the setup as necessary, and take care to hold the stock firmly, feeding it through the blade with slow, steady pressure.

3 **Smooth the panels.** When making broad bevel cuts on the table saw, even the sharpest blade will leave some burn marks or rough spots on raised panels. Now is the time to smooth out these imperfections. You can sand the panel bevels smooth, using a sanding block and fine-grit sandpaper. A scraper also does a good job of removing rough spots and burn marks.

Assembling the Frames and Panels

1 **Test fit the frame-and-panel assemblies.** Assemble each frame and panel set to make sure that frame joints fit well and the panels fit in their frames.

2 **Assemble the frame-and-panel units.** Glue each mortise-and-tenon joint together while slipping each panel into its frame. Use a wooden mallet to coax the joints together around the panels, as shown in *Photo 8*. Remember, the panels need to float in their frames, so keep glue out of the panel grooves

Photo 8: The lower rail tenon in this side assembly goes into its mortise with a little coaxing from the mallet. Be sure to spread glue on the mortise-and-tenon joints only, allowing each panel to float in its grooves.

Photo 9: *The upper back assembly goes together by fitting the center stiles and panels into the bottom rail.*

Photo 10: *Then the top rail is installed, and finally, the side stiles go on. Clamp each frame-and-panel assembly until the glue dries.*

Photo 11: *Hand plane each completed frame-and-panel assembly to eliminate any irregularities along joint lines and to give the completed bench its handmade look.*

as each unit is assembled. (See *Photo 9*.) Check each frame to make sure it's square as you clamp the stiles and rails together.

3 Install the wooden pegs. Thanks to the wood glue available today, wooden pegs aren't necessary to hold mortise-and-tenon joints together. But pegs give this piece a traditional appearance, so they're a nice feature to include. You can install the pegs while the clamps are still on each frame-and-panel assembly, or wait until the glue has dried and the clamps are removed.

To enhance the authentic appearance of your bench, don't make the pegs from a length of dowel rod. Instead, shave pegs from small square blanks (⅜ inch on a side), using a sharp chisel. (See *Photo 10*.) Make the pegs about 1¼ inches long. Pine is soft enough to allow these shop-made pegs to be driven easily into their holes. Using a ⅜-inch-diameter bit, drill out two peg holes per joint, after the joints have been clamped in each frame-and-panel assembly. The hole centers should be at least ½ inch from each tenon shoulder, and the hole depth should be 1 inch. Dab a small amount of glue on each peg before tapping it into its hole. For now, leave about ¼ inch of the peg standing proud of the surface.

4 Clean up the frame-and-panel assemblies. Wait until the glue has cured, then scrape off any excess glue that has hardened outside the joints. Trim the pegs flush with the frame with a backsaw and chisel. Then plane down the high spots where the stiles and rails meet. A jack plane is good for this type of work because you can use both hands on the plane, applying pressure with good control. (See *Photo 11*.) Planing has an added benefit: It can give your bench the hand-planed look of a fine antique. For this effect,

give the entire outside face of each panel a once-over, shaving the pegs flush and removing thin curls of wood to leave the surface smooth. Don't sand after planing, since this will obliterate the subtle marks left by the plane.

Assembling the Bench

1 Join the sides and the lower front frame-and-panel assembly. The front corners of the bench are formed by gluing the front and side frames together. Spread glue along the joining edges, then clamp the sides and front together as shown in *Photo 12*. Make sure the top edges of all three parts are flush with each other. Use a framing square to keep

Photo 12: To assemble the bench, start by joining the front assembly to the sides; then glue and screw the lower back assembly between the rear legs. The top edges of these frame-and-panel assemblies should be level and flush with each other.

the corners square while driving 2¼-inch-long trim-head screws through the front stiles and into the side stiles. Trim-head screws are good to use for this kind of work, since they don't require pilot holes. (See the Shop Savvy on page 11.) Three or four screws per joint should be adequate.

2 **Attach the lower back assembly.** The stiles of this frame-and-panel assembly fit inside the rear legs. The outside face of the frame is flush with the back edges of the legs, and the top edge of the frame is level with the top edges of the front and side assemblies, as shown in *Drawing K.* Glue and screw these joints together, again using 2¼-inch-long trim-head screws.

3 **Install the bottom.** The bottom rests on four cleats that are screwed along the inside of the storage compartment. (See *Drawing K.*) Cut the cleats from ⁵⁄₄ stock, and screw them with their wide faces along the lower rails. Exact lengths aren't crucial, but make sure the top edges are level and flush with each other. Cut the bottom to size and notch the back corners to fit around the rear legs. Then simply place the bottom on top of the cleats. Leaving the bottom unattached will allow it to expand and contract with humidity changes.

Completing the Seat

1 **Notch the side seat members.** The seat members are notched to fit around the legs, as shown in *Drawing I.* To lay out the notches, first test fit the rear seat member and side seat members together. Place this assembly on top of the storage compartment so the end grain of the side seat members butts against the front edges of the rear legs. Lay out

notch cuts, then separate the seat members amd cut the notches.

2 **Assemble and install the rear seat member and side seat members.** Glue the tenons in the rear seat member in their mortises, then glue and screw this three-piece assembly to the top edges of the compartment opening using 2¼-inch screws.

3 **Bevel the bottom rail of the upper back assembly.** As shown in *Drawing K,* this rail needs to be beveled to fit squarely against the seat members. Adjust a bevel gauge to the angle between the front edge of the rear leg and the side seat member. Use the gauge to adjust the blade angle on the table saw. Then cut the bevel, using the rip fence to guide the top edge of the assembly's top rail. Adjust the fence to remove a narrow triangular section of waste from the bottom rail.

4 **Install the upper back assembly.** As shown in *Drawing K,* the front edges of the seat back frame sit back about ¼ inch from the front edges of the legs. Glue joining edges together, and secure all joints with trim-head screws.

When the upper back assembly is in place, top it off with a small cap molding, cut from ¾-inch-thick, 1¾-inch-wide pine. Cut the cap to length; then, for feel and appearance, use a hand plane and fine-grit sandpaper to round-over the top edges. Then spread some glue along the top edge of the top rail, and center the cap over the rail. Nail it in place with 4d finishing nails.

5 **Lay out and cut the arm tenons.** Make sure the bench is on a level surface. Then hold an arm against the outside face of a rear leg, at mortise height, and use a small level to

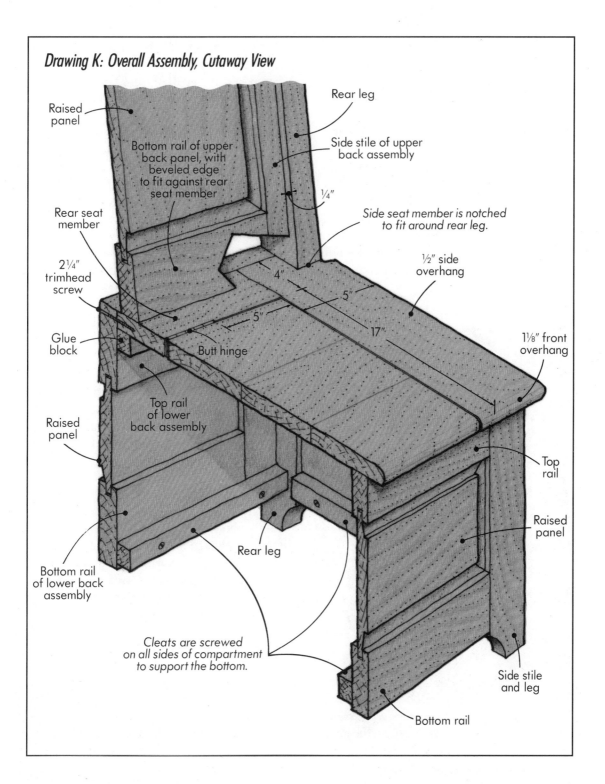

Drawing K: Overall Assembly, Cutaway View

Raised panel

Rear leg

Bottom rail of upper back panel, with beveled edge to fit against rear seat member

Side stile of upper back assembly

Rear seat member

¼"

Side seat member is notched to fit around rear leg.

2¼" trimhead screw

4"

5"

½" side overhang

Glue block

5"

17"

1⅛" front overhang

Raised panel

Butt hinge

Top rail of lower back assembly

Top rail

Raised panel

Bottom rail of lower back assembly

Rear leg

Side stile and leg

Cleats are screwed on all sides of compartment to support the bottom.

Bottom rail

keep the straight bottom edge of the arm level. In this position, you can lay out the shoulder line for the arm tenon by marking along the rear leg and against the arm. Use a square to transfer this shoulder line to the opposite side of the arm. Complete the layout by marking the tenon cheeks, which should yield a ⅜-inch-thick tenon, centered on the arm's thickness. Make each arm tenon 1 inch long, measured from the angled shoulder.

Cut out each arm tenon with a backsaw. Make the shoulder cuts first. After the cheek cuts have been made, test each tenon for fit in its mortise. If necessary, use a chisel to trim tenons for a better fit.

Photo 13: Install the upper back assembly next, followed by the three-piece seat assembly. Then the arms and spindles can be joined to the rear leg and to the side seat member.

6 **Make the spindles for the arms.** Each arm is supported by three spindles, as shown in *Drawing B*. All spindles are 9 inches long, including tenons that are ¾ inch long and ⅝ inch in diameter. The bench shown has turned spindles, with profiles as shown in *Drawing B*. If you don't have a lathe to turn these spindles, you can use a spokeshave to shape your own from dowel rod or even from clear, square pine stock. To make the tenon, cut the shoulder with a backsaw, and then pare the tenon to fit with a chisel.

7 **Drill the holes in the arms and side seat members for spindles.** Hole spacing is shown in *Drawing B*. Lay out and drill the arm holes first. Make these holes ¾ inch deep, ⅝ inch in diameter, and centered along the bottom edge of each arm. Drill each hole perpendicular to the top edge of the arm. When the arm holes are complete, fit the arm tenon in its mortise, and use a square to mark hole locations in the side seat member. Make the seat member holes ⅝ inch in diameter and ⅞ inch deep.

8 **Install the arms and spindles.** Glue the three spindles for an arm in their seat member holes. Then spread glue on the arm tenon, on the tenon shoulders, and in the arm spindle holes. Fit the arm tenon in its mortise and over its spindles at the same time, as shown in *Photo 13*. Repeat this procedure for the remaining arm.

9 **Install the seat.** Cut the seat to fit its opening, allowing 1/16-inch clearance between the seat ends and side seat members. Make sure the seat overhang at the front of the bench matches the overhang of the seat side members. Mortise a pair of butt hinges into the back edge of the seat and into the rear seat member. Locate each hinge 5 inches from a seat end. (See *Drawing K*.) Then attach the hinges to the seat and to the rear seat member.

10 **Fill the nail and screw holes and sand the bench.** If the frame-and-panel assemblies were planed earlier, they won't require sanding, except where the assemblies join at corners. All exposed corners and edges should be rounded slightly with sandpaper. Go over these areas carefully, rounding them over so that the bench will have the look and feel of a family heirloom. (See *Photo 14*.)

Photo 14: The seat swings on a pair of butt hinges that are mortised into the seat's back edge and into the front of the rear seat member.

Kitchen
&
Bathroom

Towel Rack

When a boat builder was hired to finish a house on the Maine coast, he decided to outfit the "head" in true nautical style. This small, shapely project can be a well-crafted replacement for the nondescript towel rack in your bathroom. The friendly supports can be fastened against a door or wall, and you can adjust the length of the dowel to suit your space. Alternatively, you might want to adapt this design for use as a paper towel holder. If you do, just use a 14-inch-long dowel and eliminate Step 9, which calls for screwing the dowel to the supports. With either option, you'll have a storage solution that's eye-catching as well as useful.

1 **Trace support pattern onto ¾ (five-quarters) stock.** Enlarge the pattern shown in *Drawing B* to full size. (See "Using Patterns" on page viii.) Trace this shape onto cardboard or ¼-inch-thick plywood. When making your pattern, don't cut out the 1-inch-diameter hole for the dowel; just mark the hole's center point in your pattern.

Place the pattern with its flat back edge against a straight, square edge on a piece of clear ¾ pine. Make sure that the grain of the wood runs parallel with the pattern's straight edge.

2 **Drill a 1-inch-diameter hole in each support.** If you have a Forstner bit, use it to drill these holes. It will make a cleaner hole than a spade bit. To avoid tear-out, put some scrap beneath where the bit will exit. Also, don't force the bit through the stock. Use a

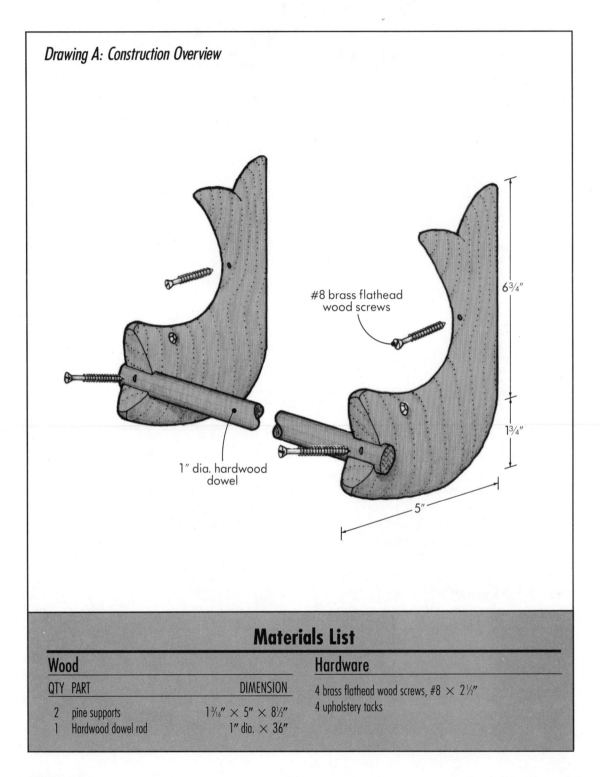

Drawing A: Construction Overview

#8 brass flathead wood screws

6³⁄₄″

1³⁄₄″

5″

1″ dia. hardwood dowel

Materials List

Wood

QTY	PART	DIMENSION
2	pine supports	1³⁄₁₆″ × 5″ × 8½″
1	Hardwood dowel rod	1″ dia. × 36″

Hardware

4 brass flathead wood screws, #8 × 2½″
4 upholstery tacks

drill press if you have one. If you don't, use an angle square as a guide, as shown in *Photo 1*. As you drill, keep the bit shank parallel with the square's vertical edge.

3 **Cut out the supports.** This work can be done on the band saw, or with a jigsaw.

4 **Shape and sand the supports.** It's time to transform the supports' square edges into more seaworthy curves. This is the most time-consuming part of the project. But some extra care here will bring good results when you finish and install your "fish."

Shave sharp corners with a ½-inch chisel. To sculpt curved edges and to taper the area between the tail and the head, use a medium-grit sanding drum with a diameter of 2 inches or less. You'll find these drums at most hardware stores and home centers, as well as in mail-order catalogues. Most drums can be used in portable electric drills or in drill presses. If you're using a portable drill, clamp each support in your bench vice, and work your way around the piece. (See *Photo 2*.) If you're working on the drill press, move the support around against the drum.

Use the sanding drum creatively to give each fish a graceful form. As the shape starts to emerge, avoid removing too much wood from around the dowel hole, since this might weaken the mouth area that will support the weight of the dowel and towels.

When you've drum-sanded the contours you want, sand by hand with 100-grit or 120-grit sandpaper. Sand with the grain of the wood to remove any scratches left by the drum sander. Shape and smooth tight areas around the tail and mouth that you couldn't reach with the drum sander. Then switch to 200-grit or 220-grit sandpaper for final smoothing. Work until the wood surface is

Photo 1: Drill out a hole for the "mouth" of each support. A square set next to the drill helps keep the bit shank perpendicular to the stock.

Photo 2: After rough shaping with a chisel, use a sanding drum in the electric drill to give each support graceful contours.

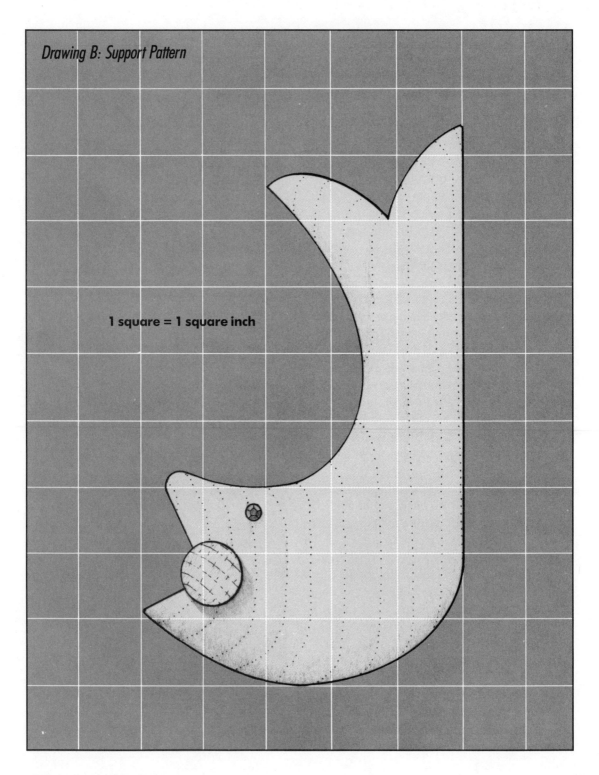

Drawing B: Support Pattern

1 square = 1 square inch

uniformly smooth to the touch.

5 **Cut the dowel to finished length.** The rack will look best if the dowel ends extend about ¼ inch beyond the mouth of each fish. In deciding on dowel length, consider how you will attach the fish supports to the wall. For a drywall or plaster wall, plan to position the supports over studs. This means, for example, that if the studs are 16 inches on center, you'll probably want to skip a stud and make the dowel about 33¾ inches long. After cutting the dowel, chamfer the ends of the dowel with a chisel.

6 **Drill pilot holes in the supports.** Drill a countersunk #8 pilot hole through the narrowest section of each fish support as shown in *Photo 3*.

7 **Apply finish to the supports and the dowel.** It's best to finish these parts separately. To finish your rack like the one shown here, give the fish an antique pine stain, followed by three coats of high-gloss urethane. Give the cherry dowel two coats of penetrating oil finish. After finish dries, give each fish some vision by adding a couple of upholstery tacks to simulate eyes.

You can also paint your fish. With paint, you can animate your project with scales, gills, and a more realistic color.

8 **Install supports.** Position one fish support over a stud or on a door. Mark the location of the attachment hole. Predrill into the door, or through the drywall, or plaster and lath, into a stud. Attach the support to the wall or door with a #8 brass flathead wood screw, using 2½-inch screws for a wall, and ¾-inch screws for a door. Use a level to align the top of the other support, and attach it to

the wall or door the same way you did the first.

9 **Attach the dowel to the supports.** The dowel is attached to each support with a brass #8 × 2½-inch flathead wood screw. Drill countersunk pilot holes for the screws, taking care to bore through the center of the dowel and into the center of the hole. Before driving screws through the dowel and into the supports, dab a bit of clear epoxy adhesive around the pilot hole in the mouth. This will strengthen the joints. Once the epoxy has cured, you can put your fish to work.

Photo 3: Drill a countersunk pilot hole through the narrowest section of the support for a single screw.

Basic Box

The basic box is an excellent storage project for the beginner. Its simplicity makes it extremely versatile, so you are bound to have use for it. You can tackle it with limited carpentry skills while learning techniques that are basic to all cabinetmaking. With the jig described in "Make a Straight-Cutting Guide for Your Circular Saw" on page 19, you can build the box even if you don't have a table saw.

In this project, you'll learn how to cut several parts to exactly the same size. You'll learn how to hide exposed plywood edges. And you'll learn to miter trim to fit a box without ever touching a ruler. These techniques will be useful for many of the projects in this book.

A major reason the basic box is so versatile is that you can use it alone or combine boxes in various ways. Small boxes can be stacked, as shown on the facing page, creating storage that can fit just about anywhere. You can make the boxes larger than shown here, or make them rectangular instead of square. Boxes can be used to support shelves as shown in "Design Ideas" on page 145. Or, as described in "Beyond the Basic Box" on page 146, it doesn't take much more work to refine the box into a chest.

The box shown here is made from ¾-inch-thick lauan plywood, which is easy to work with and takes paint well. If you want to give your boxes a clear or stained finish, you might want to use plywood with hardwood face veneers. Plywood veneered with birch, oak, or cherry can be ordered from most lumberyards. For less-expensive boxes, use common fir or pine plywood. For more information about plywood grades and types, see "Buying Wood" on page 9.

As you can see, you'll probably want to build several boxes. Although the Materials List gives the parts that go into a single box, the techniques shown here take advantage of

Drawing A: Construction Overview

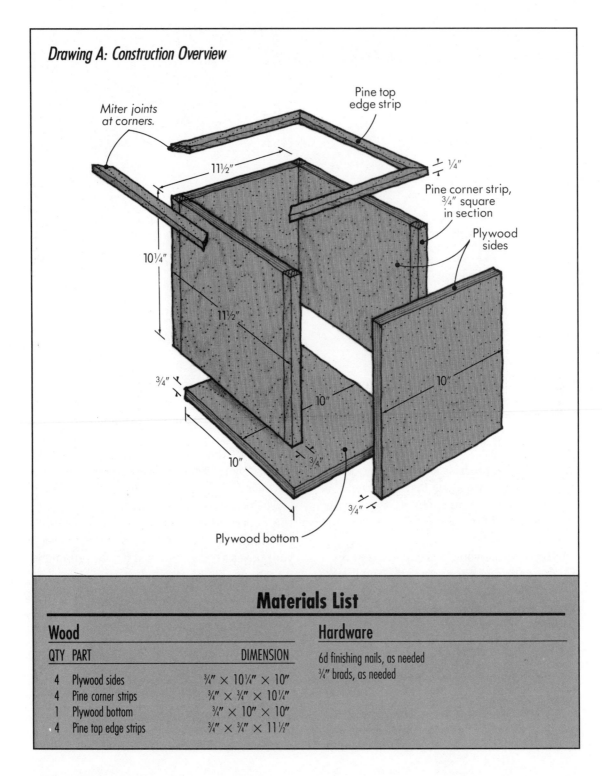

Miter joints at corners.

Pine top edge strip

11½"

¼"

Pine corner strip, ¾" square in section

Plywood sides

10¼"

11½"

10"

¾"

10"

¾"

¾"

10"

Plywood bottom

Materials List

Wood

QTY	PART	DIMENSION
4	Plywood sides	¾" × 10¼" × 10"
4	Pine corner strips	¾" × ¾" × 10¼"
1	Plywood bottom	¾" × 10" × 10"
4	Pine top edge strips	¾" × ¾" × 11½"

Hardware

6d finishing nails, as needed
¾" brads, as needed

clamping, cutting, and assembly setups that are specifically designed to let you produce a number of boxes efficiently.

Making the Sides

1 Rip the plywood to length. To produce four sides for a single box, rip a piece of ¾-inch plywood to 10 inches wide, and cross-cut it to at least 42 inches long.

2 Attach the corner strips. As shown in *Drawing A,* the sides of the boxes are joined with ¾ × ¾-inch solid pine corner strips. This edge treatment covers plywood edges that would show if the sides were simply butted together.

Rather than cut and attach corner strips individually, attach all the corner edging you'll need in one glue-up. Later you'll cross-cut the edged plywood. If you are making one box, cut a 42-inch-long strip. Glue and clamp this strip to one edge of the plywood piece. If you are making two boxes, glue and clamp strips to both edges of one plywood piece as shown in *Photo 1.* Use wood blocks to distribute clamping pressure and protect edge strips from the clamp feet. As you tighten the clamps, make sure that each edge strip remains aligned on the plywood edges.

3 Smooth the edge strips flush with the plywood. Once the glue has cured, remove the clamps and scrape any hardened glue from around the joint lines. If necessary, use a belt sander with an 80-grit sanding belt to smooth the pine edges flush with the plywood. (See *Photo 2.*)

4 Cut the sides to size. Cut one end of each plywood piece square. Then cut all sides to their finished height of 10¼ inches. A

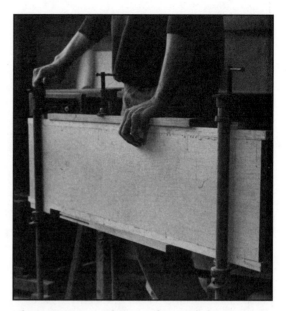

Photo 1: For two boxes, glue and clamp corner strips along both long edges of a plywood piece as shown here. For one box, glue the strips to one edge.

Photo 2: Scrape hardened glue from along joint lines, and sand sides flush, using an 80-grit sanding belt in the belt sander.

Photo 3: A stop on the miter gauge fence ensures exact dimensions when cutting side pieces from the edged board.

Photo 4: Use a simple H-shaped jig and a pair of spring clamps to hold plywood sides upright while gluing and nailing edged sides against them.

good way to make identical cutoffs on the table saw is to use a stop on the miter gauge, as shown in *Photo 3*. If your miter gauge isn't equipped with a built-in stop, attach a wood extension fence to the miter gauge; then screw or clamp a stop to the extension fence.

Assembling the Box

1 Assemble the sides. Put the box together with glue and 6d finishing nails. An H-shaped jig like the one shown in *Photo 4* will provide you with a "third hand" as you nail the glued joints together. Make the jig from scrap wood or plywood, cutting the center part of the "H" so that the overall width of the jig is 10 inches (the finished inside dimension of the box). Screw the jig together with 1⅝-inch drywall screws. Attach opposing plywood sides of the box to the jig with spring clamps, and you'll have an easy time aligning the joints for nailing. When all four sides are together, remove the jig and wipe off excess glue with a damp rag. Once the glue has dried, sand the inside of the box. It's much easier to smooth the inner faces of the sides before the bottom goes on.

2 Cut and install the bottom. Cut the bottom from ¾-inch-thick plywood to fit inside the box. Spread a light coat of glue on the bottom's edges, then fit the piece into place. Secure it by driving 6d finishing nails through the sides and into the bottom edges. Set all nails, and fill the holes with wood putty.

3 Cut and install the top edge strips. Make the edging by ripping strips ¼ inch thick from the edge of a ¾-inch board. Then cut miter joints. For best results, start by holding a length of edge stock in position on the box, and mark the locations of the miters on both ends. Cut both miters, then install the strip with glue and ¾-inch brads. Miter one edge of each remaining piece. Now work your way around the top of the box. Fit a miter against an installed edge, mark the length of the edging, and cut it to fit. (See *Photo 5*.) Set all brads, and fill the holes with wood putty.

When the putty has dried, give the entire box a thorough sanding. Pay particular attention to corners on the front and sides of the box. These sharp edges should be rounded-over for appearance and feel. You may even want to use a chamfering bit or roundover bit in your router to mill a consistent edge treatment. If so, avoid milling too deep, since this will put the bit close to nails or brads.

Photo 5: Cover the top edge of the box with ¼-inch-thick edging, cutting miter joints where pieces meet at corners.

Design Ideas

With a little imagination, you can use the basic box as a module in a variety of storage schemes. Rectangular boxes can be oriented horizontally or vertically. Sets of boxes can be used to support shelves. Another option is to create a stepped storage unit by staggering boxes in stairway fashion. In a design like this, boxes need to be screwed together, and to the wall or walls they abut. Compared to other storage projects, the box module is remarkably flexible. Without much trouble, you can break down one storage scheme and set up another. When it's time to move to another home, use your boxes individually to transport possessions.

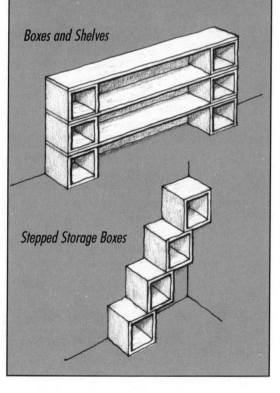

Boxes and Shelves

Stepped Storage Boxes

Beyond the Basic Box

With a little trim and some brass hardware, the basic box can masquerade as a fine frame-and-panel chest. In this design, lattice molding is applied at box corners, covering plywood butt joints and simulating frame members in the finished project. Lattice molding usually measures about ¼ inch thick and is available in different widths.

To make a chest like this one, first build a totally enclosed box, and then cut it apart to create a perfectly matching box and lid. Choose a box size that fits your needs. Assemble all joints with glue and 6d finishing nails, then install the molding. Start on one of the sides, cutting four pieces to fit, as shown. Do the opposite side next. On the remaining sides, cut the lattice molding long enough to cover the ends of the molding you've already installed. Nail and glue it into place. There's no need to install trim on the top or bottom of the box.

Now cut your creation in two. To separate the top of the chest from its base, use your circular saw and a fine-cutting blade. Guide the cut with a straight board clamped to the box. On the chest shown here, the cut is made 3 inches down from the top surface.

As soon as top and base are apart, put them back together again —this time with hinges and latches. You can also install handles, as shown in the bottom photo. Remove all hardware before applying a finish to your chest. Once the finish has dried, reattach the hardware using the screw holes you've already made.

Cutting the completed box to create the top

Attaching hinges, handles, and latches

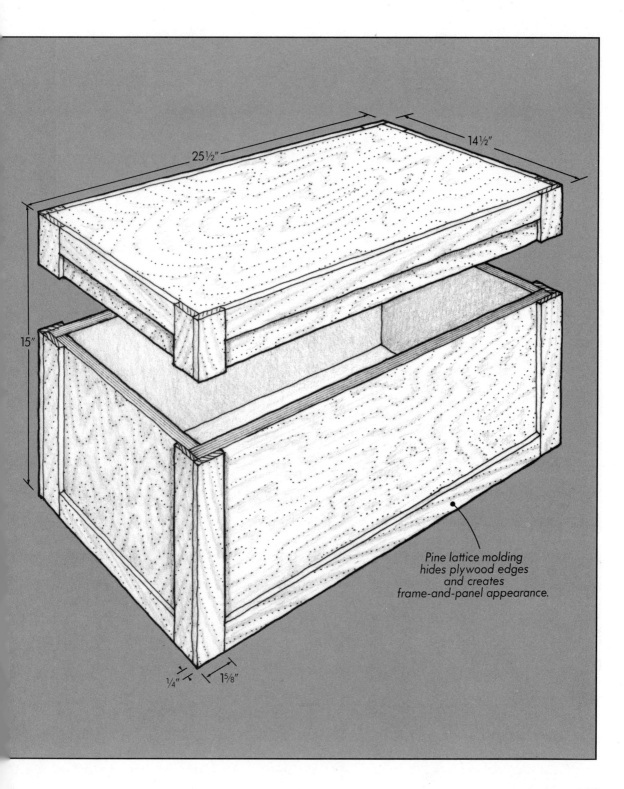

25½"

14½"

15"

Pine lattice molding
hides plywood edges
and creates
frame-and-panel appearance.

¼"   1⅝"

Knife Block

With just a few small pieces of hardwood, you can make a knife storage block that will be a proud addition to any kitchen. The knife block shown here includes a central slot for a pair of kitchen scissors, as well as slots for five knives. In making your own version of this project, you'll need to adjust the sizes and number of knife slots to fit the knives you'll be storing. You may want to replace the scissors slot with a slot to hold a sharpening rod or another knife.

This knife block is made from white oak, but other hardwoods would work equally well in terms of appearance, durability, and weight. Weight is actually an asset in a freestanding knife block, because it adds stability. Good alternatives to oak are maple, walnut, or cherry. Whatever species you choose, make sure that your stock is free of knots.

Even though this is a small project, it calls for some tricky operations. Specifically, it's very important for all four block pieces to be precisely the same size. These four pieces also have to be glued together with edges square and flush. You can solve both problems with the two jigs you'll learn about here.

Cutting the Parts

1 **Cut block and front support patterns.**
Using the dimensions given in *Drawing A,* lay out the shape of a block piece and the shape of the front support on ¾-inch-thick scrap stock. Carefully cut out these patterns on the table saw.

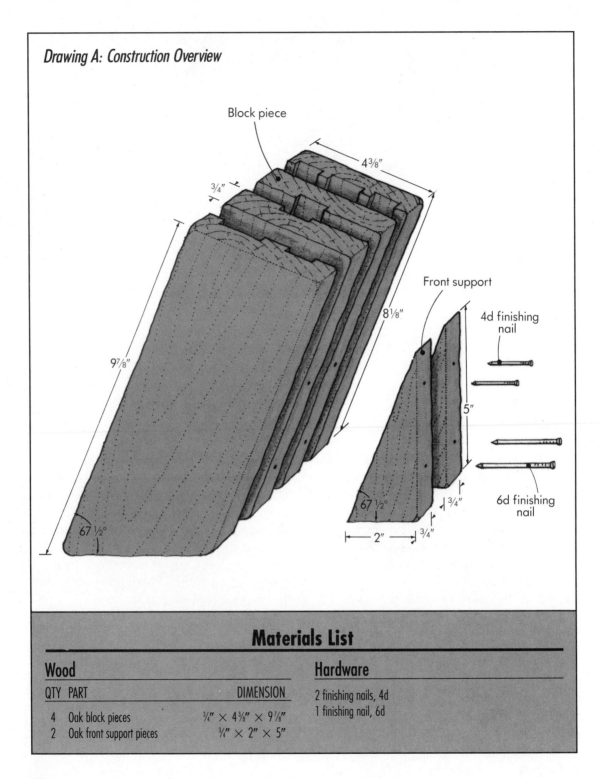

Drawing A: Construction Overview

Block piece

4³⁄₈"

³⁄₄"

9⁷⁄₈"

8¹⁄₈"

67¹⁄₂°

Front support

4d finishing nail

5"

67¹⁄₂°

³⁄₄"

2"

³⁄₄"

6d finishing nail

Materials List

Wood

QTY	PART	DIMENSION
4	Oak block pieces	³⁄₄" × 4³⁄₈" × 9⁷⁄₈"
2	Oak front support pieces	³⁄₄" × 2" × 5"

Hardware

2 finishing nails, 4d
1 finishing nail, 6d

2 Cut block pieces and front supports. Cut four block pieces and two front supports on a table saw duplicating jig, as explained in "Make a Table Saw Duplicating Jig" on page 154. This jig is easy to set up, and it will ensure that each piece you cut matches its pattern. Once you've made the jig, tack the pattern piece to a slightly larger piece of wood, and cut out the parts one at a time. (See *Photo 1*.)

3 Lay out slot locations in block pieces. Laying out slots for your knives is like putting together a puzzle. (See *Photo 2*.) The slot layout for this knife block is shown in *Drawing B*. But you should try out different arrangements with the knives (and scissors or sharpener) that you plan to store in the block. Keep in mind that the slots in a given block piece should be separated by at least ¼ inch, and there should be at least ¼ inch of wood between the shoulder of a slot and the outside edge of the block. You'll sacrifice convenience if the slots are too close together.

4 Cut slots in the block pieces. Set up a dado cutter in the table saw, and adjust the cutter to its maximum width. Then raise the cutter to show just ⅛ inch above the table. A slot depth of ⅛ inch should be sufficient for knives; but for scissors or for a knife-sharpening rod, you may need a deeper dado. For the knife block shown here, mill a pair of ³⁄₁₆-inch-deep scissors slots in adjacent pieces. In the completed block, the scissors slot measures ⅜ inch wide and 1½ inches long.

Adjust the rip fence to guide the long edges of the block pieces when milling the slots. Complete each slot by making a series of overlapping passes across the dado cutter, as shown in *Photo 3*. If you make mating slots, such as for the scissors, make each pass over

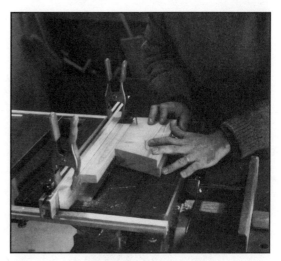

Photo 1: A pattern piece, tacked on top of an oak blank, rides against the edge of the guide board that is part of this table saw duplicating jig. For instructions on making and using the jig, see page 154.

Photo 2: Place knives on block pieces to lay out the storage slot locations.

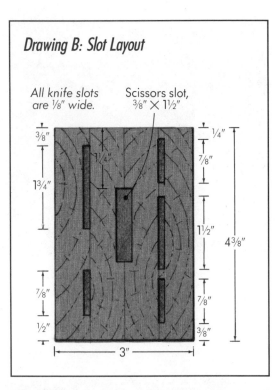

Drawing B: Slot Layout

All knife slots are ⅛" wide.

Scissors slot, ⅜" × 1½"

⅜"

1¾"

1¼"

⅞"

½"

3"

¼"

⅞"

1½"

4⅜"

⅞"

⅜"

the blade with both pieces before moving the fence. Once you've cut all the slots, smooth the bottoms of the slots as necessary, using a ½-inch or ¾-inch chisel. Remove any excess material you might have missed with the dado cutter.

Gluing Up

1 Make a clamping jig. A simple three-sided jig like the one shown in *Drawing C* keeps the four block sections properly aligned with each other during glue-up. Make the jig from some scrap pieces of ¾-inch plywood. For strength, assemble the jig using 1¼-inch drywall screws instead of nails. The important thing to remember when joining side and end pieces is that the inside corner must form right angles on all three faces. Use a square when assembling the jig to ensure this uniformity.

Photo 3: Mill the slots by making repeated passes through a dado cutter on the table saw. Use the rip fence to guide the block piece.

2 **Glue and clamp the block sections together.** Use a small brush to coat the joining surfaces on each block section with yellow wood glue. Coat these surfaces thoroughly, but keep the glue layer thin to minimize the amount of glue that squeezes into the slots during clamping.

Assemble the glued-up parts, and fit the block into the jig. Force the square top edges of all four pieces against the end of the jig while clamping across the width of the block. If you have a bench vise, it can be used as shown in *Photo 4* to clamp one side of the assembly together. Use several clamps to even up clamping pressure, checking to make sure that the top edges of the block pieces remain flush and against the square end of the jig.

3 **Glue the front pieces together.** Spread glue on mating surfaces, and use a single

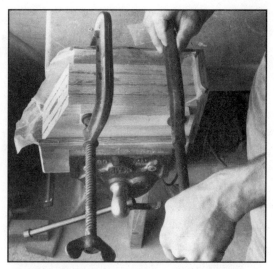

Photo 4: After coating mating surfaces with glue, clamp the block pieces together in a three-sided jig that provides a square corner to keep pieces aligned. Waxed paper, folded around the block assembly, prevents glue from adhering to the jig.

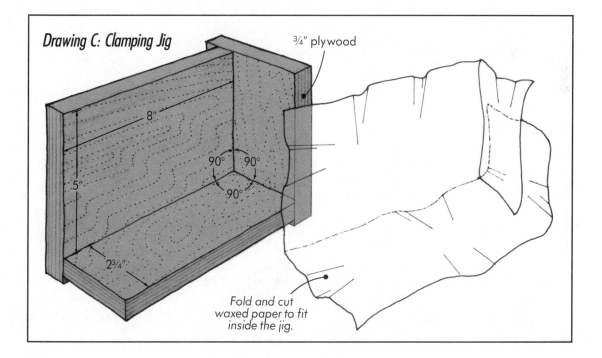

Drawing C: Clamping Jig

3/4" plywood

8"

5"

90° 90°

90°

2 3/4"

Fold and cut
waxed paper to fit
inside the jig.

Make a Table Saw Duplicating Jig

To precisely duplicate angled parts such as those used to make the knife block, nothing beats this simple duplicating jig you can make for your table saw. The only materials required are several 1⅝-inch-long flathead or drywall screws and two straight, square-edged boards at least ¾ inch thick. One of the boards should be at least 14 inches long, and wide enough to be clamped or temporarily screwed to your saw's standard rip fence. The other board, which forms a horizontal guide, should be about 10 inches long and about 2 inches wide.

While you're cutting these parts to size, also make patterns of the parts you wish to duplicate. Then cut the *blanks*, or pieces from which you will make the duplicate parts. Each blank should be slightly larger than the pattern, so that when the pattern is placed on top of the blank, between ¼ inch and ¾ inch of waste shows around the pattern's edges. You can do this rough cutting quickly with a portable circular saw; there's no need to make precise cuts.

To set up the jig, screw the horizontal guide to the vertical support as shown in the drawing. The space between the bottom of the horizontal guide and the bottom of the vertical member should be slightly more than the thickness of the blanks. To get the right distance, put the blank on the

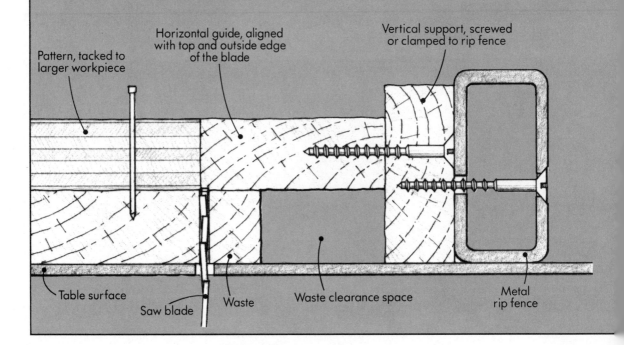

Pattern, tacked to larger workpiece

Horizontal guide, aligned with top and outside edge of the blade

Vertical support, screwed or clamped to rip fence

Table surface

Saw blade

Waste

Waste clearance space

Metal rip fence

bench with two pieces of paper on top of it. Put the horizontal guide on top of the paper. Then put the vertical support on the bench, and screw through it into the horizontal guide.

Clamp or screw the vertical support to the rip fence. Raise the blade until it touches the bottom of the horizontal guide, and position the fence to align the guide's vertical edge with the outside edge of the saw blade. Turn the saw on and raise the blade so that it cuts about ⅛ inch into the bottom of the horizontal guide. This extra ⅛ inch will ensure that the blade cuts cleanly through the workpiece.

To put the jig to work, temporarily tack the pattern on top of a blank with a couple of 4d or 6d finishing nails. Nail into sides that won't show in the completed knife block. Make sure that the pattern is roughly centered, so that some waste material shows on all sides of it. Then turn on the saw, and cut the blank to its finished dimensions by running the edges of the pattern against the vertical edge of the horizontal guide. With the edge cuts complete, your blank is now a duplicate of the pattern. Repeat the procedure with additional blanks to produce more duplicate pieces.

To use the jig safely, turn the saw off and remove waste pieces from beneath the horizontal guide after each cut. If these cutoffs accumulate between the fence and the blade, they might be thrown back at dangerous speeds.

C-clamp or spring clamp to hold the pieces together while the glue dries.

To avoid gluing the jig to the block pieces, cut and fold a piece of waxed paper to fit into the corner of the jig and up along its inside faces. Secure the waxed paper inside the jig with some tape.

Sanding, Rounding-Over, Final Glue-Up, and Finishing

1 **Flatten block and front support on the belt sander.** After the glue has cured, remove clamps from both assemblies. Fit an 80-grit sanding belt on your belt sander, and secure it upside down on the workbench. Most belt sanders can easily be clamped in this position. Press the trigger, and engage the trigger lock to keep the sander operating without constant trigger pressure. Now sand the block and front support by alternately holding the edges, ends, and sides against the moving abrasive belt. The object is to remove hardened glue and flatten all surfaces, so apply even pressure over the flat shoe of the sander. Avoid sanding over the rollers, or between the rollers and the shoe. (See *Photo 5*.)

If your sander doesn't have a trigger lock, you'll have to use the sander right side up and clamp the block in place.

2 **Round-over the block edges.** Chuck a ⅜-inch roundover bit in the router table, and adjust bit height to rout the full radius on the edge of a board. For this operation, both the bearing and the fence guide the stock. To set up the cut, adjust the fence until it is flush with the bearing. On some router tables, you may have to cut a small hole in the fence in order to "bury" the bit to this extent.

Turn on the router, and run the block through the bit to transform square edges into rounded ones. (See *Photo 6*.) The only two edges that shouldn't be rounded-over are the bottom front corner and the bottom back corner of the block.

If you don't have a router, you can round-over the edges with a block plane and sandpaper.

3 Fasten the front support to the block. First, smooth the front support with some 120-grit sandpaper. You can smooth all parts of the support more easily before you attach

it to the main block.

The supports are nailed and glued into place. Drill pilot holes for the nails to prevent the wood from splitting as you drive the nails. To locate the holes, put the block on a flat surface and put the support in position, centered from side to side. Mark the location of the supports' sides lightly in pencil. With a 1/16-inch-diameter bit, drill pilot holes for two 4d finishing nails in the narrower part of the support. Drill a pilot hole for a 6d finishing nail in the wider lower section of the support with

Photo 5: With the belt sander clamped upside down, remove hardened glue from the block and flatten the sides.

the same bit. Keep the support aligned against the block while drilling, and make sure to drill through the support and into the block.

Start the finishing nails in the support, then spread a light coat of glue on the face of the support that will join the block. Fit both parts together, making sure that each finishing nail enters its pilot hole in the block. Drive and set the nails, and remove glue that squeezes out of the joint. Fill the nail holes with wood putty.

4 Apply finish. A penetrating oil finish is a good choice for a project like this one. In addition to sealing and protecting the wood, oil highlights the grain without forming a film that will show scratches or wear off with use.

Before applying any finish, be sure to give your block a thorough sanding. Sand off darkened sections left by the router bit, and smooth corners and edges with 120-grit sandpaper. Then wipe the wood surface down with a dampened cloth. Finally, give the piece a once-over with 180-grit or 220-grit sandpaper. Wipe the wood down with a dry cloth, and apply a finish according to the manufacturer's instructions. (See *Photo 7*.)

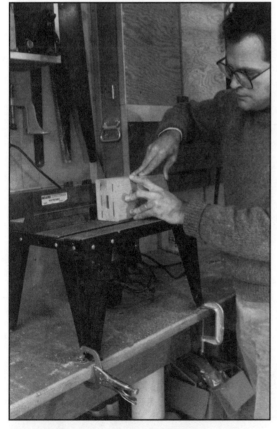

Photo 6: Round-over the block edges on the router table, using a ⅜-inch-radius roundover bit.

Photo 7: After a thorough sanding, apply a penetrating oil finish. Coat all surfaces of the knife block.

Cubbyholes

If small objects seem to accumulate in your home, a set of cubbyholes is a nice way to keep track of them. Even if you have knickknacks under control, this project makes a fine display case for tiny treasures. The cubbies are great for kids who love to collect stuff like rocks or sea shells.

The 12 compartments in this set of cubbyholes are arranged in a 3 × 4 grid. Compartment width and depth are uniform, but compartment height increases by ½ inch from bottom to top, giving these cubbies graceful proportions. The carcase is made from pine, while the interior partitions are made from lauan. A clear oil finish shows off the contrast between the woods.

1 Cut the parts to size. For this project, it's especially important for certain parts to be identical in size. Start by ripping the top, bottom, and sides to width; then change the fence setting to rip the crosspieces and dividers.

After ripping the parts to width, square one end of each piece of stock. Fasten a wood auxiliary fence to the miter gauge. Make the fence from a straight one-by board about 2 inches high and 30 inches long. Square the auxiliary fence to the saw blade. This auxiliary fence will help you steady longer pieces as you cut them to their finished lengths.

Another advantage of the long auxiliary fence is that it lets you use a stop block as

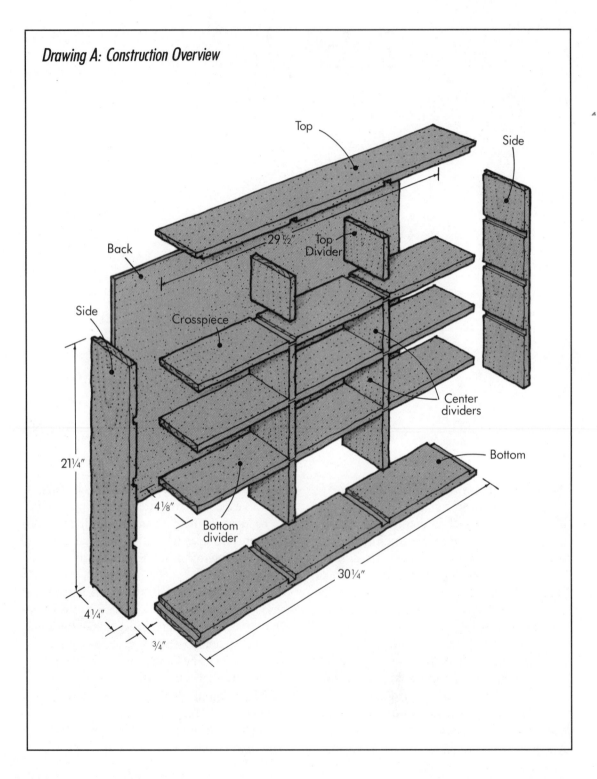

Drawing A: Construction Overview

Top

Side

Back

Top Divider

29½"

Side

Crosspiece

Center dividers

21¼"

Bottom

4⅛"

Bottom divider

30¼"

4¼"

¾"

Materials List

Wood

QTY	PART	DIMENSION
Carcase		
2	Pine sides	¾" × 4¼" × 21¼"
1	Pine top	¾" × 4¼" × 30¼"
1	Pine bottom	¾" × 4⅜" × 30¼"
1	Plywood back	⅛" × 21¼" × 29½"
Partitions		
3	Lauan crosspieces	½" × 4¼" × 29½"
2	Lauan dividers	½" × 4¼" × 4½"
2	Lauan dividers	½" × 4¼" × 4¾"
2	Lauan dividers	½" × 4¼" × 5¼"
2	Lauan dividers	½" × 4¼" × 6"

Hardware

1" paneling nails, as needed
⅝" brads, as needed

shown in *Photo 1* to cut matching parts to precisely the same length. Lay out the length on the top piece. Align your layout mark to the cut you have made in the auxiliary fence. Butt the stop block against the other end of the top and clamp it in place. Make the cut. Now there is no need to lay out the length of the bottom piece. Just butt the piece against the block and make the cut. Repeat this procedure for other sets of parts of the same length: the sides, the crosspieces, and each pair of dividers.

2 Rabbet and dado the carcase. Replace your table saw blade with a dado cutter. Adjust the cutter width to ½ inch and the height to ⅜ inch. Then mill a test dado in some scrap stock. If necessary, adjust the cutter width until the crosspieces and dividers fit snugly in the dadoes.

Now lay out one rabbet on the top, and lay out dadoes on the top and on one side. (See

Photo 1: By using a stop block, you can cut parts to exactly the same length. Clamp the stop block to a wood auxiliary fence, fastened to the miter gauge.

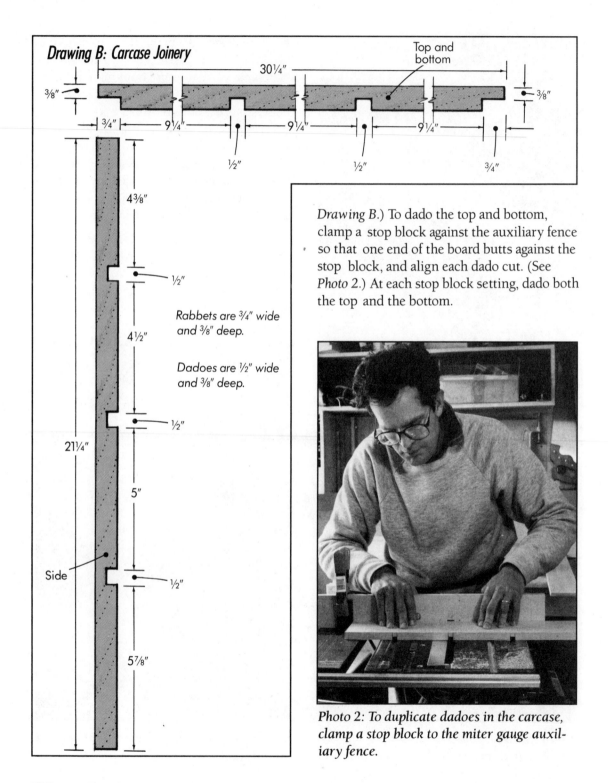

Drawing B: Carcase Joinery

Top and bottom

30¼"

3/8"

3/8"

3/4"   9¼"   9¼"   9¼"

½"   ½"   3/4"

4⅜"

½"

Rabbets are ¾" wide and ⅜" deep.

4½"

Dadoes are ½" wide and ⅜" deep.

½"

21¼"

5"

Side

½"

5⅞"

Drawing B.) To dado the top and bottom, clamp a stop block against the auxiliary fence so that one end of the board butts against the stop block, and align each dado cut. (See Photo 2.) At each stop block setting, dado both the top and the bottom.

Photo 2: To duplicate dadoes in the carcase, clamp a stop block to the miter gauge auxiliary fence.

You could cut the rabbets in one pass each by widening the dado cutter setting. But here is a much faster method: Set up the stop block so that the dado cutter cuts the shoulder of the rabbet. Make the cut, leaving ¼ inch of waste at the end of the rabbet. Do the same at the other end of the top and at both ends of the bottom. Now remove the stop block and cut away the remaining waste.

To rabbet the top and sides for the back, remove the miter gauge, leaving its auxiliary fence attached. Set the rip fence 4⅛ inches from the dado cutter. Then run each piece through the cutter with its front edge against the fence and its inside face against the table. (See *Photo 3.*)

Photo 3: Guide the carcase pieces against the rip fence to rabbet their back edges.

Photo 4: After assembling the carcase, square it up with a square, and secure opposite corners with temporary braces.

Photo 5: Use an auxiliary miter gauge fence with a stop block to mill perfectly aligned crosspiece dadoes.

Photo 6: Tap the crosspieces into the carcase dadoes, using a scrap block of wood to cushion the hammer blows. Secure each joint with three paneling nails.

3 Assemble the carcase. Spread glue on the rabbets in the top and bottom. Then join these pieces to the sides. Use two 4d finishing nails at each joint, driving the nails through the top and into the sides. Use temporary diagonal braces to keep the carcase square until the crosspieces and dividers are installed. Square up the cabinet by holding a square against the inside of the carcase, and nail braces to the opposite corners, against the carcase's back edges. (See *Photo 4.*)

4 Dado the crosspieces. As shown in *Drawing C,* each crosspiece has two dadoes on each face to create the finished cubbyhole grid. Lower the dado cutter so that it's just ⅛ inch above the table. Then clamp a stop block to the auxiliary fence to set up the dadoing operation. Flip each crosspiece side-for-side and end-for-end, always butting an end against the stop block to align each pass through the cutter. (See *Photo 5.*)   Lower the dado cutter to ⅛ inch above the table. Leave the cutting width at ½ inch. Clamp a stop block 9⅝ inches from the cut in the auxiliary miter gauge fence. Use this setup to cut all four dadoes in each crosspiece.

5 Install the crosspieces. Spread a light coat of glue in the dadoes for the crosspieces. Then fit the crosspieces into the carcase. If necessary, tap these pieces into place, using a scrap wood block to protect the crosspieces from the hammerhead. (See *Photo 6.*) Secure each joint with two or three 1-inch paneling nails. Set the nails, and fill the holes with wood putty.

6 Install the dividers. Apply glue to the dadoes. Install one bottom divider and then the dividers above it, as shown in *Photo 7.* To secure the middle dividers, drive a ⅝-

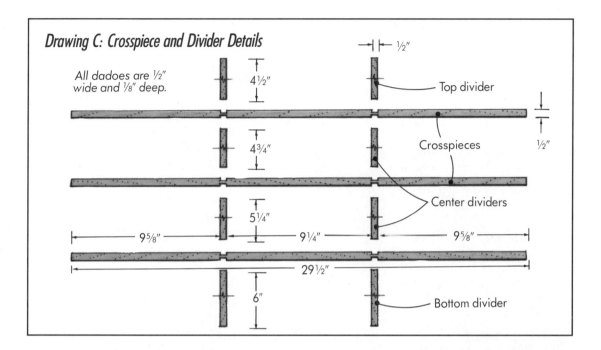

Drawing C: Crosspiece and Divider Details

All dadoes are ½" wide and ⅛" deep.

½"

4½"

Top divider

Crosspieces

4¾"

½"

Center dividers

5¼"

9⅝" 9¼" 9⅝"

29½"

6"

Bottom divider

Photo 7: Install the dividers one column at a time. Drive a single ⅝-inch brad into each middle divider from above to secure the dado joint. Set the brad before installing the next divider.

inch brad into the top of each from the dado just above it. Set the brad before installing the next middle divider. Nail the dividers to the top and bottom with 1-inch paneling nails. Repeat this procedure for the remaining two columns of dividers. When all dividers have been installed, remove the temporary diagonal braces from the carcase.

7 **Round-over the front edges.** Chuck a ¼-inch roundover bit in your router, and adjust the cutting depth to show the full radius (but not the shoulder) of the bit. Then turn on the router, and round-over all the front edges. Moving the router clockwise, run the bit's pilot bearing around all four sides of each opening. (See *Photo 8*.) It will be easier to steady the router if you use an offset base like the one shown in the photo. (Also see the Shop Savvy on page 282.)

8 **Cut the back to size.** Size the back to fit into the rabbets in the back of the carcase, as shown in *Drawing D*. Cut the back from ⅛-inch-thick plywood.

9 **Sand and apply the finish.** Give the outside of the carcase a thorough sanding, starting with 120-grit sandpaper and finishing with 220-grit paper. Then vacuum the sawdust from the wood, and apply the finish in a dust-free work area. Finish the back separately. The cubbyholes shown here have a painted back, but you might want to finish the back with stain or varnish. Whatever the finish, it's easier to apply it before the back is installed.

10 **Install the back.** Put the back in place, and nail it to the top, bottom, sides, and dividers with ⅝-inch brads.

Photo 8: Round-over the front edges of the cubbyholes with a ¼-inch roundover bit. The offset base makes it easier to keep the router steady as you move around each opening.

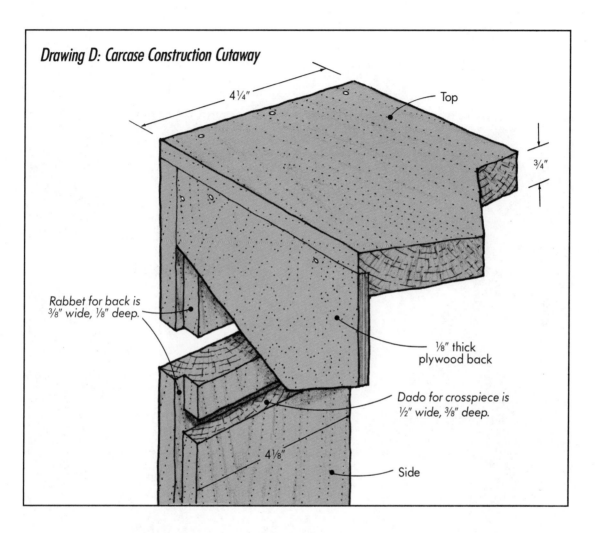

Drawing D: Carcase Construction Cutaway

4¼"

Top

¾"

Rabbet for back is ⅜" wide, ⅛" deep.

⅛" thick plywood back

Dado for crosspiece is ½" wide, ⅜" deep.

4⅛"

Side

Medicine Cabinet

D oes your bathroom feature one of those chrome and steel medicine cabinets that fit right into the decor of a '50s Buick? It was a very "modern" look in its day, but perhaps you've decided it's getting kind of dated. The replacement medicine cabinet shown here has a classic look that will never go out of style. The design harks back to earlier days, when oak was the material of choice for washroom woodwork.

This cabinet has an open lower shelf that's great for everyday items. Above, a pair of sliding mirror doors conceals an ample storage compartment with three glass shelves. The glass shelf heights are adjustable. You'll need to order the doors and shelves from a glass supplier.

The cabinet's sides, top, bottom, and middle shelf are made of oak plywood. If you don't have oak plywood for these parts, it's fine to cut these parts from solid oak stock. Just be sure that your pieces are straight, flat, and free of checks or cracks. Oak trim molding on the outside of the cabinet fits against the wall sur-

face, covering the rough opening in the wall.

As with most woodworking projects, the main reason to build your own medicine cabinet is that you will create a hand-crafted piece that is nicer than one you can buy. In this case, there is an additional reason to build it yourself: Before building the new cabinet, you can remove and measure the old one. Then build the new cabinet for an exact fit in the existing opening. Just make any adjustments necessary to the widths and/or lengths of parts given in the Materials List. This means no cutting drywall or, worse, plaster and lath, and no wall-patching to do. Best of all it means you get to spend your time making sawdust in your workshop instead of a mess in your bathroom.

Cutting the Carcase and Trim Parts

1 **Cut the carcase members.** Cut the sides, top, bottom, and middle shelf to size, making any necessary changes to the dimensions in the Materials List.

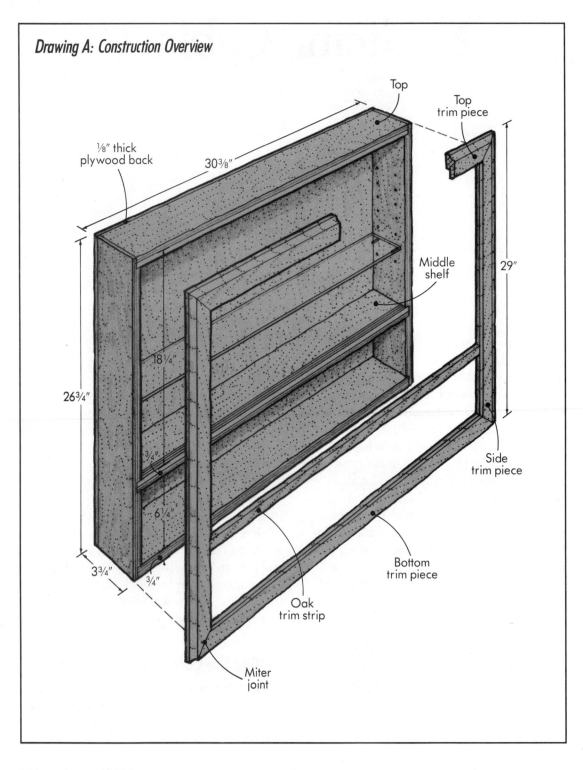

Drawing A: Construction Overview

Top

Top trim piece

⅛" thick plywood back

30⅜"

Middle shelf

29"

18¼"

26¾"

Side trim piece

¾"

6¼"

3¾"

¾"

Bottom trim piece

Oak trim strip

Miter joint

Materials List

Wood

QTY	PART	DIMENSION
2	Oak plywood sides	$\frac{3}{4}'' \times 3\frac{3}{4}'' \times 26\frac{3}{4}''$
1	Oak plywood top	$\frac{3}{4}'' \times 3\frac{3}{4}'' \times 29\frac{5}{8}''$
1	Oak plywood bottom	$\frac{3}{4}'' \times 3\frac{3}{4}'' \times 29\frac{5}{8}''$
1	Oak plywood middle shelf	$\frac{3}{4}'' \times 3\frac{3}{4}'' \times 29\frac{5}{8}''$
1	Plywood back	$\frac{1}{8}'' \times 26\frac{3}{4}'' \times 30\frac{3}{8}''$
1	Oak top trim	$\frac{3}{4}'' \times 1\frac{1}{8}'' \times 32\frac{5}{8}''$
1	Oak bottom trim	$\frac{3}{4}'' \times 1\frac{1}{8}'' \times 32\frac{5}{8}''$
2	Oak side trim	$\frac{3}{4}'' \times 1\frac{1}{8}'' \times 29''$
1	Oak trim strip	$\frac{3}{4}'' \times \frac{3}{8}'' \times 28\frac{1}{8}''$

Hardware

1 wooden upper track for ¼-inch-thick
   sliding doors, $\frac{1}{2}'' \times 1\frac{1}{8}'' \times 29\frac{5}{8}''$

Hardware

1 wooden lower track for ¼-inch-thick
   sliding doors, $\frac{3}{8}'' \times 1\frac{1}{8}'' \times 29\frac{5}{8}''$
   Available from Woodworker's Supply,
   5604 Alameda Place NE, Albuquerque, NM 87113;
   (800) 645-9292. Part #810-053.
2 mirror doors, $\frac{1}{4}'' \times 18\frac{3}{16}'' \times 29\frac{5}{8}''$
3 glass shelves, $\frac{1}{4}'' \times 2\frac{1}{2}'' \times 29\frac{1}{2}''$
2 wooden knobs, 1" dia., with mounting screws
6 brass shelf support pins, ¼" dia.
⅝" brads, as needed
1" paneling nails, as needed
¾" paneling nails, as needed

2 **Cut blanks for the trim pieces.** Use clear, straight oak for the trim. To create the molding profile in all four trim pieces, start off with two straight, clear oak boards that are ¾ inch thick and at least 4 inches wide. Make the boards at least an inch longer than the trim pieces will be. For the cabinet shown here, you'd need one piece, or blank, at least 30 inches long to make both side trim pieces and one piece at least 33⅜ inches long to make the top and bottom trim pieces. You'll rout both sides of the stock and then rip it in two. This method is faster than cutting the stock to final width first, and it provides more bearing surface for the router base.

Making the Trim

Most cabinetmaking projects begin with car-case construction. For this project, though, you will start by making the oak trim that will surround the finished cabinet. This is done simply for convenience: By following this sequence, you'll need to switch from table saw blade to dado cutter only once.

1 **Mill coved edges on the trim piece blanks.** As shown in *Drawing B,* the molding profile includes a ½-inch-radius cove. Chuck a piloted cove bit in the router, and set the bit depth to ½ inch. Then rout coves on both long edges of each blank, as shown in *Photo 1.*

2 **Rip the trim pieces to finished width.** Do this cutting on the table saw, using the rip fence to guide the stock. Position the fence 1⅞ inches from the saw blade.

3 **Chamfer the trim.** In the finished cabinet, the chamfered part of the trim will face in. Chuck a 45-degree chamfering bit in

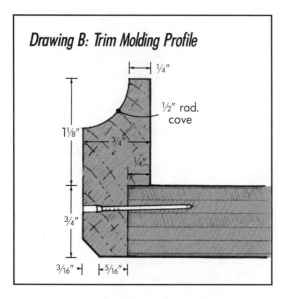

Drawing B: Trim Molding Profile

1/4"

1/2" rad.
cove

1 1/8"

3/4"

1/4"

3/4"

3/16"   5/16"

the router and adjust the cutting depth to 3/16 inch. Chamfer the inside edge of each trim piece.

4 Rabbet the trim. The trim pieces are rabbeted to fit over the front edges of the cabinet. After squaring the miter gauge to the saw blade, replace the blade with a dado cutter and set the miter gauge temporarily aside. Adjust the cutter width to match the thickness of the cabinet top, bottom, and middle shelf. The plywood is nominally 3/4 inch thick, but measure it—it may be slightly thinner. Then raise the cutter to 3/4 inch. Position the rip fence 1/2 inch from the cutter. Guide each trim piece through the cutter as shown in *Photo 2*.

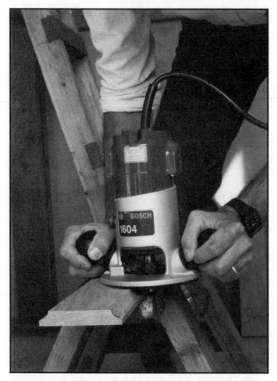

Photo 1: Start the molding profile by milling coved edges. This 4-inch-wide board will yield two pieces of trim.

Photo 2: Rabbet each trim piece to fit over the front edges of the carcase. Guide the outside face of the trim against the rip fence.

Building the Carcase

1 **Rabbet and dado the sides.** As shown in *Drawing C*, each side is rabbeted at its ends, and dadoed to hold the middle shelf. Adjust the dado cutter height to ⅜ inch. Then fasten a wood auxiliary fence to your miter gauge. Make this fence about 2 inches high and at least 30 inches long. Attach the fence so that one end extends about 9 inches beyond the dado cutter's path.

Lay out the dado on one of the side pieces. Position that piece against the auxiliary fence, aligning the layout lines with the dado cutter. Clamp a stop block to the fence as shown in *Photo 3*. Mill the dado, and then use the stop block to align the other side for its dado cut. Use the same procedure for the rabbets: Align a side to cut the first rabbet, clamp on the stop block, and then mill the remaining three rabbets.

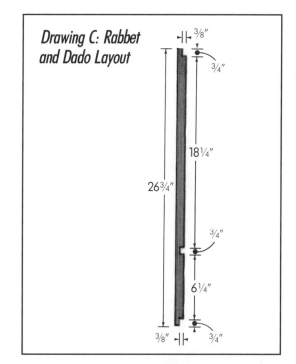

Drawing C: Rabbet and Dado Layout

Photo 3: Secure a wood auxiliary fence to the miter gauge, and use the dado cutter to rabbet and dado the sides. Clamp a stop block to the fence to align the joints in both pieces.

2 Rabbet the middle shelf and the top.
As shown in *Drawing D,* the middle shelf and the top are rabbeted to receive door tracks. To make these rabbets, raise the dado cutter to a height that matches the width of your sliding door tracks (1⅛ inches for the tracks used here). Now position the rip fence to guide the middle shelf and the top as you mill rabbets to hold the tracks. This setup is similar to that shown in *Photo 2,* except that the rabbet dimensions are different. As shown in *Drawing D,* the rabbet for the upper track should be ½ inch deep, while the rabbet for the lower track needs to be ⅜ inch deep.

3 Fasten door tracks to the middle shelf and the top. Spread glue evenly on the shoulder and bottom of the rabbets that hold the tracks. Then clamp the tracks in place until the glue dries. (See *Photo 4.*) Take care not to get any glue on the inner surfaces of the tracks, where the mirror doors will run.

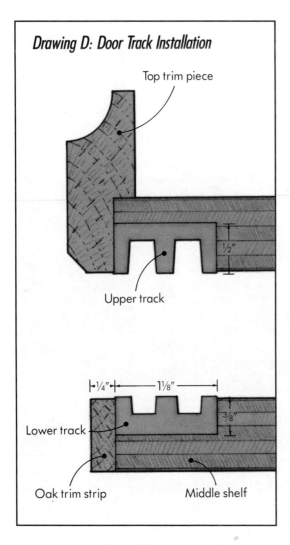

Drawing D: Door Track Installation

Top trim piece

½″

Upper track

|¼″| 1⅛″ |

⅜″

Lower track

Oak trim strip

Middle shelf

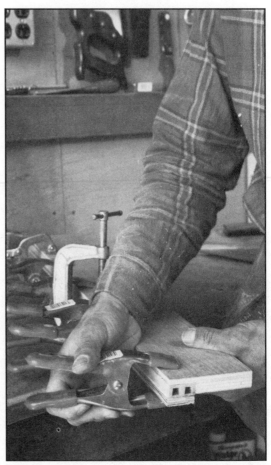

Photo 4: Glue each sliding door track in its rabbet, and use clamps to secure the joint until the glue cures.

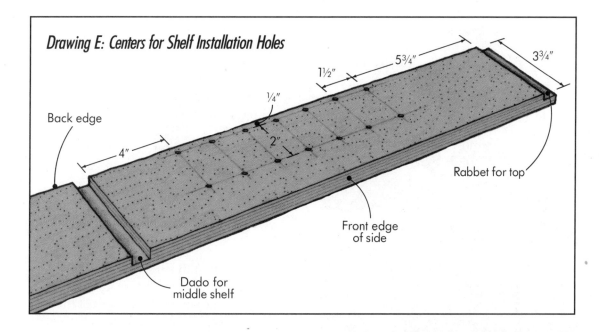

Drawing E: Centers for Shelf Installation Holes

Back edge

4"

1½"

5¾"

3¾"

¼"

2"

Rabbet for top

Front edge of side

Dado for middle shelf

4 **Drill holes for shelf supports.** Each cabinet side has two rows of ¼-inch-diameter holes to hold the pins that support the glass shelves. The hole spacing is shown in *Drawing E.* Start by laying out the centers for the lowermost pair of holes in each side. Use a sharp awl to make starter holes exactly on these first two centers; then drill the holes to a depth of ⅜ inch, using a ¼-inch-diameter bit.

To simplify the work of drilling precisely spaced holes above your first two holes, make a jig like the one shown in *Photo 5.* Start with a short, rectangular piece of wood cut to the same width as the sides (3¾ inches). With a square, lay out centers for four holes. On these centers, drill four ¼-inch-diameter holes all the way through the jig. Then make a right-angled cut across the width of the jig, through a pair of holes. Complete your jig by nailing a piece of wood against one edge. This piece will keep jig and side member edges flush.

Photo 5: With a simple jig like this one, you can drill two rows of precisely spaced holes in each side for shelf support pins.

To put the jig to work, fit two short, ¼-inch-diameter dowels into the holes you've made in one side. Now rest the jig's half-holes over the dowels as shown in *Photo 5,* and drill out the next pair of holes in the side, using the jig's holes to guide the bit. Wrap tape around the bit to indicate when the hole depth reaches ⅜ inch. Place the dowels into the new holes, and reposition the jig to drill out the next pair of holes. Stop when you've made seven pairs of holes; then repeat this procedure to make the holes in the other side.

5 **Assemble the sides, top, bottom, and middle shelf.** Spread glue in the rabbet and dado joints where the top, bottom, and middle shelf will fit. Then nail each joint together, using 1-inch paneling nails. (See *Photo 6.*)

6 **Cut and install the back.** Check the cabinet frame to make sure it's square. Then spread glue on the back edges of the top, bottom, and middle shelf. Use ¾-inch paneling nails to nail down the plywood back.

Installing the Trim

The four trim pieces fit around the outside edges of the carcase like a large picture frame, with miter joints at each corner. For some tips on cutting tight-fitting miter joints on the table saw, see the Shop Savvy on the opposite page.

1 **Cut and tack trim pieces to the carcase.** Begin by mitering one end of a side trim piece. Place this piece on the side where it will be installed, aligning the mitered end exactly on its corner. Now mark the opposite end for its miter cut. After making the second miter cut, predrill 1¹⁄₁₆-inch holes for 1-inch paneling nails, and tack this first trim piece into place, nailing through the front of the trim and into the edge of the side. Drive the nails just far enough to hold the trim.

Cut the bottom trim piece next. Start with the miter that fits against the side piece

Photo 6: Glue and nail the carcase sides to the top, bottom, and middle shelf.

already tacked into place. Lay out the second miter directly from the cabinet. Then tack the bottom trim piece to the carcase. Repeat this procedure with the remaining side trim. (See *Photo 7*.) Cut the top trim piece last, again fitting one miter joint together in order to mark the opposite miter's cutoff line.

2 **Install the trim pieces.** Temporarily remove the trim. Glue and nail the trim pieces to the carcase and to each other, following the same order outlined in the previous step. Use a damp cloth or sponge to wipe off glue that squeezes out of the joints. Set all nails, and fill the holes with wood putty.

3 **Install the trim strip.** As shown in *Drawing D*, this oak strip covers the plied edge of the middle shelf and the front edge of the lower door track. Cut the strip to fit between the side trim pieces; then install it with glue and ⅝-inch brads.

Ordering and Installing the Doors

1 **Order the mirror doors.** Each door should be cut from ¼-inch-thick mirror glass. To understand how the sliding doors fit in the upper and lower tracks, look again at *Drawing D*. The door height should be ⁵⁄₁₆ inch greater than the height of the compartment opening. This allows you to lift each door up against the top of the upper track's groove. When you do this, the door bottom is high enough to clear the trim and the bottom door track. Lower the door into the appropriate groove: The top edge of the door will remain in the upper door track.

Order your mirror doors from a glass and mirror supplier. Specify door height as dis-

Photo 7: Fit the mitered end of a trim piece against an adjoining miter. Lay out the opposite miter directly from the cabinet.

cussed above, and make each door 1 inch wider than half the finished width of the compartment opening. Have your supplier smooth all corners so that no sharp edges remain on the mirror. On each door, have the supplier drill an installation hole for a 1-inch-diameter wooden knob. Center the hole 4 inches from the outside bottom corner of the door, and 1 inch from the door's outside edge. Also have your supplier spray the edges and back of each mirror with a mirror sealant. This treatment protects the mirror's reflective coating.

2 **Install the door knobs.** If the installation screws supplied with your wooden knobs are designed for ¾-inch-thick material, you'll have to cut the screws to a shorter length (about ¾ inch) so that they will work on a ¼-inch-thick door. When installing each knob, fit a plastic washer (available from most glass suppliers) between the screw head and the back of the mirror. This washer will cushion the glass against pressure exerted by the screw.

3 **Install the door.** First, buff a light coat of paste wax in all door track grooves. Then lift each door into place as described in Step 1.

Installing the Cabinet

1 **Drill pilot holes.** From inside the cabinet, drill a countersunk pilot hole in each side and in the top and bottom. It's not necessary to drill pilot holes into the wall framing inside the opening.

2 **Screw the cabinet into the wall.** Hold the cabinet in its opening so that all four trim pieces fit flat against the wall. Screw the cabinet to the wall framing below first, then to the sides, and finally to the top.

Living
&
Family Rooms

Bookends

These bookends will add convenience and elegance wherever they're used. Unlike conventional bookends, this design incorporates runners to connect a pair of bookends. One bookend is fixed; the other can be moved easily but locks into place by the weight of the books being stored. The runners keep both bookends aligned, providing extra stability. (See *Drawing A*.) A design like this is especially good for holding books that are used frequently. Or you might choose to display a special set of books with this small, well-crafted storage project.

The contrasts of light oak and dark walnut are used to make the bookends shown here, but other hardwoods could do equally well in a project like this. Maple and birch are other light-colored woods to consider.

Making the Parts

1 **Cut the bookend parts to size.** On the table saw, cut stock for the walnut center pieces and oak bookend pieces to the width and thickness dimensions given in the Materials List. You'll need one 14-inch-long piece of walnut and two 14-inch-long pieces of oak. Edges to be glued should be straight and square, so it's a good idea to joint them, as described in "Straight, Square Edges" on page 22.

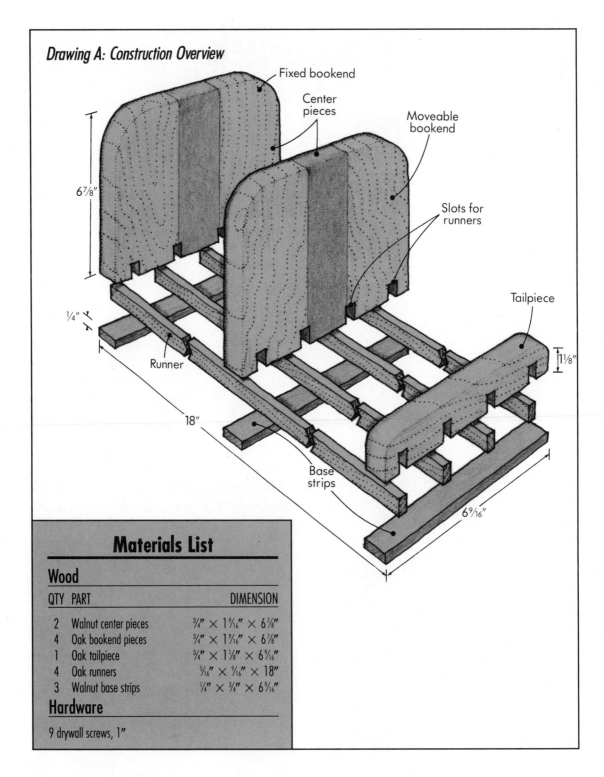

Drawing A: Construction Overview

Fixed bookend

Center pieces

Moveable bookend

Slots for runners

Tailpiece

$6\frac{7}{8}$"

$\frac{1}{4}$"

Runner

$1\frac{1}{8}$"

18"

Base strips

$6\frac{9}{16}$"

Materials List

Wood

QTY	PART	DIMENSION
2	Walnut center pieces	$\frac{3}{4}$" × $1\frac{1}{16}$" × $6\frac{7}{8}$"
4	Oak bookend pieces	$\frac{3}{4}$" × $1\frac{1}{16}$" × $6\frac{7}{8}$"
1	Oak tailpiece	$\frac{3}{4}$" × $1\frac{1}{8}$" × $6\frac{9}{16}$"
4	Oak runners	$\frac{5}{16}$" × $\frac{9}{16}$" × 18"
3	Walnut base strips	$\frac{1}{4}$" × $\frac{3}{4}$" × $6\frac{9}{16}$"

Hardware

9 drywall screws, 1"

2 **Glue up the bookend parts.** Spread glue evenly along joining edges of the walnut and oak bookend parts. Then clamp the walnut piece between the two oak pieces, as shown in *Photo 1*. Use at least three pipe clamps, and place wood pads between the clamping feet and the oak. Tighten the clamps evenly while keeping all three pieces flat.

3 **Cut the bookends to size.** When the glue cures, remove the clamps and scrape off any hardened glue along the joint lines. Then use an 80-grit sanding belt on the belt sander to sand both sides of the panel smooth. Set the miter gauge to 90 degrees and cut the ends of the panel square. From the panel cut two pieces each 6⅞ inches long. These pieces become the fixed bookend and the movable bookend.

Next, lay out the curves on the top corners of each bookend. As shown in *Drawing B*, each curve is part of a circle with a radius of 1½ inches. To mark the pivot points, measure 1½ inches from the top and 1½ inches from each side. By clamping both bookend pieces together as shown in *Photo 2*, you can cut them simultaneously, using a jigsaw with a fine-cutting blade.

After making the curved cuts, hold the pieces together and sand them smooth and even on the belt sander, using an 80-grit sanding belt. For this work, it's best to have the belt sander stationary, so that you can move the rounded bookend corners carefully across the sanding belt as shown in *Photo 3*. If you don't have a stand like the one shown in the photo, you can clamp your sander in the bench vice while you smooth the curves. If your belt sander doesn't have a locking switch, clamp the pieces in the bench vice and move the sander over the work.

Photo 1: Glue and clamp the walnut center piece between the oak bookend pieces. Wood blocks on both sides protect the oak from the steel clamp feet.

Photo 2: With both bookend pieces clamped together, lay out and then cut curves into the top corners with a jigsaw.

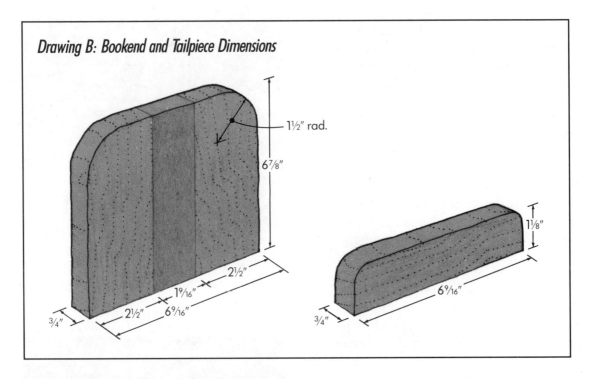

Drawing B: Bookend and Tailpiece Dimensions

1½" rad.

6⅞"

2½"

1⁹⁄₁₆"

2½"   6⁹⁄₁₆"

¾"

1⅛"

6⁹⁄₁₆"

¾"

Photo 3: Hold the bookends together to even up curved cuts on the belt sander. This sanding stand will steady the bookends at a right angle to the sanding belt.

4 **Cut the tailpiece to rough size.** Mill the tailpiece to the thickness and length in the Materials List, but make it at least 2½ inches wide. You'll need the extra width when cutting the notches.

5 **Lay out notches in the tailpiece.** Using the dimensions given in *Drawing C,* lay out all four dadoes along the bottom edge of the tailpiece. Use a square to transfer the dado shoulder lines up along one side of the piece.

6 **Mill notches in the bookends and tailpiece.** You need a guide board in this step, both as a miter gauge extension and to help prevent chip-out. Clamp the bookends, tailpiece, and a guide board together so that all bottom edges are flush with each other. Orient these parts as shown in *Photo 4,* sandwiching the bookends between the tailpiece and the guide board. Make the sandwich so that all

Drawing C: Slot Layout

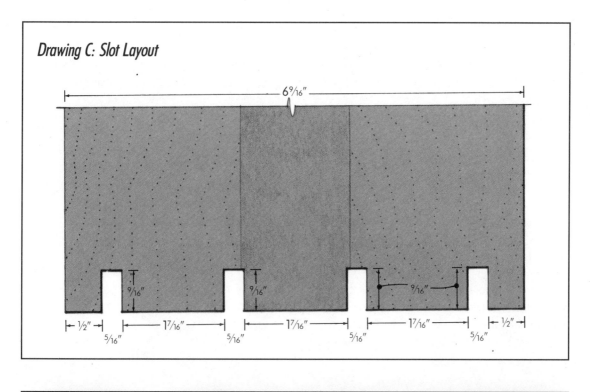

Photo 4: To mill runner slots, clamp the bookends between the tailpiece blank and a guide board. Holding the guide board against the miter gauge, align the dado cutter with the slot layout marks on the tailpiece before milling each slot.

four pieces are flush on the left end. Make sure that the notch layout is visible on the front of the tailpiece. Also check that your clamps won't get in the way as you mill notches.

Adjust the dado cutter in your table saw to a width of ⁵⁄₁₆ inch. Raise the cutter ⁹⁄₁₆ inch above the table, and set the miter gauge for a 90-degree cut. Mill a trial notch in some scrap stock to test the dado dimensions, and adjust the cutter if necessary.

Place the guide board against the miter gauge. Align the cutter with a notch layout on the tailpiece, and hold the guide board firmly against the miter guide as you cut the first dado. Cut all the way through the guide board, keeping the bottom edges of all pieces flat against the table surface. Mill the remaining dadoes using the same technique, as shown in *Photo 4.*

7 **Cut base strips and runners.** On the table saw, cut base strips to the dimensions given in the Materials List. For safety, be sure to use a push stick when moving small parts against the rip fence and through the saw blade.

Cut the runners from a clear, straight oak board. First adjust the rip fence so that it's ⁵⁄₁₆ inch from the blade. Rip a test strip from some scrap stock and see how it fits into the dadoes you've milled in the bookends and tailpiece. The strip should just slip into the dado without being forced. Adjust the rip fence if necessary; then cut the oak runners to their finished thickness. Now set the rip fence ⁹⁄₁₆ inch from the saw blade, and rip the runners to their finished width. Again, it's a good idea to test the fence position on some scrap stock before making final cuts. Cut all four runners to a finished length of 18 inches.

Shop Savvy

Gluing Assistance from Your Medicine Cabinet

To solve the problem of applying small amounts of glue, raid your medicine cabinet. Cotton-tipped swabs make it easy to get glue into tight spots. You can also use swabs to remove glue that squeezes out of a small joint. Just moisten the swab slightly before dabbing at the squeezed-out glue.

Assembly and Finishing

1 **Screw base strips to the bookends and tailpiece.** First, clamp a bookend in your bench vice, with its bottom edge up. Firmly hold a base strip in position along the bottom edge, and drill countersunk pilot holes for three 1-inch-long drywall screws. Center these holes between the runner slots.

Spread a small amount of glue along the bottom edge of the bookend. Avoid getting glue in the slots. Then fasten the base strip to the bookend by driving a drywall screw into each pilot hole. Wipe away any glue that squeezes out into the slot. (See the Shop Savvy on opposite page.) Glue and screw a base strip to the remaining bookend and to the tailpiece.

Set the table saw's rip fence 1⅜ inches from the blade, and rip the tailpiece/base-strip assembly to its finished width.

2 **Shape and smooth the tailpiece, bookends, and runners.** Set up the belt sander as before, and round-over the edges of the tailpiece and bookends. (See *Photo 5*.) All but the bottom edges of these assemblies should get this roundover treatment, easing sharp corners into gentle curves. Follow up this power sanding with some hand sanding. Start with 120-grit sandpaper, and finish with 220-grit paper.

Now go over the runners with 220-grit sandpaper. Ease corners very slightly, and smooth out saw marks so that the runners will allow the center bookend to move easily.

Another way to round-over the edges is with a piloted ⅜-inch roundover bit in a table-mounted router.

3 **Apply a finish.** First, wrap ¾-inch-wide masking tape around the ends of the run-

Photo 5: After installing base strips, round-over all bookend and tailpiece edges, working against a stationary belt sander.

Photo 6: Glue the runner ends into the tailpiece and the fixed bookend slots. Align the parts using clamps and a couple of scraps of wood.

ners. This will prevent the last ¾ inch of each runner from absorbing finish, so that it can be glued into place. After taping off the runner ends, apply a penetrating oil finish to the runners, bookends, and tailpiece. Take care to keep finish out of the runner slots.

When the finish has dried, apply a light coating of paste wax to the runners. Use a clean rag to buff the wax thoroughly into the wood, then peel off the masking tape to reveal the unfinished ends of the runners.

4 Glue the runners to the outer bookend and tailpiece. Slip the runners through the movable bookend. On the workbench, set up the bookends upside down, using scrap wood and spring clamps or C-clamps to hold the bookends up, as shown in *Photo 6*. Pour yellow wood glue into a small dish or container. Then use cotton-tipped swabs to spread a thin coat of glue on the runner ends, in the slots of the fixed bookend, and in the slots of the tailpiece. Glue the runners into place. Make sure the ends are flush with the outside of the fixed bookend and tailpiece. Use a clean, damp cloth to wipe away excess glue that squeezes out from around the runner slots. When the glue has cured, your project is ready to use.

Formal Bookcase

This formal bookcase features the classical beauty of a solid cherry top, yet it is simple to build because the carcase is made of plywood. The rich, dark grain of the cherry top contrasts nicely with the painted finish on the cabinet and shelves. Cornice trim, made in the workshop from cherry stock, adds to the project's well-crafted appearance. Brass-plated shelving standards, let into the cabinet sides, make shelf heights adjustable; and they are even easier to install than fixed shelves. Tall baseboard trim pieces, mitered together at the bottom corners of the cabinet, give these shelves the solid stance of built-in cabinetry. (See *Drawing A*.) In fact, once the project is finished, you might choose to build it into the wall by cutting the back edges to fit around your wall's baseboard molding.

Birch-veneered plywood is used for the carcase and shelves in this project. Birch is usually less expensive than other hardwood plywood, and it takes a painted finish very well. The plywood paneling used for the back is beaded to look like the wood wainscot you'd find in an old house. Both types of plywood are available from most lumberyards. Instead of birch plywood, you might use oak-veneered plywood, applying a clear or stained finish and topping off your bookcase with a solid oak top and cornice. Cherry-veneered plywood is also available, if a natural finish suits your fancy. The choice of finish won't affect the construction techniques described here.

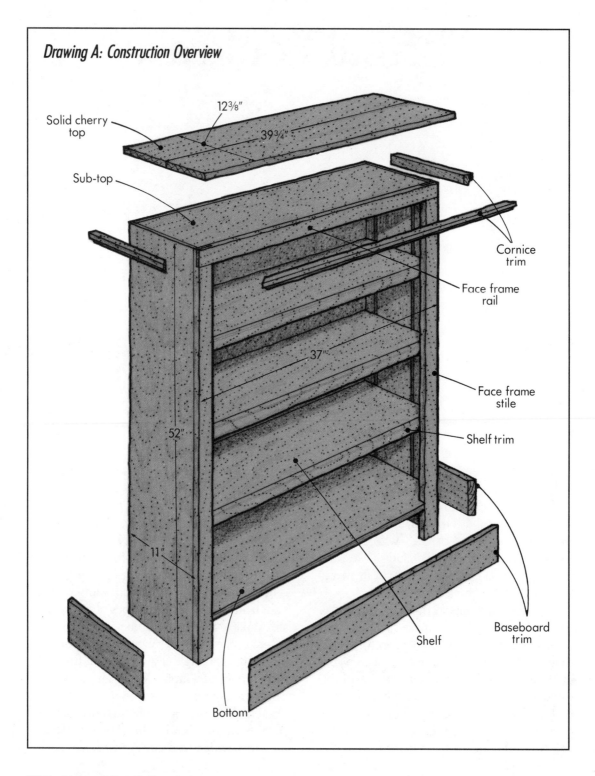

Drawing A: Construction Overview

Solid cherry top

12⅜"

39¾"

Sub-top

Cornice trim

Face frame rail

37"

Face frame stile

Shelf trim

52"

11"

Shelf

Baseboard trim

Bottom

Materials List

Wood

QTY	PART	DIMENSION
Carcase		
2	Plywood sides	¾″ × 10¼″ × 52″
1	Plywood bottom shelf	¾″ × 10¾″ × 36¼″
1	Plywood sub-top	¾″ × 10″ × 36¼″
1	Plywood back	¼″ × 36″ × 47⅝″
1	Plywood upper cleat	¾″ × 2″ × 35½″
Face Frame, Top, and Trim		
2	Poplar stiles	¾″ × 2″ × 52″
1	Poplar top rail	¾″ × 2″ × 37″
1	Poplar front baseboard	¾″ × 5⅛″ × 38½″
2	Poplar side baseboards	¾″ × 5⅛″ × 11¾″
1	Cherry top	¾″ × 12⅜″ × 39¾″
1	Cherry front cornice	¾″ × 1⅛″ × 38½″
2	Cherry side cornices	¾″ × 1⅛″ × 11¾″

Wood

QTY	PART	DIMENSION
Adjustable Shelves		
3	Plywood shelves	¾″ × 9⅛″ × 35⅜″
3	Poplar edge trim pieces	¾″ × 1½″ × 35⅜″

Hardware

6 roundhead wood screws, #6 × 1¼″
6 washers to fit over screw shanks
4 brass-plated shelving standards, 46″ long, with mounting nails
6 shelf supports
4d finishing nails, as needed
¾″ paneling nails, as needed

Building the Carcase

Carcase construction details are shown in *Drawings B and C*. For this project, the work of milling dadoes, grooves, and rabbets can be done quickly and accurately with the help of an adjustable guide fence on the router. If you don't have a router fence, you can mill dadoes and rabbets with the router jig described in "Make a Jig for Square Cutoffs and Dadoes" on page 270. Grooves for shelf standards can be cut with a dado cutter on the table saw.

Drawing B: Top View of Side

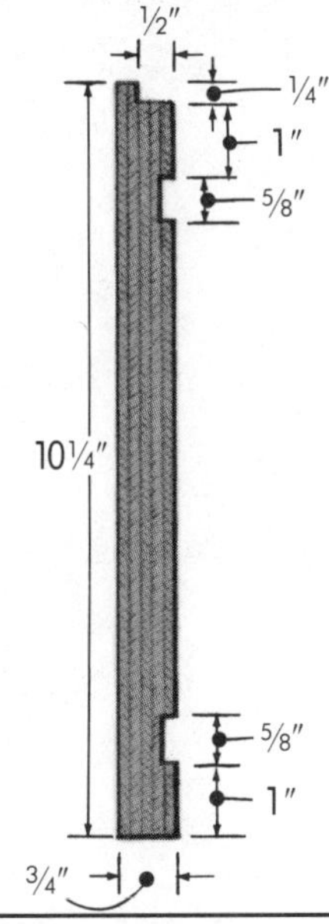

1 Cut the sides, bottom, sub-top, and upper cleat to size. Use the dimensions given in the Materials List when cutting these parts from ¾-inch-thick plywood. After cutting the bottom to width and length, lay out a ¾-inch-deep, 1⅝-inch-long notch in each corner. (See *Drawing C*.) Make your layout lines

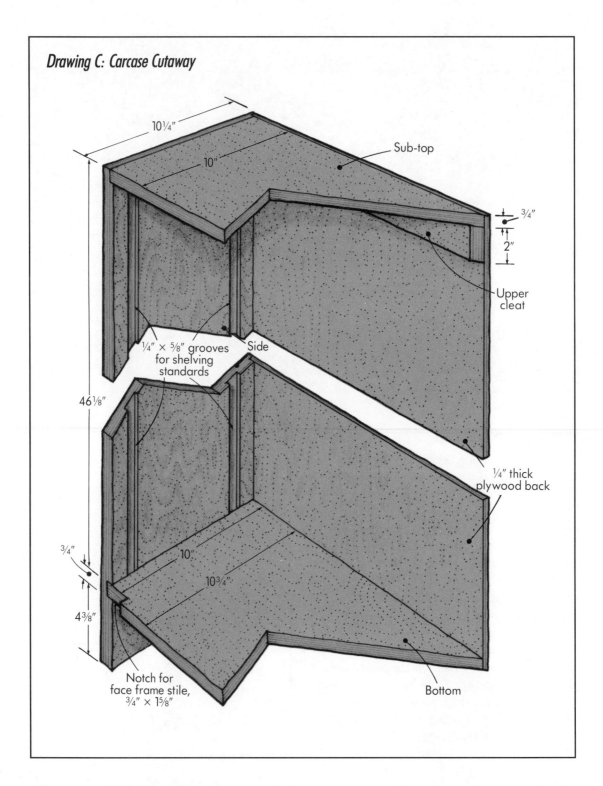

Drawing C: Carcase Cutaway

10¼"

10"

Sub-top

¾"

2"

Upper
cleat

¼" × ⅝" grooves
for shelving
standards

Side

46⅛"

¼" thick
plywood back

¾"

10"

10¾"

4⅜"

Notch for
face frame stile,
¾" × 1⅝"

Bottom

on the "good" side of the bottom that will be visible in the finished bookcase. Before cutting out each notch with a backsaw, score layout lines with a sharp utility knife. This will prevent the face veneer from splintering as you saw.

2 Rabbet back edges of sides. Chuck a ¾-inch straight bit in the router. Now screw a wood auxiliary fence to the router's guide fence. For the auxiliary fence, use a straight piece of pine ¾ inch thick and about 1½ inches wide and 12 inches long. With the router bit positioned slightly above the base surface, position the auxiliary fence to overlap all but ¼ inch of the bit's diameter.

If you have a plunge router, brace the fence securely, turn on the router, and plunge the bit into the fence until the depth of cut is ½ inch. This should allow your bit to show ¼ inch of cutting width and ½ inch of cutting depth outside the auxiliary fence. (See *Drawing D*.) If your router doesn't plunge, chisel out a depression in the auxiliary fence so that the bit will show the same cutting width and depth.

Test the setup of your router on some scrap stock, and adjust bit height or fence position if necessary. Then clamp the bookcase side securely, turn on the router, and mill each rabbet by moving the wood auxiliary fence against the back edge of the side, while keeping the router base flat against the inside face of the side. (See *Photo 1*.)

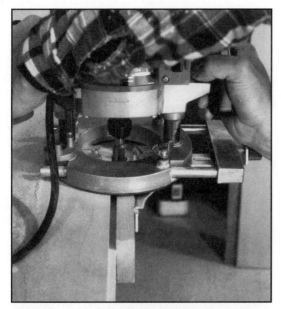

Photo 1: A wood auxiliary fence, secured to the router's adjustable fence, makes it possible to perform several milling operations quickly, using the same ¾-inch straight bit. Here the fence is adjusted to run against the back edge of the side, rabbeting it at the same time.

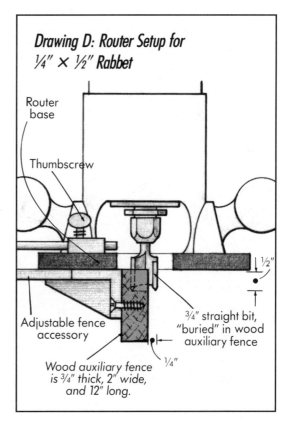

Drawing D: Router Setup for ¼" × ½" Rabbet

Router base

Thumbscrew

Adjustable fence accessory

Wood auxiliary fence is ¾" thick, 2" wide, and 12" long.

¾" straight bit, "buried" in wood auxiliary fence

½"

¼"

3 **Dado sides for the bottom.** Adjust the
router bit's depth of cut to ⅜ inch. Then
adjust the router's fence so that the wood auxiliary fence is 4⅜ inches from the bit. This
setup is shown in *Drawing E*. Mill each side's
dado by running the wood auxiliary fence
against the bottom edge of the side, as shown
in *Photo 2*. Use slow, steady pressure, keeping
the router base flat against the inside face of
the side.

4 **Rabbet sides for the sub-top.** This
setup is shown in *Drawing F*. Maintain
the router bit's ⅜-inch depth of cut, but adjust
the fence so that the working edge of the wood
auxiliary fence just touches the bit's cutting
edges. Mill each of these rabbets as shown in
Photo 3, guiding the wood auxiliary fence

against the top edge of the side while exerting
pressure downward on the router base.

5 **Groove sides for the shelving standards.** For this work, give your ¾-inch
straight bit a well-deserved rest, and replace it
with a ⅝-inch straight bit. Adjust the depth of
cut to ³⁄₁₆ inch, and adjust the router's fence so
that the wood auxiliary fence is 1 inch from
the bit.

Mill a test groove in scrap stock to make
sure that the dado depth matches the thickness of your shelving standards. If it checks
out, mill the front dado in each side, using the
fence to guide the router. To mill the dadoes
near the back edges of the sides, adjust the
fence so that the wood auxiliary fence is 1¼
inches from the bit.

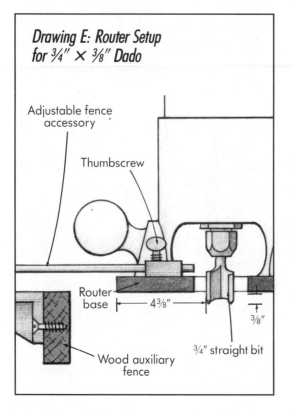

*Drawing E: Router Setup
for ¾″ × ⅜″ Dado*

Adjustable fence
accessory

Thumbscrew

Router
base |← 4⅜″ →|

⅜″

¾″ straight bit

Wood auxiliary
fence

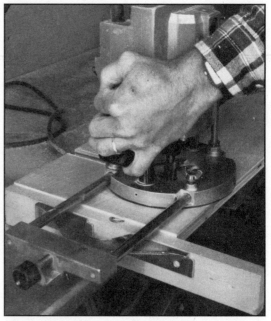

*Photo 2: Dado each side for the bottom after
adjusting the wood auxiliary fence to run
against the bottom edge of the side. Bit depth is
⅜ inch.*

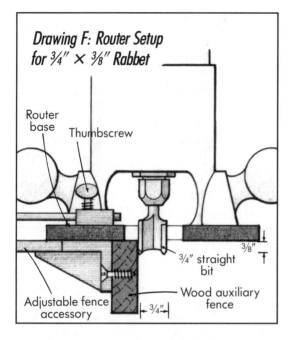

Drawing F: Router Setup for ¾″ × ⅜″ Rabbet

Router base

Thumbscrew

¾″ straight bit

⅜″

Wood auxiliary fence

Adjustable fence accessory

¾″

Photo 3: Bit depth remains at ⅜ inch to rabbet the top edge of each side. Adjust the auxiliary fence so that it can be guided by the top edge.

6 Assemble the sides, bottom, and sub-top. With glue and 4d finishing nails, join the bottom and sub-top to one side, then to the other. (See *Photo 4*.) Take care to align these parts so that the front edges of sides and sub-top are flush. Align the bottom so that the back edges of its notches are flush with the front edges of the sides.

Place the assembly on its back edges, and square it up with a framing square. Install a temporary diagonal brace across a top corner by nailing through the brace and into the front edges of the sub-top and one side.

7 Install the upper cleat and back. Turn the assembly over so that back edges are facing up, and cut the upper cleat to fit between the sides and underneath the sub-top. Install the cleat with glue and 4d finishing nails. The back side of the cleat should be flush with the shoulders of the rabbets that are milled in the back edges of the sides. Cut

Photo 4: Glue and nail the bottom and sub-top to the sides.

the back to fit into the side rabbets without binding. Test fit the back, then install it with glue and ¾-inch paneling nails.

Making the Face Frame and Baseboard Trim

In this design, the face frame consists of two stiles and a top rail. These members meet at the top corners of the carcase with half-lap joints. The three baseboard trim pieces are installed over the cabinet sides and face frame stiles, also covering the front edge of the bottom. (See *Drawing G*.)

1 **Cut the stiles and rail to size.** Rip the stile and rail members to a finished width of 2 inches. Then cut these parts to their finished lengths, checking the dimensions in the Materials List against the actual height and width of the carcase.

2 **Mill lap joints in the stiles and rail.** For this joinery work, make sure that the miter gauge is perpendicular to the table saw blade before you replace the blade with a dado cutter. Then attach a wood auxiliary fence to the miter gauge. Make the fence from straight, ¾-inch-thick pine or plywood, about 2 inches

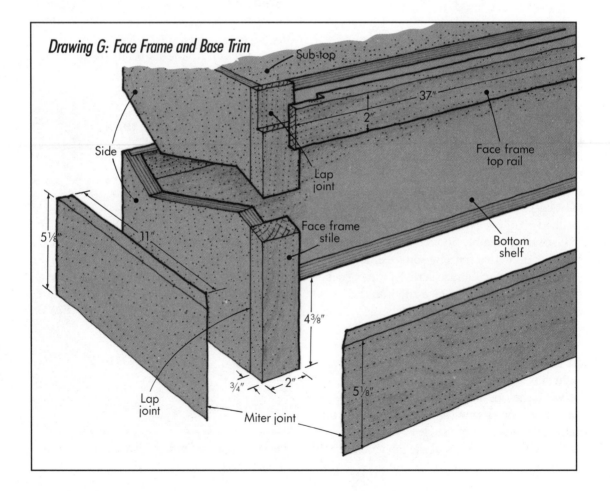

Drawing G: Face Frame and Base Trim

high and 14 inches long. When attaching this wood fence to the miter gauge, allow one end of the fence to extend about 4 inches beyond the cutting line of the dado cutter.

Adjust the dado cutter to its maximum width, and raise it to a height of ⅜ inch. Make test cuts in face frame scrap pieces to fine-tune the dado height until it equals half the thickness of the face frame stock.

Now turn on the saw and push the miter gauge forward until the dado cutter cuts all the way through the auxiliary fence. Shut the saw off, and measure exactly 2 inches over from the groove you just made in the auxiliary fence. The 2 inches will include the width of the groove. Screw a stop block against the fence. Make sure that the working edge of the block is perpendicular to the table.

This setup makes it easy to mill half-lap joints quickly and precisely. Hold each stile or rail with one edge against the auxiliary fence, and butt the end of the workpiece against the stop block to align it for the pass through the dado that will cut the joint's shoulder. (See *Photo 5.*) Once the shoulder cut is made, slide the workpiece away from the stop block and make a series of overlapping passes to complete the joint. (See *Photo 6.*)

Photo 5: Cutter height must equal half the stock thickness. Cut the shoulder of each lap joint with the end of the workpiece butted against the stop block.

Photo 6: To complete the joint, move the end of the workpiece away from the stop block, and make successive passes through the cutter.

3 **Install the face frame.** Run a bead of glue along the front edges of the carcase sides and sub-top. Then spread glue in the face frame lap joints. With 4d finishing nails, fasten the face frame members to the carcase and to each other. (See *Photo 7*.) To pull each lap joint tight, tighten a pipe or bar clamp across each top corner. Use scrap wood blocks between the clamping feet and the face frame. Set all nails, fill the resulting holes with wood putty, and use a damp cloth to wipe off excess glue.

4 **Cut and install the baseboard.** This three-piece assembly is mitered around the sides and front of the carcase, as shown in

Drawing G. Start with a piece of stock at least 68 inches long, enough to make all three trim pieces. Then rip the stock to a finished width of 5⅛ inches. Cut the front and side pieces a couple of inches longer than the finished lengths given in the Materials List. Tilt the table saw blade to a 45-degree angle. Test the trueness of the angle by making cuts in two pieces of scrap and then fitting the joint together against a square. Adjust the blade angle until your sample joint fits tight and square.

Miter one edge of the front baseboard. Put it into place on the case and scribe where the other miter should start. Cut that miter. Attach the front with 4d nails and glue, nail-

Photo 7: The lap joints in the face frame join over the top corners of the carcase. Glue and nail the face frame to the front edges of sides, bottom, and sub-top.

Photo 8: Miter the baseboard pieces where they meet at corners; then install the three-piece assembly with glue and 4d finishing nails.

ing just far enough to hold it in place in case you have to finely adjust its position. Miter one end of each side baseboard. Hold each side baseboard in position on the case, and scribe for a square cut that is flush with the back. Make these cuts. Glue and nail these sides to the carcase, also putting glue on the miter joints. (See *Photo 8.*) Set all nails.

5 Mill a decorative top edge on the baseboard. Chuck a ¼-inch roundover bit in the router, and set the depth adjustment so that the bit will mill a ⅛-inch-deep shoulder in the top front corner of the baseboard. (See *Drawing H.*) Test this setup on some ¾-inch-thick scrap stock; then mill the baseboard

edge. (See *Photo 9.*) Start on the left side of the bookcase, milling this side baseboard first. Then mill the front piece, followed by the remaining side piece.

Making the Shelves

As shown in *Drawing I,* these bookcase shelves are made from ¾-inch-thick plywood with poplar edge trim. The poplar edge treatment covers the front edge of the plywood, adding strength to each shelf and also bringing the shelf profile into scale with the face frame.

Photo 9: The decorative top edge of the baseboard can be routed in place, using a ¼-inch roundover bit.

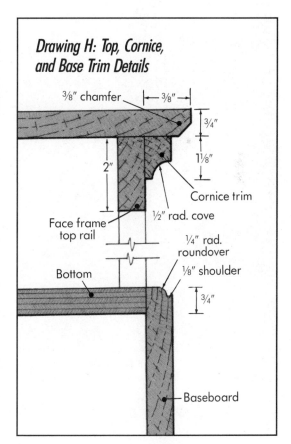

Drawing H: Top, Cornice, and Base Trim Details

⅜" chamfer

⅜"

¾"

1⅛"

2"

Cornice trim

Face frame top rail

½" rad. cove

¼" rad. roundover

⅛" shoulder

¾"

Bottom

Baseboard

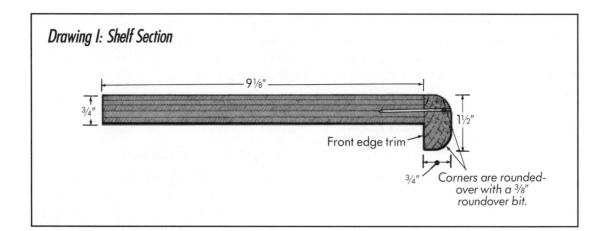

Drawing I: Shelf Section

9⅛"

¾"

1½"

Front edge trim

¾"

Corners are rounded-over with a ⅜" roundover bit.

Photo 10: Round-over the front corners of the shelf trim pieces on the router table, using a ⅜-inch roundover bit. Wood featherboards, positioned vertically and horizontally, force the stock against the fence and table.

1 **Cut the plywood shelves to size.** The dimensions given in the Materials List allow for about ⅛ inch of space between the shelf ends and bookcase sides. The finished width of the shelves is also about ⅛ inch less than the depth of the shelf opening. These clearances will allow shelf heights to be adjusted easily, without binding. Rip the shelves to width first; then cut them to length.

2 **Round-over the shelf trim on the router table.** First, cut all trim pieces to length and width. Then set up a ⅜-inch roundover bit in the router table. Adjust the table's fence so that the trim pieces will bear against it and the pilot bearing. Set the bit height to mill an even roundover on ¾-inch-thick stock. Use scrap wood to test your setup.

To complete your setup, clamp wooden featherboards to the table and to the fence, as shown in *Photo 10.* These safety devices are easy to make on your table saw, and their purpose is to force the workpiece against the table and fence. (See the Shop Savvy on the opposite page.) Be sure to position the featherboard fingers so that they slant forward against the workpiece, toward the outfeed side of the table. Run each edge against the fence.

Shop Savvy

Featherboards Are Fine Shop-Made Helpers

Featherboards offer a firm grip in wood-working operations where an extra hand is needed, and they are easy to make on the table saw. Start with a piece of clear pine that is ¾ inch thick, about 3½ inches wide, and about 10 inches long. Cut off the working end of your featherboard at a 60-degree angle. Then use the rip fence (at different settings) to guide the edge of the board as you make a series of closely spaced cuts, as shown in the photo. Make each cut about 5 inches long, and separate cuts by about ¼ inch.

When using featherboards, always position them so that the fingers are pressing forward against the stock, pointing toward the outfeed side of the bit or blade. This allows the stock to slide forward but not backward, helping to prevent kickback.

3 Fasten the edge trim to the shelves. Using a ¹⁄₁₆-inch-diameter bit, predrill holes for 4d finishing nails in all three trim pieces. Space the nails about 10 inches apart and ⅜ inch from the top edge of each trim piece. Run a bead of glue along the front edge of each plywood shelf; then secure the edge strips with 4d finishing nails. Wipe off excess glue with a damp cloth, set the nails, and fill the holes with wood putty.

Making the Top and Cornice Trim

1 Make the cherry top. The top's dimensions allow it to overhang the sides and front of the bookcase by 1⅜ inches. (See *Drawing H*.) To make the top, you'll probably have to edge-glue two or three cherry boards together, creating a solid piece at least 11⅝ inches wide. Make sure that all joining edges are straight and square, and arrange the boards to create the most pleasing grain pattern. When glue has cured, remove the clamps, scrape off any hardened glue, and sand both sides flat and smooth. If there are no high or low spots on either side, you can do this smoothing work with a belt sander and a 100- or 120-grit sanding belt. Now cut the top to its finished dimensions, and give it a finer sanding with an orbital sander and 200-grit or

220-grit sandpaper. If you don't have an orbital sander, do this sanding by hand.

Using a chamfering bit in the router, mill a ³⁄₈-inch-wide chamfer along the bottom front edge and bottom side edges of the top. With 220-grit sandpaper, gently round-over the edges of the chamfer and the top edges of the top.

Brush the top free of loose sawdust, move to a dust-free work area, and apply a penetrating oil finish. Be sure to apply finish on both sides and on all edges of the top. This will reduce the possibility of cracking or warping due to humidity changes.

2 Install the top. First, position the cherry top on the plywood sub-top. Make it flush with the back, with equal overhangs on the sides. Use C-clamps to keep the top in position, protecting the top with wood scraps between the clamping feet and the top.

From inside the bookcase, drill ¹⁄₈-inch-diameter pilot holes through the sub-top into the top. Put a piece of tape around the bit about 1¼ inches from the tip as a depth guide. This will help you make sure you don't drill all the way through the top. Make a total of six holes—one near each corner, and two near the middle. Then enlarge the sub-top pilot holes with a ⁵⁄₁₆-inch diameter drill bit. Drive a #6 × 1¼-inch roundhead screw into each hole, first slipping a washer over each screw. The oversized holes in the sub-top will allow the top to expand and contract with changes in humidity.

3 Make the cornice. As shown in *Drawing H,* the cornice profile contains a coved edge, which is milled with a ½-inch cove bit. Start by cutting a trim blank from clear cherry stock. The blank should be ¾ inch thick, 1⅛ inches wide, and 62 inches long.

Chuck the cove bit in the router table, and set up featherboards to help you hold the cornice blank firmly against the fence and table while milling the coved edge. The setup is similar to that used for milling shelf edge trim. (See *Photo 10.*) For safety and smoothness of finish, make the profile in several passes, taking a deeper cut with each pass.

4 Pre-finish the cornice trim. By finishing the cornice at this stage, you won't need to worry about getting excess finish on the painted sides and face frame of the bookcase. For the cornice trim, use the same penetrating oil finish that the cherry top received.

5 Cut the cornice to size. Like the baseboard, the cornice pieces are mitered where they meet. Cut and fit the cornice the same way you cut the baseboard. (See *Step 4,* page 202 .) Don't install the cornice yet.

Finishing Up

1 Apply a painted finish. The bookcase shown here has a painted two-tone finish. The shelves and interior of the bookcase are ivory, while the outside surfaces are tan. Apply sealer and finish coats of paint according to the manufacturer's instructions.

2 Install the cornice trim. Predrill ¹⁄₁₆-inch-diameter nail holes in the trim pieces. Make three holes in the side pieces and five holes in the front piece. Drill these holes in the flat upper section of the trim profile, not in the coved section.

Spread glue on the miter joints, but don't glue the trim pieces to the top, since the top needs to respond to humidity changes independently of the trim. Nevertheless, these cherry parts should appear to be all one piece in the finished bookcase. So in addition to forcing the miter joints tightly together, push the trim up against the underside of the top as you drive nails into the top rail or side. Set all nails, and fill the holes with cherry-tinted wood putty. (See *Photo 11*.) Wipe any excess putty from around each hole.

3 **Install shelving standards.** The standards have numbers stamped on them to help line up shelf supports. Orient the standards so that the numbers will be right-side up and then use a hacksaw to cut the top end to 46 inches. Cutting them off at the top ensures that all the shelf supports will be in the same plane, even if your cuts are slightly off. Fit each standard in its groove, with its bottom end butted against the plywood bottom piece. Double-check that the numbers are facing up. Insert the short installation nails into standard holes, and drive the nails into the side of the bookcase. Now fit the adjustable shelving clips in the standards, install the shelves, and decide what books you'd like to show off in your new project.

Photo 11: Install cornice trim after carcase and face frame have been painted.

Project construction and installation by Bethlehem Woodworks

Storage Wall

A built-in storage wall is an efficient and attractive way to get a room organized. It takes advantage of the entire floor-to-ceiling height in a room, transforming a bare wall into useful space while giving the room custom-built character. The project shown here consists of two identical units installed on either side of a large pocket door. Each wall unit consists of a base cabinet and an upper cabinet. (See *Drawing A*.) Electrical outlets are built into the base cabinet so that the units can hold stereo equipment. Shelf heights are adjustable in the base cabinet and in the upper cabinet, except for the lowermost upper cabinet shelf.

While these cabinets are "built-in," they actually are made in the workshop and then joined together when installed. When measuring a room for a storage wall, make sure the walls are plumb and the floors are level. In houses old and new, corners can be out of square, walls can be off plumb, and floors can

stray from level and flat. In these situations, you'll need to build some "scribe" space into each wall unit. (See "Scribe Fitting for Built-In Results" on page 226.) This will allow you to shim up the base cabinet carefully, so that all shelf space will be level regardless of floor and wall conditions. Moldings or other trim pieces can then be used to cover the shim space. If the room is carpeted, add the carpet thickness to the unit's height; you will remove the carpet from under the cabinets later.

This unit was painted, so the builder decided to make it from birch-veneered plywood. Birch grain is not prominent, making it an excellent base for paint. Maple is another relatively inexpensive veneer that takes paint well. More expensive hardwood-veneered plywood can be used if you prefer a storage wall with a stained or clear finish. If oak-veneered plywood is used, for example, then the face frames, cabinet doors, shelf edges, and trim should be cut from solid oak stock.

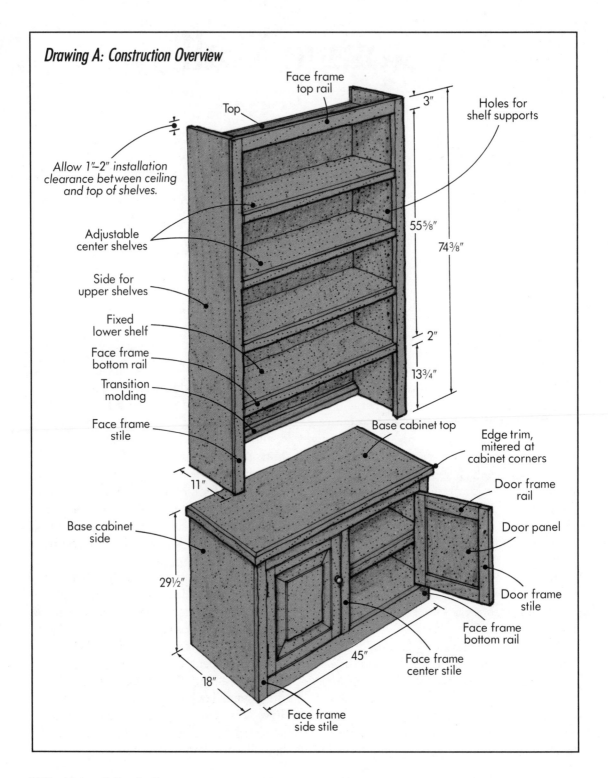

Drawing A: Construction Overview

Face frame top rail

Top

3″

Holes for shelf supports

Allow 1″–2″ installation clearance between ceiling and top of shelves.

Adjustable center shelves

55⅝″

74⅜″

Side for upper shelves

Fixed lower shelf

2″

Face frame bottom rail

13¾″

Transition molding

Face frame stile

Base cabinet top

Edge trim, mitered at cabinet corners

11″

Door frame rail

Door panel

Base cabinet side

29½″

Door frame stile

Face frame bottom rail

Face frame center stile

45″

18″

Face frame side stile

Materials List

Wood

QTY	PART	DIMENSION
Base Cabinet Carcase		
2	Sides	¾" × 17¼" × 29½"
1	Top	¾" × 17¾" × 45"
1	Bottom shelf	¾" × 17" × 44¼"
1	Plywood back	¼" × 30¼" × 44¼"
Base Cabinet Face Frame		
2	Side stiles	¾" × 2" × 29⅛"
1	Center stile	¾" × 2" × 23⅛"
1	Top rail	¾" × 2" × 41"
1	Bottom rail	¾" × 4" × 41"
Frame-and-Panel Doors (2 required)		
4	Stiles	¾" × 2" × 23"
4	Rails	¾" × 2" × 16⅜"
2	Panels	¾" × 16¼" × 19⅞"
1	Base cabinet shelf	¾" × 16" × 43¼"
Upper Cabinet		
2	Sides	¾" × 10¼" × 74⅜"
1	Fixed bottom shelf	¾" × 10" × 44¼"

Wood

QTY	PART	DIMENSION
1	Top	¾" × 10" × 44¼"
3	Adjustable shelves	¾" × 10" × 43¼"
3	Lips for adjustable shelves	¾" × 1½" × 41"
1	Plywood back	¼" × 44½" × 72⅛"
2	Face frame stiles	¾" × 2" × 74⅜"
1	Face frame top rail	¾" × 3" × 41"
1	Face frame bottom rail	¾" × 2" × 41"
1	Transition molding	¾" × 1½" × 43½"

Hardware

6d finishing nails, as needed
¾" paneling nails, as needed
8 drywall screws, 2¼"
4d finishing nails, as needed
⅜" dia. wood plugs, as needed
2 pairs brass (or brass-plated) butt hinges, ⅝" × 2"
2 brass (or brass-plated) doorknobs
2 sets magnetic door catches
16 adjustable shelf supports

Note: Materials listed are for one full storage wall unit—a base cabinet and a set of shelves.

Making the Base Cabinet Carcase

1 **Cut the sides, top, and bottom shelf to size.** Whether you're doing this cutting on a large table saw, or with a circular saw and edge guide (see "Cutting Plywood Panels" on page 25), have a helper assist you in handling the plywood sheets. Take extra care to make sure the side pieces are identical in size.

2 **Dado the sides to receive the bottom shelf.** As shown in *Drawings B and C*, each dado should be 3¼ inches from the bottom edge of its side. If you're doing this on the table saw, adjust the width of the cutter to

Photo 1: A pair of pocket doors divides this living room wall into two equal parts. This storage wall project consists of two units designed to fit on either side of the doorway.

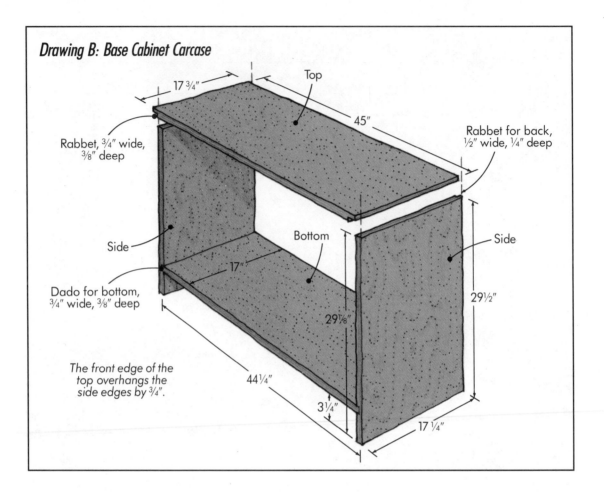

Drawing B: Base Cabinet Carcase

17 3⁄4"

Top

45"

Rabbet, 3⁄4" wide, 3⁄8" deep

Rabbet for back, 1⁄2" wide, 1⁄4" deep

Side

Side

Bottom

17"

Dado for bottom, 3⁄4" wide, 3⁄8" deep

29 1⁄2"

29 1⁄8"

The front edge of the top overhangs the side edges by 3⁄4".

44 1⁄4"

3 1⁄4"

17 1⁄4"

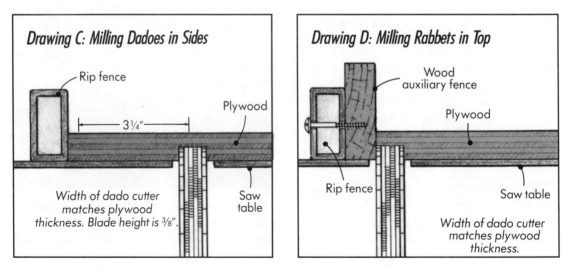

Drawing C: Milling Dadoes in Sides

Rip fence

Plywood

3 1⁄4"

Saw table

Width of dado cutter matches plywood thickness. Blade height is 3⁄8".

Drawing D: Milling Rabbets in Top

Wood auxiliary fence

Plywood

Rip fence

Saw table

Width of dado cutter matches plywood thickness.

match the thickness of the plywood. Then adjust cutter height to ⅜ inch, and position the rip fence 3¼ inches from the cutter. Run each side through this setup, keeping the bottom edge against the rip fence, and the inside face against the table surface.

3 **Rabbet the ends of the top piece.** These rabbets will fit over the top edges of the sides. To make these rabbets on the table saw, first protect your fence and blade by attaching a wood auxiliary fence to the rip fence using a straight board at least 1 inch thick and 3 inches wide. Leave height and width settings on the dado cutter the same as for Step 2. Move the wood fence over next to the dado cutter. When the saw is turned on, the cutter should just graze the fence. Cut the rabbet as shown in *Drawing D*.

4 **Mill rabbets along back edges of the sides.** These rabbets are ½ inch wide and ¼ inch deep to receive the ¼-inch-thick cabinet back. To set up the table saw for this operation, first lower the dado cutter beneath the table surface. Then move the wood auxiliary

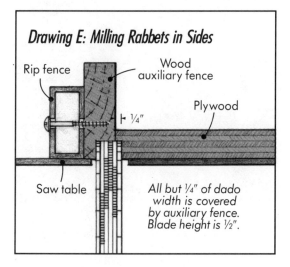

Drawing E: Milling Rabbets in Sides

Rip fence

Wood auxiliary fence

Plywood

⊢ ¼"

Saw table

All but ¼" of dado width is covered by auxiliary fence. Blade height is ½".

fence over the cutter, so that only ¼ inch of the cutter shows beyond the edge of the wood fence. Make a mark on the wood fence directly over the saw's arbor and ½ inch above the table surface. Now turn the saw on, and slowly raise the cutter into the wood fence. Stop when the cutter height reaches the mark. "Burying" part of the dado cutter in an auxiliary fence is a good way to mill small rabbets. (See *Drawing E*.) With the inside face of each side facing down, run the back edge of the side against the fence to mill each rabbet.

5 **Assemble the carcase.** To make this job go smoothly and accurately, it helps to have a large, flat work area. Glue and nail the bottom and top of the cabinet to one side, then the other, using 6d finishing nails. (See *Photo 2*.) Make sure that the front edge of the bottom is flush with the front edges of the sides. The back edge of the top should be flush with the bottom of the side rabbets while the front edge of the top should extend ¾ inch beyond the front edges of the sides.

Use a framing square to test for square corners where the sides meet the top and the bottom. If necessary, force the carcase square and secure it that way by nailing a temporary diagonal brace across one corner. Set all nails, and fill holes with wood filler.

6 **Install the back.** First, turn the assembly over so that all front edges are facing down. Now measure, cut, and install the back of the cabinet. Spread glue on the back edges of the top and bottom pieces, and along the side rabbets. Then drop the back in place, and nail it fast with ¾-inch paneling nails. Once the back is secured, it will keep the carcase square, and you can remove the temporary diagonal brace installed as part of Step 5.

Making the Base Cabinet Face.Frame

1 **Cut and fit the stiles and rails.** As shown in *Drawing F,* the base cabinet's face frame consists of five parts: two side stiles, a center stile, a bottom rail, and a top rail. The bottom rail is 4 inches wide, while all remaining face frame members are 2 inches wide. The lengths of face frame members are also given in *Drawing F,* but it's best to take these lengths directly from the front of the carcase. Cut the side stiles to size and temporarily tack them to the front edges of the sides. Then cut top and bottom rails to fit between the side stiles. Finally, cut the center stile to fit between the rails. Leave all these members in

their positions on the carcase.

2 **Drill counterbores and pilot holes for face frame screws.** In this project, stiles and rails meet with simple butt joints, which are glued and screwed together to assemble the face frame. As shown in *Drawing F,* each side stile is joined to the top rail with a single 2¼-inch-long drywall screw. The side stile is connected to the bottom rail with two screws. The center stile requires two screws—one driven through each rail.

Counterbore each screw hole with a ⅜-inch-diameter bit and drill pilot holes with a ⅛-inch-diameter bit. Make sure that the pilot

Photo 2: A flat work surface is important when assembling the cabinet carcase. The bottom is dadoed into the sides, and the top is rabbeted to fit over the top edges of the sides. Glue and nail these joints together, using 4d finishing nails.

holes extend into the member where the point of the screw will lodge. To save time, counterbores and pilot holes can be drilled in one step using a #6 combination pilot bit. For more details, see "Drilling and Driving" on page 8. Center each counterbored hole on the width of the frame member, and take care to drill with the bit perpendicular to the edge of the stock. In the side stiles and the top rail, make each counterbored hole 1 inch deep. Make the counterbored hole in the bottom rail 2½ inches deep. When making fairly deep counterbored holes like these, it's important to withdraw the bit frequently while drilling, to clear accumulated sawdust. When all counterbores and pilot holes have been drilled, remove face frame members from the carcase.

Photo 3: After the back of the carcase is attached, the face frame can go on. Join stiles and rails with glue and counterbored screws. Glue and nail the frame members to the front of the carcase.

3 Assemble and attach the face frame.
First, spread glue on center stile ends. (See *Photo 3*.) Clamp the center stile against the top

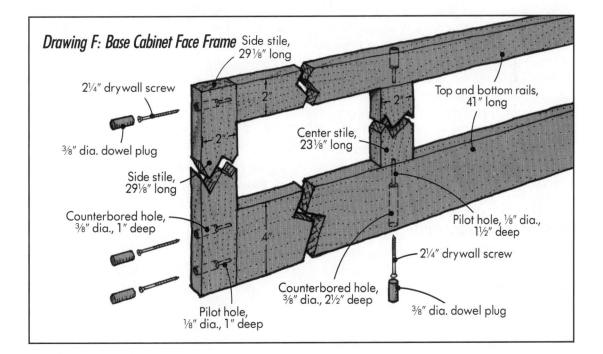

Drawing F: Base Cabinet Face Frame Side stile, 29⅛" long

2¼" drywall screw

⅜" dia. dowel plug

Side stile, 29⅛" long

Counterbored hole, ⅜" dia., 1" deep

Pilot hole, ⅛" dia., 1" deep

Center stile, 23⅛" long

Top and bottom rails, 41" long

Pilot hole, ⅛" dia., 1½" deep

2¼" drywall screw

⅜" dia. dowel plug

Counterbored hole, ⅜" dia., 2½" deep

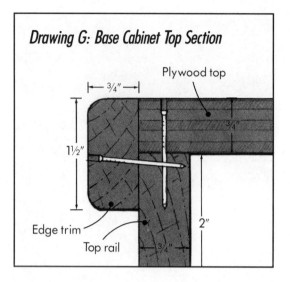

Drawing G: Base Cabinet Top Section

Plywood top

3/4"

3/4"

1½"

2"

Edge trim

Top rail

3/4"

and bottom rails, and drive screws through the rails and into stile pilot holes to secure this three-part assembly. Next, glue and nail the side stiles to the carcase sides, using 4d finishing nails. Complete the face frame by gluing and screwing the rails to the side stiles. Make sure to spread glue along the top edge of the top rail, since this edge will butt against the underside of the carcase top. (See *Drawing G.*) Use 4d finishing nails to secure the carcase top to the top rail, and to join the bottom rail against the bottom shelf. Glue ⅜-inch-diameter wood plugs in all counterbored holes. Allow each plug to stand slightly proud of the surface so that it can be trimmed flush after the glue dries. Set all nails, and fill the resulting holes with wood filler.

Making the Frame-and-Panel Doors

1 Glue boards together to make two panels. At this stage, it's smart to make panels at least ½ inch longer and wider than the anticipated final dimensions given in the Materials List. Set glued-up boards aside overnight until the glue cures.

2 Mill inside edges of stiles and rails. As shown in *Drawing H,* the inside edge profile includes a groove where the raised panel will fit, and a rounded-over edge that faces outward in the finished cabinet. You can mill this profile on the router table, using a special "stile-and-rail" bit, or you can use a shaper cutter with a similar profile. If you don't have these special bits or cutters, you can use the table saw to construct the door frames. (See "Making the Stiles and Rails" on page 254.)

Before you begin milling, cut the stiles and rails to the lengths and widths in the Materials List. Use scrap from the stile and rail stock to make test cuts until your bit or cutter is at the correct height. Then mill the groove and the roundover profile into the inside edge of each frame member.

3 Cope the ends of the rails. These cuts, also made on the router or shaper, must be set up carefully. Precisely set the cutter height so that each coped rail end will fit against the contoured inside edge of the stile. Again, make test cuts in scrap until you get it right. Use a miter gauge (set at 90 degrees) and a backup block to guide the rails through the cutter.

4 Test fit the door frames, and cut panels to final size. Test fit the stiles and rails, checking the joints as you square up the frame. To calculate the proper length and width of the panel, follow this simple formula: Double the depth of the panel groove, add this sum to the width (or length) of the opening, and subtract ⅛ inch. This gives the panel room to expand and contract inside the frame without stressing it. Cut panels to final size following these measurements.

5 **Cut raised panels.** For this project, panels are "raised" on the table saw, using the setup shown in *Drawing I*. Adjust blade angle to 12 degrees off square, and raise the blade about 1¾ inches above the table. Then attach an auxiliary fence to the standard rip fence. The fence should be 12 inches high and at least 14 inches long. For best results, make the fence from ¾-inch-thick hardwood plywood. It will provide a smooth vertical surface to guide the inside face of the panel blank as each bevel is cut. As shown in *Drawing I*, the auxiliary fence should be positioned ⁷⁄₁₆ inch from the blade to make the bevel cuts.

Test the setup (and your technique) on some ¾-inch-thick scrap stock. Adjust fence position if necessary, then cut bevels on all the panel blanks. On each blank, always make the two cross-grain cuts first, then finish up by cutting with the grain.

6 **Rabbet back edges of panels.** As shown in *Drawing H,* these rabbets keep panel and frame surfaces approximately flush in the finished door. Remove the panel-raising auxiliary fence, and replace it with a lower auxiliary fence of solid pine as shown in *Drawing J*. Install the dado head in the table saw and adjust cutter for maximum width of cut. Lower the dado cutter below the table surface. Then move the rip fence, with its auxiliary fence attached, over the cutter, so that just ⁹⁄₁₆ inch of the cutter shows beyond the wood fence. Make a mark on the fence directly over the cutter, ³⁄₁₆-inch from the table surface. Now turn the saw on and slowly raise the cutter into the wood. Stop when the cutter height reaches ³⁄₁₆ inch. Use this setup to rabbet all four back edges of each panel. Once all the cutting is done, sand the saw and cutter marks off the panels, especially the beveled edges that will show on the outside face of each door.

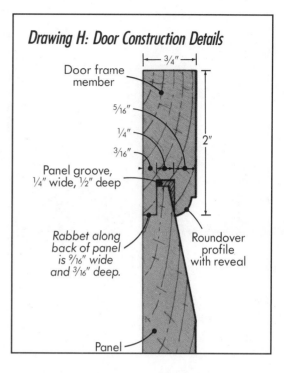

Drawing H: Door Construction Details

Door frame member

¾"

⁵⁄₁₆"

¼"

³⁄₁₆"

2"

Panel groove, ¼" wide, ½" deep

Rabbet along back of panel is ⁹⁄₁₆" wide and ³⁄₁₆" deep.

Roundover profile with reveal

Panel

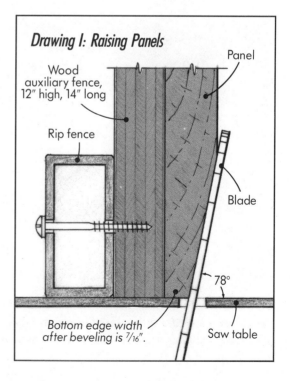

Drawing I: Raising Panels

Panel

Wood auxiliary fence, 12" high, 14" long

Rip fence

Blade

78°

Bottom edge width after beveling is ⁷⁄₁₆".

Saw table

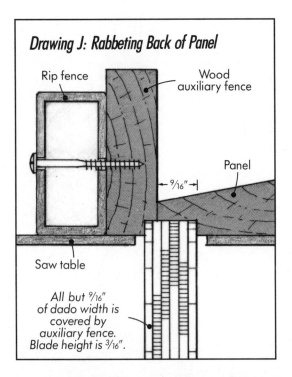

Drawing J: Rabbeting Back of Panel

Rip fence

Wood auxiliary fence

Panel

9/16"

Saw table

All but 9/16" of dado width is covered by auxiliary fence. Blade height is 3/16".

7 **Assemble the doors.** To make this job easier, use drywall screws and two straight boards to make a right-angled jig. Lay out the 90-degree angle with a framing square, and screw both boards to your workbench or to a flat work surface. Spread glue on the coped areas of the rail ends before joining them to the stiles. Slip the panel into place before joining all frame members together (see *Photo 4*); then use pipe clamps to pull stile-and-rail joints tight.

8 **Test fit and adjust doors.** Place each door in its opening to check how it fits. To look good, flush-fit doors like these should show an even gap of between 1/16 inch and 1/8 inch around all four sides. If necessary, mark stiles or rails that require trimming, and do this delicate work with a jointer or a hand plane. With pencil marks, key each door to its

Photo 4: A right-angle jig, screwed to the top of the workbench, helps keep door frames square as they're assembled. Fit the raised panel into its grooves after joining a stile and rail together; then glue the remaining stile and rail to these frame members. Keep glue out of the panel grooves so that the panel can float in its frame.

opening as adjustments are completed.

9 **Cut hinge mortises for doors and side stiles.** The butt hinges for these doors are spaced 2 inches from the door corners. Follow the instructions in "Mortising for a Butt Hinge" on page 93.

10 **Drill holes for doorknobs and install door catches.** Position the knobs on either side of the carcase center stile. To make sure the knobs are horizontally aligned, hang the cabinet doors before marking centers for the knobs and drilling holes. Wait until finish has been applied to install the knobs. Fasten magnetic (or other) door catches to doors and carcase center stile.

Making the Upper Cabinet

1 **Dado sides to receive top and bottom shelves.** Each top shelving unit has a fixed bottom shelf, a top, and three adjustable shelves. Upper cabinet construction details are shown in *Drawing K*.

Mill the dadoes with the dado cutter head on the table saw as shown in *Photo 5*. Adjust dado width to match the thickness of the shelves, then raise the cutter ⅜ inch above the table. Mill the dadoes by guiding the top and bottom edges of each side against the rip fence. The setup is similar to that shown in *Drawing C*, except that the fence must be positioned 2¼ inches away from the cutter (for the top shelf dadoes) and 15 inches away from the cutter (for the bottom shelf dadoes).

2 **Rabbet the back edges of the sides.** These rabbets will hold the ¼-inch-thick plywood back, so each should be ½ inch wide and ¼ inch deep. Use the table saw setup shown in *Drawing E*.

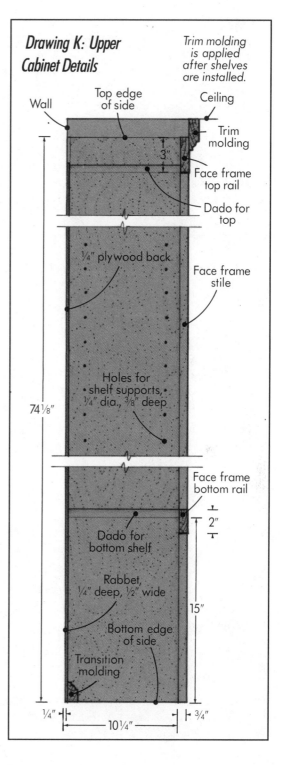

Drawing K: Upper Cabinet Details

Trim molding is applied after shelves are installed.

Wall

Top edge of side

Ceiling

Trim molding

3"

Face frame top rail

Dado for top

¼" plywood back

Face frame stile

Holes for shelf supports, ¼" dia., ⅜" deep

74⅛"

Face frame bottom rail

2"

Dado for bottom shelf

Rabbet, ¼" deep, ½" wide

Bottom edge of side

15"

Transition molding

¼"

10¼"

¾"

Storage Wall Design Options

With a little imagination, you can adapt this storage wall design to fit a variety of room conditions. Both the base cabinets and the upper shelves can be combined to create built-in storage around a fireplace or closet. To cope with a broad expanse of wall area, you can build several complete units and join them together, side-by-side. This will produce a single continuous countertop surface and several banks of shelves. Flank a window with floor-to-ceiling storage by installing full units on either side of the window. Then install a base cabinet beneath the window. You might build a fixed shelf above the window, between upper shelving units.

When designing a storage wall, adjust the width of the base cabinets and the length of the upper shelves to fit your space. Keep in mind, however, that the shelves shown in this project (3/4-inch plywood reinforced with a solid wood edge) shouldn't be longer than 48 inches to avoid sagging under a load. To join adjacent base cabinet and upper shelf units, glue and screw the face frames together.

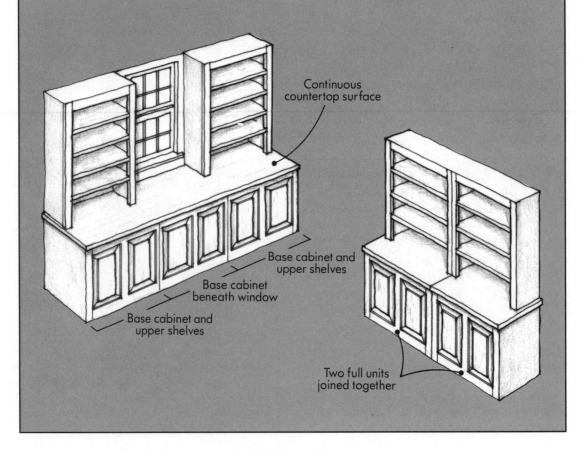

Continuous countertop surface

Base cabinet and upper shelves

Base cabinet beneath window

Base cabinet and upper shelves

Two full units joined together

3 Cut and install bottom shelf and top. Cut these parts to the dimensions in the Materials List. Working on a flat surface, glue and nail the shelf and the top into their dadoes. Make sure the front edges of these pieces are flush with the side front edges.

4 Cut and install the back. Carefully place the upper shelves on the floor, or other flat work surface, with the front edges facing down. With a framing square, make sure that the sides are square with the bottom shelf and the top. Spread glue along the back edges of the shelf and top, and in the rabbets along the back edges of both sides. Then slip the back into place. Make sure that the bottom edge of the back is flush with the bottom edges of the sides. The position of the back's top edge isn't critical, as long as it can be fastened against the back edge of the top. Nail the back to the sides, bottom shelf, and top, using ¾-inch paneling nails, as shown in *Photo 6*.

Photo 5: Mill dadoes in sides to hold fixed shelves using the dado cutter in the table saw. The dado width should match shelf thickness, and the dado height should be ⅜ inch. Guide the end of the side against the rip fence to mill each dado.

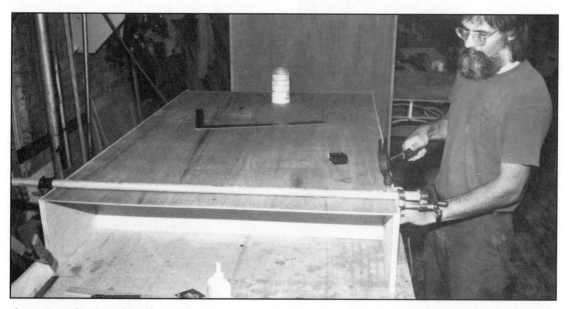

Photo 6: Make sure that the sides are square with the top and bottom shelves before attaching the back. Glue and nail this ¼-inch-thick plywood panel to the back edges of the sides and shelves.

5 **Cut and install the face frame.** Cut the stiles to the lengths in the Materials List and then glue and nail them into place with 4d finishing nails. Then cut the rails to fit snugly between stiles (see the Shop Savvy on page 13), and install them with glue and 4d finishing nails. Like the face frame for the base cabinet, make the stile-to-rail connections with 2¼-inch-long drywall screws. (See *Photo 7.*) Drive screws into pilot holes that include 1-inch-deep counterbores. Drill a single pilot hole where each stile joins the bottom rail. When drilling, take care to center the hole on

Photo 7: After fastening the face frame members to the sides and shelves, join stiles to rails with glue and counterbored screws. Drill counterbored holes 1 inch deep, using a ⅜-inch-diameter bit. With a long Phillips bit chucked in the drill, drive 2¼-inch drywall screws into the rails. Then glue wood plugs into the counterbored holes.

the stile edge, and keep the bit perpendicular to the edge. Drill a pair of pilot holes where each stile joins the top rail. Drive screws into all holes, and fill holes with dowel plugs.

6 **Cut and install transition molding.** As shown in *Drawings A and K,* this trim piece, which can be cut from a length of ¾-inch-thick stop molding, fits along the bottom edge of the plywood back. Later you'll screw into it from the bottom of the base cabinet. Spread glue along the back and ends of the molding, and secure it to the plywood with several spring clamps. Make sure that the bottom edge of the molding is flush with the bottom edge of the plywood.

Making the Adjustable Shelves

1 **Cut base cabinet shelf and upper shelves to length and width.** Depending on what you plan to store in a wall unit, a single base cabinet shelf, three adjustable shelves, and one fixed upper shelf should be adequate. The cutting list dimensions allow for ⅛ inch of clearance between each shelf end and the side where the shelf supports are installed.

2 **Glue and nail shelf edges onto plywood shelves.** The edge treatment shown in *Drawing L* serves two purposes: It adds strength, helping the shelf support loads without sagging, and it also conceals the plywood edge, creating a smoother, thicker edge that looks good on the finished piece.

The edge for the base cabinet shelf runs the full length of the shelf. Edges for the adjustable upper shelves stop 1⅛ inches shy of each shelf end. This allows the shelf ends to extend behind the face frame, where they're held up by round shelf support pins that fit in holes drilled in the sides. Use 4d finishing nails to secure the shelf edges to the plywood, and set all nails using a nailset.

3 Round-over shelf edging. Clamp each shelf with its solid wood edge facing up. Then rout the top edges of the wood edging with a ¼-inch roundover bit. Set the nails with a nailset, fill holes with wood putty, and sand surfaces smooth when the putty dries.

4 Drill holes for shelf supports. The brass, pin-type supports used for these shelves are designed to fit in ¼-inch-diameter holes that are drilled ⅜ inch deep into the

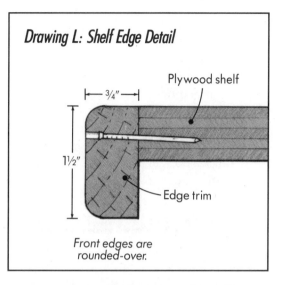

Drawing L: Shelf Edge Detail

Plywood shelf

¾"

1½"

Edge trim

Front edges are rounded-over.

Shop Savvy

Making a Pegboard Jig for Drilling Holes

It would be nearly impossible to drill accurately aligned holes for shelf support pins without using some kind of jig. Fortunately, you can make a simple but extremely accurate jig from a sheet (or partial sheet) of perforated hardboard (also known as pegboard). Sawing parallel with the holes in the hardboard, cut a piece about 10½ inches wide and 60 inches long. Clamp this guide strip against the inside surface of the side, and use the holes in the pegboard as guides for drilling out two columns of holes As long as you drill the lowermost hole in each column at the same elevation on the side, all remaining holes will be equally spaced, providing four level support points at each shelf height. A short block of wood with a hole drilled in it can be slipped over the drill bit to act as a depth stop. You can

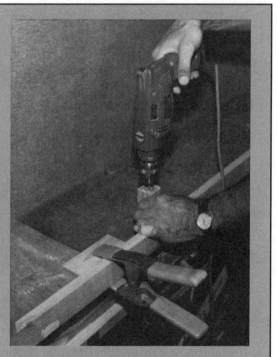

reuse this jig on other shelving and cabinetry projects. You can also make a shorter, wider version for base cabinets with adjustable shelves.

sides of the shelving unit. Each side requires two columns of holes. Separate the two columns on each side by at least 7 inches, and space holes equally to provide four level support points at different shelf height adjustments. Start the lowermost holes about 12 inches from the bottom shelf, and end each column of holes about 10 inches from the top. For a quick, accurate way to drill these holes, see the Shop Savvy on page 223.

Installing the Cabinet and Shelves

1 Sand cabinet and shelves and apply first finish coats. Sanding, painting, staining, and sealing operations are all easier to do before this storage unit is built into the wall. Detach all hinges and hardware, and

Photo 8: Use a prybar to remove baseboard molding from the wall where the storage unit will be installed.

detach base cabinet doors from the face frame. Sand and finish these items and all adjustable shelves separately.

2 Remove baseboard molding, crown molding, and other trim from wall and ceiling areas where wall unit will be installed. By working carefully with one or more prybars, you can remove most trim pieces with minimal damage to trim or wall and ceiling surfaces. (See *Photo 8.*) This is also the time to remove wall-to-wall carpet from the floor area that the base cabinet will occupy. For stability, the cabinet should rest on the floor, not on carpet or carpet padding.

3 Complete necessary wiring and ductwork changes. The storage unit may cover existing outlets and switches, so these will need to be safely terminated or rerouted. Alternatively, you may want to wire an outlet into the base cabinet for stereo equipment, or bring in cable for television. If heating or air-conditioning ducts will be covered by the unit, these should be rerouted or capped off.

4 Position and level the base cabinet. Use wood shims to level the top of the base cabinet from front to back and from left to right. Wedges and short, narrow lengths of wood will both work well as shims. To secure the base cabinet's position, drive screws through the back and into the wall framing or masonry. In this installation, screws are also driven through one side and into the adjacent wall, and through the remaining side and into the door casing. (See "Against the Wall," on page 10.)

5 Install the upper cabinet. Since the base cabinet top will be level, the upper shelves should be easy to position. Push the cabinet against the wall, and align the cabinet's sides so that they're flush with the ends of the base cabinet. (See *Photo 9.*) Screw the sides to the wall and toescrew through the edge of the door casing into the framing behind. From inside the base cabinet, drive screws through the base cabinet top and into the transition molding.

6 Install edge trim around the base cabinet top. As shown in *Photo 10,* this ¾-inch-thick, 1½-inch-wide trim covers the plywood edge of the top and part of the face frame's top rail. Before cutting trim pieces to length, round-over the two outside corners of the trim stock, using a ⅜-inch roundover bit in the router table. Then cut miter joints where trim pieces meet at corners. (See page 177 for more information on mitering.) Glue and nail the trim to the cabinet using 4d finishing nails, as shown in *Photo 10.* Set the nails, and fill nail holes with wood putty.

7 Install the trim. The exact trim you use will depend on the trim scheme of the room. Quarter-round molding is good to use between the floor and the bottom of the base cabinet. Stop molding works well between the sides of the unit and the wall. In this installation, stop molding is also used to cover the

Photo 9: Base cabinets are installed first, followed by upper cabinets. Use shims as necessary beneath the base cabinet to make its top surface perfectly level. The scribe space between the storage unit and the ceiling and wall surfaces will be covered by trim pieces.

Scribe Fitting for Built-In Results

A carpenter might define a perfect world as a place where walls are flat and plumb, always meeting at exact 90-degree angles. Ceilings and floors would be level, too, with no irregularities to impede the installation of built-in shelves and cabinets. Unfortunately, these conditions rarely occur. To cope with less-than-perfect conditions, it's important to learn about scribe fitting. Scribe-fit details are crucial to give cabinetry a truly built-in appearance.

There are various ways to scribe fit a cabinet against a wall or ceiling. In the storage wall project shown here, common stop molding is used to cover the scribe space between the top of the upper cabinet and the ceiling. It's also used to cover the scribe space between the wall and face frames of the base and the upper cabinets. The contoured edge of the stop molding fits against the face frame, and is kept plumb or level to stay even with the face frame edges. The edge of the stop molding that fits against the wall or ceiling is scribed to conform to its irregularity. This strategy usually yields the best-looking results.

To scribe fit a molding like this, tack it in place against the cabinetry so that it is plumb (for wall installation) or level (for ceiling installation) and parallel with the edge of the face frame or cabinet side it will fit against. Then use a compass as shown in the left photo to transfer the existing slope and contour of the wall (or ceiling) to the molding. Remove the molding and use a jigsaw or coping saw to cut along the scribe line. Test fit the molding, trim it for a better fit if necessary, and then install it (right photo).

Scribe fitting with a compass

Installing a scibe-fit molding

Photo 10: Trim for the base cabinet top can be installed after the upper cabinet is in place. Miter the trim pieces where they join at the cabinet corner.

space between the upper shelves and the ceiling. As an alternative, you could use crown or cornice molding along the ceiling.

Where walls aren't plumb and ceilings aren't level, individual trim pieces have to be tapered or contoured to compensate for out-of-plumb walls and out-of-level ceilings. Usually, you can achieve the best appearance by

scribe fitting the outside edges of the pieces, keeping inside edges (those that fit against the shelves or cabinet) level or plumb. For more details, see "Scribe Fitting for Built-In Results" on the opposite page.

8 Finish up. Apply finish coats, and install base cabinet doors and adjustable shelves.

Dining Room

Buffet Cart

Roll it where you need it; roll it out of the way when you're done. That's the beauty of this handsome buffet cart that features two broad shelves below a large work surface. The cart's frame is sturdy and attractive oak. The shelves and work surface are covered with plastic laminate for durability and easy cleaning. Locking casters enable you to give the cart a stationary stance.

While the cart was designed as a kitchen work island, it's certainly elegant enough to find its way into the dining room as a sideboard. If you want to dedicate it to dining room use, you might consider substituting oak-veneered plywood for the plastic laminate. If you elect to use laminate, be sure to start out with oversized pieces (at least an inch longer and wider than the final dimensions given in the Materials List). This way, you'll be able to flush-trim the laminate after it's glued to the shelves and countertop. Instead of buying a large sheet of laminate, you may be able to save money by using several "scrap" pieces from a millwork or cabinetmaking shop.

Cutting and Mortising the Legs and Rails

1 Prepare and cut the stock. Make your frame members from clear, straight oak. After ripping the frame members to rough dimensions (1⅝ inches thick and 2⅜ inches wide) on the table saw, plane one face of each piece flat on the jointer. Then run your stock through the thickness planer, planing off alternate faces until you reach a finished thickness of 1½ inches. Next, joint one edge of each piece straight and square. Then return to the thickness planer to plane stock down to a finished width of 2¼ inches. Once this dimensioning work is complete, cut all frame members to their finished lengths.

If you can't find 1½-inch-thick stock, you can glue up ¾-inch-thick material to make the legs and rails. You'll still need to use the jointer and thickness planer to dimension the pieces as discussed above. If you don't have access to a jointer or a thickness planer, you can have your stock dimensioned at a millwork or cabinetmaking shop.

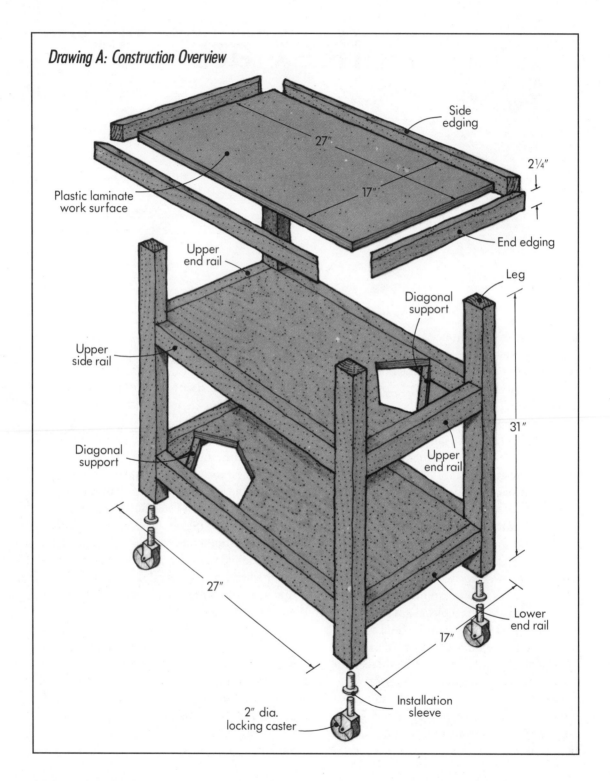

Drawing A: Construction Overview

Side edging

27"

17"

2¼"

Plastic laminate work surface

End edging

Upper end rail

Diagonal support

Leg

Upper side rail

31"

Diagonal support

Upper end rail

27"

Lower end rail

17"

Installation sleeve

2" dia. locking caster

2 **Lay out the mortises.** As shown in *Drawing B*, all mortises are ½ inch wide, 1¼ inches long, and 1¹⁄₁₆ inches deep. Use a right-angle jig like the one shown in *Photo 1* to lay out the mortises. To make this jig, screw a straight piece of stock to a flat surface, and then use a framing square to position another piece perpendicular to the first. Place all four legs in the frame, with wide faces up.

With a try square, lay out mortise shoulders across all four legs at once, as shown in *Photo 1*. Turn the legs and lay out a second set of mortise shoulders on narrow faces. Now label the top of each leg relative to its position in the finished cart. For example, use "LR" to label the left rear leg. Leg labels are important because the mortises for the end rails will not be centered on the leg sides. (See *Drawing B*.)

3 **Rout the side rail mortises.** The mortising work for this project was done with a mortising base designed for use with plunge routers. You can also do a fine job of mortising with the adjustable fence that's available for most plunge routers. (See "Mortising with a Plunge Router" on page 236.) With either accessory, the object is to set up the base or fence so that the bit can be guided in a straight line while the full length of the mortise is routed. Use the same base (or fence) adjustment to mill all eight side rail mortises. (See *Photo 2*.)

Materials List

Wood

QTY	PART	DIMENSION
4	Oak legs	1½″ × 2¼″ × 31″
4	Oak side rails	1½″ × 2¼″ × 24½″
4	Oak end rails	1½″ × 2¼″ × 16″
8	Diagonal supports	¾″ × 1½″ × 6″
2	Plywood shelves	¾″ × 14″ × 22½″
1	Plywood top	¾″ × 17″ × 27″
2	Oak edge boards	¾″ × 2¼″ × 28½″
2	Oak edge boards	¾″ × 2¼″ × 18½″

Hardware

16 drywall screws, 1¼″
4d finishing nails, as needed
1 sheet plastic laminate for top, 17″ × 27″
2 sheets plastic laminate for shelves, 14″ × 22½″
4 locking casters, 2″ dia.

Photo 1: Lay out the shoulders of leg mortises with legs ganged together in a right-angle jig.

4 **Rout the end rail mortises.** As shown in *Drawing B,* the mortises for the end rail tenons are ½ inch from the outside edge of each leg. Check the leg labels to avoid milling mortises close to the inside face of a leg.

Rout these mortises as before. If you are using the Woodhaven mortising base, discussed in "Mortising with a Plunge Router," adjust one side of the base so that the dual fences can fit over the 2¼-inch-wide side of the leg.

5 **Square up the mortises.** Start squaring up the ends of the mortises by driving a sharp, ½-inch chisel straight down with a hammer. Work with the chisel's bevel facing into the mortise, and with its cutting edge parallel to, and about 1/16 inch inside, the shoulder line. Pare to the line using hand pressure, removing a thin shaving. (See *Photo 3.*) Also check the bottom of the mortise to see if it needs to be cleaned up. Repeat this technique to finish off each mortise.

Photo 2: Mill mortises with a plunge router. The mortising base accessory shown here has a pair of fences to keep the bit aligned. You can also use a standard fence to do this.

Photo 3: Square up the rounded ends of each mortise with a ½-inch chisel.

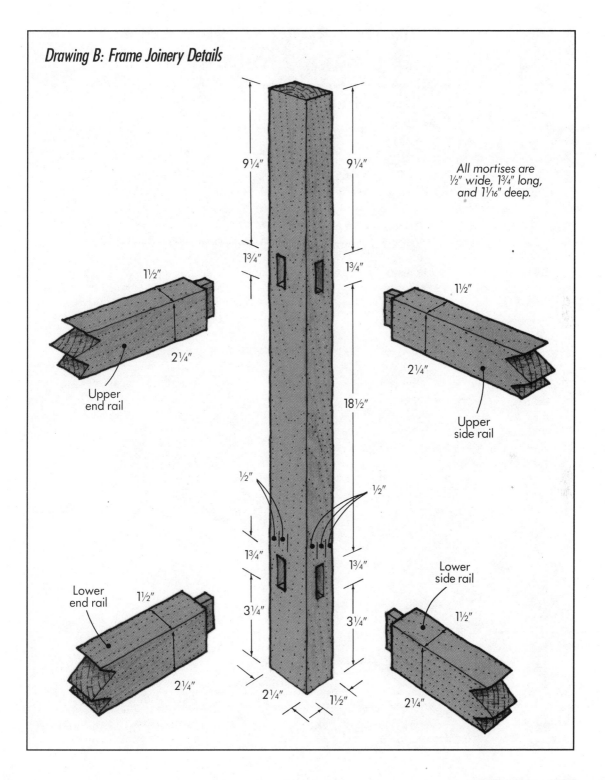

Drawing B: Frame Joinery Details

All mortises are ½" wide, 1¾" long, and 1¹⁄₁₆" deep.

9¼"   9¼"

1¾"   1¾"

1½"

2¼"

Upper
end rail

1½"

2¼"

Upper
side rail

18½"

½"   ½"

1¾"   1¾"

Lower
side rail

Lower
end rail

1½"

2¼"

3¼"   3¼"

1½"

2¼"

2¼"   1½"

Mortising with a Plunge Router

With plunge-cutting action and variable depth adjustments, plunge routers are well suited for mortising work. The best bit for mortising is a straight bit with an up-spiral pattern. The spiral flutes on this type of bit (high-speed steel or solid carbide) will pull waste wood out of the mortise as you work, leaving clean cheeks that are free of burn marks. These mortising bits are available in different diameters from many mail-order tool suppliers.

To guide the router and keep the bit moving in a straight line as you mill the full length of the mortise, you'll need to use a fence. Put the fence on the side of the mortise that is closest to you. Adjust the fence so that when it bears against the side or edge of the workpiece, the bit is perfectly aligned to mill the mortise. In situations where the mortise layout isn't centered on an edge or side, make sure the fence is bearing against the correct side.

As an alternative to using a standard router fence for mortising work, you can buy a special mortising base for your router. The clear acrylic mortising base made by Woodhaven (see "Sources" on page 360) has a pair of adjustable fences that improve stability and alignment when mortising with a plunge router.

Start the mortise by making two plunge-cuts at each end of the mortise, as if you were boring a pair of holes with a drill bit. Then remove the waste that remains between these holes. Do this in several passes, each about ¼-inch deeper than the one before. If you are using a standard fence which is guided on one side of the workpiece, be sure to rout from left to right; that way, the router rotation direction will work with you to keep the fence against the workpiece. With the double-fenced Woodhaven, this won't matter.

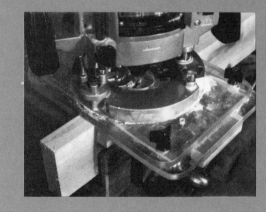

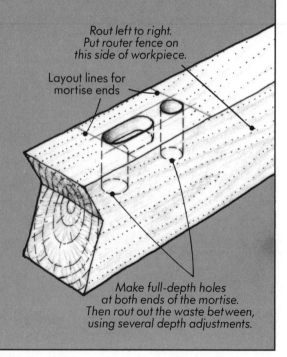

Rout left to right. Put router fence on this side of workpiece.

Layout lines for mortise ends

Make full-depth holes at both ends of the mortise. Then rout out the waste between, using several depth adjustments.

Making Rail Tenons

The tenons are cut on the table saw with a shop-made tenoning jig. This jig lets you cut several kinds of joints with speed and precision. (See "Make a Table Saw Tenoning Jig" on page 238.)

1 Make shoulder cuts. The tenon dimensions are shown in *Drawing C*. To make the tenons, adjust the table saw blade height to ½ inch. Attach a stop block to the rip fence, on the infeed side of the blade. Adjust the rip fence so that when you hold the end of the rail against the stop block, the rail is aligned for the shoulder cuts. Cut the shoulder on the 2¼-inch-wide sides of each rail. (See *Photo 4*.) Guide the rail with the miter gauge, set at 90 degrees. Cut shoulders in a scrap piece of rail stock, too. You'll use this scrap for test cuts.

Lower the blade height to ¼ inch and cut the shoulders in the edge of each rail. Hold the rail against the miter gauge, as before, and align each cut by butting the rail end against the stop block.

2 Make cheek cuts with the tenoning jig. With a rail held vertically in the jig, raise the height of the saw blade until it reaches the tenon's shoulder line. Adjust the

(continued on page 240)

Photo 4: Align the tenon shoulders by clamping a stop block to the rip fence. Guide the rail against the miter gauge to make each cut.

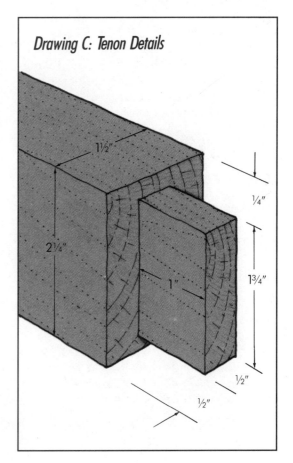

Drawing C: Tenon Details

1½"

2¼"

¼"

1"

1¾"

½"

½"

Make a Table Saw Tenoning Jig

The table saw tenoning jig shown here works the same way as the expensive manufactured jigs that you'll find in many commercial cabinetmaking shops. This jig is especially useful when you've got lots of tenons to cut. It's precise and easy to adjust for different tenon thicknesses. For best results, use clear hardwood for your jig's runners, and ¾-inch-thick hardwood plywood for the the fence, base, brace, and bottom. When building your own jig, you may have to adjust certain dimensions based on the design of your table saw.

Start by cutting the bottom, adjustable base, and fence to size. When cutting out these parts, make sure that they are all exactly the same width (10 inches). Let the length of the bottom and adjustable base run long, since both parts need to be trimmed square as the jig is made.

Cut a ⁵⁄₁₆-inch-wide, 6-inch-long adjustment slot in the adjustable base. You can do this using a plunge router and a straight bit, or by drilling a pair of ⁵⁄₁₆-inch-diameter holes and then cutting between them with a jigsaw.

Using the table saw dado cutter, mill matching dadoes in the bottom and the adjustable base, guiding edges against the rip fence. Position the rip fence 1¼ inches from the cutter. As shown in the drawing, it's important for the bottom and adjustable base dadoes to line up, so that the runners will work smoothly. Cut a pair of hardwood runners that fit snugly in these dadoes, and fasten them to the adjustable base, driving #6 × ¾-inch flathead wood screws into holes that are counterbored about ⅛ inch. Use three screws for each runner.

Now place the adjustable base on the bottom, with the runners in their slots, and drill a ⅛-inch-diameter guide hole, centered in the adjustment slot. On the underside of the piece, cut a recess around the hole so that a T-nut (sized to accept a ¼-inch-diameter carriage bolt) will fit flush with the wood surface. Enlarge the installation hole as necessary to accommodate the T-nut; then install it. Drill a hole in the wooden adjustment knob with a ¼-inch-diameter bit to hold the carriage bolt. The bolt must be long enough to extend through the knob and adjustment slot, engaging the T-nut without extending through the bottom of the sliding base. Attach the carriage bolt to the knob with epoxy.

Next, cut a hardwood guide strip to fit snugly in the table saw's miter gauge groove. Screw the strip to the underside of the bottom, at a right angle to the bottom's long edges. Counterbore these screws about ⅛ inch.

With the bottom and adjustable base clamped together by the knob and carriage bolt, place this assembly on the saw table, with the bottom's guide strip in the miter gauge groove. Now turn on the saw, and trim off the front edges of the bottom and adjustable base. This will make both edges exactly parallel with the miter gauge groove that will guide the jig.

Fasten the fence and brace to the adjustable base, driving 1⅝-inch drywall screws into countersunk holes. Make the working side of the fence flush with the front edge of the adjustable base, and make sure that the fence forms a right angle with the adjustable base, as shown in the drawing.

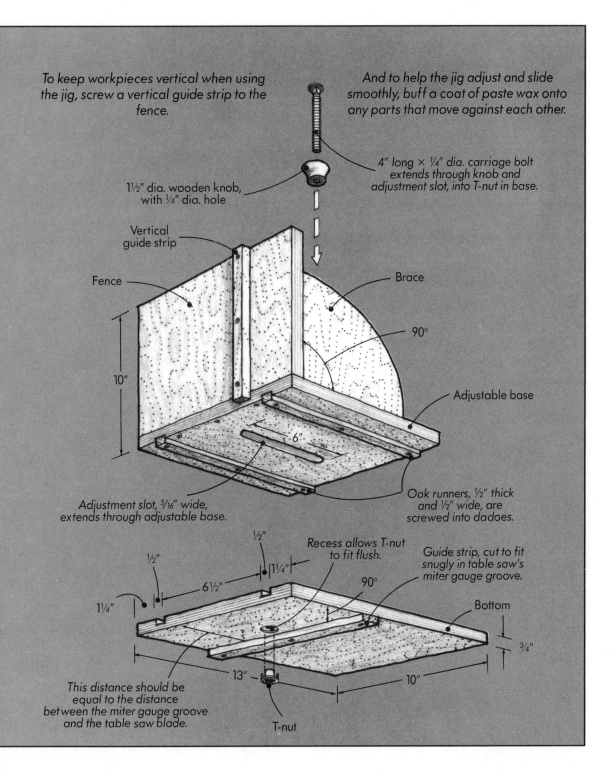

To keep workpieces vertical when using the jig, screw a vertical guide strip to the fence.

And to help the jig adjust and slide smoothly, buff a coat of paste wax onto any parts that move against each other.

4" long × ¼" dia. carriage bolt extends through knob and adjustment slot, into T-nut in base.

1½" dia. wooden knob, with ¼" dia. hole

Vertical guide strip

Fence

Brace

90°

10"

Adjustable base

6"

Oak runners, ½" thick and ½" wide, are screwed into dadoes.

Adjustment slot, ⁵⁄₁₆" wide, extends through adjustable base.

½"

½"

1¼"

1¼"

6½"

Recess allows T-nut to fit flush.

90°

Guide strip, cut to fit snugly in table saw's miter gauge groove.

Bottom

¾"

13"

10"

This distance should be equal to the distance between the miter gauge groove and the table saw blade.

T-nut

position of the jig's vertical fence to align the saw blade for a cheek cut. (See *Photo 5*.) Check this setup by making two cheek cuts in 2¼-inch-wide sides of the scrap piece you cut earlier. Test fit the tenon in the mortises. If the tenon fits too loosely, move the jig's vertical fence a little farther away from the blade. Move it closer if the tenon fits too tightly.

Cut two cheeks in each tenon. (See *Photo 6*.) When all these cuts have been made, reposition the jig's fence to cut out the top and bottom of each tenon. For these cuts, you'll be holding the rail edges against the fence. Keep the blade height the same.

Assembling the Cart

1 Test fit the joints. Do a trial assembly, without glue, to make sure that all mortise-and-tenon joints fit together well.

2 Glue the side rails to the legs. Put glue in the mortises that will hold side rail tenons. Use a small brush to spread glue evenly over the inside of each mortise. Then join a pair of side rails to a pair of legs. Because the legs are beefy and won't bend, you can pull these joints tight with a single pipe clamp, as shown in *Photo 7*. When the tenon shoulders have snugged up against the leg edges, check each assembly with a square to make sure that the legs and rails meet at right angles.

3 Glue the end rails to the side assemblies. Spread glue in the remaining mortises, and on the side rail tenons. Fit the side rails into their mortises, and tighten pipe

Photo 5: Adjust the fence of the tenoning jig to align the tenon cheek with the blade.

Photo 6: Cut each tenon cheek by holding the rail against the jig's fence and guide strip.

clamps to pull these joints together, checking as you clamp to make sure that the assemblies are square.

4 **Cut and install the diagonal supports.** Cut eight identical supports, mitering the support ends at a 45-degree angle. Position each support with its bottom edge flush with the bottom of the rails. Counterbore pilot holes for one 1¼-inch drywall screw at each joint. Glue and screw the supports into place. (See *Photo 8*.)

5 **Install casters.** Turn the cart upside down, and mark the center of each leg end by crossing diagonals. Then follow the manufacturer's instructions to install your casters. The casters used on this cart require a ½-inch-diameter installation hole 1¾ inches

deep. (See *Photo 9*.) A plastic sleeve fits in each hole and the metal stem of the caster fits in the sleeve.

Making the Shelves and Top

1 **Cut the shelves, top, and plastic laminate.** Check the measurements in the Materials List against the actual inside dimensions of the cart's frame. Cut the shelves and the top to finished sizes. Cut three pieces of plastic laminate, making each about 1 inch wider and longer than the plywood piece it will cover.

2 **Glue down the plastic laminate.** Using a clean brush, spread contact cement on the top surfaces of the shelves and top, and on the bottom surface of each piece of plastic

Photo 7: After spreading glue on the mortise-and-tenon joints, join the side rails to the legs, and pull the joints tight with pipe clamps.

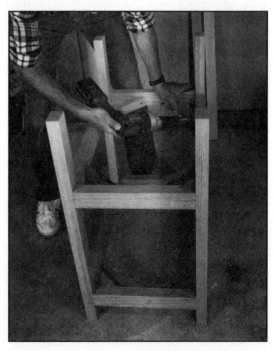

Photo 8: Glue and screw the diagonal supports between the rails.

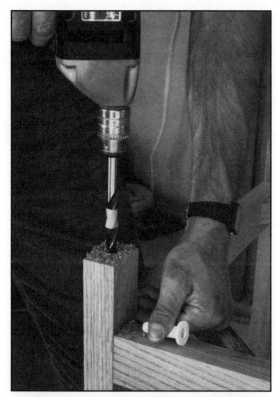

Photo 9: In the bottom of each leg, drill an installation hole for the plastic sleeve that holds the stem of the caster.

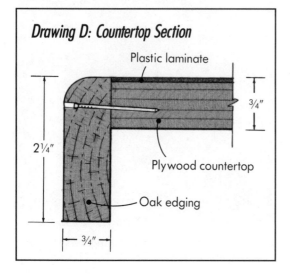

Drawing D: Countertop Section

Plastic laminate

3/4"

Plywood countertop

2¼"

Oak edging

3/4"

laminate. Work quickly with the brush, aiming for a thin but thorough coat. When the cement dulls after about 10 minutes, recoat the wood surfaces. (See *Photo 10*.) Wait another 15 minutes, or until the contact cement no longer sticks to your finger when you touch it. Then carefully hold a piece of laminate over the plywood, making sure that excess laminate will overhang all four plywood edges. Press both materials together, and then force the laminate firmly down, using hand pressure or a roller. Make sure you get the laminate positioned right the first time; you won't be able to lift it up or slide it.

3 Trim the laminate flush. Chuck a piloted flush-trimming bit in your router, and adjust the depth so that the pilot bearing will be guided against the plywood edge while the cutter trims the laminate. Clamp the top or shelf on the workbench, turn on the router, and then trim the laminate flush, as shown in *Photo 11*. Move the router counterclockwise, taking care to keep the base flat against the laminate surface. It will be easier to keep the router flat if you use an offset router base like the one shown in *Photo 11*. (See the Shop Savvy on page 282.) Use this technique to complete the flush-trimming work on the shelves and countertop.

4 Install the top edging. As shown in *Drawings A and D,* the countertop is edged in oak. The edging pieces are installed with their top edges flush with the laminate surface and meet at the corners with miter joints.

Begin by mitering one end of an edge piece. Align the mitered end against a corner of the countertop, and mark the opposite end for its miter cut. After making the second miter cut, predrill holes in this edge piece for two 4d finishing nails, and tack the piece into place. Now miter one end of a second edge piece and fit it against the first piece so that the second miter can be marked and cut. Tack this piece into place as well; then mark and cut the remaining two pieces.

After all four edge pieces have been cut, glue and nail them to the countertop's plywood edge and to each other. Tighten pipe clamps across the length and width of the countertop to pull edging joints tight. Wipe off any excess glue with a damp cloth.

Working by hand, or with an orbital sander, round-over the four mitered corners where the edging pieces join, as shown in *Photo 12*. Then rout a ⅜-inch roundover around the countertop.

To avoid damaging the laminate surfaces, sand and finish the cart's frame with the countertop and shelves removed. Give the countertop edging the same finish treatment as the rest of the cart. Once the final application of finish has dried, fit the shelves and countertop in place and roll the cart to work.

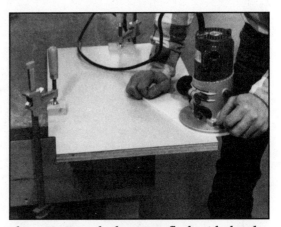

Photo 11: Trim the laminate flush with the plywood using a flush-trimming bit in the router.

Photo 10: Spread a thin coat of contact cement on the plywood shelves and on the underside of each piece of plastic laminate. Recoat the shelves with a second thin layer after the first layer soaks in. Once the cement dries to the touch, you can adhere the laminate.

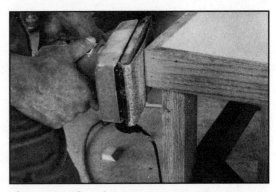

Photo 12: After the countertop's oak edging has been installed, round-over the sharp corner at each miter joint.

Jelly Cupboard

This jelly cupboard takes its name from Colonial times, when every household "put food by." Today its storage function can be a bit more versatile. It still works well as a pantry cabinet in the kitchen, but you're just as likely to find stereo equipment behind its door.

Patterned after an antique, this cupboard is authentic in proportion and style. It's even built like the original, with mortise-and-tenon joints and a frame-and-panel door. Like the original, this cupboard has a back made from pine boards that are joined together with wood splines—an early variation on the tongue-and-groove joint.

The cupboard's carcase is made from ¾-inch-thick "one-by" pine. The face frame and door frame are made from ⁵⁄₄ pine. The actual thickness of ⁵⁄₄ stock can vary slightly from one lumberyard to the next. For the projects in this book, we're assuming an actual thickness of 1³⁄₁₆ inches. If your ⁵⁄₄ stock measures out to a different thickness, you'll have to adjust the project dimensions slightly, or plane your ⁵⁄₄ boards down to 1³⁄₁₆ inches thick.

Building the Carcase

1 Glue up blanks for the sides and top. For these parts, you'll need to edge-glue some one-by boards. Make sure the edges are straight and square before gluing and clamping up. Once the glue has cured, scrape off any hardened glue and use a belt sander with an 80-grit sanding belt to smooth both sides of each blank.

2 Cut sides, shelves, and top to size. Finished dimensions of the sides and shelves are given in the Materials List. To lay out the shape of the top, see *Drawing B*. Right-angled stopped cuts are required to cut out the "ears" on the front corners of the top. Start each long cut on the table saw, using the rip fence to guide the waste side of the blank. Stop each of these cuts about 1½ inches before the blade crosses the layout line. Then finish the cutout by hand, using a fine-toothed crosscut saw (one with 10 or more points per inch).

3 Dado the sides and groove the top. Each side requires five dadoes. To lay out
(continued on page 248)

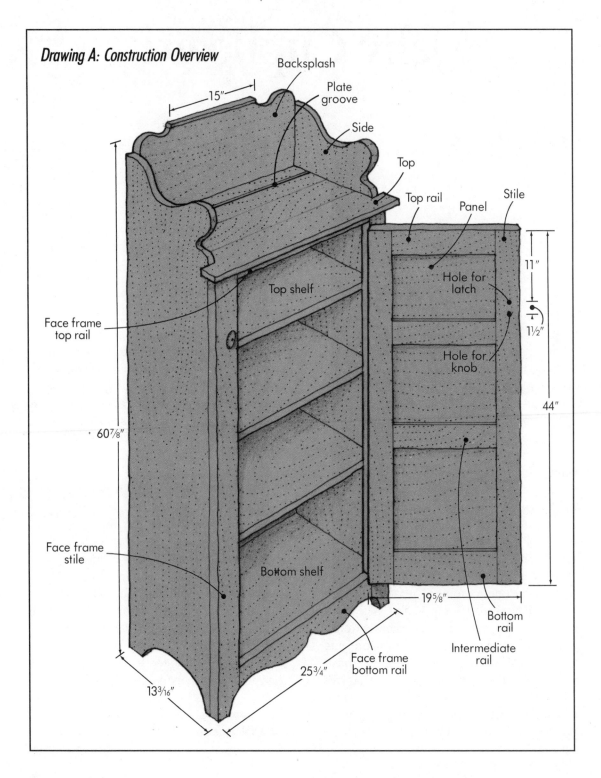

Drawing A: Construction Overview

Backsplash

Plate groove

15"

Side

Top

Top rail

Panel

Stile

Face frame top rail

Top shelf

Hole for latch

11"

1½"

Hole for knob

44"

60⅞"

Face frame stile

Bottom shelf

19⅝"

Bottom rail

Intermediate rail

13³⁄₁₆"

25¾"

Face frame bottom rail

Materials List

Wood

QTY	PART	DIMENSION
Carcase		
2	Pine sides	$\frac{3}{4}'' \times 12'' \times 59\frac{1}{4}''$
4	Pine shelves	$\frac{3}{4}'' \times 11\frac{1}{4}'' \times 25''$
1	Pine top	$\frac{3}{4}'' \times 13\frac{7}{16}'' \times 27\frac{1}{4}''$
2	Pine back boards	$\frac{3}{4}'' \times 11\frac{1}{4}'' \times 50\frac{7}{8}''$
1	Pine back board	$\frac{3}{4}'' \times 2\frac{1}{2}'' \times 50\frac{7}{8}''$
2	Pine splines	$\frac{1}{4}'' \times 1'' \times 50\frac{7}{8}''$
1	Pine backsplash	$\frac{3}{4}'' \times 10'' \times 25''$
1	Pine molding	$\frac{7}{8}'' \times 1'' \times 25''$
Face Frame		
2	Pine stiles	$1\frac{3}{16}'' \times 3'' \times 50\frac{1}{2}''$
1	Pine top rail	$1\frac{3}{16}'' \times 1\frac{1}{2}'' \times 22\frac{3}{4}''$
1	Pine bottom rail	$1\frac{3}{16}'' \times 3'' \times 22\frac{3}{4}''$
Frame-and-Panel Door		
2	Pine stiles	$1\frac{3}{16}'' \times 3'' \times 44''$

Wood

QTY	PART	DIMENSION
1	Pine bottom rail	$1\frac{3}{16}'' \times 4'' \times 16\frac{5}{8}''$
2	Pine intermediate rails	$1\frac{3}{16}'' \times 3'' \times 16\frac{5}{8}''$
1	Pine top rail	$1\frac{3}{16}'' \times 3'' \times 16\frac{5}{8}''$
1	Pine bottom panel	$\frac{3}{4}'' \times 13\frac{3}{4}'' \times 14\frac{5}{8}''$
1	Pine center panel	$\frac{3}{4}'' \times 11'' \times 14\frac{5}{8}''$
1	Pine top panel	$\frac{3}{4}'' \times 9\frac{1}{4}'' \times 14\frac{5}{8}''$
1	Wooden latch	$\frac{3}{4}'' \times 1'' \times 1\frac{1}{2}''$

Hardware

1 flathead wood screw, #8 $\times$ 1½"
2 pairs butt hinges, 1½" $\times$ 2½"
6d finishing nails, as needed
6d spiral-shank flooring nails, as needed
1 turned wooden knob, 1½" dia., with mounting screw

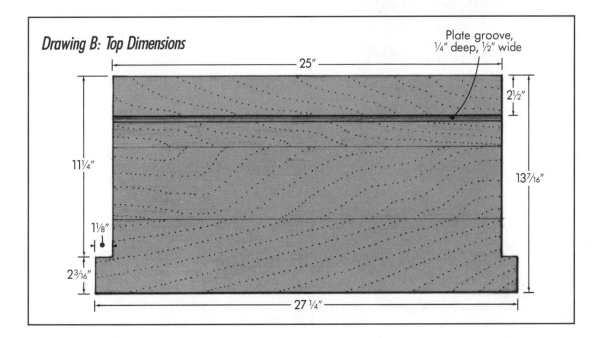

Drawing B: Top Dimensions

Plate groove, ¼" deep, ½" wide

25"

2½"

11¼"

13⁷⁄₁₆"

1⅛"

2³⁄₁₆"

27 ¼"

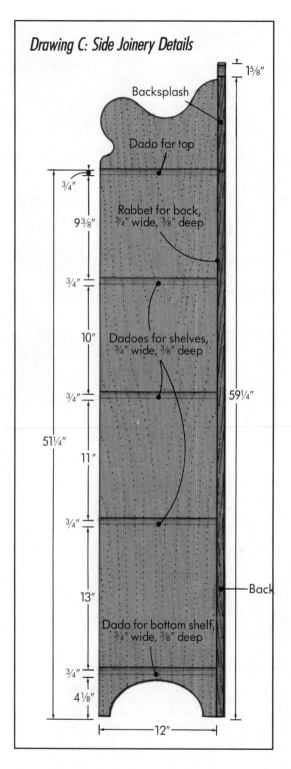

Drawing C: Side Joinery Details

Backsplash

Dado for top

1⅝"

¾"

9⅜"

Rabbet for back,
¾" wide, ⅜" deep

¾"

10"

Dadoes for shelves,
¾" wide, ⅜" deep

¾"

59¼"

51¼"

11"

¾"

13"

Back

¾"

Dado for bottom shelf,
¾" wide, ⅜" deep

¾"

4⅛"

12"

the dadoes, see *Drawing C*. A good way to mill these dadoes is to use a router and a right-angle jig like the one shown in "Make a Jig for Square Cutoffs and Dadoes" on page 270. Chuck a ¾-inch straight bit in the router, and adjust the depth of cut to ⅜ inch. Then use the jig to align each dado and to guide the base of the router.

The groove in the top will serve as a plate groove in the finished cupboard. Lay out and cut this groove as shown in *Drawing B*.

4 Rabbet the back edges of the sides. As shown in *Drawing D*, the back edge of each side is rabbeted to hold the back of the cupboard. You can mill these joints on the table saw, using a dado cutter. To guide the back edge of each side, fasten a wood auxiliary fence to the saw's rip fence. Adjust the cutter width to ¾ inch, and raise the cutter ⅜ inch above the table. Position the auxiliary fence so that the cutter just grazes it. To mill each rabbet, run the back edge of the side against the auxiliary fence, keeping the inside face of the piece flat on the saw table.

5 Bead the shelf edges. Beaded edges are traditional in a piece like this. As shown in *Drawing E,* the front edge profile of the three upper shelves includes a bead and a sanded roundover. You can mill these beads with your router, using a ¼-inch-radius beading bit. If you don't have this bit, or if you want to try a classic carpenter's trick, see the Shop Savvy on page 258.

6 Assemble sides, shelves, and top. Spread glue in the dadoes in one side, and then fit a shelf into each dado. Make sure that the bead on each shelf's front edge is facing down. The flat portion of each shelf's front edge should be flush with the front edge of the side. Secure each joint by driving three 6d finishing nails through the side and into the shelf ends. When the top and shelves have been joined to one side, join the remaining side as shown in *Photo 1*, again using glue and 6d finishing nails. Set all nail heads and fill the resulting holes with wood putty.

7 Cut curves into the sides. Each side extends above the top in a decorative curve. There's also a curved cutout at the bottom end of the side, to give the cupboard a lighter stance and to minimize rocking on an uneven floor. Patterns for both curves are shown in *Drawing F.* Enlarge these patterns to full-scale, and trace the curves onto the sides. (For tips on making and using patterns, see "Using Patterns" on page viii.) As an alternative, you can create a curved detail of your own that pleases your eye. After tracing the outline onto each side, cut the curves with a portable jigsaw. (See *Photo 2.*)

8 Make splines and grooved boards for the back. The traditional back for this cupboard consists of one-by boards with grooved edges that are joined together with wood splines. The groove-and-spline construction allows the back boards to expand and contract freely with changes in humidity.

Photo 1: Glue and nail the top and shelves to one side, then to the other.

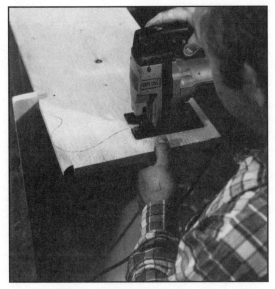

Photo 2: After tracing the pattern onto the side, make the curved top cut with the jigsaw.

The splines keep the board edges aligned while spanning any gaps between boards. (See *Drawing D*.)

The back boards for the cupboard shown are a pair of 1 × 12s (actual width is 11¼ inches) butted together and a single 2½-inch-wide board. You can use boards of different widths to yield a combined width of 25 inches. Cut all boards to a finished length of 50⅞ inches.

Mill grooves in the board edges on the table saw, guiding each board against a high wooden auxiliary fence screwed to the rip fence. Adjust the dado cutter to ¼ inch wide and ½ inch high. Then position the auxiliary fence ¼ inch from the dado cutter. Test the fence position on some scrap one-by stock to make sure that the grooves you'll be milling will be

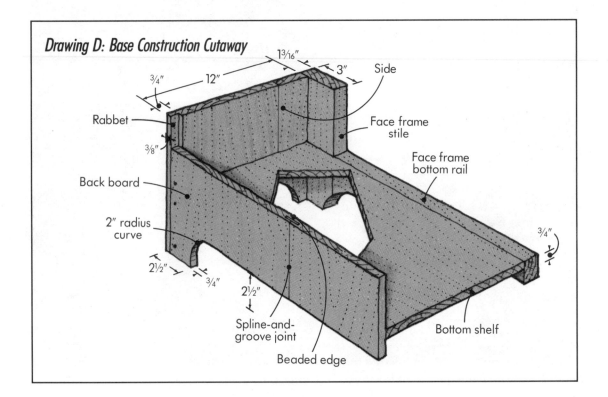

Drawing D: Base Construction Cutaway

13/16"
3/4"
12"
3"
Side
Rabbet
Face frame stile
3/8"
Face frame bottom rail
Back board
2" radius curve
3/4"
2½"
3/4"
2½"
Spline-and-groove joint
Beaded edge
Bottom shelf

centered on the board edges. Then mill grooves in all edges that will receive splines.

When all the grooves have been milled, rip splines from ⁵⁄₄ stock or from lattice molding. Make the splines ¼ inch thick, ¹⁵⁄₁₆ inch wide, and 50⅞ inches long. Test fit the board-and-spline assembly across the back of the cupboard; then mill a ¼-inch-diameter bead along one inside edge where boards meet each other. In other words, there should be a single bead along each edge-to-edge joint. This traditional edge treatment is shown in *Drawing D*. Again, you can use the method in the Shop Savvy on page 258, or use a ¼-inch beading bit in the router.

9 **Install the back.** When positioning the back boards and splines, make sure that the top edge of each board falls on the center of the top's back edge, as shown in *Drawing G* and in *Photo 3*. For an authentic look, use 6d spiral-shank flooring nails to fasten back boards against the top and shelves. The small heads on these nails resemble those on the old-fashioned wrought nails that were often used to fasten back boards onto Colonial cabinets. The spiral shanks on the flooring nails offer superior holding power. To avoid splitting the wood near the board edges, use a ⅛-inch-diameter bit to predrill nail holes. Drive several nails through back boards and into rabbeted sides as well. Take care not to drive nails through the splines.

10 **Cut and install the backsplash.** The pattern for the curved top of the backsplash is shown in *Drawing H*. Trace this shape onto some 1 × 12 stock, and cut out the curve with a jigsaw. Then cut a bead along the straight center section of the top edge. You can create this embellishment using a router and ¼-inch beading bit, or use the hand-

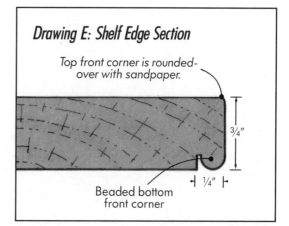

Drawing E: Shelf Edge Section

Top front corner is rounded-over with sandpaper.

¾"

¼"

Beaded bottom front corner

Photo 3: Back board edges are grooved to accept ¼-inch-thick splines. Note that the top edges of the back boards fall on the center line of the top's back edge.

Jelly Cupboard **251**

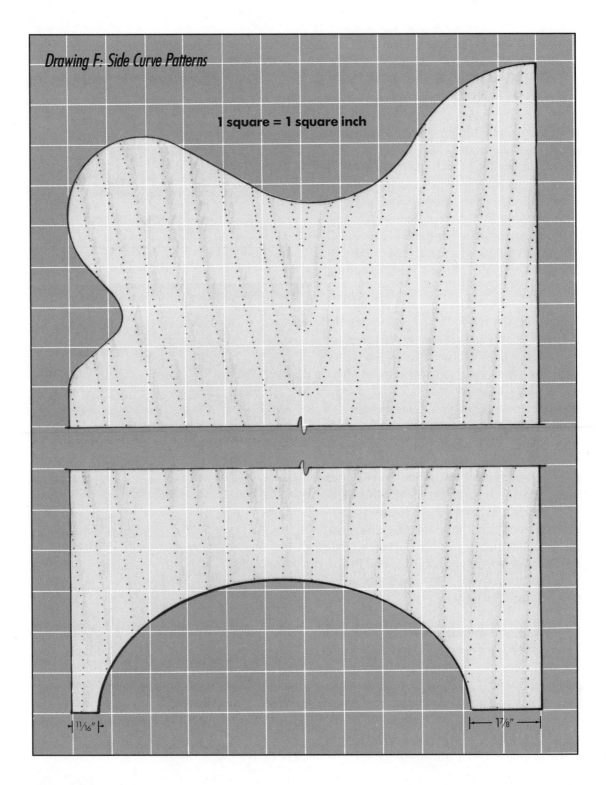

Drawing F: Side Curve Patterns

1 square = 1 square inch

$^{11}/_{16}"$

$1^{7}/_{8}"$

worked approach described in the Shop Savvy on page 258. Using a half-round file, shape the bead around the corner of the straight section, as shown in *Drawing H*.

Install the backsplash by driving 6d spiral-shank flooring nails into predrilled holes through the backsplash edges and into the back edges of the top and sides.

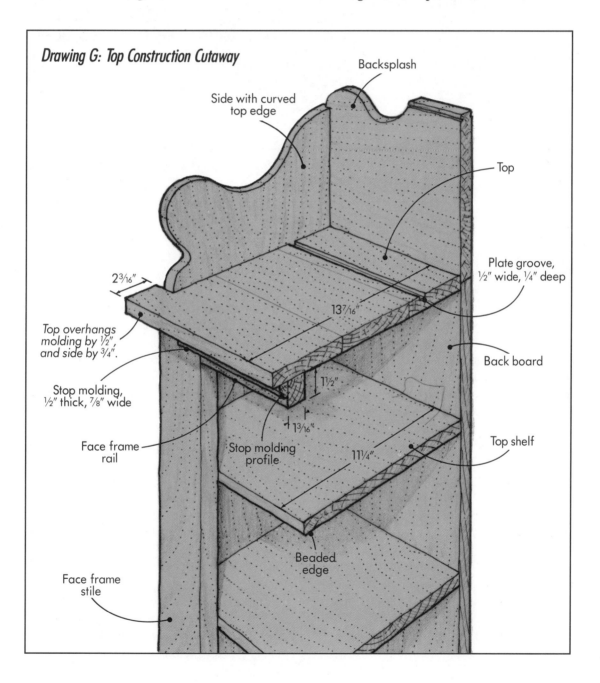

Drawing G: Top Construction Cutaway

Backsplash

Side with curved top edge

Top

Plate groove, $\frac{1}{2}$" wide, $\frac{1}{4}$" deep

$2\frac{3}{16}$"

$13\frac{7}{16}$"

Top overhangs molding by $\frac{1}{2}$", and side by $\frac{3}{4}$".

Back board

Stop molding, $\frac{1}{2}$" thick, $\frac{7}{8}$" wide

$1\frac{1}{2}$"

$1\frac{3}{16}$"

Face frame rail

Stop molding profile

$11\frac{1}{4}$"

Top shelf

Beaded edge

Face frame stile

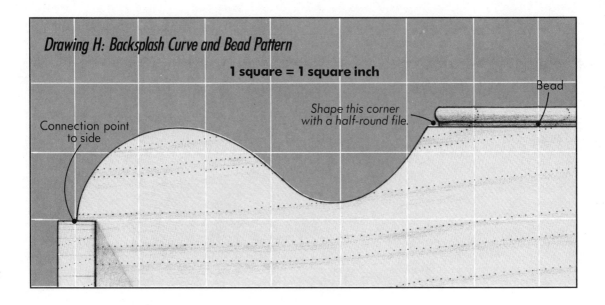

Drawing H: Backsplash Curve and Bead Pattern

1 square = 1 square inch

Connection point to side

Shape this corner with a half-round file.

Bead

Making the Stiles and Rails

As shown in *Drawing A,* the cupboard's face frame and door frame consist of vertical members called stiles, and horizontal members called rails. Both frames are assembled with mortise-and-tenon joints. (See *Drawing I* and *Drawing J*.) Because there are quite a few mortises and tenons in this project, it's important to do the cutting and joinery work in the right order. The sequence presented here allows you to take full advantage of each setup on the table saw before changing blade height or fence position for another operation.

1 Cut the stiles and rails to size. Before cutting the stiles and rails to the dimensions given in the Materials List, check the front of the carcase to make sure it measures 25¾ inches wide and 50½ inches high (from bottom of side to underside of top). If not, adjust the face frame members to fit. In this design, the height and width of the door are ⅛ inch smaller than the face frame opening.

Cut all frame members from ⁵⁄₄ stock, and label each frame member as it's cut.

2 Cut grooves for the door panels. Put a dado cutter on the table saw with its width set to ⅜ inch. Raise the cutter ⁹⁄₁₆ inch above the table. Then position the rip fence so that the grooves are centered along the edges of door frame members. Test your setup by milling sample grooves in some scrap ⁵⁄₄ stock, and adjust as necessary. Then run frame members through, applying pressure against the fence and table, as shown in *Photo 4.*

3 Mortise the stiles. Lay out the face frame mortises as shown in *Drawing I* and the door frame mortises as shown in *Drawing J.*

Chuck a ⅜-inch-diameter drill bit in your electric drill, and wrap a piece of masking tape around the bit 1½ inches from its tip. Then bore a series of closely spaced holes inside the layout lines for each mortise. Use the tape on the bit as a depth-stop indicator.

(See *Photo 5*.) Once you've roughed out all the mortises, use a ⅜-inch-wide chisel to square up the ends of each mortise. Then smooth mortise cheeks with a ¾-inch-wide chisel. For an alternative method of milling mortises—using a plunge router—see "Mortising with a Plunge Router" on page 236.

4 Mill tenons in the rails. All rail tenons are 1½ inches long and ⅜ inch thick, but their widths vary. To minimize setup changes, you'll mill all the tenons to length and thickness. Then you'll go back and cut them to width. To avoid confusion, the top rail on *Drawing I* is labeled to show which tenon dimensions are referred to as length, thickness, and width.

Photo 4: Mill grooves in frame members on the table saw, using the dado cutter. Adjust cutter width to ⅜ inch, and cutter height to 9/16 inch.

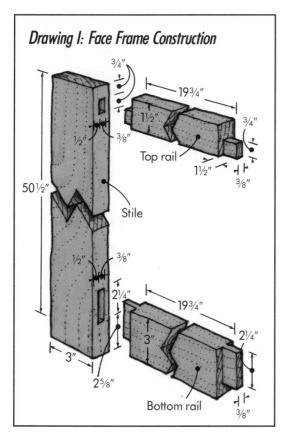

Drawing I: Face Frame Construction

¾"

19¾"

1½"

¾"

½"

⅜"

Top rail

1½"

⅜"

50½"

Stile

½"

⅜"

2¼"

19¾"

3"

2¼"

3"

2⅝"

Bottom rail

⅜"

Photo 5: Drill out mortises with a ⅜-inch-diameter bit. Tape wrapped around the bit acts as a depth stop.

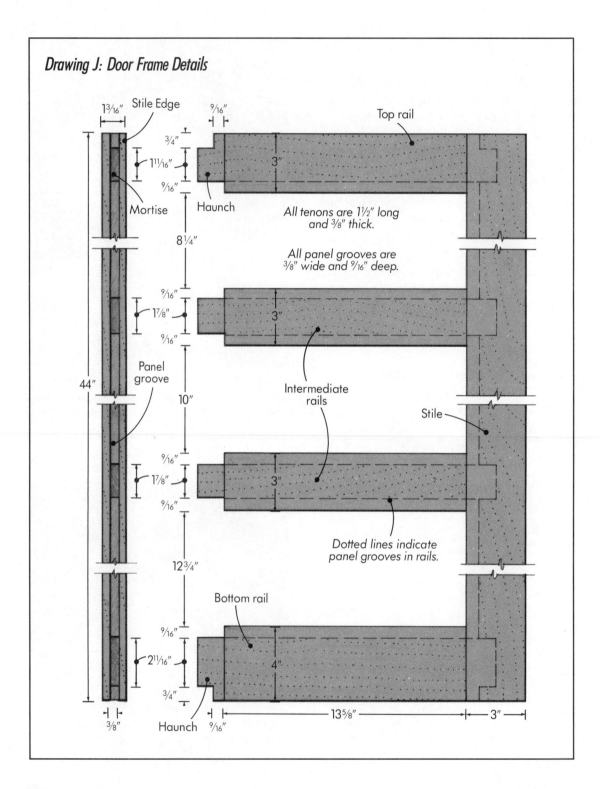

Drawing J: Door Frame Details

Stile Edge

1³⁄₁₆"

⁹⁄₁₆"

Top rail

Mortise

¾"

1¹¹⁄₁₆"

⁹⁄₁₆"

Haunch

3"

All tenons are 1½" long and ⅜" thick.

All panel grooves are ⅜" wide and ⁹⁄₁₆" deep.

8¼"

⁹⁄₁₆"

1⅞"

⁹⁄₁₆"

3"

Panel groove

Intermediate rails

10"

⁹⁄₁₆"

1⅞"

⁹⁄₁₆"

3"

Stile

44"

Dotted lines indicate panel grooves in rails.

12¾"

Bottom rail

⁹⁄₁₆"

2¹¹⁄₁₆"

4"

¾"

⅜"

Haunch

⁹⁄₁₆"

13⁵⁄₈"

3"

Make the tenons in a series of cuts with the dado cutter. Start by adjusting the dado cutter to its maximum width and by setting its height to ⅜ inch. Turn on the saw, and use the miter gauge (set to 90 degrees) to guide a scrap piece of ¾ stock through the cutter. Flip the stock over and make another pass through the cutter to complete a short sample tenon. Check how this tenon thickness matches your mortise width. If necessary, adjust the cutter height and try again until you get a tenon that will fit snugly without being forced. Adjustments will be minute: Raising the blade ¹⁄₃₂ inch will reduce tenon thickness by ¹⁄₁₆ inch.

To set up the saw to give you the right tenon length, attach a guide block to the rip fence on the *infeed* side of the cutter, as shown in *Photo 6*. To position the fence, put a rail into the miter gauge, face down. Align the layout line for the tenon shoulder with the edge of the dado cutter, and ease the fence over until the guide block butts against the end of the rail. Lock the fence in place, and check your setup on a piece of scrap. Cut the shoulder first, then move the rail end away from the guide block as you make repeated overlapping passes to "nibble" away the rest of the tenon cheek. Cut all the tenons this way.

Now cut all the face frame tenons to width. Raise the dado cutter to ¾ inch, but don't change the fence setting. Use the guide block to align the face frame rails as you cut their tenons. For these cuts, hold the rail on edge, with its side against the miter gauge.

To cut the haunched tenons, first cut one shoulder as above. Then move the fence ⁹⁄₁₆ inch closer to the blade, and then cut the second shoulder to create the haunch. (See *Drawing J*.)

Test fit the face frame and door frame assemblies to make sure that all joints go together well. Use a chisel as necessary to pare down tenons or enlarge mortises when the joints are too tight.

Photo 6: Cut rail tenons using the table saw dado cutter. A stop block, attached to the rip fence on the infeed side of the blade, aligns each rail for its shoulder cut. Guide the rail against the table saw's miter gauge to make shoulder and cheek cuts.

Shop Savvy

Beading with a Flathead Screw

Long before routers and beading bits came on the scene, old-time carpenters relied on a quick and easy way to bead the edge of a board. You can duplicate this simple technique with a flathead screw and a small block of wood. For a bead with a radius of about ¼ inch, use a #8 flathead screw that's at least an inch long.

Drive the screw into the squared-off end of a block of wood, allowing the head to stand about ¼ inch proud of the surface. Now run the end of the block against the edge of the stock as shown in the top photo. Keeping the block (and screw shank) horizontal, bear down so that the edge of the screw's head shaves a small channel into the stock. Move your beading tool up and down the edge of the stock repeatedly until you've cut an even channel. For more effective shaving action, you can sharpen the screw's cutting surfaces with a file. Complete the bead's profile by rounding-over the corner with a block plane or some sandpaper.

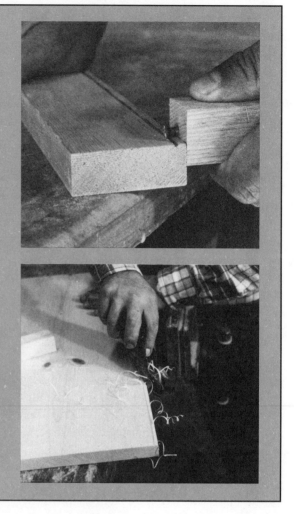

Raising Panels on the Table Saw

The panel-raising technique described here is a good one to use if you prefer to work strictly on the table saw. But there are other ways to make panels for use in frame-and-panel construction. For more information, see "Panel Alternatives" on page 263.

1 Cut panel blanks to size. Frame dimensions are important when sizing panels: Panels should float in their frames, with about ¹⁄₁₆ inch of clearance at each edge, so that they can expand and contract with humidity changes. Since the grooves are ⁹⁄₁₆ inch deep, each panel should be 1 inch larger than the length and width of the opening where it will fit. So use the panel dimensions in the Materials List only as a guide. To calculate exact panel sizes, always measure the actual dimensions of the frame opening. To make the larger panels for the two lower frame openings, you'll probably have to glue two or more boards together.

2 **Make reveal cuts.** The reveal cuts define the border of the flat "raised" field in the middle of each panel. Adjust the table saw blade to show just ⅛ inch above the table. Then set the rip fence 1⅝ inches away from the blade. Guiding the panel edges against the rip fence, make four cuts in the outside face of each panel. (See *Photo 7.*)

3 **Make bevel cuts.** To set up the table saw for beveling panel edges, adjust the angle of the saw blade to 78 degrees (12 degrees off square) and raise the blade 1⅝ inches above the table. Screw a tall auxiliary fence to the rip fence, using a straight piece of wood that's at least 14 inches long and 12 inches high. Position the rip fence so that the blade tilts away from the auxiliary fence, and so that there's 5/16 inch of space between the auxiliary

fence and the blade at the table surface. Before running your panels through this setup, it's a good idea to make one or more bevel cuts in some scrap one-by stock. You should remove a triangular section of waste, cutting just high enough to reach the reveal that was cut in the previous step. (See *Photo 8.*)

When all bevel cuts have been made, smooth any saw marks from beveled areas using 150-grit sandpaper or a scraper.

Completing the Face Frame and Door

1 **Install the face frame.** Rest the cupboard on its back and test fit the frame on the cabinet, as shown in *Drawing A.* Butt the face frame under the top and make sure the top of the bottom rail is flush with the top of the bottom shelf. The outside edges of the face

Photo 7: Make reveal cuts for raised panels with the table saw blade ⅛ inch high. Position the rip fence 1⅝ inches from the blade.

Photo 8: Tilt the blade 12 degrees off vertical to make bevel cuts, completing the raised panel profile. Position the rip fence 5/16 inch from the blade.

frame stiles should be flush with the sides of the cupboard. If these edges stand slightly proud of the sides, plane them flush. Then disassemble the parts, and glue the frame together and to the front of the cupboard. Secure the frame while the glue dries by driving 6d finishing nails through the face frame and into the front edges of the sides. Also nail the bottom rail to the bottom shelf.

With a portable jigsaw, make the curved cut in the face frame stiles and bottom rail to finish off the bottom of the cupboard. The pattern for this cutout is shown in *Drawing K*.

2 Assemble the door. Before gluing the door frame members together, put the entire door assembly through a dry run, fitting panels into their openings while joining rails to stiles. You may find it necessary to

sand or plane down one or more beveled areas so that a panel can fit into its grooves. When you're sure that all parts go together smoothly, permanently assemble the door by gluing rail tenons into their mortises. Keep glue out of panel grooves, so that panels can float in their frames. It's a good idea to clamp one stile horizontally in your bench vice, and then secure rails and panels as shown in *Photo 9*. Attach the opposite stile last. Check that the assembly is square, then use several pipe clamps to pull joints tight while the glue sets. Check again to see if the assembly is square, to make sure uneven clamping pressure hasn't racked the assembly.

3 Install the door. First, mortise a pair of butt hinges into the stile on one side of the door. (See "Mortising for a Butt Hinge" on

Photo 9: Fit raised panels after joining door rails to a door stile.

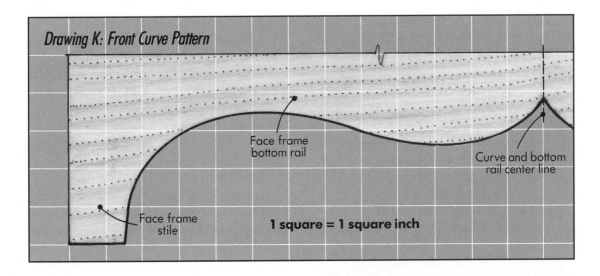

Drawing K: Front Curve Pattern

Face frame
bottom rail

Curve and bottom
rail center line

Face frame
stile

1 square = 1 square inch

page 93.) Locate each hinge 4 inches from the top or bottom corner of the door. Next, put the cupboard on its back and place the door in its opening. Position the door so there's equal space between the frame and the top and bottom of the door. Then lay out hinge mortises in the face frame stile as shown in *Photo 10*. Remove the door from its opening, complete the hinge layout, and chisel out hinge mortises in the face frame stile. When this is done, screw the door hinges into place.

Installing the Latch, Knob, and Trim

1 Install the doorknob. The knob specified in the Materials List can be bought at most hardware stores. In the door stile, drill the hole for the doorknob's installation screw 11 inches down from the top corner of the door. Center the hole across the stile's width, and use a bit whose diameter matches that of the screw.

2 Make and install the door latch. The handmade latch on this cupboard is a nice

Photo 10: After installing hinges on the door, fit the door into its opening and lay out hinge mortises in the face frame stile.

traditional touch. Trace a football-shaped pattern around a ¼-inch-diameter hole drilled in ¾-inch pine. Make the pattern about 1 inch wide and 1½ inches long. Then cut out the catch with a coping saw, and chisel it into a tapered form. (See *Photo 11*.) Using a 1½-inch-long #8 flathead wood screw, secure the latch to the face frame stile about 1½ inches above the doorknob location. Drill a pilot hole for the screw before driving it.

3 Cut and install molding beneath the top. The profile and location of this molding are shown in *Drawing G*. If you can't find a match for this profile at the lumberyard, you can substitute a simple stop or cove molding. It's also possible to make your own molding using the router and one or more bits. With a coping saw, cut the ends of the molding into a curve that matches the molding profile. To do this, simply place a short scrap piece of the molding against the flat back face of the molding that will be installed. Now trace the molding profile onto the workpiece. Cut out this profile using a coping saw. When both ends have received this treatment, soften their edges with sandpaper.

Photo 11: The handmade latch is cut out around a ¼-inch-diameter hole and shaped with a chisel.

Panel Alternatives

Frame-and-panel construction doesn't always require the use of raised panels made from solid wood. As an alternative, you can use flat plywood panels that are as thick as the frame grooves are wide. Most lumberyards can order plywood in different thicknesses and with different face veneers. This makes it possible to achieve a traditional frame-and-panel appearance without the work of raising panels. For example, if your frame members are made from pine, and frame grooves are 1/4 inch wide, you'll need to order 1/4-inch-thick plywood with pine face veneers.

If true raised panels are what you're after, you can raise them with your router instead of on the table saw. Mail-order tool catalogues offer a wide selection of panel-raising bits. (See "Sources" on page 360.) Most panel-raising bits have a pilot bearing, so they can be guided along the edges of the panel blank. But because these bits are big, it's safer to use them in a router table. Always mill the panel in several passes, deepening the cut with each pass until you reach the final profile.

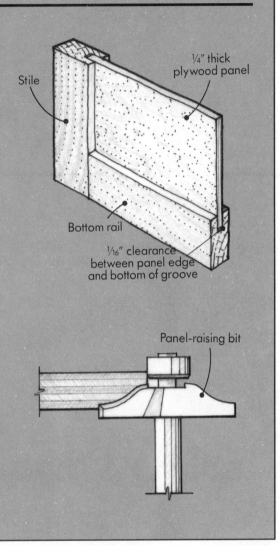

Stile

1/4" thick plywood panel

Bottom rail

1/16" clearance between panel edge and bottom of groove

Panel-raising bit

Office
&
Study

Basic Bookcase

This basic bookcase is both sturdy and elegant. It's designed to be built easily from a single sheet of ¾-inch-thick plywood and a small amount of pine one-by stock. The birch plywood used for the sides and shelves shown here is a wise choice if you plan a painted finish. If you want to use a stained or clear finish, you might want to consider another type of hardwood-veneered plywood. You can make the face frame from wood of the same species as the plywood face veneers. For contrast, you could mix a light plywood, like oak, with a dark hardwood, like walnut.

Making Sides and Shelves

1 **Cut sides, shelves, and top to size.**
Unless your table saw is set up with large extension tables, it's easier to use a circular saw to cut parts to rough size than to wrestle a 4 × 8-foot sheet of plywood over your table saw. Make all of your pieces about ¼ inch wider and longer than the finished dimensions in the Materials List. Then set up the rip fence on your table saw to rip sides and shelves to their finished widths. (See *Photo 1*.)

Photo 1: Cut shelves and sides to their finished widths on the table saw.

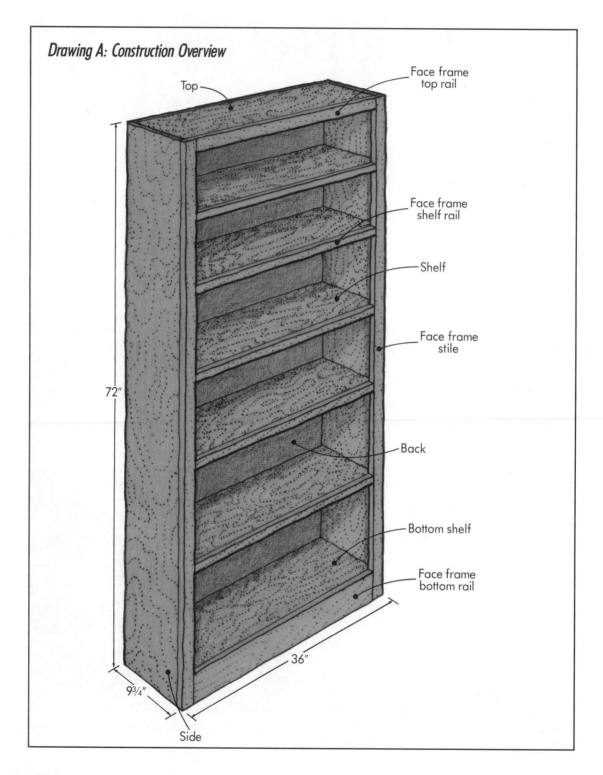

Drawing A: Construction Overview

Top

Face frame top rail

Face frame shelf rail

Shelf

Face frame stile

Back

Bottom shelf

Face frame bottom rail

72"

36"

9¾"

Side

For this project to come out well, it's important for sides and shelves to have square ends. Sides should also be identical in length. The same is true for the shelves and top.

It's difficult to crosscut long pieces like these on the table saw. For precise cutoff work, you can make a jig like the one shown on page 270 ("Make a Jig for Square Cutoffs and Dadoes") and in *Photo 2*.

2 Rabbet back edges of the sides. As shown in *Drawing B*, these rabbets will hold the ¼-inch-thick plywood back of the bookcase. Mill these ½-inch-wide, ¼-inch-deep rabbets on the router table, using a straight bit with a diameter of ½ inch or greater. Adjust the router so that the bit shows ½ inch above the table. Then adjust the fence so that only ¼ inch of the bit extends beyond

(continued on page 273)

Materials List

Wood

QTY	PART	DIMENSION
Carcase		
2	Plywood sides	¾" × 9" × 72"
7	Plywood shelves and top	¾" × 8¾" × 35¼"
1	Plywood back	¼" × 35½" × 68¾"
Face Frame		
2	Pine stiles	¾" × 1¾" × 72"
1	Pine bottom rail	¾" × 4" × 32½"
1	Pine top rail	¾" × 1¾" × 32½"
5	Pine shelf rails	¾" × 1" × 32½"

Hardware

6d finishing nails, as needed   4d finishing nails, as needed
¾" paneling nails, as needed

Photo 2: Cut the shelves and bookcase sides square with a square-cutting jig. The base of the circular saw rides against a straightedge guideboard.

Make a Jig for Square Cutoffs and Dadoes

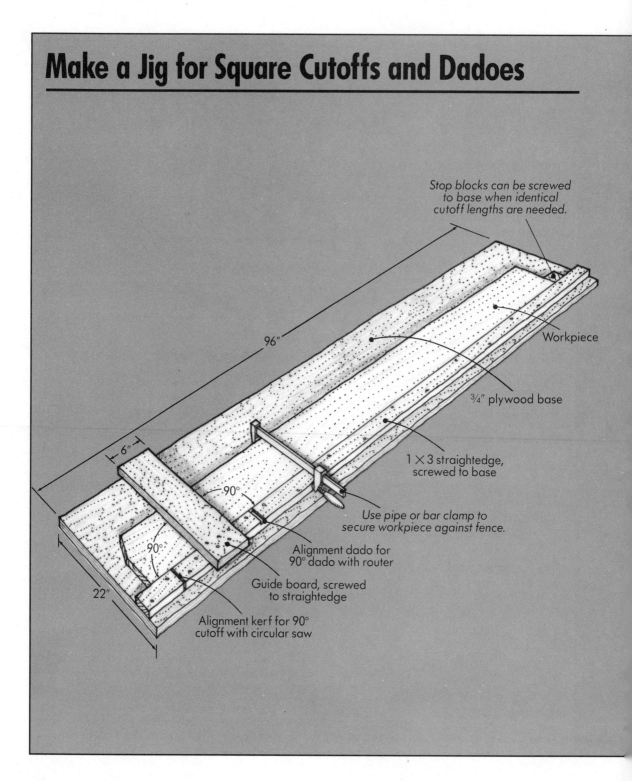

Stop blocks can be screwed to base when identical cutoff lengths are needed.

96"

Workpiece

¾" plywood base

1 × 3 straightedge, screwed to base

6"

90°

Use pipe or bar clamp to secure workpiece against fence.

Alignment dado for 90° dado with router

Guide board, screwed to straightedge

90°

22"

Alignment kerf for 90° cutoff with circular saw

When large parts have to be cut, it's usually best to keep the *workpiece* stationary and move the *tool* to make the cut. Radial arm saws and panel cutters are two power tools that work on this principle. With the jig shown here, you can duplicate the precision of a radial arm saw or a panel cutter, using a circular saw or a router.

To make the jig, start with a base of ¾-inch-thick AC plywood. You can use the full 96-inch length of a 4 × 8 panel as shown in the drawing, or make a smaller version of the jig. Jig width can also vary, depending on the scale of your projects.

The most important parts of the jig are the straightedge and the guide board that are fastened to it. For the straightedge, choose a clear, flat board (either pine or plywood) that has at least one perfectly straight edge. You can use the "factory" edge from a plywood panel, or run the edge of a pine 1 × 3 across the jointer to get a straight, square surface. Make the straightedge at least 2½ inches wide and as long as the base. Fasten the straightedge to the base as shown in the drawing, driving 1¼-inch drywall screws into countersunk pilot holes.

The guide board length should equal the base width. You can locate the guide board anywhere along the jig, or move it to different spots after one operation is complete. The edges of the guide board must be parallel, straight, and square. Rip one edge on the table saw and then set the fence to make a slightly narrower rip. Turn the

board edge for edge, and make a rip at the new fence setting. The resulting edges will be parallel, straight, and square.

Attach the guide board to the straightedge, as shown. Use a framing square to keep the guide board perpendicular to the straightedge as you work. Screw the guide board into place by driving 1¼-inch drywall screws into countersunk pilot holes.

To use the jig for square cuts, put a fine-cutting crosscut blade in your circular saw, square the blade to the base, and adjust the depth of cut to ¾ inch. Then make an alignment kerf in the straightedge by guiding the edge of the saw base against one edge of the guide board. With the workpiece held against the straightedge, you can line up the cutoff line with the alignment kerf and make your cut. To produce identical lengths, measure from the alignment kerf and screw a stop block to the base, as shown in the drawing.

Use a similar technique for milling dadoes, although dado depth will usually be less than ¾ inch. Rout an alignment dado in the straightedge. Align the layout lines with the dado to position the board.

If necessary, you can move the guide board for different cutting or milling work. You can also attach a guide board at a predetermined angle to the straightedge, and use the jig to make precise cuts (or dadoes) at different angles. Replace the straightedge when it becomes too full of alignment kerfs or dadoes.

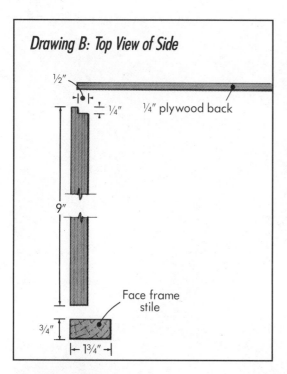

Drawing B: Top View of Side

½"

¼" plywood back

¼"

9"

Face frame
stile

¾"

1¾"

Photo 3: Rabbet the back edge of each side on the router table, using a straight bit. Bit height is ½ inch, and the bit should show ¼ inch beyond the fence.

Photo 4: Mill dadoes in both sides at once using the square-cutting jig. Sides are clamped against the jig's straightedge. The router base rides against the edge of the guide board, which is screwed to the straightedge.

it. Test this setup on some scrap stock, and adjust the bit height and fence position if necessary. Then mill each rabbet by holding the back edge of the side against the fence, and the inside face of the side against the table. (See *Photo 3.*)

3 **Lay out dadoes for the shelves and rabbets for the top.** Each side requires six dadoes for the shelves and a single rabbet for the top, as shown in *Drawing C*. This layout provides the tallest shelf space at the bottom of the bookcase. You can alter shelf spacing to fit your needs.

Place the sides together in the cutoff and dadoing jig, with rabbetted back edges butting against each other and facing up. Align the boards so the ends are flush. Run your tape measure up the length of the sides, near the center rabbets, and lay out the dadoes with a sharp pencil. Then use a framing square to extend these marks across the width of both sides.

Mill shelf dadoes and rabbets as shown in *Photo 4*, using the router (with ¾-inch straight bit) and the cutoff and dadoing jig. Adjust bit depth to ⅜ inch, and clamp sides together against the jig's straightedge, as shown in the photo. Note: If the plywood you're using doesn't measure exactly ¾ inch thick, then you should dado and rabbet the sides using a ½-inch straight bit, and follow the instructions in "Rabbet and Dado Joinery Solves Shelf Thickness Problems" on page 275.

Assembling the Bookcase

1 **Glue and nail shelves to sides.** Before assembling the case, start 6d finishing nails into the outside face of one side. Drive three nails along the rabbet and into each

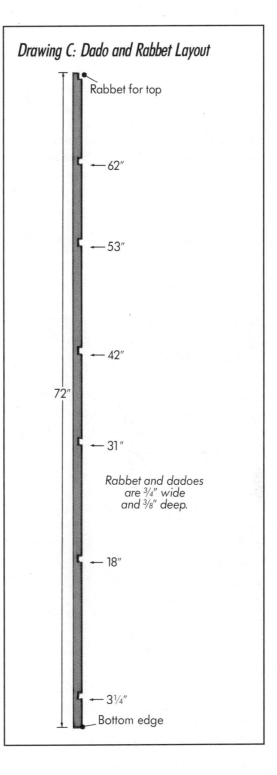

Drawing C: Dado and Rabbet Layout

Rabbet for top

← 62″

← 53″

← 42″

72″

← 31″

Rabbet and dadoes
are ¾″ wide
and ⅜″ deep.

← 18″

← 3¼″

Bottom edge

dado. Center the nails in the width of the dadoes and rabbet and drive them just far enough into the wood to stay there, but not so far that they come through the other side.

Assemble the bookcase on a large, flat work surface. Spread glue along the bottom and sides of a single dado. Working with front edges facing up, make sure the front of the shelf is flush to the front of the side and then nail the joint together. Repeat this gluing and nailing process until all six shelves and the top are secured to one side.

Position this subassembly so that the free ends of the shelves face up. Spread glue in the remaining shelf joints, and fit the opposite side

Photo 5: Glue and nail the shelves first to one side and then to the other.

over the ends of the shelves. (See *Photo 5*.) Check each joint to make sure the front edges of the sides and shelves are flush as you nail joints fast with 6d finishing nails.

2 **Square up shelves and sides.** Place the assembly on a flat surface, with front edges facing up. Make sure the assembly is square by comparing diagonal measurements. If it is square, the distance between opposite corners should be equal. If necessary, carefully rack sides and shelves until diagonal measurements are equal. Secure this position by nailing a temporary diagonal brace across one corner of the assembly. The brace should extend from a side across at least one intermediate shelf to the top.

3 **Install the back.** Turn the bookcase over so that back edges face up. Measure the back from top to bottom and across the rabbets and cut the back to fit, adjusting the dimensions in the Materials List if necessary. Spread a light coat of glue along the side rabbets and along the back edges of the shelves. Then slip the back into position. Its top edge should be flush with the top of the case. The back's lower edge should cover the back edge of the bottom shelf. Nail the back to the sides and shelves with ¾-inch paneling nails.

Installing the Face Frame

The face frame covers the front edges of the plywood sides and shelves. Both the vertical stiles and the horizontal rails are cut from pine one-by stock. (See *Drawing D*.) For best results, cut face frame members from clear, straight boards.

1 **Rip stock and install stiles.** Rip ¾-inch-thick pine boards to the widths in

Rabbet and Dado Joinery
Solves Shelf Thickness Problems

Plywood sold as ¾-inch-thick material usually doesn't measure up. Because the manufacturer often sands the plywood, it's common to buy "¾-inch-thick" plywood that actually measures ¹¹⁄₁₆ inch thick.

While this discrepancy doesn't affect the strength of the plywood, it can cause some joinery problems. An ¹¹⁄₁₆-inch-thick shelf will not fit snugly in a dado that is milled with a standard ¾-inch straight router bit. To cope with differences between router bit diameter and plywood thickness, use the dado and rabbet strategy shown here.

You'll need a ½-inch straight bit and a ⅜-inch rabbeting bit. With the straight bit, rout ½-inch-wide, ⅜-inch-deep dadoes in the sides for each shelf. To hold the top shelf, mill a rabbet ½ inch wide and ⅜ inch deep. Guide the router against a straight-edge as you cut. The jig shown in *Photo 4* and described on page 270 ensures straight, square milling.

Now chuck the ⅜-inch rabbeting bit in your router. Adjust the bit's depth of cut to leave a tongue that is exactly ½ inch thick. Test your setup by milling rabbets in a scrap piece of plywood cut from the same panel as your shelves. When the setup is correct, rabbet all the shelves.

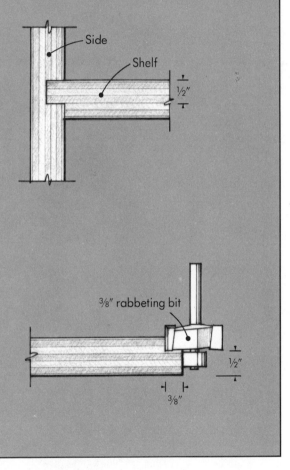

the Materials List. Cut the stiles to length and then glue and nail each stile to the sides and shelves with 4d finishing nails. Make sure the outside edge of the stile is flush with the outside face of the side.

2 Install rails. To make sure that the rail ends fit snugly between the stiles, cut each one to fit, instead of measuring with your tape measure. (See the Shop Savvy on page 13.)

Align the top edge of each rail with the top surface of the plywood shelf, as shown in *Drawing D*. Put glue on the rails and use 4d finishing nails to secure each rail against its shelf. *(See Photo 6.)*

At the bottom corners of the face frame, drive two 6d finishing nails through each stile and into the ends of the bottom rail. Set all nail heads, and fill holes with wood putty. When the putty dries, sand it flush before finishing.

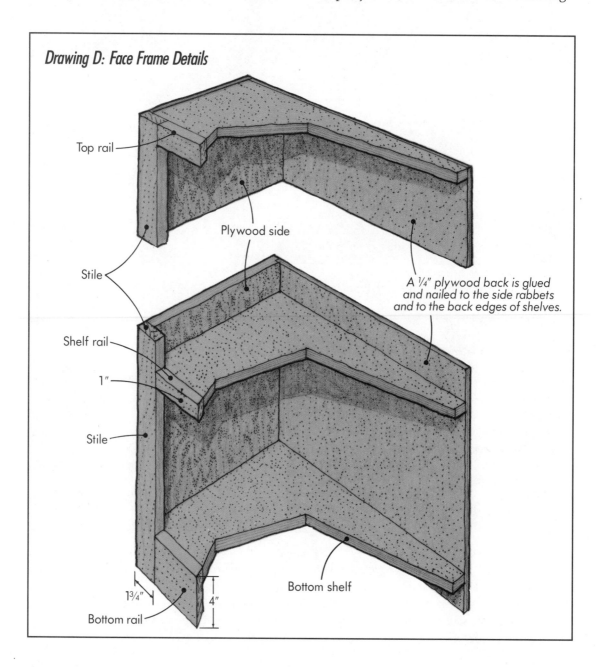

Drawing D: Face Frame Details

Top rail

Plywood side

Stile

A ¼" plywood back is glued and nailed to the side rabbets and to the back edges of shelves.

Shelf rail

1"

Stile

Bottom shelf

1¾"

4"

Bottom rail

Shop Savvy

Shelf Support Cleats

Using dado joints where shelves join sides adds strength to the bookcase using shelf support cleats instead of dadoes. Cleats are fine in this design because in the finished project, they'll be almost completely hidden by the face frame.

Cut your cleats from clear pine one-by stock; make them 1½ inches wide and (for this project) 8¾ inches long. After laying out cleat locations on both sides, glue and screw each cleat against its layout line, using three 1¼ inch drywall screws per cleat. Drill counterbored pilot holes for the screws, but take care to limit the depth of the counterbore to ⅛ inch. After driving the

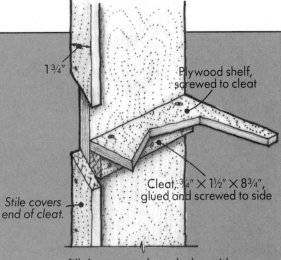

1 ¾"

Plywood shelf, screwed to cleat

Stile covers end of cleat.

Cleat, ¾" × 1½" × 8¾", glued and screwed to side

screws, fill the counterbore holes with wood putty.

To install the shelves, glue and screw each shelf against its cleats. Again, drill counterbored pilot holes for two screws at each cleat connection. Fill the holes with wood putty.

Photo 6: Use glue and 4d finishing nails to secure pine face frame members to shelves and sides. Install the stiles first, then cut the rails to fit between them.

Magazine Rack

This little rack will be a big help in organizing the magazines that pile up around the house. Its two-tier design holds plenty of magazines while keeping them all accessible.

The rack is equally at home in the living room, bedroom, or bathroom. You might want to make two or three, installing one wherever magazines accumulate. Once you've made a pattern, as explained here, it's easy to duplicate the curved sides. The rack shown here is made of walnut. You can choose cherry, maple, birch, or any native hardwood that suits your taste and decor.

Making Sides and Slats

1 Prepare the stock. If you are dimensioning the stock yourself, start by jointing one face of each board and then planing all boards to ½-inch thick. Then joint one edge of each board.

2 Make a routing template. Use *Drawing A* to make a full-scale side pattern on a piece of ¼-inch-thick hardboard or plywood. Cut out the template with a jigsaw or bandsaw. Then smooth and straighten the straight cuts with 80-grit sandpaper wrapped around a sanding block. Wrap the sandpaper around a dowel to smooth the curved sections. Or you can make a sanding stick to help you with this

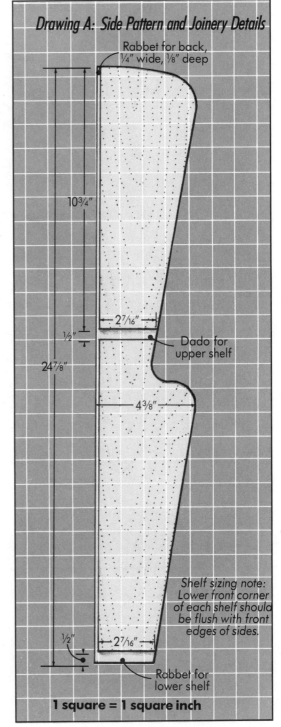

Drawing A: Side Pattern and Joinery Details

Rabbet for back, ¼" wide, ⅛" deep

10¾"

½"

24⅞"

2⁷⁄₁₆"

Dado for upper shelf

4⅜"

Shelf sizing note: Lower front corner of each shelf should be flush with front edges of sides.

½"

2⁷⁄₁₆"

Rabbet for lower shelf

1 square = 1 square inch

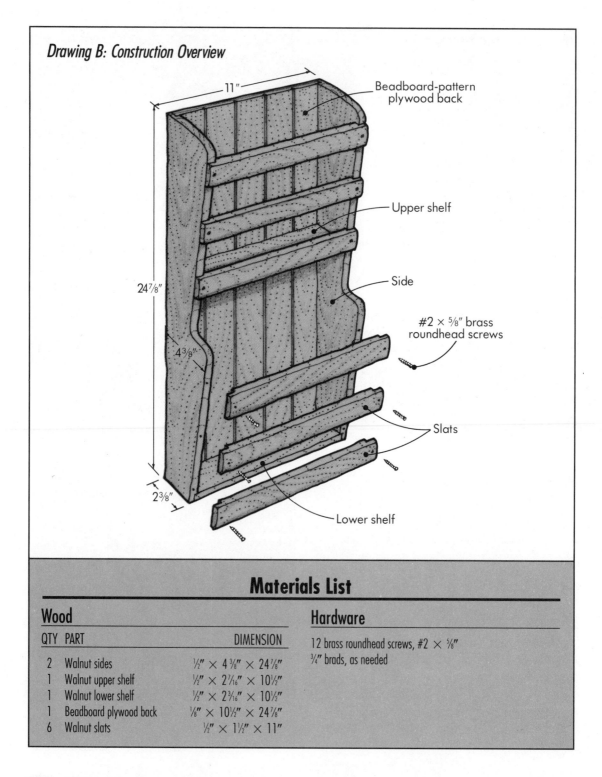

Drawing B: Construction Overview

11″

Beadboard-pattern
plywood back

Upper shelf

Side

#2 × 5/8″ brass
roundhead screws

24 7/8″

4 3/8″

Slats

2 3/8″

Lower shelf

Materials List

Wood

QTY	PART	DIMENSION
2	Walnut sides	1/2″ × 4 3/8″ × 24 7/8″
1	Walnut upper shelf	1/2″ × 2 7/16″ × 10 1/2″
1	Walnut lower shelf	1/2″ × 2 3/16″ × 10 1/2″
1	Beadboard plywood back	1/8″ × 10 1/2″ × 24 7/8″
6	Walnut slats	1/2″ × 1 1/2″ × 11″

Hardware

12 brass roundhead screws, #2 × 5/8″
3/4″ brads, as needed

Photo 1: Trace the rough size of the side by keeping the pencil line about ⅛ inch away from the template.

smoothing and shaping work. (See the Shop Savvy on page 60.) Sand until the front edge of the pattern is uniformly smooth. This is important because this edge will guide the pilot bearing of the pattern-cutting router bit. Rough spots, voids, or other irregularities in the template's edge will show up on the side pieces.

3 **Cut the sides to rough size.** First take a careful look at your stock, noting knots, checks, sapwood, and other imperfections you'll want to avoid when planning your cuts. Place the template on a piece of stock with its back edge flush with the jointed edge of the stock. Trace the outline of the front edge onto the stock. Instead of running the pencil hard against the template, make your outline about ⅛ inch outside of the template edge, as shown

Photo 2: Adjust the depth of the pattern-cutting bit so that the bearing rides against the template edge.

Shop Savvy

Make an Offset Base for Your Router

When you are doing pattern routing or any other edge-forming work, less than half of the router base is riding on the surface of the workpiece or pattern. An offset base makes your router more stable for this kind of work by greatly increasing the base area in contact with the surface. You can make this type of base from various sheet materials, including hardboard, plywood, and plastic. The base shown here was cut from ¼-inch-thick Corian, a synthetic product that's often used for countertops and tub surrounds.

To make your own offset base, unscrew the standard plastic base from your router and scribe its circumference and screw hole locations onto the new base. Drill and countersink the installation holes on your new base. Then lay out the shape of the offset base, and cut it out with a jigsaw. The offset base shown in the photo is 11¼ inches long and tapers from a 6-inch diameter to a 2¼-inch diameter. Smooth the cut edges of your offset base, and

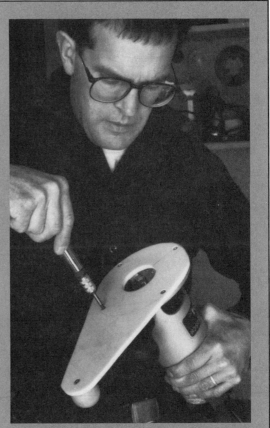

install a knob at the narrow end of the base. Unless the standard and offset base thicknesses are significantly different, you will be able to attach the offset base using the screws you removed earlier.

in *Photo 1*. Repeat this operation for the second side.

Use a jigsaw to cut each side to its rough size. Keep the jigsaw blade centered on the pencil line, so that each side will be slightly larger than the template.

4 Rout the sides to final size. Using several ⅝-inch wire nails, temporarily tack the template to one side. Make sure that the back edge of the side piece is flush to the

back edge of the template.

Rout the sides to final size with a pattern-cutting bit. This type of bit has a pilot bearing mounted above a straight bit. The bearing and bit diameters are identical, so you can duplicate parts with a full-scale template. Adjust the bit depth so that the bearing will ride on the template edge. (See *Photo 2*.) The standard base on your router will work fine if you are careful, but you'll gain stability if you replace it with an offset base like the one used here.

Photo 3: Tack the template temporarily to the workpiece. Guide a pattern-cutting bit against the template to cut each side to shape.

(See the Shop Savvy on opposite page.)

Hold the router firmly on the template near the template's bottom corner, making sure that the bit is not touching anything. Turn on the tool, then move the bit into the side and against the bottom corner of the template. With slow, steady pressure, run the bit's bearing along the template edge, trimming the side to its final size. (See *Photo 3.*)

5 Make the slats. Rip stock for the slats to width. Chuck a ¼-inch roundover bit in a table-mounted router and adjust the bit height so that the full cutting radius is above the table. Now position the fence so that it is aligned with the edge of the bit's bearing. Set up a featherboard to help hold the slat pieces down against the table. (For details on featherboards, see the Shop Savvy on page 205.) Then run your slat stock through this setup, rounding-over all four edges on each piece. (See *Photo 4.*) When this is done, cut the slats to their finished length.

Photo 4: Round-over the slat edges on the router table, using a ¼-inch roundover bit.

Photo 5: Rabbet for the back by guiding the sides against a wooden fence screwed to your saw's rip fence.

Photo 6: Guide each side with the miter gauge to mill the rabbet and dado for the shelves.

Milling Rabbets and Dadoes

1 Rabbet the back edges of the sides. These rabbets receive the back as shown in *Drawing C*. Square the table saw's miter gauge to its blade, and then replace the blade with a dado cutter. Adjust the cutter width to the thickness of your stock (½ inch). This thickness setting isn't important now, but you will use it in the next step. Attach a ¾-inch-thick wood auxiliary fence to the rip fence. Make the wood fence at least as high and long as a standard saw fence. Position the auxiliary fence so that it covers all but ⅛ inch of the cutter's width; then turn on the saw and slowly raise the dado cutter to ¼-inch height. Run the back edge of each side against the auxiliary fence as shown in *Photo 5*.

2 Mill the rabbets and dadoes for the shelves. The sides are rabbeted for the lower shelf and dadoed to receive the upper shelf as shown in *Drawing A*. Remove the auxiliary and rip fences, and mill these rabbets and dadoes by guiding the back edge of each side against the miter gauge. (See *Photo 6*.)

3 Rabbet the slat ends. As shown in *Drawing C,* the ends of each slat are rabbeted to fit over the sides. Mill these joints with the dado cutter at the same setting used in the previous step.
    Attach a wooden stop block on the infeed side of the table saw's rip fence. Adjust the fence so that when the slat's end is butted against the stop block, the slat is aligned for its rabbet. (See *Photo 7*.)

4 Rabbet the bottom edge of two slats. Rabbet the bottom edge of two slats to fit over the front edges of the shelves as shown in *Drawing C*. To mill these joints, keep the dado cutter at the same setting, and position the rip fence 1 inch from the cutter. Guide the top edge of the slat against the fence to cut the rabbet. (See *Photo 8*.) When this joinery work is complete, give each slat a final sanding. Round-over the ends of the slats, starting with 100-grit sandpaper and finishing up with 200-grit or 220-grit paper.

5 **Cut the shelves to their finished sizes.** These are the last parts you'll cut before assembly. Each shelf should be 10½ inches long. To determine the finished widths of the top and bottom shelves, it's best to measure a side rabbet and dado where each shelf will fit. Note in *Drawing A* that the bottom front edge of each shelf should be flush with the front edge of the side. The back edge of each shelf should be flush with the shoulder of the rab-

Photo 7: A stop block, fastened to the rip fence on the infeed side of the saw, aligns each slat while the end rabbets are milled.

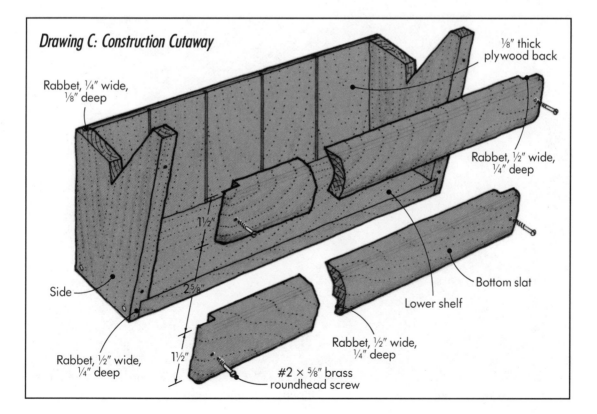

Drawing C: Construction Cutaway

⅛" thick plywood back

Rabbet, ¼" wide, ⅛" deep

Rabbet, ½" wide, ¼" deep

Side

1½"

2⅝"

Bottom slat

Lower shelf

Rabbet, ½" wide, ¼" deep

Rabbet, ½" wide, ¼" deep

1½"

#2 × ⅝" brass roundhead screw

Photo 8: Rabbet the bottom edge of two slats by guiding each slat against the rip fence.

bet where the back will fit. Take these details into account when cutting each shelf to its finished width.

Assembly and Finishing

1 Join the sides and shelves. Sand the sides thoroughly, taking extra care to smooth their front edges and outside faces. Put glue into the rabbet and dado joints that will hold the shelves; then fit the parts together. (See *Photo 9*.) Secure each joint by driving two ¾-inch brads through the sides and into the shelf ends.

2 Stain and install the back. After cutting the back to fit, stain it to match the natural tone of the walnut parts. Once the

Photo 9: Start the assembly process by fastening the sides to the shelves.

stain has dried, spread glue on the back edges of the shelves, and along the rabbeted back edge of each side. Fit the back into place, and secure it by driving ¾-inch brads into the shelves and sides. (See *Photo 10*.)

3 **Apply finish.** In a dust-free area, apply finish to the slats and to the subassembly of sides, shelves, and back. It's easier to apply finish before the slats are installed. A penetrating oil finish was used on the rack shown here. A satin polyurethane or varnish would also look good.

4 **Install the slats.** First, install the two slats that are rabbeted along the bottom. Predrill and install these slats by driving one ⅝-inch brass roundhead screw centered through each end rabbet into the front edge of the side, as shown in *Drawing C*.

To help position the remaining slats, rip a scrap of plywood to a width of 2⅝ inches. Use the plywood as a spacer, placing it across both sides, and between the installed shelf slat and the slat that you're about to install. (See *Photo 11*.) Use two screws to attach each slat.

Photo 10: The plywood back fits into rabbeted sides and against the back edge of both shelves.

Photo 11: Drill pilot holes for the slat-installation screws. Install the shelf slats first; then use a 2⅝-inch-wide piece of plywood as a spacer when installing the remaining slats.

Wall Organizer

D on't let the diminutive size of this wall organizer fool you—it can handle a lion's share of storage. Contrasting with the dark grain of the walnut, the thin pine dividers in the "letterbox" section of this wall unit keep bills, letters, and envelopes in order. The organizer would work well above the dresser in a bedroom, holding small items like brushes, wallets, cologne, and a current novel or two. Or you may find these shelves equally useful in the kitchen, or by the front door. The shelves are wide enough to hold magazines, and the drawer can fit in either of two openings on different levels. You can fasten these shelves to the wall, or simply set the unit down on top of a larger flat surface.

The walnut used for this project offers both strength and beauty. While it wouldn't be a good idea to use a softwood like pine to make the ½-inch-thick shelves, you could easily substitute another hardwood like cherry, maple, or birch for the walnut. Since most lumber dealers don't have ½-inch-thick hardwood in stock, you'll probably have to order it.

Alternatively, you can use a thickness planer to plane down ¾-inch-thick stock, or have a millwork shop do this work for you. If you have trouble finding 7-inch-wide boards, buy narrower stock and edge-glue your boards to make up the 7-inch width.

Making the Parts

For sides, shelves, and dividers to go together squarely, opposing dadoes must be milled in matching locations. To accomplish this, lay out all your joints carefully, making sure not to confuse one part or side for another, and follow the instructions below for using an auxiliary fence and stop block arrangement.

1 **Cut sides, shelves, and ½-inch dividers to size.** All these parts are 7 inches wide, so rip enough stock now to make all of them. Then cut shelves and sides to the finished lengths given in the Materials List. Don't cut the dividers to length now; wait until you've assembled shelves and sides.

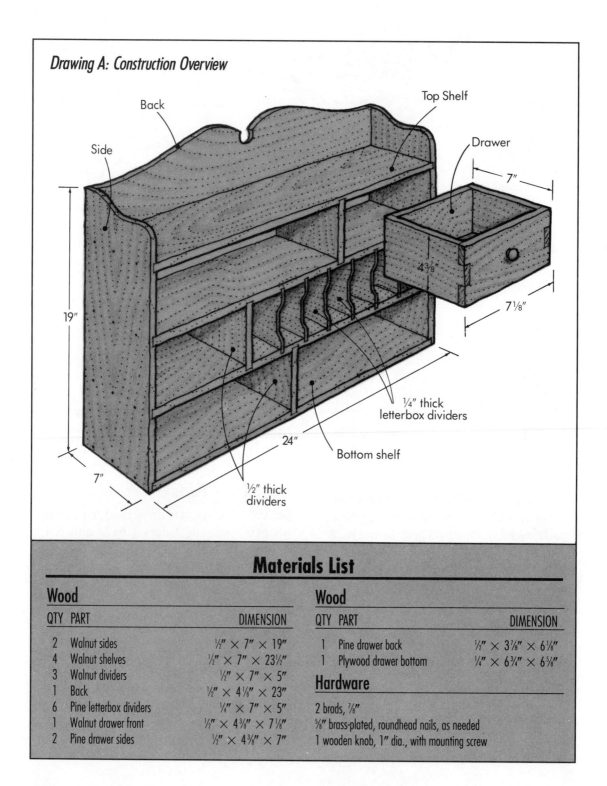

Drawing A: Construction Overview

Back

Top Shelf

Side

Drawer

7"

19"

4⅜"

7⅛"

¼" thick
letterbox dividers

7"

24"

Bottom shelf

½" thick
dividers

Materials List

Wood

QTY	PART	DIMENSION
2	Walnut sides	½" × 7" × 19"
4	Walnut shelves	½" × 7" × 23½"
3	Walnut dividers	½" × 7" × 5"
1	Back	½" × 4⅛" × 23"
6	Pine letterbox dividers	¼" × 7" × 5"
1	Walnut drawer front	½" × 4⅜" × 7⅛"
2	Pine drawer sides	½" × 4⅜" × 7"

Wood

QTY	PART	DIMENSION
1	Pine drawer back	½" × 3⅞" × 6⅛"
1	Plywood drawer bottom	¼" × 6¾" × 6⅝"

Hardware

2 brads, ⅞"
⅝" brass-plated, roundhead nails, as needed
1 wooden knob, 1" dia., with mounting screw

2 **Set up for dadoing and rabbeting.** First, square your table saw's miter gauge to the saw blade. Then replace the blade with a dado cutter and adjust the cutter width to match the stock thickness. Adjust the cutter height to ¼ inch.

Attach a wood auxiliary fence to the miter gauge. Use a straight, ¾-inch-thick board about 20 inches long and 2½ inches wide. Secure it to the gauge so that one end extends about 4 inches beyond the cutting line of the dado cutter. Now turn on the saw, and push the miter gauge forward so that the dado cutter makes a notch in the bottom edge of the auxiliary fence. Extend the shoulder lines of the notch by making two vertical marks on the auxiliary fence. These lines will let you align the layout marks on shelves and sides with the dado cutter.

Now lay out the locations of dadoes and rabbets on the shelves and sides. (See *Drawings B and C*.) Mark dado and rabbet shoulder lines across the edges and sides of these parts.

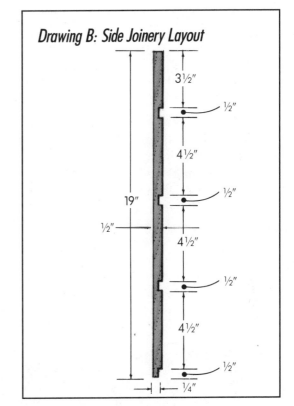

Drawing B: Side Joinery Layout

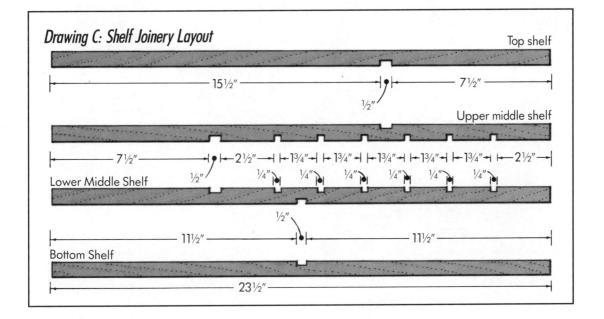

Drawing C: Shelf Joinery Layout

To avoid confusing one shelf for another as the dadoes are milled, label the top right rear corner of each shelf with a pencil. Use a "T" for the top shelf, a "UM" for the upper middle shelf, and so on.

3 **Mill dadoes and rabbets in the sides and shelves.** Align the layout marks on a shelf or side with the notch shoulder lines on the fence. Keeping the workpiece aligned against the fence, butt a small stop block against one end of the board, and clamp the block to the fence. Turn on the saw and cut the joint, holding the workpiece firmly against the fence. Leave the stop block in place to align the opposing dado or rabbet in another shelf or side. (See *Photo 1*.) Remember, for each stop block setting, one piece will be cut

Photo 1: A wood auxiliary fence and a stop block secured to the miter gauge will enable you to duplicate dadoes in different pieces.

with its back edge against the fence, while the other piece is cut with its front edge against the fence. Be sure to check your labels for orientation.

When you've milled all rabbets and dadoes for shelves and ½-inch-thick dividers, readjust the width of the dado cutter to ¼ inch, or to match the thickness of your letterbox dividers. Shift the auxiliary fence over about an inch, and mill a new ¼-inch-wide and ¼-inch-deep alignment notch in the fence. Extend the notch shoulder lines and use the stop block to dado the two center shelves for the letterbox dividers.

4 **Cut curves in sides.** The pattern for the ogee-style curve on the top of each side is shown in *Drawing D*. (For information on enlarging patterns to full-scale size, see "Using Patterns" on page viii.) Trace a full-scale pattern onto one side, and then clamp both sides together so that you can cut them at the same time. Before cutting, make sure all edges are flush. Once you've made the curved cut, separate the sides and sand the curves smooth.

Assembling the Shelves, Sides, and Back

1 **Join the shelves and sides.** In this design, the brass-plated roundhead nails used to fasten shelves to sides are left exposed as decoration. Driven with a tack hammer, they should set flush with the wood surface. To avoid splitting the wood or bending the nails, predrill nail holes in sides only, using a ¹⁄₁₆-inch-diameter bit. Drill holes for three nails at each rabbet or dado joint. Put one hole in the middle of each joint and the others 1 inch from the front and back.

Spread a light, even coat of glue in the rabbet and dadoes in one side piece, then fit the shelves into the joints. Make sure that the front edges of all parts are flush. Now glue and nail the other side to the shelves. (See *Photo 2*.)

2 Cut and install the back. The pattern for the curved back is shown in *Drawing D*. Cut the back to fit between the sides. Then trace and cut the curve. Sand the curved edge thoroughly, smoothing out saw marks and softening corners. Spread glue on the bottom and end edges of the back, then fit it into place. Clamp the back down against the top shelf. To protect the round cutout in the back and keep the clamp in position, use a small clamping block, as shown in *Photo 3*. Also clamp the sides against the ends of the top by tightening a clamp across the width of the unit.

Adding the Dividers

1 Cut and install the ½-inch dividers. Cut these walnut pieces to fit in the dadoes in the shelves. Select straight stock, and make your cuts so that the grain will run in the same direction as the sides. This hides

Photo 2: Make sure that all front edges are flush when joining shelves and sides.

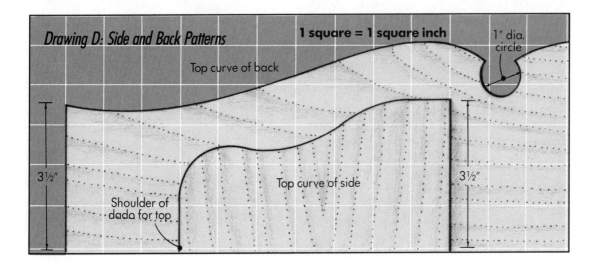

Drawing D: Side and Back Patterns

1 square = 1 square inch

1" dia. circle

Top curve of back

Top curve of side

Shoulder of dada for top

3½"

3½"

Photo 3: After cutting and sanding the back, glue it to the top shelf and to the sides. A large C-clamp should provide adequate downward pressure. Use a clamping block between the clamp and the back's circular cutout.

the end grain and allows the dividers to expand and contract in the same direction as the sides. Spread glue in the joints before slipping the dividers into place. Don't nail these joints. Use a pair of C-clamps or pipe clamps for each divider.

2 Cut and smooth the ¼-inch letterbox dividers. Cut these pine dividers to fit between the dadoes in the shelves. Again, run the grain in the same direction as the sides.

Drawing E shows the curved cut on the front edges of the letterbox dividers. Trace this pattern onto one divider blank. Clamp two more divider blanks below the first. Check that all edges are flush. Then make the curved cut in three pieces at once, as shown in *Photo 4*. To make installation easier, chisel a chamfer into the divider edges that will fit into the dadoes. (See *Photo 5*.) When chamfering, leave the two front corners of the divider square. Don't install these dividers yet.

Shop Savvy

Divide Distances the Easy Way

Using a tape measure, framing square, or ruler, you can easily and accurately divide the width of a board into three or more equal parts. Simply measure diagonally across the board, selecting a distance that is a multiple of the number of divisions desired. (See drawing.) For example, to divide a board into three parts, use increments such as 6 inches, 9 inches, and 12 inches. Mark division points along the ruler or tape measure to divide the space into equal parts.

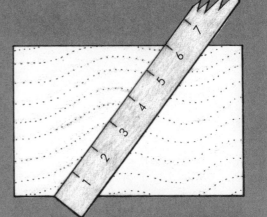

To divide a board into thirds across its width, make a diagonal measure that is a multiple of 3; then mark the division points.

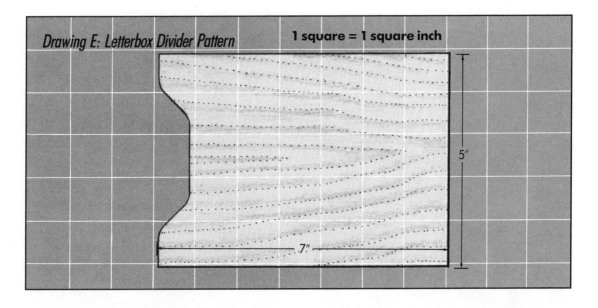

Drawing E: Letterbox Divider Pattern 1 square = 1 square inch

5"

7"

Photo 4: The curved front edges of the letterbox dividers can be cut three at a time, using a fine-tooth blade in the jigsaw.

Photo 5: For an easier fit in shelf dadoes, use a chisel to chamfer the top and bottom edges of the letterbox dividers. Note that the grain runs parallel to the divider's 5-inch dimension.

3 **Sand and apply a finish.** Thoroughly sand the assembled shelves, sides, and dividers. Use 120- or 180-grit sandpaper to soften corners and edges. Then go over all surfaces with 200- or 220-grit sandpaper. Do the same for the letterbox dividers.

Wipe wood surfaces free of sawdust, then apply a penetrating oil finish. Be sure to coat all parts evenly, so that the shelf undersides and back edges also receive a finish. Apply the oil finish to individual ¼-inch-thick dividers.

4 **Install the ¼-inch dividers.** Slip these parts carefully into their dadoes. Position the divider front corners flush with the shelf front edges.

Making the Drawer

The three-finger joint connecting the drawer sides to the front provides good strength and a pleasing appearance. You can cut these joints the same way you cut rabbets and dadoes.

1 **Cut front, sides, and back to size.** Use the Materials List as a guide, but cut the drawers to fit their actual openings. Cut the drawer parts to allow the drawer ⅛ inch of free play from side to side and from top to bottom.

2 **Lay out the finger joint in one side.** The dimensions given in *Drawing F* divide the side's height into three parts that are

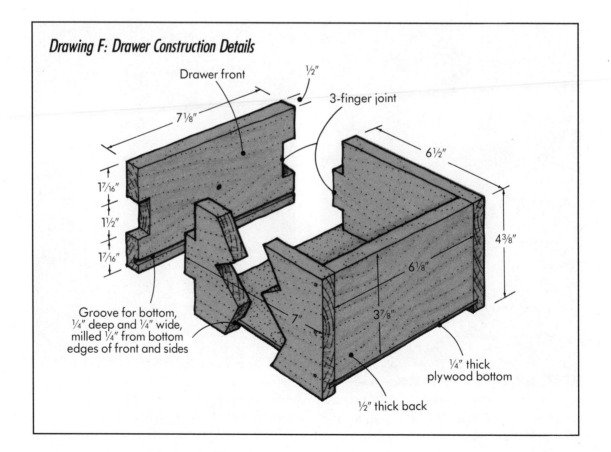

Drawing F: Drawer Construction Details

Drawer front

½"

3-finger joint

7⅛"

6½"

1⁷⁄₁₆"

1½"

1⁷⁄₁₆"

4³⁄₈"

6⅛"

Groove for bottom, ¼" deep and ¼" wide, milled ¼" from bottom edges of front and sides

7"

3⁷⁄₈"

¼" thick plywood bottom

½" thick back

approximately equal. For a quick, precise way to lay out equal divisions across a given length or width, see the Shop Savvy on page 294. Use a combination square to lay out the shoulders of the side's single finger.

3 Cut the three-finger joint in the front and sides. Adjust the dado cutter in the table saw to maximum width, and adjust the cutter height to equal the thickness of front and sides (½ inch). Using several ⅝-inch brads, temporarily nail the sides together, with all edges flush and the joint layout showing. Now turn on the saw, position the sides as shown, and line up the joint layout with the cutter. Clamp a stop block against the fence, as

shown in *Photo 6,* and make the first shoulder cut. Then flip the workpiece so that the opposite side and opposite edge are held against the fence and the stop block, respectively. Cut the second shoulder while holding the workpiece in this position. (See *Photo 7.*) With both shoulders cut, you can now "nibble" away the remaining waste, removing the stop block and running the sides through the cutter repeatedly. Be sure to keep the bottom edge of the workpiece flat against the saw table.

Next, remove the brads that hold the sides together. Put one side on top of the drawer front. Trace around the finger to lay out the notch on the drawer front. Reset the stop block to cut out the notch. Test fit these joints;

Photo 6: A stop block, clamped to a miter gauge auxiliary fence, establishes the shoulder line for the finger joint in the drawer sides.

Photo 7: After making the first shoulder cut, flip the workpiece side-for-side, and make the second shoulder cut. Then make successive passes to remove the remaining waste on both sides of the joint.

use a chisel if necessary to pare the surfaces for a better fit.

4 **Groove the front and sides to hold the bottom.** Adjust the dado cutter to cut a groove ¼ wide and deep. Position the rip fence ¼ inch from the cutter. Running the bottom edge of each part against the fence, mill grooves in the front and sides.

5 **Assemble the front, sides, bottom, and back.** With glue and ⅞-inch brads, fasten the sides to the front. Drive a single brad through each side's finger into the notch in the front. You shouldn't need more than these two nails to secure these joints. Set the nails and fill holes with wood putty.

Cut the bottom to fit into its grooves, then slip it into place. Now cut the back to fit between the sides. The back's top edge should be flush with the top edges of the sides, as shown in *Drawing F*. Install the back with glue and ⅞-inch brads. Drive brads through the sides and also through the bottom. Check to make sure your drawer is square. If necessary, clamp it against two straight-edged boards that are screwed to a work surface to form a right angle. Check to see that it is square.

6 **Install the wooden knob and finish the drawer.** Find the center point of the drawer front by crossing diagonals, then drill a hole for the knob's installation screw. Give the entire drawer a thorough sanding before installing the knob. Check the drawer's fit in both openings, and sand where necessary to eliminate any binding as the drawer opens and shuts. Finally, apply a penetrating oil finish to all surfaces of the drawer.

Bedroom

Under-Bed Drawer

Here's a project that takes advantage of a storage area that goes unused in many homes. This drawer is designed to fit underneath a bed frame. Small wooden wheels, mounted at the bottom corners of the drawer, allow it to slide in and out easily. A lightweight lid keeps the drawer's contents free of dust. The aromatic cedar panel that lines the bottom makes this storage unit ideal for out-of-season clothes. Depending on the size of your household, you may want to make several of these drawers at once. Before you begin, be sure to check the clearance underneath your bed or beds. The drawer lid adds ¼ inch to the overall height of this project; the wheels add another ¼ inch. There should be at least ¼ inch of clearance space between the lid and the bottom of the bed or bed frame. Take these measurements into account when you determine the finished width of the drawer's sides, front, and back.

Sizing Stock and Making the Locking Joints

As shown in *Drawing A,* the sides of this drawer join the front and back with locking joints. This is a strong and attractive corner joint for drawers and boxes. Make it with a fine-cutting, carbide-tipped combination blade in your table saw.

1 Cut the front, back, and sides to size. Rip all four parts to width, always making sure that you have a straight, square edge to guide against the rip fence. Then cut the front, back, and sides to length. Put a scrap piece of this stock aside; you'll use it to test the setup in Step 4.

2 Groove the ends of the front and back. This groove is the first step in making the locking joint, which is shown in more detail

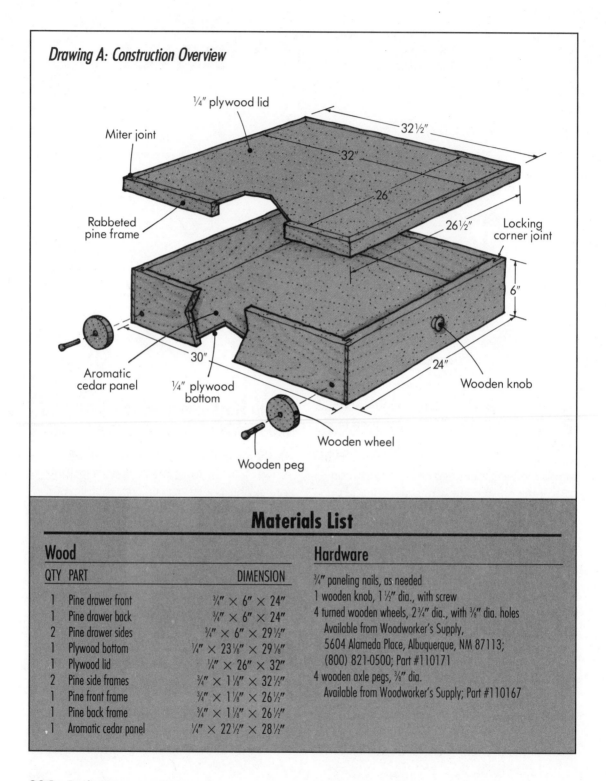

Drawing A: Construction Overview

¼" plywood lid

Miter joint

32½"

32"

26"

26½"

Rabbeted
pine frame

Locking
corner joint

6"

Aromatic
cedar panel

30"

¼" plywood
bottom

24"

Wooden knob

Wooden wheel

Wooden peg

Materials List

Wood

QTY	PART	DIMENSION
1	Pine drawer front	¾" × 6" × 24"
1	Pine drawer back	¾" × 6" × 24"
2	Pine drawer sides	¾" × 6" × 29½"
1	Plywood bottom	¼" × 23⅛" × 29⅛"
1	Plywood lid	¼" × 26" × 32"
2	Pine side frames	¾" × 1⅛" × 32½"
1	Pine front frame	¾" × 1⅛" × 26½"
1	Pine back frame	¾" × 1⅛" × 26½"
1	Aromatic cedar panel	¼" × 22½" × 28½"

Hardware

¾" paneling nails, as needed
1 wooden knob, 1½" dia., with screw
4 turned wooden wheels, 2¾" dia., with ⅜" dia. holes
   Available from Woodworker's Supply,
   5604 Alameda Place, Albuquerque, NM 87113;
   (800) 821-0500; Part #110171
4 wooden axle pegs, ⅜" dia.
   Available from Woodworker's Supply; Part #110167

in *Drawing B*. Each groove is made by making two passes across the saw.

Before you begin, attach a tall wood auxiliary fence to your table saw's rip fence. Make your fence from a straight piece of ¾-inch-thick plywood that's at least 10 inches wide and 12 inches high. Use screws or clamps to attach the auxiliary fence to the rip fence. Make sure that the fence is square with the table surface. (See *Photo 1*.)

Adjust the blade height of your table saw to match the thickness of the drawer front, back, and sides. Now position the auxiliary fence ¼ inch from the saw blade. Turn on the saw, and run one end of the back piece through the blade as shown in *Photo 2*. Guide the side of the workpiece against the auxiliary fence while running the end through the saw and against the table surface. Use both hands to keep the piece steady as you make the cuts.

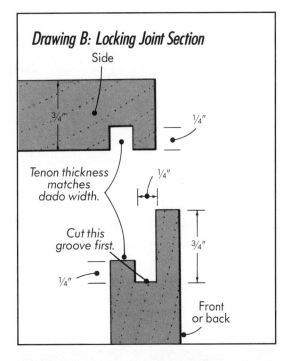

Drawing B: Locking Joint Section

Side

¾″

¼″

Tenon thickness matches dado width.

¼″

Cut this groove first.

¼″

¾″

Front or back

Photo 1: Attach a tall auxiliary fence to the rip fence, and make sure that it is square with the table.

Photo 2: With the auxiliary fence positioned ¼ inch from the blade, rip one shoulder of the end groove. Use both hands to guide the workpiece.

Once you've made the first cut, turn your workpiece so that the other face is against the auxiliary fence and the same edge is on the table. Run it through the blade again as shown in *Photo 3*. This will cut the opposite shoulder of the groove and will ensure that the groove is centered. Make two shoulder cuts like this on the opposite end of the back piece and both ends of the front piece. Note: If your saw blade cuts a kerf slightly thinner than ⅛ inch, a thin strip of waste will remain after the shoulder cuts are made. If this is the case, reposition the auxiliary fence so that you can saw out the waste with a third cut.

3 Cut the tenons. Cutting the grooves creates two tongues on each end of the stock. The next step is to trim one of the tongues,

creating a ¼-inch tenon at each end of the stock. As shown in *Drawing B,* these tenons fit into dadoes in the side pieces. Lay out this cut on one end of the back or the front piece.

To cut the tenons on the front and back pieces, start by lowering the saw blade height to ⁵⁄₁₆ inch. Now clamp a wooden stop block on the infeed side of the rip fence as shown in *Photo 4*. Adjust the rip fence so that putting the stock against the stop block properly aligns the cut. Guide the cut with a miter gauge, and cut all four tenons.

4 Cut dadoes in the sides. Lay out this dado in a short piece of pine scrap left over from Step 1. Place the finished end of a front or back piece against the scrap piece as shown in *Photo 5;* then mark the shoulders of

Photo 3: *To rip the other shoulder of the end groove, place the opposite face of the workpiece against the fence.*

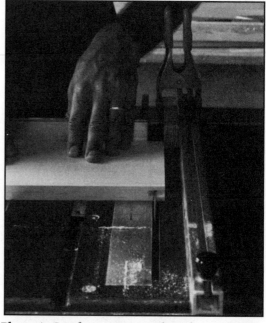

Photo 4: *Cut the tenons, guiding the workpiece against the miter gauge. A stop block, clamped to the rip fence on the infeed side of the blade, aligns each tenon cut.*

a "test" dado on the scrap piece with a sharp pencil. Set up the saw to cut the dadoes in two passes. First, adjust blade height to equal tenon length. Then set up a stop block on the rip fence as you did to cut the tenons. (See *Photo 6*.) Cut a sample shoulder, check it against the tenon for fit, and adjust the stop block position if necessary. When the tenon and dado align, cut shoulders on both ends of both drawer sides. Then reposition the stop block to align each side for its final shoulder cut. Again, test your setup by finishing the dado in the scrap piece before completing the dadoes in the sides.

Cutting Grooves and Assembling the Drawer

1 **Groove the bottom edges of the sides, front, and back.** These grooves will hold the ¼-inch-thick plywood bottom. Make them with two passes through the table saw blade as shown in *Drawing C*. To set up for the first cuts, adjust the blade height to ⅜ inch, and position the rip fence 5⅜ inches from the blade. Cut the bottom shoulder of the groove in the front, back, and side pieces, running the top edge of each piece against the rip fence. Now adjust the rip fence so that it's 5¼ inches from the blade. Run the top edge of each piece against the rip fence to cut the opposite shoulder of the groove in each piece.

2 **Cut the bottom to size.** Test fit the front, back, and sides. Make sure the locking joints fit smoothly, and then measure for the bottom. Add ⅝ inch to the inside dimensions (length and width) of the drawer to get the finished length and width of the bottom.

3 **Assemble the drawer.** Put glue in the corner joints and in the grooves for the

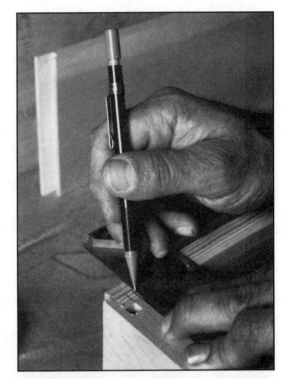

Photo 5: Lay out the dado cut by holding the locking joint's tenon against a drawer side.

Photo 6: Dado the sides to hold the tenon, guiding the cut with the miter gauge. Clamp a stop block to the rip fence to align the joint's shoulder cuts.

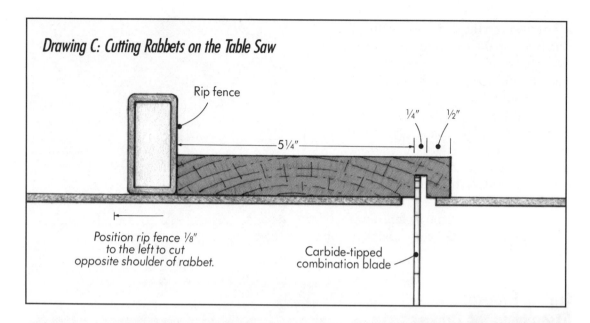

Drawing C: Cutting Rabbets on the Table Saw

Rip fence

5¼"

¼"   ½"

Position rip fence ⅛"
to the left to cut
opposite shoulder of rabbet.

Carbide-tipped
combination blade

Photo 7: After gluing the corner joints and assembling the drawer, place pipe clamps across the width of the drawer. Make sure that the drawer stays square as you tighten the clamps.

Photo 8: Rabbet the lid's frame members by making two kerfs, guiding the bottom edge of each piece against the rip fence.

bottom. Place a side on a flat surface, and assemble one corner joint by attaching the front. Then fit the bottom in the grooves in these two pieces. Next, attach the back to the side, fitting the back's groove over the bottom at the same time. Finally, install the remaining side.

Pull the sides against the front and back by tightening pipe clamps across the width of the drawer. This should close up the locking joints. (See *Photo 7.*) As you tighten the clamps, use a framing square to check that the sides remain square with the front and back.

Making the Lid

1 Cut the lid panel to size. The lid panel's 26 × 32-inch size will give the finished lid a loose fit on the drawer, making it easy to remove and replace the lid. Cut the panel from a sheet of ¼-inch plywood, taking care to lay out and cut square corners.

2 Cut and rabbet the lid frame. As shown in *Drawing D,* these pine pieces cover the edges of the lid, holding the plywood panel in rabbets that measure ¼ inch deep and ½ inch wide. Cut the side lid frame pieces to a rough length of 34 inches, and cut the front and back frame members to a rough length of 28 inches. Then rip all four pieces to a finished width of 1⅛ inches.

Rabbet the frame pieces in two cuts on the table saw, guiding the bottom edge of the frame member against the rip fence. (See *Photo 8.*) Make the first cut in each frame

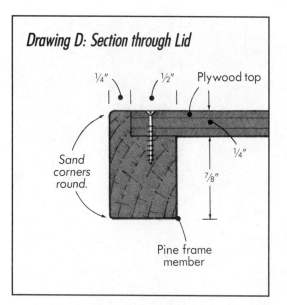

Drawing D: Section through Lid

1/4"   1/2"   Plywood top

Sand corners round.

1/4"

7/8"

Pine frame member

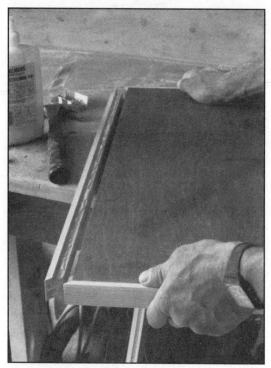

Photo 9: The frame is mitered together at the lid's corners. Glue the miter joints together while gluing the lid in each rabbet.

member with the fence 1 inch from the blade. Then set the fence 7/8 inch from the blade for the second kerf.

3 Install the frame members. The frame is mitered to fit around the lid. (See *Photo 9.*) To get good, tight-fitting miters on all four corners, it's best to miter a single piece and work your way around all four edges. For tips on making precise miter cuts, see the Shop Savvy on page 177.

Miter the end of one side frame member. Position it on the lid and lay out the miter on the frame member's other end. After making this miter cut, glue and nail the frame member to the plywood panel with 3/4-inch paneling nails. Now miter one end of an adjoining frame piece and position it on the lid. Lay out the miter on the opposite end, cut it, and install this piece. Repeat this cut-and-fit procedure to install the remaining two frame members. You'll have to mark the last miter cut by holding the back frame member against the bottom edge of the first miter.

Adding the Wheels and the Cedar Panel

1 Sand and finish the drawer and lid. Now is the time to go over your project with sandpaper, rounding over sharp corners, removing glue stains, and smoothing joints. Sand flat areas with an orbital or random-orbit sander, starting out with 120-grit sandpaper, and then switching to 180-grit or 200-grit sandpaper. Round-over corners by hand, sanding with 180-grit or 200-grit paper.

To seal and protect the wood, apply two coats of satin polyurethane varnish. Be sure to coat all surfaces of the drawer and lid.

2 Drill holes for the axles. The wheels turn on hardwood axles that are glued into holes drilled in the drawer sides. Chuck a ⅜-inch-diameter bit in your drill, and lay out the centers for the axle holes. Each center should be 1⅛ inches from the bottom edge, and 1⅜ inches from the front or back of the drawer. Mark each of the center points with an awl or a sharp nail, then drill all the way through the drawer side at each axle location. (See *Photo 10*.)

3 **Install the wheels and axles.** First fit an axle through a wheel, and then insert the axle into an installation hole. If the end of the axle extends through the hole and into the drawer, trim off this excess with a backsaw or other fine-cutting saw. Install and trim the remaining three axles in the same way.

Remove the axles. Spread a generous amount of glue in each axle hole, using a small brush or cotton swab. (See the Shop Savvy on page 188.) Then fit each axle through its wheel, and insert the axle into its hole. Use a damp cloth to wipe up excess glue that squeezes out inside the drawer.

4 **Cut the cedar panel to size.** Take the inside dimensions of your drawer, and use them to cut a bottom liner from an aromatic cedar panel. As an alternative, you can line the bottom of your drawer with tongue-and-groove aromatic cedar boards. Both closet-lining materials are available at most lumberyards.

Photo 10: Using a ⅜-inch-diameter bit, drill two axle installation holes in each side. Then insert each axle through its wheel, and glue the axle's end in the hole.

Closet Makeover

Has your bedroom closet become a deep, dark jumble of clothes, shoes, and other items you may never see again? Here's a project that will transform an underused closet into a well-designed storage area for shoes, socks, shirts, jackets, and plenty of other items that can easily get "lost" in a disorganized space. The heart of this design is a tall, narrow storage unit, or chest, that divides the closet into two sections. You can build drawers to fit in the chest compartments, or simply use the compartments alone for storage. For this project, four drawers were built. On one side of the chest there is a single clothes pole for dresses, coats, and other long items. On the other side of the chest are upper and lower clothes poles for items like shirts and jackets. (See *Drawing A*.) This three-pole configuration increases hanging space and

versatility, while the chest offers both drawers and shelf space.

Because of the chest, which also acts as a closet divider, this closet makeover isn't suited for single-door closets or closets that are less than 48 inches wide. If your closet has bi-fold doors, like the closet shown here, you can center the chest in the door opening. If your closet has sliding doors (also called bypass doors), you'll have to position the chest to one side of the center. You might also choose to position the chest off-center in order to have a long clothes pole (or two) on one side and a shorter pole on the other.

The interior dimensions of your closet(s) may vary from those of the closet shown here. Adjust the dimensions of the poles, shelves, and ledgers to fit your space. The chest and drawer dimensions can remain the same.

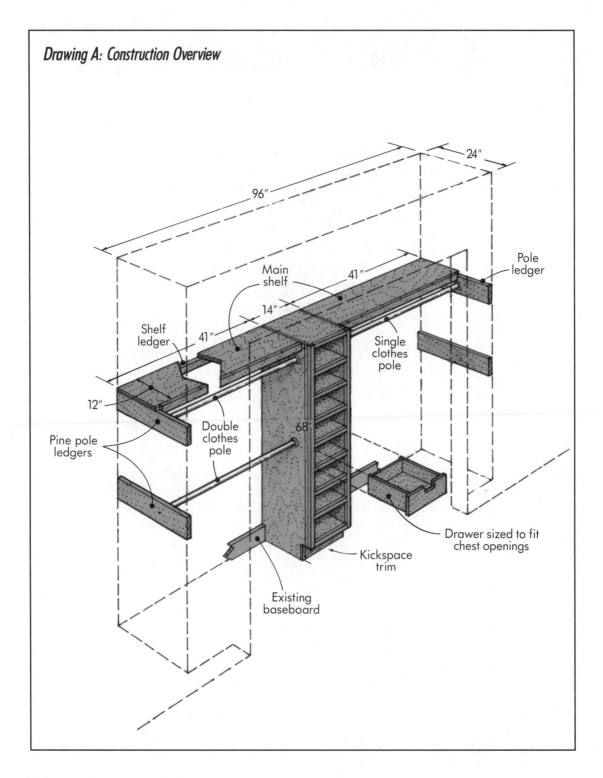

Drawing A: Construction Overview

96"

24"

Pole ledger

Main shelf

41"

14"

Shelf ledger

41"

Single clothes pole

12"

68"

Double clothes pole

Pine pole ledgers

Drawer sized to fit chest openings

Kickspace trim

Existing baseboard

Making the Chest Carcase

1 Cut the sides, dividers, and top to size. These parts make up the carcase, or body, of the chest. If you're cutting these parts from a larger plywood panel, see "Cutting Plywood Panels" on page 25.

Materials List

Wood

QTY	PART	DIMENSION
Carcase		
2	Plywood chest sides	3/4" × 15 1/2" × 68"
8	Plywood chest dividers	3/4" × 13 1/4" × 15 1/2"
1	Plywood chest top	3/4" × 13 1/4" × 15 1/2"
2	Poplar chest trim pieces	1/2" × 3/4" × 62 3/4"
9	Poplar chest trim pieces	1/2" × 3/4" × 12 1/2"
1	Pine kickspace trim	3/4" × 5 1/4" × 14"
1	Pine shelf ledger	3/4" × 1 1/2" × 96"
3	Pine pole ledgers	3/4" × 4 1/2" × 24"
2	Plywood shelves	3/4" × 11 1/4" × 41"
2	Pine cleats	3/4" × 3/4" × 10 1/2"
2	Pine shelf trim pieces	3/4" × 1 1/2" × 40 1/4"
Drawers (4)		
8	Plywood sides	1/2" × 6 7/8" × 15"
4	Plywood fronts	1/2" × 6 7/8" × 11 7/8"
4	Plywood backs	1/2" × 6 1/8" × 11 7/8"
4	Plywood bottoms	1/4" × 11 7/8" × 13 3/4"
4	Pine false fronts	3/4" × 7 5/8" × 15 1/2"

Hardware

6 wooden pole supports
3 wooden clothes poles 1 1/4" dia. × 39 1/4"
4d finishing nails, as needed
1" brads, as needed
3/4" paneling nails, as needed
16 drywall screws, 1"
6 drywall screws, 1 1/4"
1 1/4" drywall screws, as needed
2 1/2" drywall screws, as needed
6 flathead wood screws, #8 × 3/4"

Drawing B: Carcase Side Details

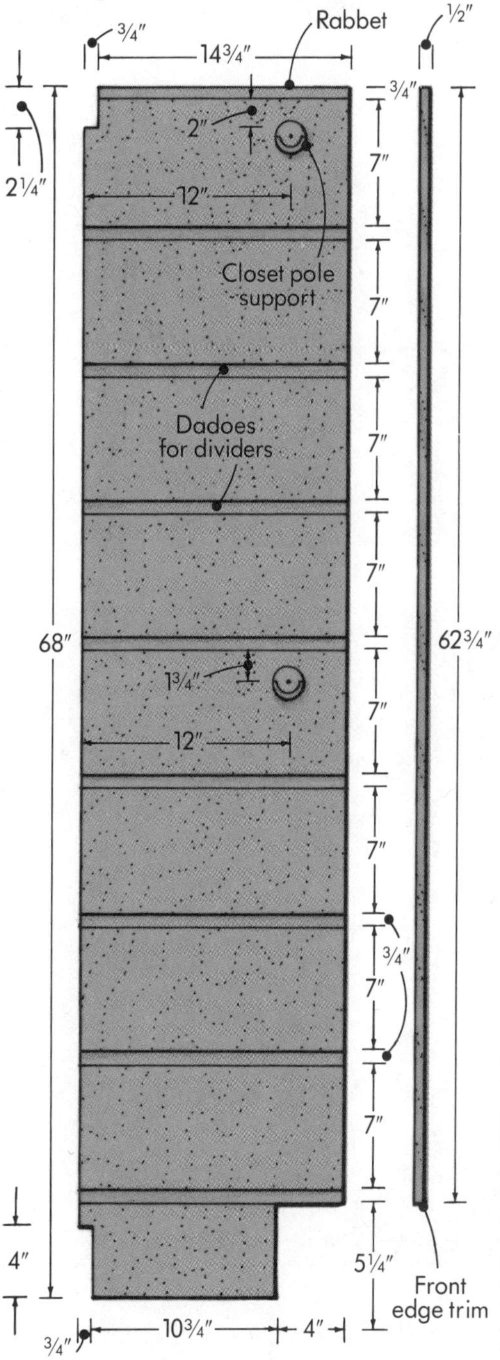

3/4"
14 3/4"
Rabbet
1/2"
3/4"
2"
2 1/4"
12"
7"
Closet pole support
Dadoes for dividers
68"
62 3/4"
1 3/4"
12"
3/4"
4"
5 1/4"
Front edge trim
3/4"
10 3/4"
4"

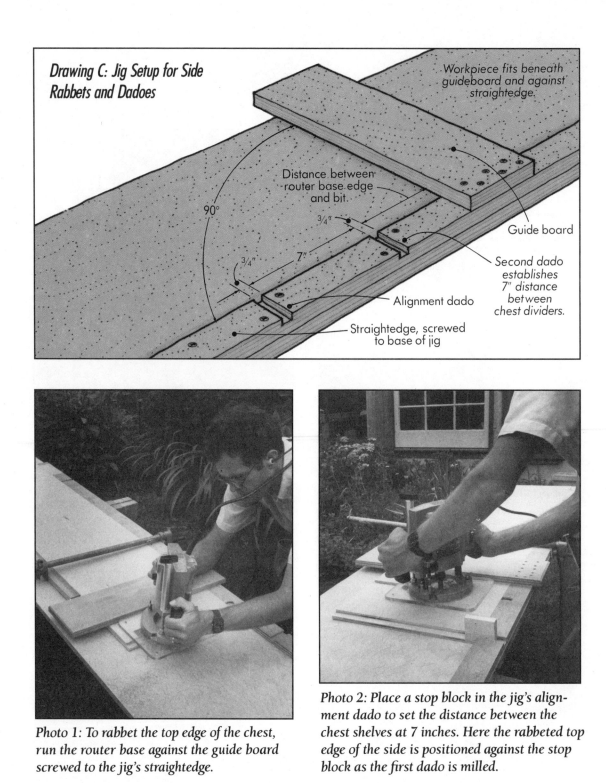

Drawing C: Jig Setup for Side Rabbets and Dadoes

Workpiece fits beneath guideboard and against straightedge.

Distance between router base edge and bit.

90°

3/4"

7"

3/4"

Guide board

Second dado establishes 7" distance between chest dividers.

Alignment dado

Straightedge, screwed to base of jig

Photo 1: To rabbet the top edge of the chest, run the router base against the guide board screwed to the jig's straightedge.

Photo 2: Place a stop block in the jig's alignment dado to set the distance between the chest shelves at 7 inches. Here the rabbeted top edge of the side is positioned against the stop block as the first dado is milled.

2 **Rabbet and dado the sides.** As shown in *Drawing B,* the chest sides are rabbeted and dadoed to hold the dividers and top. In the finished chest, compartment openings are all 7 inches high and 12½ inches wide. To mill evenly spaced joints, use the jig shown in *Photos 1, 2, and 3* and described in detail on page 270 ("Make a Jig for Square Cutoffs and Dadoes").

To set up the jig for the rabbets and dadoes in this project, refer to *Drawing C.* First, chuck a ¾-inch straight bit in your router, and set the depth to ⅜ inch. Running your router against the jig's guide board, mill an alignment dado in the jig's straightedge, near the middle of the jig. Now reposition the guide board to mill a second dado in the straightedge, exactly 7 inches from the alignment dado.

Position a side in the jig, aligning the side's

Photo 3: Keep using the alignment dado and stop block to set up successive dadoes in each side.

top edge with the second straightedge dado. This sets you up to rabbet the top edge of the side, as shown in *Photo 1.* Use a pipe clamp to clamp the side against the straightedge. Then rout the rabbet, guiding the router against the guide board.

After completing the rabbet, loosen the pipe clamp, and reposition the side in the jig so that its rabbeted top edge aligns with the alignment dado. Use a scrap of ¾-inch-thick stock as an indexing guide, fitting it in the alignment dado and in the rabbet. This sets you up to mill the uppermost dado. Tighten the pipe clamp and mill the dado, again running the router against the guide board. (See *Photo 2.*) Now loosen the clamp, and shift the side until the uppermost dado is even with the alignment dado. Make sure that your indexing guide fits in the alignment dado and side dado before clamping the side in the jig. Continue to mill the dadoes in this way, using the indexing guide to reposition the side after milling each dado. (See *Photo 3.*) Mill a total of eight dadoes in the side; then duplicate this joinery work on the remaining side.

3 **Cut the side notches.** Notch the top back corner and the bottom corner of each side as shown in *Drawing B.* The top notch will fit around the shelf ledger, while the bottom notch will fit around the baseboard. Adjust the size of each bottom notch so that it will fit neatly around the baseboard in your closet. Lay out each notch with a tape measure and a square. As you mark up both sides, make sure that you'll be creating two sides that are mirror images of each other, not duplicates. Cut out the notches by hand, using a crosscut saw.

4 **Assemble the carcase.** Join the dividers and top to one side with glue and 4d finishing nails. As you attach the dividers, make sure their front edges are flush to the front of the side. Likewise, fit the top in its rabbet with its front edge flush with the side's front edge. Drive three or four nails to secure each joint.

When you've fastened the dividers and top to one side, glue and nail the remaining side to the top and dividers. Again, take care to keep all front edges flush. Make sure the dividers are square with the sides. Then set all nail heads, and fill the resulting holes with wood putty.

5 **Install the poplar edging.** First, cut the strips to fit against the sides' front edges.

Glue and nail them in place with 1-inch brads. Then cut and install the strips that fit against the dividers. (See *Photo 4*.) Set the heads of the brads, and fill the holes with wood putty.

Making the Drawers

1 **Cut the parts to size.** As shown in *Drawing D*, the drawers for this project have solid pine false fronts that are sized to overlap the front edges of the carcase. Drawer fronts, sides, and backs are made from ½-inch-thick plywood; the bottom is ¼-inch-thick plywood. Cut all these parts to the dimensions given in the Materials List.

Photo 4: With sides and shelves together, glue and nail the trim pieces to the front edges of the carcase.

Photo 5: Use the dado cutter to rabbet the front edge of each drawer side. A stop block, clamped to the miter gauge auxiliary fence, aligns the workpiece.

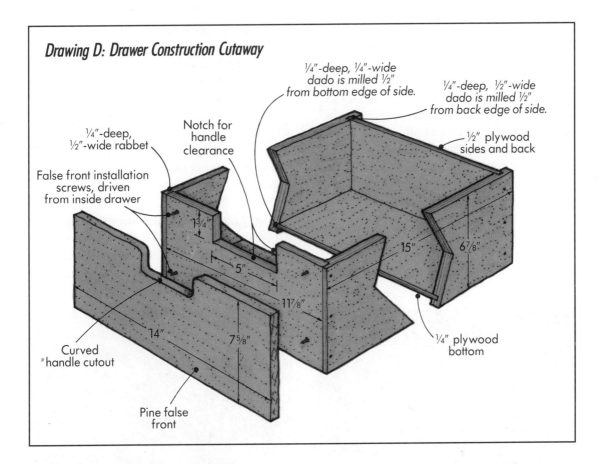

Drawing D: Drawer Construction Cutaway

¼"-deep, ¼"-wide dado is milled ½" from bottom edge of side.

¼"-deep, ½"-wide dado is milled ½" from back edge of side.

¼"-deep, ½"-wide rabbet

Notch for handle clearance

½" plywood sides and back

False front installation screws, driven from inside drawer

1¾"

15"

6⅞"

5"

11⅞"

Curved handle cutout

14"

7⅝"

¼" plywood bottom

Pine false front

2 **Rabbet, dado, and groove the drawer sides.** Fit the dado cutter in your table saw, and adjust cutter width to ½ inch. Mill a test dado in scrap stock to make sure that dado width matches the thickness of the drawer fronts, sides, and backs. Adjust the cutter height to ¼ inch. Then attach a wood auxiliary fence to your miter gauge. Use a straight piece of ¾-inch-thick wood for the auxiliary fence, and make it about 2 inches wide and 14 inches long. Attach the wood fence so that it extends several inches past the cutting width of the dado.

Turn on the saw, and mill an alignment dado in your auxiliary fence. Now clamp a stop block to the auxiliary fence, aligning the working edge of the stop block with the outside shoulder of the alignment dado. This will set you up to rabbet the front edges of the drawer sides. Cut each of these rabbets while holding the side against the miter gauge with its inside face on the saw table and its front edge against the stop block. (See *Photo 5*.)

To dado the sides for the back, reposition the stop block so that it's ½ inch from the shoulder of the alignment dado. Mill each of these dadoes as shown in *Photo 6*, with the back edge of the side butted against the stop block.

Adjust the dado cutter's width to ¼ inch so that you can mill grooves for the drawer bottoms. Position the rip fence ½ inch from the dado cutter; then mill grooves in the fronts and sides, always running the bottom edge of each part against the rip fence. (See *Photo 7*.)

3 **Notch the drawer fronts.** As shown in *Drawing D,* these drawers have cutout handles instead of conventional applied handles. Each drawer front is notched to create a handhold for the cutout handle on the false front that is fastened against it. Centered along the top edge of the drawer front, each notch is 1¾ inches deep and 5 inches long.

To simplify the layout and cutting of the notches, clamp all four drawer fronts together, with top and side edges flush. Lay out the notch on the drawer on top of the stack. Adjust your table saw blade height to 1¾ inches. Hold the clamped-together fronts against the miter gauge with all top edges against the saw table. Now align the blade with a notch shoulder layout line, and cut through your stack of fronts. Repeat this operation to make the opposite shoulder cut. Once the shoulder cuts are made, unclamp the fronts and finish the notches using a jigsaw.

4 **Make handle cutouts in the false fronts.** The cutout pattern is shown in *Drawing E.* To duplicate the cutout in each false front, you can use a pattern-cutting bit in

Photo 6: *To dado the sides for the drawer back, position the stop block ½ inch from an alignment dado milled in the wood auxiliary fence.*

Photo 7: *Groove the drawer sides and fronts with the rip fence set ½ inch from the dado cutter. Guide the bottom edge of each side or front against the rip fence to cut each groove.*

your router, along with a full-scale template. A pattern-cutting bit is a straight router bit with a bearing on the shank, directly above the cutters. The bearing's diameter is identical to the bit's cutting diameter.

Cut a piece of ¼-inch hardboard or plywood to the same length and width as the false front, and trace the handle cutout pattern onto it. For best results, drill out the two curved corners of the template, using a 1-inch-diameter bit in your drill. Cut out the rest of the template with a jigsaw. Sand the cutout area of the template smooth.

Temporarily attach the template to a false front by driving two ⅝-inch nails through the template and into the inside face of the false front. Make sure the template is flush with the edges of the false front. Now use your jigsaw to cut out the rough shape of the handle. Saw between ⅛ inch and ¼ inch inside the template. This will leave a small amount of waste to be removed by the router and pattern-cutting bit. Adjust the depth of your pattern-cutting bit so that the bit's bearing runs against the template edge. With the template and false front held securely, turn on the router, and run the bit's bearing against the edge of the template to rout each notch. (See Photo 8.) Repeat this technique to mill handles on all remaining false fronts.

Photo 8: Mill the curved notch into each false front using a template and a pattern-cutting bit. Mounted on the bit's shank, above the cutters, the bit's bearing is guided against a ¼-inch-thick template.

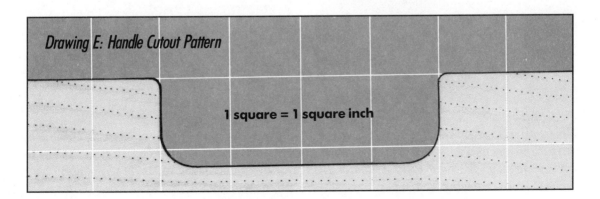

Drawing E: Handle Cutout Pattern

1 square = 1 square inch

5 **Assemble the drawers.** Begin the drawer assembly by joining the fronts to the sides using glue and ¾-inch paneling nails. Use three nails for each joint. Make sure that the bottom edges of each three-piece assembly are flush with each other. For each drawer, spread some glue in the grooves where its bottom will fit, then slip the bottom into place. Spread glue along the bottom edge of the back, and glue the back into the two side dadoes. The back's bottom edge should fit

against the drawer bottom. Secure each dado joint with three ¾-inch paneling nails. Square up the drawer as shown in *Photo 9,* holding an angle square against the front and a side. Then nail the drawer bottom to the bottom edge of the back, using three ¾-inch paneling nails.

6 **Finish the false fronts and drawers.** Give the drawers and false fronts a thorough sanding, paying particular attention to edges, corners, and to the handle cutouts on the false fronts. Round-over all sharp corners, and work to make flat areas and edges uniformly smooth. Then brush the parts free of sawdust, and apply finish. The false fronts shown here have a coat of "antique pine" stain followed by an application of satin polyurethane varnish. The drawers are finished with a primer-sealer coat, followed by a coat of acrylic latex semigloss enamel.

7 **Install the false fronts.** Install each false front by driving four 1-inch drywall screws through the front and into the false front from inside the drawer. Place a screw near each corner of the front. Be sure to center each drawer front on its false front before driving installation screws.

Photo 9: The last nails to drive when assembling a drawer are those that extend through the bottom and into the bottom edge of the back. Hold an angle square against the front and a side while driving these nails.

Preparing the Closet

1 **Clean out and clean up the closet.** If you haven't done so already, strip your closet back to its bare walls. Remove all existing shelves, ledgers, and poles. If this work damages drywall surfaces, repair holes or cracks as necessary, and prime the repaired areas. If the interior of your closet needs repainting, it will be easier to do this work now, before the new ledgers, shelves, and poles are installed.

2 **Attach the main shelf ledger.** As shown in *Drawing A,* this ledger board extends horizontally across the closet's back wall. To mark the exact height of the ledger, put the chest into position in the closet. Mark where the lower back edge of the chest's top contacts the wall; then remove the chest from the closet. Using a level, extend this mark into a line along the back wall. This line marks the ledger's top edge. Just above the line, mark where wall studs are located. For tips on locating studs in a wood-frame wall, see the Shop Savvy on page 32.

Cut the ledger to fit along the back wall, and install it by driving 2½-inch drywall screws through the ledger, through the drywall, and into wall studs. At the back corners of the closet, secure each ledger end by driving a screw at an angle (toescrewing) so that the screw will hold fast in the corner framing.

3 **Install the pole ledgers.** Cut all three of these ledgers to fit at the ends of the closet. Notch both upper pole ledgers to fit around the shelf ledger as shown in *Drawing F.* Make both notches ¾ inch deep and 1½ inches wide. Fit the upper pole ledgers into position so that their top edges are level with the top edge of the shelf ledger. Secure the pole ledgers by toescrewing them at the closet corners, using 2½-inch drywall screws. To avoid splitting the wood, predrill countersunk pilot holes for the ledger installation screws. Install the lower pole ledger so that its top edge is level and about 36½ inches from the floor.

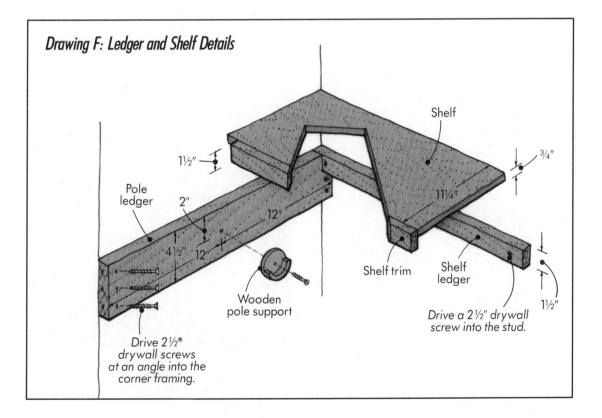

Drawing F: Ledger and Shelf Details

Shelf

1½″

3/4″

Pole ledger

2″

12″

11¼″

4½″   12″

Wooden pole support

Shelf trim

Shelf ledger

1½″

Drive a 2½″ drywall screw into the stud.

Drive 2½″ drywall screws at an angle into the corner framing.

Installing the Chest, Shelf, and Poles

1 **Sand and finish the chest.** It's much easier to do this work before the chest is installed. Begin sanding with 100-grit or 120-grit sandpaper, smoothing edges, corners, and flat surfaces. Then switch to 180-grit sandpaper, and go over the entire chest again. When you've finished sanding, brush all sawdust from the chest, and apply sealer and finish coats.

2 **Install the chest.** Center the chest on the closet's back wall. Fit the notches in the chest under the shelf ledger and over the baseboard. Use a level to make sure that the chest sides are plumb. Then anchor the chest to the wall by toescrewing 2½-inch drywall screws through the sides and into the shelf ledger and baseboard. Drill a countersunk pilot hole for each of the four installation screws—two

driven into the shelf ledger, and two driven into the baseboard. This should pull the chest firmly against the wall.

3 **Install the kickspace trim.** This rectangular piece of pine covers the opening at the bottom of the chest. Install it with glue and 4d finishing nails, driving three nails into each side's front edge.

4 **Cut and install the shelf sections.** The continuous shelf in the finished project actually consists of three parts: the top of the chest, and a pair of shelf sections that are installed on either side of it. To support each shelf end that fits against the chest, fasten a cleat against the chest side ¾ inch below the chest top. (See *Drawing G.*) Attach each cleat with three 1¼-inch drywall screws, driving them in countersunk pilot holes.

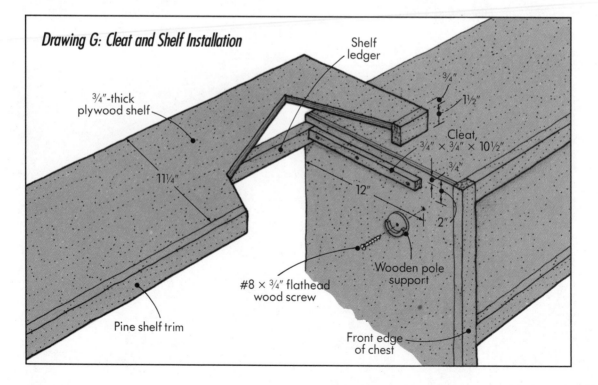

Drawing G: Cleat and Shelf Installation

Shelf ledger

¾"-thick plywood shelf

¾"

1½"

Cleat, ¾" × ¾" × 10½"

¾"

11¼"

12"

2"

#8 × ¾" flathead wood screw

Wooden pole support

Pine shelf trim

Front edge of chest

From ¾-inch-thick plywood (or a 1 × 12 pine board), cut both shelf sections to fit between the ends of the closet and the chest sides. Install each shelf section by driving 4d finishing nails through the top of the section and into the shelf and pole ledgers.

5 Cut and install the shelf trim pieces.

Each trim piece is ¾ inch thick, 1½ inches wide, and ¾ inch shorter in length than the shelf it's attached to. (See *Drawings F and G*.) These trim pieces are not just for appearance; they will prevent the shelves from sagging. After cutting both trim pieces to their finished dimensions, attach them to the front edges of both shelf sections, using glue and 4d finishing nails. The top edge of each trim piece should be flush with the top surface of the shelf. Set all nail heads, fill the resulting holes with wood putty, and sand the putty smooth after it has dried. Round-over the trim piece edges with 120-grit sandpaper.

6 Install the pole supports and poles.

The pole supports and poles are available at lumberyards and home centers. Finish these parts before installing them. In the project shown here, the closet poles and turned wood pole supports are finished with the same stain used on the drawer false fronts. Lay out the centers for installing the pole supports as shown in *Drawings B, F, and G*. Then install each upper support by driving a #8 × ¾-inch flathead wood screw through the support's installation hole and into either a pole ledger or a chest side. (See *Photo 10*.) Drill pilot holes for the installation screws using a ⅛-inch-diameter bit.

To install the lower pole support against its ledger, locate the center of the installation hole 12 inches from the back edge of the ledger and 2 inches from the ledger's top edge. Fit the lower pole into its supports, and see whether it's level by placing a level along the top of the pole. If a slight adjustment is needed to make the lower pole level, you can move either of its supports up or down.

Remove the drawers, poles, and pole supports while you paint the ledgers and shelves. After the paint has dried, reattach these parts and put your revamped closet to work.

Photo 10: Poles are held by wooden pole supports that are screwed to the chest and to pole ledgers at each end of the closet.

Toy Chest

Your kids will begin enjoying this toy chest even before you get a chance to stow a single plaything inside. Just hand them a box of chalk and let them decorate the box. Its front, rear, and side panels are coated with a special blackboard paint that cleans with a chalk eraser or damp cloth, just like any blackboard. When your kids get tired of drawing, they'll find that the toy chest makes a relaxing seat, complete with kid-sized armrests and backrest.

This toy chest uses applied frames which make it quite easy to build. The panels are made of plywood, which doesn't expand and contract with humidity changes as solid wood does. This eliminates the need to "float" the panels in frame grooves as you must do for solid wood. Instead of cutting grooves, mortises, and tenons, you'll simply screw the frame members to the panels.

The panels are made of medium-density overlay (MDO) plywood. This plywood has a factory-applied paper lamination. The paper offers a smooth, durable surface that is ideal for painting. For this reason, many road signs are made of MDO.

You'll probably have to special-order your MDO. It's available with the paper lamination on one or both sides. For this project you need only one MDO side. If your lumber dealer can't find a source for MDO board, use cabinet-grade birch, poplar, or maple plywood instead.

The toy chest has wheels instead of feet, making it easy to move around and giving it a playful appearance. The chest's seat is fitted with spring-dampening supports. These supports are a very important safety feature. They make the seat close slowly, so it can't slam shut on a head or hand.

Making the Chalkboard Panels

1 **Cut the panels to size.** If you are cutting the parts from a full sheet of MDO, start by using your circular saw to rough-cut a 38-inch-wide, 96-inch-long piece. Then set your table saw rip fence 18½ inches from the blade, place the piece's factory edge against the fence, and rip it into two 96-inch-long pieces. After you've made the cut, run the wider piece through the same fence setting, removing the edge which you cut with the circular saw.

Cut the front and back panels and the bottom to rough length and the side panels to rough width, adding about ½ inch to the

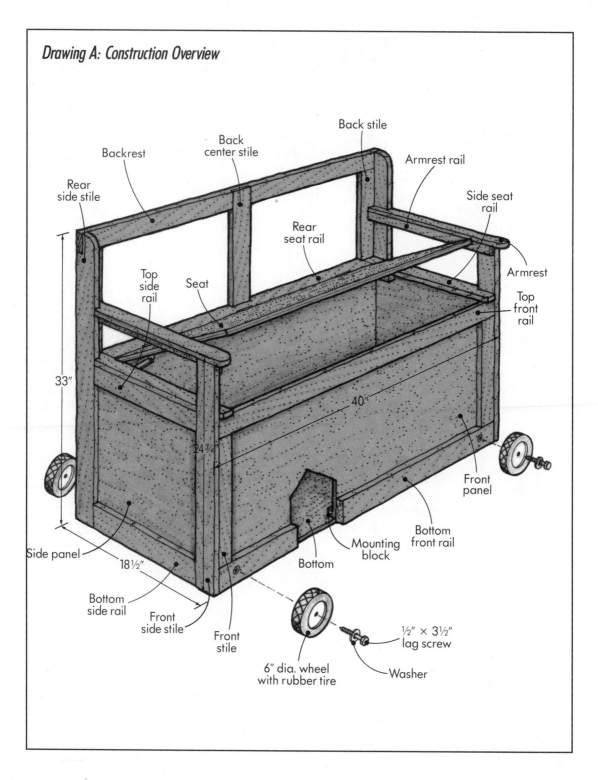

Drawing A: Construction Overview

Backrest

Back center stile

Back stile

Rear side stile

Armrest rail

Side seat rail

Top side rail

Rear seat rail

Seat

Armrest

Top front rail

33"

40"

24¾"

Front panel

Side panel

18½"

Bottom side rail

Front side stile

Front stile

Bottom

Mounting block

Bottom front rail

6" dia. wheel with rubber tire

½" × 3½" lag screw

Washer

Materials List

Wood

QTY	PART	DIMENSION
Panels		
1	MDO* front panel	$\frac{3}{8}'' \times 18\frac{1}{2}'' \times 38\frac{1}{2}''$
1	MDO back panel	$\frac{3}{8}'' \times 18\frac{1}{2}'' \times 38\frac{1}{2}''$
2	MDO side panels	$\frac{3}{8}'' \times 16\frac{1}{4}'' \times 18\frac{1}{2}''$
1	MDO bottom panel	$\frac{3}{8}'' \times 16\frac{1}{4}'' \times 37\frac{3}{4}''$
Side Frames		
2	Poplar rear stiles	$\frac{3}{4}'' \times 2\frac{1}{2}'' \times 33''$
2	Poplar bottom rails	$\frac{3}{4}'' \times 2\frac{1}{2}'' \times 13\frac{1}{2}''$
2	Poplar top rails	$\frac{3}{4}'' \times 2\frac{1}{2}'' \times 13\frac{1}{2}''$
2	Poplar armrest rails	$\frac{3}{4}'' \times 1\frac{3}{4}'' \times 17\frac{3}{4}''$
2	Poplar front stiles	$\frac{3}{4}'' \times 2\frac{1}{2}'' \times 24''$
2	Poplar armrests	$\frac{3}{4}'' \times 1\frac{3}{4}'' \times 18\frac{1}{2}''$
Front Frame		
1	Poplar bottom rail	$\frac{3}{4}'' \times 2\frac{1}{2}'' \times 40''$
1	Poplar top rail	$\frac{3}{4}'' \times 2\frac{1}{2}'' \times 40''$
2	Poplar stiles	$\frac{3}{4}'' \times 1\frac{3}{4}'' \times 13\frac{1}{8}''$
Back Frame		
2	Poplar bottom rails	$\frac{3}{4}'' \times 2\frac{1}{2}'' \times 16\frac{1}{4}''$
2	Poplar top rails	$\frac{3}{4}'' \times 2\frac{1}{2}'' \times 16\frac{1}{4}''$
2	Poplar side stiles	$\frac{3}{4}'' \times 1\frac{3}{4}'' \times 30\frac{1}{2}''$
1	Poplar center stile	$\frac{3}{4}'' \times 2\frac{1}{2}'' \times 33''$
1	Poplar backrest	$\frac{3}{4}'' \times 2\frac{1}{2}'' \times 40''$

*MDO stands for medium-density overlay.

Wood

QTY	PART	DIMENSION
Seat		
1	Rear seat rail	$\frac{3}{4}'' \times 1\frac{1}{2}'' \times 35''$
2	Poplar side seat rails	$\frac{3}{4}'' \times 2\frac{1}{2}'' \times 17\frac{3}{4}''$
1	Poplar seat	$\frac{3}{4}'' \times 17\frac{11}{16}'' \times 34\frac{7}{8}''$
2	Poplar mounting blocks	$1\frac{3}{8}'' \times 2'' \times 3''$
2	Poplar bottom mounting blocks	$\frac{3}{4}'' \times 1\frac{1}{2}'' \times 16\frac{1}{4}''$
2	Poplar bottom mounting blocks	$\frac{3}{4}'' \times 1\frac{1}{2}'' \times 36\frac{1}{4}''$

Hardware

1 quart blackboard paint
  Manufactured by Klean-Strip, W. M. Barr, Inc.,
  Memphis, TN 38101-1879
$\frac{3}{4}''$ drywall screws, as needed
$1\frac{1}{4}''$ drywall screws, as needed
1″ drywall screws, as needed
3 butt hinges, $1\frac{1}{2}'' \times 1\frac{1}{2}''$
1 left-hand seat support
  Available from Woodworker's Supply,
  5604 Alameda Place, Albuquerque, NM 87113;
  (800) 645-9292; Part #100033
1 right-hand seat support
  Available from Woodworker's Supply; Part #100032
#4 × $\frac{3}{4}''$ roundhead wood screws, as needed
4 wheels, 6″ dia., with solid rubber tires
4 lag screws, $\frac{1}{2}'' \times 3\frac{1}{2}''$
8 washers, with $\frac{1}{2}''$ holes

Materials List dimensions. Set the bottom piece aside; you'll cut it to final dimensions after assembling the box.

Square one end of each front, back, and side panel. Do this with your circular saw, using a straight guide board clamped to the workpiece, or use the jig described on page 270. (See "Make a Jig for Square Cutoffs and Dadoes.") Now use the guide board or jig to cut these pieces to their final dimensions.

2 Apply the chalkboard finish. This special paint, available from the source listed in the Materials List, actually contains slate particles that become part of the finished surface. A good-quality, alkyd-based, flat black enamel will also make a durable chalkboard. With either finish, plan to apply two coats to the MDO side of all four panels. Use a high-quality paintbrush (2 or 2½ inches wide) made for use with oil-based paints.

Apply the finish carefully, using long brush strokes to keep each coat even. Set the panels aside to dry completely.

Cutting the Frame

1 Cut the frame parts to size. Cut the stiles and rails, as well as the armrests and seat rails, to the sizes given in the Materials List. Begin by ripping them to width. Make sure you have a straight, square edge to run against the rip fence. (See "Straight, Square Edges" on page 22.) Cut the parts in batches, arranged by width: Cut all the 1½-inch-wide pieces, then reset the fence and cut the 1¾-inch-wide pieces, and so on.

Photo 1: To cut the lap joint for the seat back, make overlapping passes through the dado cutter, guiding the workpiece with the miter gauge.

Make sure that your miter gauge is square with the saw blade, and cut the frame parts to their final lengths. When cutting the two armrest rails to final length, be sure to make a 45-degree bevel cut on one end of each rail. This angled end is shown in *Drawing C*.

2 Cut the seat back's lap joints. As shown in *Drawing B*, the backrest and the back's center stile meet in a lap joint. To cut the joint, replace your table saw blade with a dado cutter, and adjust the cutter to its maximum width. Now raise the cutter to a height of ⅜ inch, or exactly half the thickness of the frame. To test your height setting, turn on the saw and cut a sample lap joint in two scrap pieces of poplar. Fine-tune the cutter height until you're able to mill a sample joint that fits together properly. The thickness across the joint should match the thickness of the stock.

Lay out both halves of the joint, marking shoulder lines on the back's center stile and on the backrest. Guide each piece against the miter gauge, and make overlapping passes across the cutter until you've completed each half of the joint. (See *Photo 1*.)

3 Cut curves in the rear side stiles. As shown in *Drawing B*, each of these two stiles extends to support the backrest. Draw a 2-inch-radius curve on the top corner of each piece, and cut out the curves with a jigsaw.

4 Cut the notches. There are three sets of notches in this project: The rear side stiles are notched to hold the backrest. The armrests and the side seat rail are notched around the rear side stiles, and the backrest is notched around the back center stile. Notch dimensions are given in *Drawings B, C, and D*. To cut the notches, adjust the dado cutter's height to ¾ inch, and make a series of overlapping

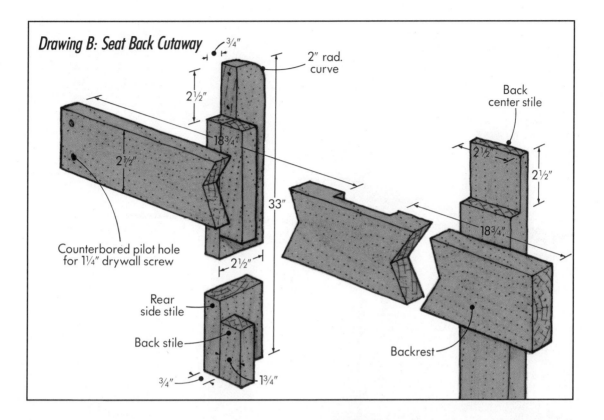

Drawing B: Seat Back Cutaway

2½"

¾"

2" rad. curve

18¾"

33"

2½"

2½"

Counterbored pilot hole for 1¼" drywall screw

Rear side stile

Back stile

¾"

1¾"

Back center stile

2½"

2½"

18¾"

Backrest

passes to complete the notch, guiding the workpiece with one side held against the miter gauge. (See *Photo 2*.)

Assembling the Chest

1 **Attach the stiles and front rails.** The vertical stiles and horizontal rails are shown in detail in *Drawings E and F*. Note that rails are always installed between stiles, except on the front panel. Note also that the 1¾-inch-wide stiles (on front and back panels) are installed with one long edge flush with a panel edge. The 2½-inch-wide stiles on the side panels are installed so that their edges extend 1⅛ inches beyond the side panel edges.

To install frame members, drive ¾-inch drywall screws through the unfinished

Photo 2: Set the dado cutter ¾ inch high and cut the notch in several passes.

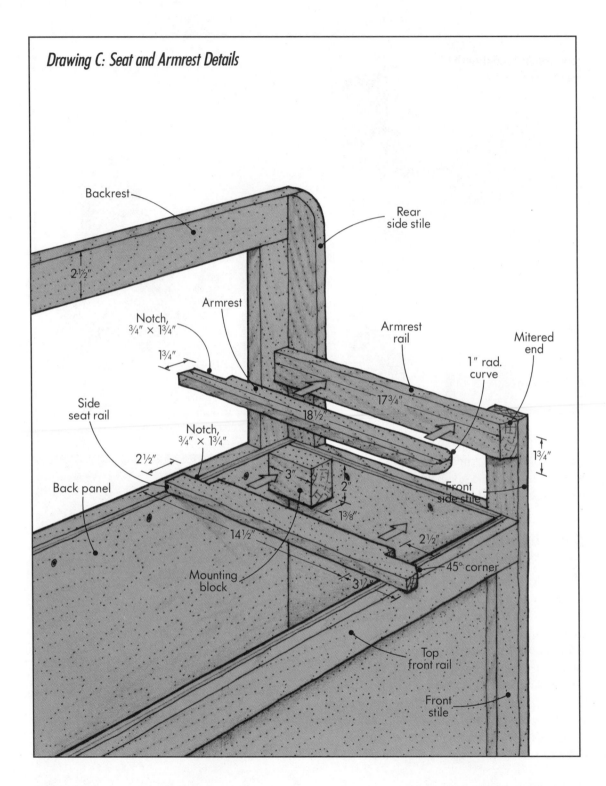

Drawing C: Seat and Armrest Details

Backrest

Rear side stile

2½"

Armrest

Notch, ¾" × 1¾"

1¾"

Armrest rail

Mitered end

1" rad. curve

17¾"

18½"

Side seat rail

Notch, ¾" × 1¾"

2½"

Back panel

3"

2"

1¾"

1⅜"

Front side stile

14½"

Mounting block

2½"

45° corner

3½"

Top front rail

Front stile

(inside) face of the panel. Spring clamps do a good job of securing the frame member against its panel while you drive screws to install it. Drill countersunk pilot holes for the screws, spacing them about 5 inches apart.

Start by installing the stiles on back and side panels, following the information in *Drawing E*. The bottom ends of these stiles should extend ⅜ inch beyond the bottom edges of the side and back panels. Next, install the front rails, again driving ¾-inch drywall screws into countersunk pilot holes. The ends of these rails should be flush with the side edges of the panel, and the bottom rail's bottom edge should extend ⅜ inch below the panel's bottom edge. Make the top rail's top edge flush with the top edge of the panel.

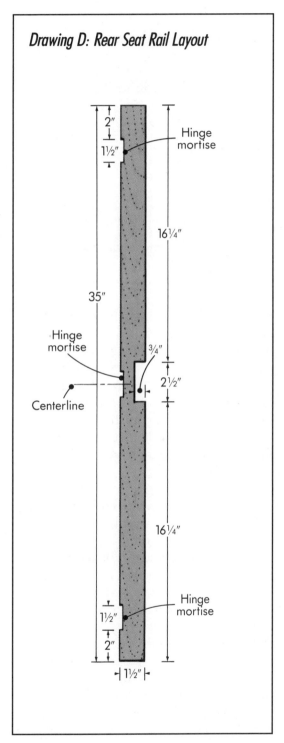

Drawing D: Rear Seat Rail Layout

Photo 3: Install the frame by driving ¾-inch drywall screws through the inside face of each panel. Drill countersunk pilot holes for the screws.

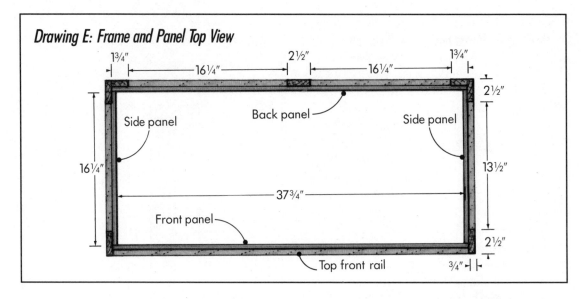

Drawing E: Frame and Panel Top View

1¾"   16¼"   2½"   16¼"   1¾"

2½"

Side panel

Back panel

Side panel

16¼"

13½"

37¾"

Front panel

2½"

Top front rail

¾"

2 Attach the remaining frame members. These include the rails for the back and side panels, as well as the stiles for the front panel. (See *Drawing F*.) Use ¾-inch drywall screws, driving them into countersunk holes, as in the previous step. (See *Photo 3*.) Make sure that the top edge of each top rail is flush with the panel's top edge. Rail bottom edges should be flush with the bottom ends of the stiles.

3 Join the sides, back, and front. When you put these frame-and-panel assemblies together, make sure the top edges of all the panels are flush. Spread glue on the corner joints, clamp them together, and secure them by driving 1¼-inch drywall screws in ⅜-inch-diameter counterbored holes. Make each counterbored hole between ¼ inch and ⅜ inch deep, and space the holes about 6 inches apart. Wipe off excess glue with a damp cloth. With the chest standing right-side up, brace the sides square with the front and back by tacking temporary braces across opposite corners.

4 Install the bottom and mounting blocks. As shown in *Drawing A,* the chest bottom fits against the bottom edges of the side, front, and back panels, and against ¾-inch-thick, 1½-inch-wide mounting blocks that are attached to the inside of the chest. Cut four mounting blocks to fit inside the chest, one mounting block against each panel. With a hand plane, chamfer one long edge of each mounting block. Using 1¼-inch drywall screws, glue and screw each block to its panel as shown in *Photo 4*. The chamfered edge should face into the chest, while the opposite edge is flush with the bottom edge of the panel.

Rip and crosscut the bottom to fit. To install the bottom, first spread glue along the bottom edges of the mounting blocks. Then place the bottom on the mounting blocks so that the overlay surface faces inside the chest. Drive 1-inch drywall screws through the bottom and into the mounting blocks. Space the screws about 8 inches apart. It shouldn't be necessary to drill pilot holes for these screws. Drive the heads flush with the wood surface.

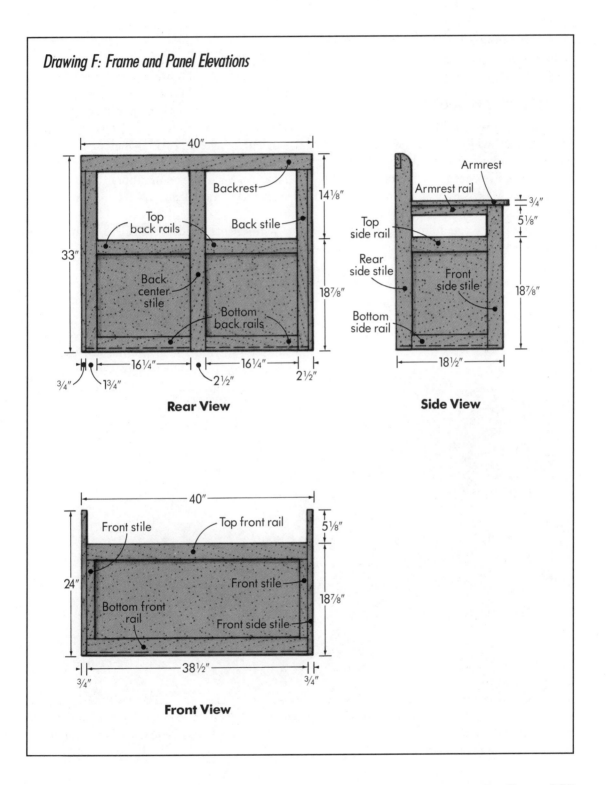

Drawing F: Frame and Panel Elevations

Rear View

40"

33"

14⅛"

18⅞"

Backrest

Top back rails

Back stile

Back center stile

Bottom back rails

16¼"

16¼"

2½"

2½"

¾"

1¾"

Side View

Armrest

Armrest rail

Top side rail

Rear side stile

Front side stile

Bottom side rail

¾"

5⅛"

18⅞"

18½"

Front View

40"

24"

5⅛"

18⅞"

Front stile

Top front rail

Front stile

Bottom front rail

Front side stile

38½"

¾"

¾"

Once the bottom is installed, turn the chest right-side up and remove the temporary diagonal braces.

Completing the Seat

1 Glue up the seat blank. To make this 17 ⅝-inch-wide seat more warp-resistant, glue up a blank approximately 18 inches wide from four or five boards, each one at least 36 inches long. Make sure your boards are clear and straight, with square edges. Arrange the boards so that the end grain patterns alternate, curving up and down across the width of the blank. Spread glue on adjoining edges. Place clamps on alternate sides of the panel to equalize clamping pressure, and protect the edges of the blank by using wood clamping blocks between the clamping feet and the workpiece.

2 Install the backrest. Installation details for this part are shown in *Drawing B*. Spread glue on adjoining surfaces, and fit the backrest's lap and notch joints together. Clamp the lap joint tight until the glue sets. Fasten each end of the backrest to the notched side rail by driving two 1¼-inch drywall screws into counterbored pilot holes. (See *Photo 5*.) Make the counterbores between ¼ inch and ⅜ inch deep.

3 Install the side seat rails. As shown in *Drawing C*, each of these pieces is notched to fit around the side panel's front and rear stile. Each side seat rail overhangs the front panel's top rail by ¾ inch. Cut a 45-degree corner on the front end of each side seat rail as shown in *Drawing C*. Drill counterbored pilot holes for three 1¼-inch drywall screws in the

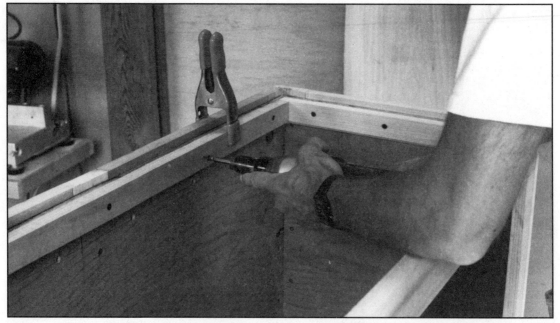

Photo 4: After assembling the sides, front, and back, install the bottom mounting blocks with glue and 1¼-inch drywall screws. The bottom edges of the mounting blocks should be flush with the bottom edges of the panels.

top of each side rail and drive the screws into the top side rail.

4 Install the armrest rails. Glue and screw these two parts in place, as shown in *Drawing C*. Drill counterbored pilot holes for a pair of ¾-inch drywall screws in each of the stiles and install these rails as shown in *Photo 6*.

5 Install the armrests. Before attaching these two parts, round the front end of each one by cutting a 1-inch-radius curve in both front corners. Don't worry if these curved cuts aren't identical; you'll smooth them out later.

Spread glue on the top of each armrest rail, and in each armrest notch. Then position each part on its rail. Secure the armrests by coun-

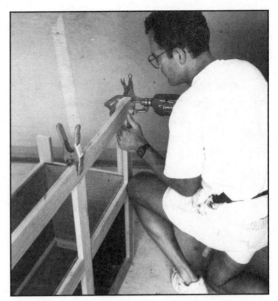

Photo 5: Glue and screw the backrest into place.

Photo 6: Install the side seat rails, armrest rails, and armrests with glue and counterbored screws.

terboring and driving 1¼-inch drywall screws through the armrests and into the armrest rail.

6 **Sand and cut the seat.** Unclamp the seat after glue has dried, and use a scraper to remove hardened glue from along joint lines. Then sand both sides smooth. This smoothing work is easiest to do with a belt sander or a random-orbit sander. With either tool, start out using a medium-grit belt or disk, then finish up with a fine-grit belt or disk.

Test fit the rear seat rail. Its notch should fit around the back panel's center stile, and its back edge should be flush with the back panel's top rail. (See *Drawing A*.) Now measure the opening for the seat. To calculate the finished width of the seat, measure from the rear seat rail to the outside edge of the top front rail. Add ⅝ inch to this measurement. To calculate the seat length, subtract ⅛ inch from the length of the opening. Cut the seat to width and length.

7 **Cut hinge mortises in the seat and rear seat rail.** The mortise layout is shown in *Drawing D*. Leave the rear seat rail in place on the chest, and take the seat over to your workbench to mortise the hinges to its back edge. (See "Mortising for a Butt Hinge" on page 93.) When you've installed the hinges in the seat, hold the seat in its opening, allowing for equal clearance between the ends of the seat and the edges of the side pieces. Now lay out your hinge mortises on the seat rail. Now you can remove the rail and cut its hinge mortises on the workbench.

8 **Install the seat and rear seat rail.** Glue and screw the seat rail into place, fitting it as described in Step 6. Secure the rail by driving six 1¼-inch drywall screws through the

Shop Savvy

A Simple Jig for Perpendicular Holes

A short piece of 2 × 4 stock with a rabbet cut along one edge makes a fine guide for drilling holes that are perpendicular to the workpiece. To make your jig, start with a straight piece of 2 × 4 stock that's at least 12 inches long. Rabbet one long edge by making two cuts on the table saw, with the blade height set at about ¾ inch. Guide the 2 × 4 against the rip fence for each cut. When you've completed the rabbet, use your miter gauge to cut off a piece about 2½ inches long. When drilling, use both edges of the rabbet to guide the drill bit.

top of the rail and into the top edge of the top back rail. Counterbore all screw holes, as before. Once the seat rail is screwed down, install the seat by screwing its hinges in their seat rail mortises.

9 **Install the seat supports.** This support hardware will prevent the seat from slamming shut and possibly injuring a hand or head as it closes. Each support has a spring-dampening mechanism that causes the seat to shut slowly. To mount each support, glue and clamp a mounting block inside the chest, as shown in *Drawing C*. When the glue dries,

hold the seat open at an 85-degree angle. You can use a protractor to set your bevel gauge to this angle. Hold the seat open against the bevel gauge, and tighten a small C-clamp against one armrest, positioning the clamp so that it holds the seat open at the proper angle.

With the seat held open, hold each support in its installed position, as shown in *Drawing G*. Now use an awl or a sharp nail to mark pilot hole locations for the four installation screws. Drill pilot holes with a 1/16-inch-diameter bit, and then install each support by driving #4 × 3/4-inch roundhead wood screws into the pilot holes. (See *Photo 7*.)

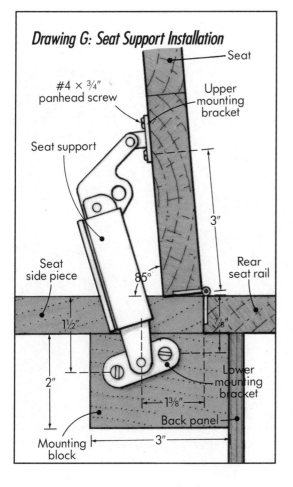

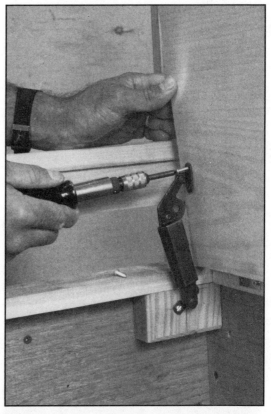

Photo 7: *Screw each seat support to its mounting block; then keep the seat open about 85 degrees when screwing the support to the seat.*

Finishing Up

1 **Fill the counterbores with dowel plugs.** Cut each plug from a dowel rod with a diameter that matches that of the counterbores. Cut each plug about ½ inch long. Then pour some glue into a small dish, dip each plug into the glue, and then tap the plug into a counterbore. (See *Photo 8*.) Wipe off excess glue from around the plug with a damp cloth.

2 **Trim the plugs and sand the chest.** When the glue has dried, use a fine-toothed saw to trim each plug flush. Take care to cut only the dowel and not the surrounding wood surface. (See *Photo 9*.) When this trimming is done, begin sanding. A random-orbit

sander with a medium-grit sanding disk is a good way to start. Pay particular attention to the dowel plugs, which should be sanded flush, and to curved parts, which should be rounded evenly. Switch to a fine-grit sanding disk to finish smoothing the flat surfaces with your sander. Then work by hand, using 200-grit sandpaper to ease the sharp corners of frame members. Take care not to sand the blackboard surfaces.

3 **Drill holes for the wheel axles.** Each wheel turns on a ½-inch-diameter, 3½-inch-long lag screw axle. The lag screws are driven into the front and back of the chest, into the bottom mounting blocks. Lay out the center for each hole 1⅛ inches from the bot-

Photo 8: After dipping each dowel plug in glue, tap it into a counterbored hole.

Photo 9: After the glue has dried, trim dowel plugs using a fine-toothed saw.

tom of the chest, and 1⅝ inches from the end. Drill 2¼-inch-deep pilot holes for the lag screws, using a ⅜-inch-diameter bit. For a quick, easy jig that helps you to keep the bit perpendicular as you drill, see the Shop Savvy on page 338.

Use a pair of washers when installing each wheel. (See *Photo 10.*) Place one washer over the screw shank, between the wheel and the head of the screw. Place the other washer over the screw shank, between the wheel and the chest.

4 Apply the finish. To make finishing easier, remove the wheels and axles and remove the seat hinges and supports. On the toy chest shown here, the frame members are finished with an alkyd primer followed by two coats of red enamel. A stained finish would also look good. For durability, apply at least one coat of satin polyurethane over the stain.

To avoid getting finish on the panels, mask them off, using newspaper and masking tape. (See *Photo 11.*) Apply the tape lightly to the panels so as not to risk peeling away blackboard finish. Also, apply your finish coats as soon as possible after masking off the panels. Allowing masking tape to stay in place for more than several days will make it more difficult to remove. If sticky tape residue remains on the panels after removing the tape, wipe it off with a rag dampened in mineral spirits.

Reattach the wheels and seat after your last coat of finish has dried.

Photo 10: Install each wheel with a lag screw and a pair of washers.

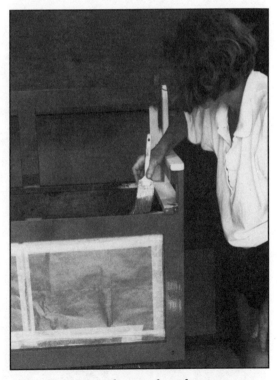

Photo 11: Protect the panels with newspaper and masking tape before applying the finish.

Chest of Drawers

This chest of drawers owes its classic good looks to the fine antique that inspired its design. But instead of being built entirely from solid oak, the new chest relies on plywood to simplify construction. The sides of the chest are oak-veneered plywood, and the drawers are made from birch-veneered plywood. The top and drawer false fronts are solid oak, as are the frame members that separate and support the drawers.

The result is a chest that not only is handsome and sturdy, but is also quite easy to build. The Materials List is long, but the joinery details consist of simple dadoes, rabbets, and grooves.

If you favor cherry, maple, or another hardwood over oak, you can combine solid stock with like-veneered plywood, as was done here. Whatever wood you choose, select your solid stock with care. Use only clear, straight boards for the solid parts.

Making the Sides

1 Cut the sides. Unless you have large extension tables around your table saw, it's easiest to cut the sides to rough width using a circular saw before cutting them to final width on the table saw. Factory edges on plywood panels are straight but usually have dings from handling. So you'll use the factory edge as a reference and then rip it off. Start by laying out an 18¼-inch-wide cut along the full length of the plywood sheet. Make the cut by following the line with the circular saw. Then crosscut this piece in half with the circular saw.

Now set the table saw fence 18⅛ inches from the blade. Rip both pieces to this width, running the factory edges against the rip fence. Next, adjust the fence so that it's 18 inches from the blade, and rip off the factory edges. This will give you clean, straight edges on both side pieces.

Crosscut the sides to finished length, making sure that these cuts are square. (See "Make a Jig for Square Cutoffs and Dadoes" on page 270.)

2 Cut oak parts for the carcase. Make sure that the oak boards for the carcase parts are uniformly ¾ inch thick. It's also important for at least one edge of each board to be straight and square. (See "Straight, Square Edges" on page 22.)

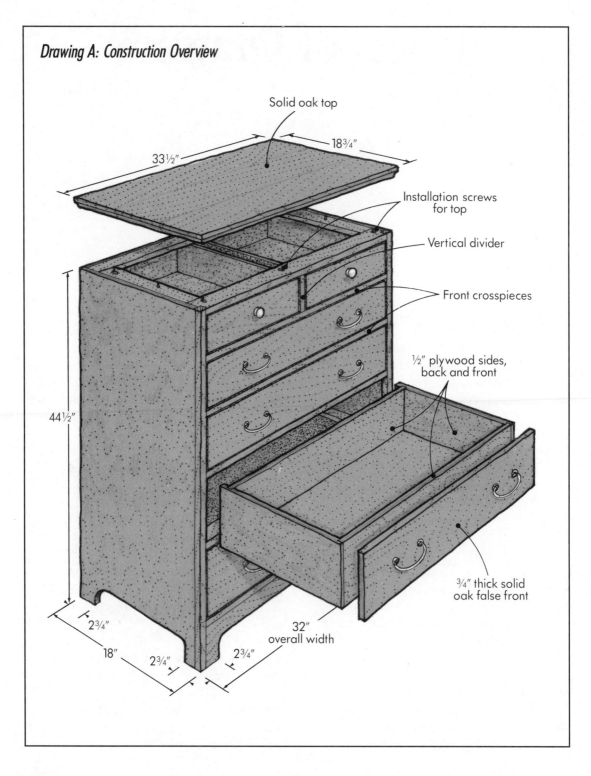

Drawing A: Construction Overview

Solid oak top

18¾"

33½"

Installation screws for top

Vertical divider

Front crosspieces

½" plywood sides, back and front

¾" thick solid oak false front

44½"

2¾"

18"

2¾"

2¾"

32" overall width

Materials List

Wood

QTY	PART	DIMENSION
Carcase		
2	Plywood sides	¾″ × 17¼″ × 44½″
2	Oak corner trim pieces	¾″ × ¾″ × 44½″
1	Plywood back	¼″ × 31¼″ × 44½″
1	Oak top	¾″ × 18¾″ × 33½″
Horizontal Frames		
6	Oak front crossmembers	¾″ × 2½″ × 31¼″
6	Oak rear crossmembers	¾″ × 1½″ × 31¼″
12	Oak side supports	¾″ × 1½″ × 13¾″
1	Oak center support	¾″ × 2½″ × 13¾″
24	Plywood splines	¼″ × 1″ × 1½″
2	Plywood center splines	¼″ × 1″ × 2½″
1	Oak vertical divider	¾″ × 2½″ × 5″
1	Oak bottom front panel	¾″ × 5″ × 30½″
1	Oak top drawer divider	¾″ × 1″ × 15¼″
Drawers		
1	Oak false front	½″ × 8⅞″ × 30⅜″
1	Oak false front	½″ × 7⅞″ × 30⅜″
1	Oak false front	½″ × 6⅞″ × 30⅜″
1	Oak false front	½″ × 5⅞″ × 30⅜″
2	Oak false fronts	½″ × 4⅞″ × 14¾″
2	Plywood sides	½″ × 8⅞″ × 17″
2	Plywood sides	½″ × 7⅞″ × 17″
2	Plywood sides	½″ × 6⅞″ × 17″
2	Plywood sides	½″ × 5⅞″ × 17″

Wood

QTY	PART	DIMENSION
4	Plywood sides	½″ × 4⅞″ × 17″
1	Plywood front	¾″ × 8⅞″ × 29⅞″
1	Plywood front	¾″ × 7⅞″ × 29⅞″
1	Plywood front	¾″ × 6⅞″ × 29⅞″
1	Plywood front	¾″ × 5⅞″ × 29⅞″
2	Plywood fronts	¾″ × 4⅞″ × 14¼″
1	Plywood back	½″ × 8⅛″ × 29⅞″
1	Plywood back	½″ × 7⅛″ × 29⅞″
1	Plywood back	½″ × 6⅛″ × 29⅞″
1	Plywood back	½″ × 5⅛″ × 29⅞″
2	Plywood backs	½″ × 4⅛″ × 14⅜″
4	Plywood bottoms	¼″ × 16″ × 29⅞″
2	Plywood bottoms	¼″ × 16″ × 14⅞″

Hardware

11 drywall screws, 1¼″
32 drywall screws, 1″
2 white knobs, 1⅜″ dia., with mounting screws.
Available from The Woodworkers' Store,
21801 Industrial Blvd., Rogers, MN 55374;
(612) 428-2199. Part #64394.
8 die-cast drawer pulls, 3″ boring, with mounting screws.
Available from The Woodworkers' Store. Part #32052.
4d finishing nails, as needed
1″ brads, as needed
⅝″ brads, as needed

When ripping parts to width from a wider board, always start by running the straight, square edge of the board against the rip fence. To minimize waste, it's usually best to cut out the widest parts first. From widest to narrowest, these parts include the bottom front panel, the front crossmembers, the center support, the vertical divider, the rear crossmembers, the side supports, the top drawer divider, and the front corner strips. If you have access to a jointer, rip parts 1⁄16 inch wider than their finished widths, and then remove 1⁄16 inch from the sawed edges on the jointer. After cutting all of these parts to their finished widths, cut them to their finished lengths.

3 Rabbet the back edges of the sides. The sides are rabbeted to receive the back. Replace the table saw blade with a dado cutter, and adjust the cutter width to ¾-inch. This

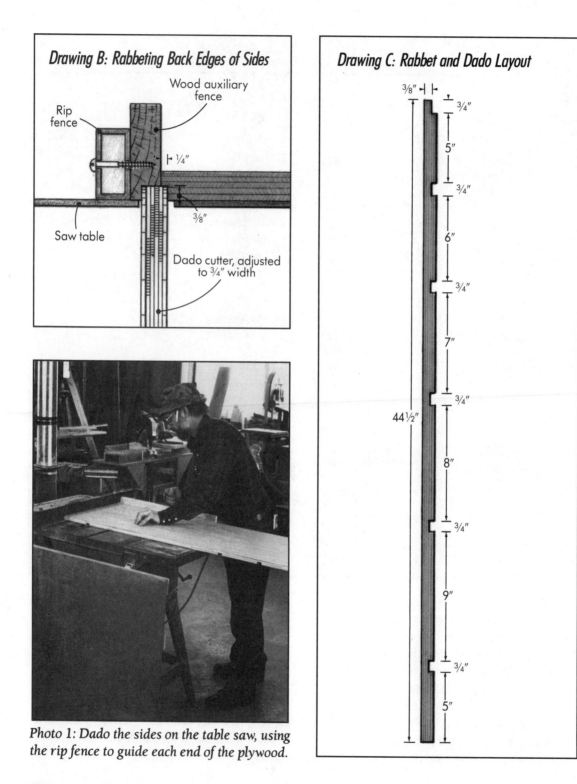

Drawing B: Rabbeting Back Edges of Sides

Wood auxiliary fence

Rip fence

1/4"

Saw table

3/8"

Dado cutter, adjusted to 3/4" width

Drawing C: Rabbet and Dado Layout

3/8"

3/4"

5"

3/4"

6"

3/4"

7"

3/4"

44½"

8"

3/4"

9"

3/4"

5"

Photo 1: Dado the sides on the table saw, using the rip fence to guide each end of the plywood.

width setting isn't important for this step, but you'll use it for the following two steps.

Lower the cutter just slightly below the table. Attach a wood auxiliary fence to the rip fence. Position the fence so that the wood covers all but ¼ inch of the dado's width. Make a mark on the wood fence exactly ⅜ inch above the table. Turn on the saw, and slowly raise the cutter into the wood auxiliary fence until the cutter reaches the mark. (See *Drawing B*.)

Examine the side pieces, and make sure to mill all rabbets and dadoes in the "bad" side of each piece so that it will face inside the finished chest. Run each side through the dado cutter with its back edge against the wood auxiliary fence.

4 Dado the sides. Lay out the dadoes on one side as shown in *Drawing C*. With a square, transfer the dado shoulders to the front and back edges of the side. To ensure that the dadoes in both sides match, guide the sides against the rip fence as you make the cuts. To mill the bottom dado, for example, position the rip fence 5 inches from the dado cutter, and run the bottom edge of each side against the fence. Reposition the fence for each new pair of dadoes. To help guide the side, brace a long edge against the miter gauge while running a short edge against the rip fence. (See *Photo 1*.)

5 Rabbet the top edges of the sides. The top frame sits in rabbets milled into the top inside edges of the sides. To make these rabbets, position the wood auxiliary fence as shown in *Drawing D*. Mill each rabbet by running the top edge of the side against the wood fence. Note: As an alternative to cutting rabbets and dadoes on the table saw, you can mill the joints using a router and a straight bit. See the project Formal Bookcase on page 192.

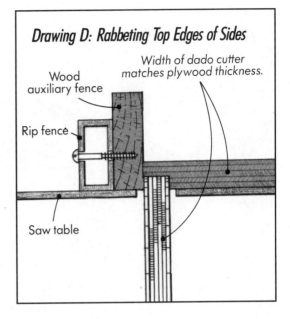

Drawing D: Rabbeting Top Edges of Sides

Width of dado cutter matches plywood thickness.

Wood auxiliary fence

Rip fence

Saw table

Building the Frames

Horizontal frames, shown in *Drawing E,* join sides together while separating and guiding the drawers. The frame members are joined with splines that fit into slots as shown in *Drawing F*. A total of six horizontal frames is required. It's important for all frames to be square and identical in size.

1 Notch the front crossmembers. The front crossmembers are notched to fit around the front trim pieces. Attach a wood auxiliary fence to your table saw's miter gauge. Adjust the dado cutter width to ⅜ inch, and the height to ¾ inch. Test these settings on some scrap stock, and adjust the cutter as necessary. Then run the wood fence through the dado cutter to make an alignment notch. Fasten a stop block to the fence, aligning it with the notch in the auxiliary fence. Hold a front

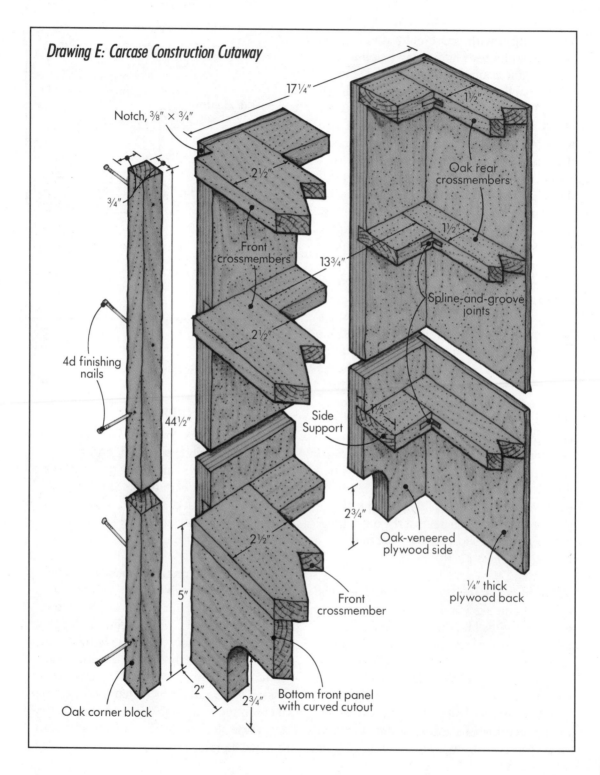

Drawing E: Carcase Construction Cutaway

Notch, 3/8" × 3/4"

17 1/4"

1 1/2"

Oak rear crossmembers

2 1/2"

3/4"

Front crossmembers

13 3/4"

1 1/2"

Spline-and-groove joints

4d finishing nails

2 1/2"

44 1/2"

Side Support

1 1/2"

2 3/4"

Oak-veneered plywood side

2 1/2"

5"

Front crossmember

1/4" thick plywood back

Oak corner block

2"

2 3/4"

Bottom front panel with curved cutout

crossmember with one side against the auxiliary fence and one end against the stop block to make the notch cuts. (See *Photo 2*.) Make a pair of notches in all six front crossmembers.

2 **Rout slots in the frame members.** Rout the slots with a ¼-inch slot-cutting bit. The bit used here has a pilot bearing that allows it to cut ½ inch deep. Adjust the bit depth so that the slots will be approximately centered.

To slot the ends of center and side supports, clamp all 13 members together with their ends flush, as shown in *Photo 3*. Run a pencil line across the top sides of these pieces. You'll need to use these *witness marks* later, when assembling the frames. Turn on the router, and slot one set of ends, then the other.

Rout the crossmember slots one at a time. Witness-mark the top side of each piece, and

Photo 2: Notch the front corners of each front crossmember with the dado cutter. A stop block, fastened to a miter gauge auxiliary fence, aligns the cut.

Photo 3: Clamp the side and center supports together, with ends flush, to rout slots for the splines.

cut a slot that extends 2 inches from each end of every crossmember. To hold the center support, rout center slots on one front crossmember and on one rear crossmember. (See *Drawing F*.) Make these slots about 3¼ inches long.

3 Cut the splines. For spline stock, you can use hardboard, plywood, or waferboard. The important thing is to use splines that are the same thickness as the slot width. The spline width should be ¹⁄₁₆ inch less than two times the slot depth. (See the Materials List.) This will leave space for glue and will ensure tight joints.

4 Assemble the horizontal frames. To ensure frame squareness and speed the assembly process, build a simple right-angle jig like the one shown in *Photo 4*. Be sure to

make your jig from a couple of boards or plywood rips with straight, square edges. Screw the long board to a plywood base; then use a framing square to keep the second board square with the first one as you screw it down.

To assemble a frame, spread glue on the splines and on the end grain of the side supports. Then join the crossmembers and supports. Make sure all witness marks are on the same side of the frame. Now hold one corner of the frame square in the jig while driving several ⅝-inch brads into the corner's spline-and-groove joint. You might find it helpful to clamp a frame member against the jig while nailing the corner, as shown in *Photo 4*. Brace and nail all four corners of each frame the same way. Then use glue, splines, and brads to secure the center support to its front and back crosspieces. Be sure to center this frame member between the side supports in the horizon-

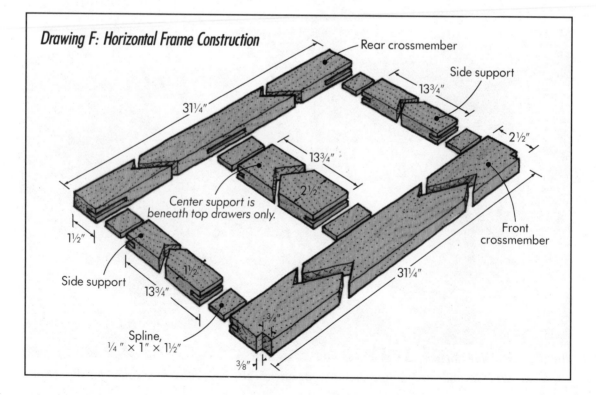

Drawing F: Horizontal Frame Construction

Rear crossmember

Side support

13¾"

31¼"

13¾"

2½"

2½"

Center support is beneath top drawers only.

Front crossmember

1½"

1½"

Side support

13¾"

31¼"

¾"

Spline, ¼" × 1" × 1½"

3/8"

tal frame. Set the completed frames aside until the glue cures.

Assembling the Carcase

1 **Cut curves in the sides and bottom front panel.** As shown in *Drawing G,* these cutouts begin 2¾ inches from the corners of the finished chest. Note that ¾ inch of this dimension is the corner block, so start the cuts 2 inches from the ends of the bottom front panel and the sides. After laying out the length and height of each cutout, mark the curve using a compass, or by tracing against a 2-inch-diameter container. Make all three cutouts with a jigsaw, using a fine-cutting blade.

2 **Join the frames to the sides.** First, use a framing square to mark nailing lines across the outside face of both sides. Center each line on a dado on the inner face of the side. Mark lightly with a pencil, so that all marks can be sanded off easily.

Carefully spread glue in the top dado and bottom dado of one side. Then fit two frames into these dadoes. Make sure that the shoulder of each crossmember notch is flush with the front edge of the side, as shown in *Drawing E.* Secure each joint by driving four 4d finishing nails through the side and into the edge of the frame. Glue and nail the remaining four frames to the same side, always taking care to align the frame notches with the side's front edge.

When all the frames have been joined to one side, turn the assembly over to rest on the outer face of the side. Now glue and nail the remaining side to the frames. (See *Photo 5.*) Use a damp cloth to wipe up excess glue that squeezes out of joints. Once the frames and

Photo 4: Assemble horizontal frames with the aid of a right-angle jig.

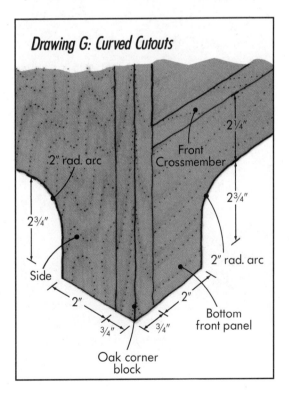

Drawing G: Curved Cutouts

2" rad. arc

Front Crossmember

2¼"

2¾"

2¾"

2" rad. arc

Side

Bottom front panel

2"

2"

¾"

¾"

Oak corner block

sides are together, put the carcase on its back in the right-angle jig to square it up. Measure across the diagonals. If the measurements are the same, the carcase is square. If not, place a long clamp between the corners of the diagonal that measured longer, and tighten the clamp until the diagonals measure the same.

3 Install the dividers. Cut the vertical divider to fit between the two uppermost frames. Spread some glue on the ends of this piece, and position it exactly halfway between the sides. Hold it in place with a bar clamp, as shown in *Photo 6*. Then drill countersunk pilot holes for two 1¼-inch drywall screws

through the top crossmember and one through the lower crossmember. You can unclamp the joint after driving all three screws.

Glue and screw the top drawer divider to the center support. Use three 1¼-inch drywall screws, driving them into countersunk pilot holes. When installing this piece, butt its front end against the back edge of the vertical divider, as shown in *Drawing H*. Also, make sure that this divider is perpendicular to the front of the drawer opening.

4 Install the corner trim pieces. Spread glue in the front crossmember notches

Photo 5: Glue and nail the six horizontal frames to one side, then to the other. Position the back of the notch flush with the edge of the side.

Photo 6: Center the vertical divider between the two uppermost horizontal dividers. Then drill countersunk pilot holes for 1¼-inch drywall screws to secure the piece.

and along the front edges of the sides. Then install the corner blocks by driving 4d finishing nails through the blocks and into the sides and crossmember notches. (See *Photo 7*.) To avoid bending nails and splitting the oak, predrill nail holes, using a ¹⁄₁₆-inch bit.

5 **Install the bottom front panel.** Spread glue along the ends and top edge of the front panel. Then put the panel into place with its top edge butted under the lowest front crossmember. Clamp the panel against the front crossmember. Predrill and drive 4d finishing nails through the crossmember into the top edge of the panel. Then predrill and drive 4d finishing nails through the corner blocks into the ends of the front panel.

6 **Cut and install the back.** Check the dimensions of the back of the carcase and cut the back to fit. Spread glue in the side rabbets and along the back edges of the rear crossmembers. Then fit the back into place, and secure it by driving ¾-inch paneling nails into the sides and rear crossmembers.

Photo 7: Solid oak corner blocks fit into crossmember notches and against the sides, covering each side's plywood edge. Install these blocks with glue and 4d finishing nails; then set the nail heads.

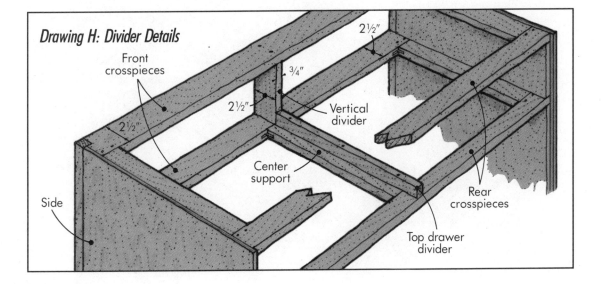

Drawing H: Divider Details

Front crosspieces

2½″

¾″

2½″

Vertical divider

2½″

Center support

Rear crosspieces

Side

Top drawer divider

Building the Drawers

The drawers for this chest have solid oak *false fronts* that are installed after the plywood drawer sides, bottom, back, and front are assembled. Construction details are shown in *Drawing I*. To avoid confusion when dealing with so many parts, keep the parts for each drawer together as you cut them to size and complete the joinery work. Mark which are the right sides and which are the left sides in each drawer, to avoid milling rabbets or dadoes in the wrong location.

1 **Cut the false fronts.** The drawer openings in your chest may be slightly different from those in the chest shown here, so measure your drawer openings carefully before sizing any drawer parts.

The false fronts need about ¹⁄₁₆ inch of clearance on all four sides. So subtract ⅛ inch from the drawer opening height and width to get the height and width of each false front.

Before cutting the oak for the false fronts, plan how you want the grain to flow across the drawers and what order will look best from top to bottom. Also, it's a good idea to cut the two top drawers from the same length of board so that the grain pattern will continue across them. Rip and crosscut the false fronts to size.

2 **Cut the plywood drawer parts.** For each drawer, rip plywood for the sides and front to the same width as the false front. Rip the drawer backs ¾ inch narrower than the sides and fronts. Before cutting the sides to length, measure inside the carcase from the plywood back to the front of the frames. Subtract the thickness of the false fronts. Cut the sides to exactly this length so that the fronts will be flush with the front of the carcase. Cut the plywood fronts and backs ½ inch shorter than the length of the false fronts. This allows for the depth of the rabbets and dadoes in the

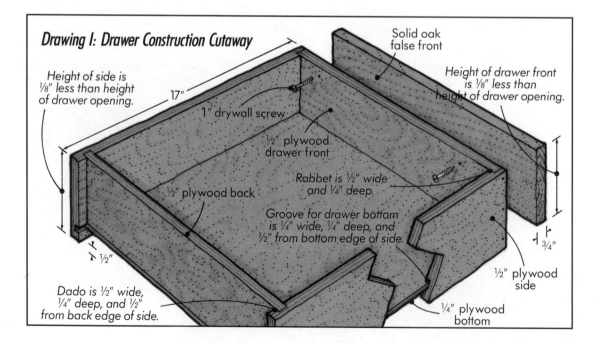

Drawing I: Drawer Construction Cutaway

Height of side is ⅛" less than height of drawer opening.

17"

1" drywall screw

½" plywood drawer front

Solid oak false front

Height of drawer front is ⅛" less than height of drawer opening.

Rabbet is ½" wide and ¼" deep.

½" plywood back

Groove for drawer bottom is ¼" wide, ¼" deep, and ½" from bottom edge of side.

¾"

½" plywood side

½"

Dado is ½" wide, ¼" deep, and ½" from back edge of side.

¼" plywood bottom

sides, as shown in *Drawing I*. When the plywood front is fitted into these joints, the sides will be flush with the ends of the false front.

3 **Groove the sides and plywood fronts for the bottoms.** Set up the dado cutter in the table saw, adjusting the cutter width to match the thickness of the plywood drawer bottoms (¼ inch). Raise the cutter to ¼ inch, and position the rip fence ½ inch from the cutter. Now cut the dadoes by running the bottom edges of the sides and plywood fronts against the rip fence. (See *Photo 8*.)

4 **Rabbet and dado the sides.** Adjust the width of the dado cutter to match the thickness of the drawer backs and false fronts (½ inch). Keep the dado height at ¼ inch. Attach a wood auxiliary fence to your miter gauge. Make the fence ¾ inch thick, about 2 inches high, and about 14 inches long. Make sure the gauge is set at 90 degrees. Turn on the saw and cut an alignment notch in the auxiliary fence. Now clamp a stop block against one shoulder of the alignment notch as shown in *Photo 9*. This setup will let you quickly and accurately rabbet the front edges of the sides.

When you have rabbetted all the front edges, reposition the stop block ½ inch from the shoulder of the alignment notch. Use this setup to dado the sides to hold the back. Butt the back edge of each side against the stop block to align the dado cut.

5 **Sand the plywood fronts, sides, and backs.** Round the top and bottom edges of your drawer parts slightly with 100- or 120-grit sandpaper. This will prevent the plywood veneer from splintering when you slide the drawer in and out and will make the drawer operate more smoothly.

Give all the drawer parts a final smoothing

Photo 8: Guide the bottom edge of each drawer side and false front against the rip fence to mill grooves for the drawer bottom.

Photo 9: Rabbet the front edge of each side using the dado cutter. An auxiliary fence and stop block, fastened to the miter gauge, will align each side for its run through the cutter.

before assembling them. This work can go quickly if you use an orbital or random-orbit sander and some 180- or 200-grit sandpaper.

6 Assemble the drawers. Use the right-angle jig to assemble the drawers with speed and accuracy. Spread glue along the rabbet-and-dado joints in the sides, where the back and plywood front will fit. Also run a bead of glue in the grooves where the drawer bottom will fit.

First fit the bottom into its grooves, and nail the sides to the plywood front with 1-inch brads. Then fit the back into its dadoes. Slide the back down against the bottom before nailing each dado joint fast. Now place the drawer upside down, and brace the plywood front and one side against the right angle of your assembly jig. Hold the drawer square while nailing

Photo 10: Before nailing the drawer bottom to the bottom edge of the back, square up the drawer against a right-angle jig.

through the bottom and into the bottom edge of the back. (See *Photo 10.*) Check again to make sure the drawer is square after nailing. Repeat this assembly process with all the drawers.

7 Attach the drawer fronts. The oak drawer fronts are installed by driving 1-inch drywall screws through the plywood fronts. For each small top drawer, four screws are required—one near each corner. The four lower drawers need six screws apiece—four corner screws and a pair of screws near the center. Drill countersunk pilot holes from the inside in the plywood fronts for all installation screws. Then slide each drawer into its opening.

To install each oak front, first place it in its opening, against the false front. Now use three shims to center the front in its opening. (See *Photo 11.*) Thin, slightly tapered pieces of wood work well as shims, but you can use cardboard or other material instead. Place one shim between the bottom edge of the oak front and the front crossmember. Place the other two shims between the front's ends and the corner blocks, or sides of the opening. Step back from the chest and make sure the drawer front looks centered in its opening. Then hold the front against the false front, reach into the chest from above the drawer, and drive the screws attaching the oak front. A cordless drill or driver comes in handy for this kind of work. Repeat this procedure to attach all the drawer fronts.

8 Drill holes for the knobs and pulls. In the chest shown here, each small top drawer has a knob, while each of the four lower drawers has a pair of pulls. Mark for screw holes with the drawers in place. Center the knobs on the top drawers and center the pulls below the knobs. Remove the false fronts. As you take each one off, mark its back with a little arrow so you'll know which end is up when you reinstall them. Drill holes in the false fronts for the knob and the pull screws. Drill these holes from the front and then countersink them from the back. Test fit the hardware on the drawer fronts, but don't fasten it in place or replace the false fronts until after you apply the finish.

Making and Installing the Top

As with the drawer fronts, make the top from clear, straight oak stock. You'll need to glue up several boards to make up the top's 18¾-inch width. For best results, use boards at least 35 inches long.

1 Glue up the top panel. Arrange the top boards to create a pleasing grain pattern. Then joint the board edges. Glue and clamp the top boards together with at least three pipe clamps. Protect the top by putting wooden pads between the top and the clamping feet. As you tighten the clamps, keep joints even, and make sure that the panel stays flat. Excessive or uneven clamping pressure will cause the boards to bow and shift.

2 Cut and smooth the top. Once the glue has cured, remove the clamps, scrape away any hardened glue, and sand both sides of the panel. To smooth down the high spots and remove glue marks, sand with 80-grit sandpaper in your belt sander.

Now cut the top to its finished size. The

Photo 11: Wood shims, placed along the drawer front's end and bottom edges, keep the front centered during installation. Attach the front to the false front by driving 1-inch screws through the false front, from inside the drawer.

dimensions given in the Materials List allow for a ¾-inch overhang on the sides and front of the chest.

Give the "good" side of the top a final sanding, using progressively finer grits up to 200- or 220-grit. Do this work by hand, or with a finish sander—either an orbital sander or a random-orbit sander. Round the top's front corners slightly, and soften all top edges.

3 **Mill the coved edge profile.** Chuck a ½-inch-radius cove bit in your router and set the depth at ½ inch. Now clamp the top to your workbench, with its good side facing down. Working counterclockwise, rout the

Photo 12: With the top clamped securely upside down, rout a cove along the end and the front edges.

coved profile along the end and front edges. (See *Photo 12*.) After routing, sand the coved surface with 220-grit sandpaper, smoothing out burn marks and other irregularities.

You will install the top after finishing the chest.

Applying Finish

1 **Sand the carcase.** Give the sides and front of your chest a final sanding. Smooth the joint between the sides and corner blocks, fill all nail holes with wood putty, and smooth all surfaces that will be visible in the finished chest. Using 220-grit sandpaper, soften the corners around the drawer openings. Then brush or vacuum the carcase free of loose sawdust.

2 **Apply finish coats.** For the chest shown here, the plywood drawers are sealed with a single coat of satin polyurethane. The chest's sides, front, top, and drawer fronts got several coats of "natural" penetrating oil finish. If you prefer the darker tone of aged oak, consider staining the sides, top, front, and drawer fronts with a "golden oak" stain. Depending on the manufacturer's recommendations, stain can be followed by a penetrating oil finish, wax, varnish, or polyurethane. Regardless of your finish choices, be sure to apply an equal number of coats to both sides of the top and the drawer fronts. This is important to prevent the oak from warping with humidity changes. It's a good idea to seal the inside of the chest with a coat of clear finish, too. Spread and buff paste wax along each side support, and along the bottom edges of the drawer sides. This will allow the drawers to slide smoothly, with a minimum of effort. Allow all finish coats to dry thoroughly before reattaching the top and the drawer fronts.

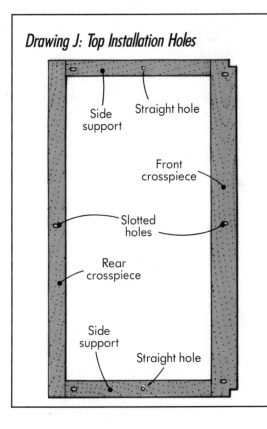

Drawing J: Top Installation Holes

Side support

Straight hole

Front crosspiece

Slotted holes

Rear crosspiece

Side support

Straight hole

Photo 13: By moving the drill from side to side, elongate the six top installation holes near the front and back of the top horizontal frame.

Completing the Assembly

1 **Install the top.** Drill eight countersunk ⅛-inch pilot holes in the uppermost horizontal frame. Locate the holes as shown in *Drawing J.* Drill all holes from inside the carcase to ensure that you'll have sufficient clearance for driving installation screws.

Enlarge the six holes at the front and back of the chest into slots. To do this, move your drill from side to side to make slots that are parallel to the side supports. (See *Photo 13.*)

Put the top in place with even overhangs on the front and sides. Hold the top down with clamps and a heavy object as shown in *Photo 14.* Now secure the top by driving 1¼-inch drywall screws into installation holes from inside the carcase.

Photo 14: Use a combination of clamps and weights to force the top down against the carcase during installation. From inside the carcase, drive 1¼-inch drywall screws through installation holes and into the top.

Sources

General Suppliers

(hardware, accessories, hand tools, portable and stationary power tools, finishes, and finishing tools)

Garrett Wade
161 Ave. of the Americas
New York, NY 10013
1-800-221-2942

Sears, Roebuck, & Company
(east of the Mississippi)
P.O. Box 780593
Wichita, KS 67278-0593
(west of the Mississippi)
P.O. Box 27900
San Antonio, TX 78227-0900
1-800-366-3000

Woodcraft
210 Wood County Industrial Park
P.O. Box 1686
Parkersburg, WV 26102-1686
1-800-225-1153

Woodworker's Supply
5604 Alameda Place NE
Albuquerque, NM 87113
1-800-645-9292

Environmentally Safe Finishes

Carver Tripp Finishes
Parks Corporation
P.O. Box 5
Somerset, MA 02726
1-800-225-8543

The Hydrocote Co., Inc.
P.O. Box 160
Tennent, NJ 07763
1-800-229-4937

Hardware, Accessories, and Portable Power Tools

(see also "General Suppliers")

Leichtung Workshops
4944 Commerce Parkway
Cleveland, OH 44128
1-800-321-6840

The Woodworker's Store
21801 Industrial Blvd.
Rogers, MN 55374-9514
(612) 428-2199

Williams Tool & Hardware Supply
2017 White Settlement Rd.
Fort Worth, TX 76107
1-800-338-6668

McFeely's
712 12th St.
Lynchburg, VA 24505-0003
1-800-443-7937

Stationary Power Tools

(see also "General Suppliers")

Farris Machinery Co.
320 N. 11th St.
Blue Springs, MO 64015
1-800-872-5489

Grizzly Imports, Inc.
P.O. Box 2069
Bellingham, WA 98227
1-800-541-5537

Jet Equipment and Tools
P.O. Box 1477
1901 Jefferson Ave.
Tacoma, WA 98402
1-800-274-6848

Router Bits and Router Accessories

Cascade
Box 3110
Bellingham, WA 98227
1-800-235-0272

Eagle America
P.O. Box 1099
Chardon, OH 44024
1-800-872-2511

MLCS Ltd.
P.O. Box 4053DA
Rydal, PA 19046
1-800-533-9298

Woodhaven
5323 W. Kimberley Rd.
Davenport, IA 52806
(319) 391-2386

684.16   Snyder, Tim.
SNY
          Shelving and
            storage.

$26.95

DATE			